D0427407

Human Rights in Korea

Studies in East Asian Law
Harvard University
16

edited by

WILLIAM SHAW

Published by
THE EAST ASIAN LEGAL STUDIES PROGRAM
OF THE HARVARD LAW SCHOOL
and
THE COUNCIL ON EAST ASIAN STUDIES / HARVARD UNIVERSITY
Distributed by the Harvard University Press
Cambridge (Massachusetts) and London   1991

Human Rights in Korea

Historical and Policy Perspectives

© Copyright 1991 by the President and Fellows of Harvard College.
Printed in the United States of America

The Harvard Law School, in cooperation with Harvard's Council on East Asian Studies, the Harvard-Yenching Institute, and scholars from other institutions, has initiated a program of training and research designed to further scholarly understanding of the legal systems of China, Japan, Korea, and adjacent areas. A series of publications called Studies in East Asian Law has been established in conjunction with this program.

Library of Congress Cataloging-in-Publication Data

Human rights in Korea : historical and policy perspectives / edited by
    William Shaw.
        p. cm. – (Studies in East Asian law)
        Includes bibliographical references (p.) and index.
        ISBN 0-674-41605-8
        1. Civil rights—Korea—History. 2. Human rights—Korea—History.
    I. Shaw, William, 1944– .   II. Series.
    LAW <Kor 7 Human 1990>
    323'.09519—dc20   90-1987
                                                        CIP

UNIVERSITY LIBRARY
Lethbridge, Alberta

To the memories of
William H. Shaw (1922–1950)
and
Gregory Henderson (1922–1988)
students of Korea, lovers of freedom

CONTRIBUTORS

EDWARD J. BAKER is Assistant Director of the Harvard-Yenching Institute and the author of numerous articles relating to modern Korea. His current research interests are in South Korean political affairs and the role of law in Korean society.

LAWRENCE W. BEER is the Fred Morgan Kirby Professor of Civil Rights, Lafayette College. He has also lectured at many other universities in Asia and the West.

VIPAN CHANDRA is Professor of History at Wheaton College, Norton, Massachusetts. A specialist in modern Korean history, he is the author of *Imperialism, Resistance and Reform: Enlightenment and the Independence Club* (Berkeley, Institute of East Asian Studies, 1988) and the book-review editor of the *Journal of Korean Studies*.

JEROME ALAN COHEN is an international lawyer and Lecturer on Law at the Harvard Law School. Formerly Associate Dean, Professor and Director of the East Asian Legal Studies Program at the Harvard Law School, he is the author of many books and essays on legal affairs relating to East Asia.

GREGORY HENDERSON (1922–1988) is the author of the classic *Korea: The Politics of the Vortex* (Harvard University Press, 1968). He served in the U.S. Foreign Service from 1947 to 1964 and was for many years affiliated with the Fairbank Center for East Asian Research at Harvard. In 1988, he was posthumously given the Human Rights Award of the North American Coalition for Human Rights in Korea.

DONALD S. MACDONALD is Professor Emeritus at Stroudsburg (Pennsylvania) State University, and the author of *The Koreans: Contemporary Politics and Society* (rev. ed. Westview, 1990). He has spent over ten years in Korea as army officer, diplomat, and scholar.

MICHAEL ROBINSON, is Associate Professor of History at the University of Southern California and the author of *Cultural Nationalism in Colonial Korea, 1920–1925* (University of Washington Press, 1988). He is presently working on the cultural history of Korea in the 1930s.

WILLIAM SHAW is an Asian specialist at the Department of Defense and conducts classes on modern Korea at the School of Advanced International Studies, Johns Hopkins University. He has lived and worked in Korea for a number of years, most recently as a Fulbright Lecturer in 1981 and 1982. He is the editor of *Legal Norms in a Confucian State* (Berkeley, Institute of East Asian Studies, 1981) and author of *South Korea: A Country Study* (Department of the Army) to be published in 1991.

JAMES M. WEST, a member of the Texas Bar since 1982, is currently engaged in teaching, research and legal consulting in Seoul, Korea. He received his S. J. D. from Harvard Law School in 1989 for a dissertation on law and social theory. While at Harvard he was an Instructor in the Graduate Program and a Research Associate in East Asian Legal Studies.

ACKNOWLEDGMENTS

Research for this volume was supported in large part by a Ford Foundation grant for the study of human rights issues in China, Korea, and Vietnam, administered through the Harvard Law School's East Asian Legal Studies Program (E.A.L.S.). Special thanks are due to the successive directors of E.A.L.S., especially to Jerome A. Cohen, Professor Arthur Von Mehren, and Professor Oliver Oldman. Professor Oldman and Professor K. C. Chang, Director of the Council on East Asian Studies, were instrumental in supporting the project in its final stages and in returning Studies on East Asian Law to its original home at Harvard University. Florence Trefethen, Executive Editor for the Council, provided invaluable advice, guidance, and editorial oversight—no easy matter with a multi-author work—from submission of the manuscript through completion of publication.

Not every contributor to this project appears in the table of contents. Before the research and writing began, much of the framework for the historical approach was developed in seminars and discussions with colleagues and sojourners at E.A.L.S. and elsewhere, including R. Randle Edwards, John O. Haley, Charles B. Thaxton, George

Ogle, Ilan Peleg, Kim Suk-joe, Stephen Young, Ta Van Tai, and Nguyen Ngoe Huy. Additional ideas and inspiration were gleaned from Brian E. McKnight and other participants in the 1978 Social Science Research Council Conference on Law and the State in East Asia. Among other exploratory exercises during the germination period was an E.A.L.S. staff seminar on human-rights thought in traditional East Asia, to which John Gibbs brought expertise concerning moral reasoning and development. Additional insights came from discussion with Dr. K. P. Yang and Dr. Sung Yoon Cho of the Library of Congress. Finally, the comments of two anonymous readers were helpful in drawing attention to the need for a synthesis of the individual chapters in the introduction. The views expressed in each chapter, of course, are solely those of its author. I alone am responsible for the Introduction, which simply represents my own interpretation and synthesis of the issues raised in the diverse contributions, and does not reflect the position of the U.S. Government or Department of Defense.

Two of the authors, Michael Robinson and Donald Macdonald, served as expert readers of two other chapters in addition to providing their own essays. At an early stage, John Merrill and Wonmo Dong took time to provide insightful and valuable comments on two other chapter drafts. Thanks go to Edward J. Baker for help with the list of suggested readings. A draft of the chapter concerning the Equalization Movement of the 1920s benefited from exposure to colleagues at a conference on the Primacy of the Political Order in East Asia held at the American Academy of Arts and Sciences in September 1982. After acceptance of the manuscript, but before final revisions, Linda Lewis provided several of the authors with an opportunity to revisit some of the issues raised in this volume at a panel on Korean Concepts of Justice at the annual conference of the Association of Asian Studies in March 1989. Additional thanks go to Professors Dae Sook Suh and Glenn D. Paige of the University of Hawaii for facilitating a seminar on the book at the University of Hawaii's Center for Korean Studies in May 1989, and to Frank Upham, who provided an opportunity to air some of the ideas in the introduction before members of his seminar and the East Asian Law speakers series at the Harvard Law School in September 1989. A special debt is owed Dr. Lawrence Beer, Kirby Professor of Law and Civil Rights at Lafayette

College, for his comparative perspective as an authority on Japanese law and politics.

As the Harvard East Asian Legal series returns to its proper home, what better occasion to acknowledge the role in Asian legal studies of Jerome A. Cohen, who for more than two decades has provided encouragement and example to specialists in many disciplines and has inspired many of us with his dedication to the subject and to human rights in Asia. On his sixtieth birthday this year, I am certain the contributors of this book would all join me in these sentiments, and in saying: "Wansui, Jerry."

William Shaw

CONTENTS

We should cease to talk about vague and—for the Far East—unreal objectives such as human rights, the raising of living standards, and democratization. The day is not far off when we are going to have to deal in straight power concepts. The less we are hampered by idealistic slogans, the better.
    George Kennan, 1948

Korea's traditional sociopolitical ideology, Confucianism, with its emphasis on order, conformity, consensus and filial piety, retains great strength, coexisting uneasily with the Western democratic ideals and industrial-age values to which Koreans have been exposed in this century.
    U.S. Department of State Report on Human Rights Practices, 1984

I came to feel that our . . . traditional concept of culture has often justified the most distorted views about primitive and non-Western societies, the "others" whom anthropologists traditionally study. It does so by stereotyping individuals and groups as mere carriers of the culture, by pressing them pancake-flat under a tyranny of culture. Individual and collective action, response, resistance, and struggle for or against "the" culture get lost in such a determinism; they are crushed under the despotism of cultural tradition.
    Richard G. Fox, Lions of the Punjab: Culture in the Making *(1985)*

Introduction

WILLIAM SHAW

RIGHTS, CULTURE, AND POLICY: THE PREVAILING MODEL

This book deals with two subjects. The first is the uneasy fate of human rights and certain ideas of human rights in twentieth-century Korea. The second is what U.S. policy should be toward human-rights problems in South Korea.

We are concerned here with what usually are termed "civil and political rights."[1] These may be traced to the "liberal" Western tradition, beginning with that tradition's foundation documents and writings of the eighteenth century. These ideas were still in development when Korean reformers first learned of them in the 1880s and 1890s, and have continued to develop, in international documents such as the Covenant on Civil and Political Rights of the United Nations and in the constitutional law and practice of various countries.

In the West, much current thinking on human rights in East Asia stresses the tension between Asian culture and human-rights thought. Americans who are concerned about human rights in China today, writes John King Fairbank, are "culture-bound" and guilty of folly or meddling in their failure to appreciate the Chinese tradition in its own terms.[2] Others speak proudly of the "metaphysical patrimony" of the West and warn against expecting human rights from non-Western governments, with their different social and ethical traditions.[3]

When applied to Korea, this view emphasizes the persistence in Korean society of premodern political values and institutions that are said to inhibit implementation of civil and political rights. Such thinking may be encountered in diverse places, including the State Department annual report on human rights in Korea and private conversations with working diplomats and military officers with experience in Korea. Some social scientists hold similar views, as may be seen in the influential interpretations of the late Hahm Pyong-Choon and sociologist Norman Jacobs.

This rights-vs.-culture model has some merits, particularly for the late traditional period, when Confucian values were still dominant. It has had other appeals, however, that sometimes have gone beyond the merits. Logically, it is difficult to understand why residual Confucianism is a barrier to human rights, but has not constrained rapid industrial growth, world-class corporate conglomerates complete with 12-hour working days for executives, modern urbanization, government by military elites, or other decidedly un-Confucian practices. One trendy solution of this contradiction has been the touting of a "Confucian work ethic" that is said to lie behind East Asian economic successes. In the case of Korea, at least, such arguments are thin, and cannot seriously be defended against a careful reading either of Korean economic history or of what Korean Confucian writers have actually said about commerce or the military vocation.

Another part of the model's appeal has been psychological. In Korea, the model has enabled apologists for authoritarian governments to portray democratic institutions as an alien transplant, ill-suited to local conditions. Because the question of national identity is one of the central preoccupations of twentieth-century Korean consciousness, this approach has often placed human-rights advocates on the defensive and required them to insist on their Koreanness.

In the West, the cultural argument against human rights in Korea has seductive affinities with a long tradition of "Orientalist" thought, including Hegel, early liberal thinkers such as John Stuart Mill, and even Herodotus. The model has also been attractive to some Western, and especially American, observers of Asia because of its appeal to the ideas of cultural relativism. To others, it has seemed compatible with realism of the George Kennan variety. For thinkers of both the cultural relativist and "realist" types it often follows that U.S. policy toward South Korea (or other Asian countries) should downplay human rights and focus on other issues, such as national security and trade.

The cultural approach to human-rights issues in Korea has numerous weaknesses. It is often poorly grounded in actual research into the Korean past. For example, the title essay of the late Professor Hahm Pyong-Choon's enormously influential 1967 book, *The Korean Political Tradition and Law,* cited a variety of Chinese sources, often from remote antiquity (and sometimes out of context), but did not discuss how individual Korean thinkers during the last traditional dynasty (from 1392 to 1910) interpreted these sources. He also failed to mention, much less analyze, a single traditional Korean source of law, legal commentary, or case book. In minimizing the role of law in both traditional and modern times, Hahm undermined the idea that rights could mean anything to Koreans. Most important, Hahm fails to note the degree to which Confucianism was discredited as a political philosophy among twentieth-century Korean thinkers and political activists. He also neglected the diversity of modern Korean values, including those of the legal profession. As a result, Hahm's Korean political tradition, which he claimed remains alive in almost unchanged form today, was populated not with actual Korean rulers, institutions, and thinkers, but with unnamed sages above the law who ruled over harmonious and passive peasants through benign ethical example and harmony according to principles strikingly (or suspiciously) like those of Plato's *Republic.*

Another problem with such accounts is that they neglect the importance both of history and of historical change. This may be seen in Norman Jacobs's recent attempt to come to terms with Korean political culture (for which he uses the term *social order*) in his study *The Korean Road to Modernization and Development* (1986). It is heavily influenced by Hahm and by the Weberian model or "ideal type" of patrimonial jurisprudence. In this model, law serves not to protect rights for all members of society, but rather as "a didactic expression of ethical rulership whose purpose is to inculcate proper conduct so that individuals will live harmonious, disciplined, productive, and . . . virtuous lives." According to Jacobs, a patrimonial social order such as that of Korea is stratified in such a way that "only the intellectual-moral role" is entitled to "formal corporate (or legal) recognition and protection of its independent rights and privileges." To simplify, those who have rights have them; those who do not, do not.

Despite many insights, Jacobs's work, like Hahm's, clearly remains captive to the notion of static, timeless characteristics of Korean society. His "Korean social order" never seems to change, despite changes in economy and social structure.[4] Consequently, one model fits all periods of Korean history, and may equally well explain Korea hundreds of years ago, today, and tomorrow.

In whichever form we take it, the model has simply ignored a number of striking facts of modern Korean history. These include:

The decline of Confucianism as a living political philosophy (despite residual strength in interpersonal relations) that began in the 1880s and sharply accelerated after the loss of Korean independence in 1910.

The growing strength, during the same period, of alternative philosophical, religious, or political traditions and forms of organization, including Catholic and Protestant Christianity, the Ch'ondogyo or "Heavenly Way" Movement, Western liberalism, and Marxism.

The strength in the postwar period of the model of militarized government and social control the Japanese exercised for thirty-five years to 1945.

The effects of national division, civil war, and the accompanying military tension on the Korean peninsula since 1945, necessitating large, often politically significant military establishments on both sides of the 38th parallel.

The chapters in this book sample the successive phases of Korea's modern century from the 1880s to the present. They represent diverse perspectives on these questions, focus on concrete historical analysis, and avoid theoretical generalization. Nonetheless, consideration of the specific historic situations explored in these chapters suggests several insights on the subject of human rights in South Korea and U.S. human-rights policy toward South Korea. These may be summarized here.

The first is that, during most of the past century, nationalism has inhibited the development of human rights as much as or more than residual elements of traditional Korean culture. For the past century, the most ardent proponents of human rights have also been strongly nationalistic and sought to strengthen the Korean state. This has engendered an ambivalent effect on the balance between state power and human rights.

A second insight that emerges from the studies is that the legacy of the recent past, and especially that of the Japanese colonial period, has been more significant than the traditional Chosŏn-dynasty legacy in influencing human-rights issues in postwar South Korea. Since the 1880s, Japanese thinkers and institutions have provided an important source of ideas and models. This influence is evident not only for economic planners and soldiers, but also for "liberal" and Marxist thinkers. Although the chapters do not touch on this question directly, it seems evident that Japanese influences on Korean ideas about governance and rights have been periodically refreshed since 1945, and remain quite vigorous and important today.

Finally, the chapters show that there is no monolithic consensus in Korean society, or even within the Korean government, on human-rights issues. There is no longer, if there ever was, a single Korean orientation or political culture concerning the subject.

NATIONALISM AND HUMAN RIGHTS: A STUDY IN AMBIVALENCE

In late-nineteenth- and twentieth-century Korea, the idea of human rights (and related institutions) has often been in tension with particularistic claims of the Korean nation and its survival. Nationalism, more than culture, has tempered and weakened the influence of human-rights thinking and institutions in modern Korean history.

Vipan Chandra's chapter is the first scholarship in English thoroughly to examine the human-rights ideas of thinkers of the late nineteenth-century Independence Club in the light of their own writings and recent Korean scholarship. He shows that these pioneering Korean human-rights thinkers were not only at odds with the current political order but also were torn between the claims of their newly acquired and Western ideas and their desire to preserve and strengthen the nation. The result was an ambivalence in their conception of rights—a latent statism mixed with the language of universal "human" rights. Nonetheless, their strong arguments for due process, freedom of expression, and responsible government mark the beginning of a century of modern Korean human-rights thought and advocacy.

Chandra's insights shed light on aspects of later Korean political thought often overlooked by historians. One may find similar ambivalencies and tensions in the political theory of a subsequent generation of Korean political thinkers and activists—those in the Korean independence movement in exile in China in the 1920s and 1930s.

When some Koreans who had fled Japanese colonial rule formed a government-in-exile in Shanghai in April 1919, they drafted a 10-article charter, much of which dealt in general terms with far-reaching civil and political rights—freedoms of religion, press, movement, and property; the right of citizens to vote and to be elected; and the abolition of discrimination between rich and poor or men and women. We don't know how the Provisional Government would have ruled Korea. It was beset with serious—even insurmountable—problems, including internal disorganization, factionalism, and, of course, unassailable Japanese control over Korea. It never was able to exercise power, much less to attempt the implementation of these or other rights. However, many of the Provisional Government's revised draft charters over the subsequent period of some twenty-odd years exhibit an unmistakable inclination toward statism. Like the Meiji Constitution, these documents combined the language of rights with a reluctance to dilute the power of the state. In many of those charters, beginning with the first constitutional revision in August 1919, provisions concerning rights were undercut by phrases such as "within the scope provided by law."[5]

Chapter 3 shows that this tension between rights and the nation—so important after 1945—was also seen in some Korean reactions to the 1920s Equalization Movement for civil rights among Korea's minority *paekchŏng* population. To a nation beginning to define social evil primarily in terms of *foreign oppression*, the universalistic "human"-rights slogans and goals of the *paekchŏng* grated against the more compelling and urgent claims of class or nation, and appeared to undermine the unity against Japan that the situation seemed to require.

It is interesting to compare this movement with the short-lived "patrician revolt" (to borrow Eric Goldman's phrase) of the Independence Club's leaders thirty years earlier. In the different social background and historical circumstances of their struggles, the two movements at first seem quite distinct. *Paekchŏng* concerns were much more immediate and less abstract than the broad public-policy issues emphasized by late-nineteenth-century reformers like Pak Yŏng-hyo, Yun Ch'i-ho, Yu Kil-chun, and Sŏ Chae-p'il. Like the earlier reformers, however, *paekchŏng* thinkers and their middle-class sympathizers were influenced both by Christian social ideals and by educational experiences and contacts in Japan. The language and concepts the *paekchŏng* used to express their concerns also were close to the liberal natural-rights concepts introduced by the earlier reformers. In fact, the Equalization Movement provides important historical evidence for the early diffusion of such ideas—and not just ideas but actions—beyond a small, Western-oriented elite.

THE COLONIAL LEGACY AND DIVERSITY IN KOREAN VIEWS OF HUMAN RIGHTS

The statism of the legal system introduced by the Japanese colonial authorities was much less ambiguous than that found in the fledgling charters of the Korean Provisional Government. In ruling Korea, Japan "modernized" many Korean institutions, and may even have set the stage for the state-led economic development of the postwar period.[6] Some Korean individuals gained exposure to liberal or socialist ideas while studying in Japan. But Japanese rule contributed little to the growth of individual political or civil rights. And, as Norman Jacobs has aptly suggested, the period of Japanese colonial rule (1910–1945) left much of the Korean population with fear of and disrespect for modern law by using it for repression and control.[7] The Japanese also left behind a model for political control through law that postwar Korean leaders were frequently to emulate.

Japanese Governors General in Korea ruled transcendently, able to issue administrative orders having the force of law entirely on their own authority . As Japanese newspapers noted at the time of annexation in 1910, Koreans lacked representation in the Diet, which had little influence over colonial policies in any case. Ordinary Koreans were not permitted even to discuss matters of government policy. The parallels with Park Chung Hee's style of rule during the heyday of the Yusin constitution from 1972 to 1979, and under President Chun Doo Hwan through 1987, as amply described in the chapter by Cohen and Baker, are evident. Other features of Japanese colonial rule, including press censorship and a strong and active government concern with policing people's thoughts[8] as well as their actions, were carried over largely intact into postwar Korean-government practice in both halves of the peninsula. One result was a political and legal inheritance contributing to authoritarian governments in post-1945 Korea, and a further setback to the development of political and civil rights.

The late Gregory Henderson's chapter shows that the state continued its dominance during the chaotic years before and after the Korean War. The effects of national division, ideological conflict, and violent confrontation even before 1950 had negative consequences for rights, both intellectually and in legal terms. Henderson's discussion of the *pŭrakchi* political trial of 1949 and 1950 also illustrates the continuing potency of the Japanese colonial model in the legal sphere. The trial, which until now has received little scholarly attention, may be seen as a link between political domination of the legal process under the Japanese and postwar South Korean political trials.

The Henderson chapter also suggests that at least some of the postwar conflict over human rights in Korea has focused on alternative Western political and legal philosophies, and not on tension between Korean and Western models of political culture. In particular, Henderson notes that German legal concepts introduced to Korea through Japanese legislation and weighted in favor of state power have had more influence than Anglo-American legal principles. This point is worth some elaboration.

A brief review of the Japanese colonial legacy will be helpful in understanding postwar developments. The Western legal doctrine that dominated Japanese legal institutions (including legal education) during the period of colonial rule over Korea was legal positivism—the view that the state and its laws come into existence before rights, and therefore create whatever rights exist. This doctrine gained widespread intellectual support in early twentieth-century European legal education as a secular counterpoise to the supposedly outmoded natural-law doctrine that rights were given by Nature or by God.

A state founded on legal-positivist doctrines may, in practice, be "better than its philosophy" and provide for ample civil and political rights. Yet, under legal positivism there is in principle nothing greater than the state itself to which appeal may be made if human rights are ignored or undermined by law. As Judith Shklar and others have noted,[9] the legal-positivist perspective was fatally undermined in the West, and natural-law doctrines given renewed life, by the European experience under Nazi legalism.

In Korea, by contrast, legal positivism retained some influence well after the end of Japanese colonial rule. As Professor Paul K. Ryu (Yu Ki-ch'ŏn) has noted in his criminal-law text in the 1950s, South Korean criminal law during the immediate postwar period was even for a time influenced by a wartime Japanese draft criminal code based on Nazi doctrines. Legal positivism was especially congenial to the rule of Park Chung Hee from 1961 to 1979,[10] and became the informal orthodoxy of the regime, especially after 1972.

Legal positivism was being undermined during the same period, however; many constitutional and legal scholars in south Korea, including those at the elite Seoul National University Faculty of Law, taught natural-law theory and doctrines of natural rights to postwar generations of law students. There is a direct link between these ideas and the ideas of the nineteenth-century Independence Club, the Korean Provisional Government, and the Equalization Movement, just as there is a close relationship between the legal positivism of Japanese colonial rule and that of the Park Chung Hee Government.

Students who learned natural-law doctrines during the postwar period—the cream of the Korean legal profession—graduated to fill the ranks of the judiciary, the procuracy and (usually at an advanced age) the legal profession. During the Park Chung Hee period, the result was tension between the unofficial orthodoxy of the regime and the natural-law theory being absorbed by generations of future judges, prosecutors, and lawyers.

This tension may be seen in several areas. For example, it is indirectly evident in the increasingly stringent political and bureaucratic controls the Park Government imposed, especially after 1972, to restrict growing judicial independence and to control the procuracy more thoroughly. These included judicial tenure limited to short terms and the forced resignation of judges on the Supreme Court and other courts. After the assassination of Park in October 1979, these controls were retained through 1987 under the succeeding regime of Chun Doo Hwan. As Jerome A. Cohen and Edward Baker discuss in their chapter, the Park Government used even more direct measures to control the outcome of specific cases, including a closed military tribunal and house arrest of defense attorneys in a political trial in 1974, and KCIA intimidation of defense witnesses in the trial of Kim Dae Jung and others in 1976. It seems clear that, by the mid-1970s, the government of South Korea was at odds with a substantial portion of the country's legal expertise.

The diversity of professional legal opinion concerning human rights also may be seen in South Korean constitutional law. The Constitution of 1962 stated that, when rights or freedoms of the citizens are curtailed by law (to preserve public order or for reasons of national security, respectively) the "fundamental nature" of such rights and freedoms "may not be transgressed." Whatever the performance of the Park Government in protecting human rights under this Constitution, this was natural-law language.

As is well known, the 1962 Constitution was influenced by American advice (and pressure) as well as by Korean legal scholars. Park Chung Hee was never happy with it. After his coup-in-office in October 1972, the new Yusin Constitution omitted the natural-law language of the chapter on rights and duties, and simply stated that legal restrictions on the rights and freedoms of citizens should be imposed "only when necessary." Other parts of this Constitution gave the president broad and unrestricted powers to rule transcendently, as the Japanese governors general had, through executive decrees.

Following the coup of General Chun Doo Hwan in May 1980, a new Constitution was drafted by a team of handpicked legal specialists. Remarkably, given the repressive political climate following the May 1980 Kwangju Incident, the natural-law language of the 1962 Constitution was restored to the chapter on rights and duties, suggesting the presence on the drafting committee of natural-law-oriented scholars. Natural-law doctrine was confirmed again in the Constitution of 1987 by an 8-member committee of government and opposition-party specialists.

Another indication of the spread of human-rights ideas may be seen in the changing and little-studied role of the Korean legal profession. In postwar Korea, there have always been individual lawyers who defended those accused of political offenses, often at great personal and professional risk. The legal profession as a whole, however, remained largely apolitical throughout the 1960s and early 1970s.

During this period, for example, the Korean Federal Bar Association seems to have been chiefly concerned with improving the social and financial standing of the profession. One reason for this may have been that the senior leadership of the profession remained in the hands of those who had received their legal training and political socialization under Japanese rule. During the mid-1970s and the 1980s, however, as a new generation came to leadership, the Bar Association became one of the few mainstream professional organizations consistently to criticize the government's violation of political rights and press freedoms.[11]

HUMAN RIGHTS AND U.S. POLICY TOWARD KOREA

As the chapters by Asian legal specialists Jerome A. Cohen and Edward Baker and retired Foreign Service Officer Dr. Donald Macdonald show, there is little disagreement about the factual record of human-rights abuses in South Korea, especially under the governments of Park Chung Hee (1961–1979) and Chun Doo Hwan (1980–1988). The authors disagree concerning the roots of the problem and the appropriate role of the United States in improving the situation.

In the debate over U.S. human-rights policy toward South Korea, the lines usually are drawn between those who implement policy and those who critique it. Those with experience in diplomacy tend to minimize U.S. responsibility for human-rights problems in the R.O.K. and also to downplay the value of official pressures in improving South Korean practice. They regard the critics as insensitive to the demands of working-level diplomacy, which must strive for uncertain success across a broad range of economic, security, cultural, and political goals. Accredited to the government, they occasionally suspect that some U.S. human-rights advocates function as surrogates or lobbyists for particular South Korean opposition leaders[12] or organizations that would like to harness U.S. diplomacy for their own goals.

The critics often are convinced that, for historical reasons, the United States bears at least indirect responsibility for South Korean government abuses and could do much more than it does to mitigate human-rights encroachments. They are less concerned with the possible role of Korean historical and political responsibility for existing problems. They are concerned that long-term U.S. political and strategic interests may become fatally undermined by failure to distance the United States sufficiently from abusive practices and regimes. Occasionally they fear that U.S. officials have slipped their democratic moorings and become "clientized," or co-opted to become apologists for the R.O.K. government where human rights issues are concerned.

Behind the respective roles of practitioner and critic often are found differing theoretical views. Through training and experience, many U.S. human-rights activists subscribe to a robust universalism, generally based on liberal ideas of civil and political rights. The activists believe that U.S. policy that slights these values denies its own roots and raison d'être. It is not surprising that human-rights activists believe that Korean culture need not pose an obstacle to democratization or the implementation of human rights. Despite disappointment or even cynicism concerning specific U.S. actions and policies, however, they remain optimistic about the future of human rights and democracy in South Korea.

As Americans, foreign-policy specialists share many of these values. But, through their own training and experience, they tend to become foreign-policy realists and cultural relativists. Willing to conduct diplomacy on human-rights issues (among others) if that is U.S. policy, they still do not see themselves as carrying out any kind of idealistic "civilizing mission." Publicly optimistic, privately they may tend to pessimism about Korean political culture and its influence on democratization and human rights.

Despite the desirability of the United States influencing South Korea on human-rights issues, such influence is, as time passes, likely to be increasingly only advisory. One senses a weakening of the levers often proposed for influencing Seoul's human-rights practices. This is due to the "graduation" of South Korea from U.S. economic and military grant assistance over the past decade, and also to the complexity of emerging economic issues, characterized by growing economic nationalism on both sides. Joint economic and military relationships between the two countries increasingly are following their own logic. This new logic cuts across the hopes of the South Korean old-line opposition that the United States could be induced to impose sanctions on the Seoul government to improve human-rights practices.

As an example taken from the field of economic rather than political rights, U.S. law calls for improvement in foreign labor law[13] and practices, threatening withdrawal of favored status or other sanctions if such improvement is not evident. However, with the advent of a U.S. current account deficit with South Korea in 1983, American pressures on Seoul to reform its labor practices or to open its markets increasingly are perceived in Seoul (on the left as well as the right) as motivated by economic factors and not concern for human rights. This perception is correct, because, in the United States, commercial pressures and free-trade doctrine deeply influence Congressional views on such sanctions, making them unavailable for use in connection with human-rights concerns. In 1987, Congress had already acted, on economic grounds, to remove South Korea from the list of countries shown preferential trade treatment under the Generalized System of Preferences (GSP). Meanwhile, it has become the South Korean dissident movement that most strongly opposes any kind of U.S. economic pressures.

The national-security relationship also is an unlikely area in which to seek U.S. human-rights pressures on the South Korean government. A small number of South Koreans may oppose U.S.-R.O.K. military ties, and pressure from Seoul to restructure the alliance has grown in recent years. However, few of even the most ardent human-rights organizations in Korea or the United States advocate linking South Korean human-rights conduct with substantial changes, such as withdrawal of U.S. ground forces, in the U.S.-R.O.K. security relationship. An effort to make such a change during the presidency of Jimmy Carter failed to muster support either from Congress or U.S. allies in the region.[14] (Although the issue seems never to have been discussed in these terms, it seems likely that unilateral U.S. troop withdrawals in 1977 or 1978 would have immeasurably strengthened the social and political role of the South Korean military and security establishment, making the 1980s even bleaker in the area of human rights than they were.)

Another security-related issue concerns the Combined Forces Command (CFC), a complex and widely misunderstood institution intended to facilitate unified command of Korean and U.S. troops in time of war. To date, it has always been commanded by a U.S. general.[15] This caused considerable misunderstanding and acrimony in December 1979, when a front-line Korean regiment under the CFC violated the chain of command by deploying to Seoul to assist in the first stage of General Chun Doo Hwan's coup d'état. A similar problem occurred during May 1980 in Kwangju, where troops not actually under the CFC brutally killed hundreds of demonstrators. In late May, the Korean Deputy Commander of the CFC returned other Korean troops to R.O.K. Army control. These troops were subsequently used to capture the city, again with loss of life. The Kwangju upheaval gave General Chun sufficient backing within the alarmed Korean military to complete the seizure of power begun in December, but permanently stained the legitimacy of his rule for many Koreans.

The resulting Korean public perception of U.S. military involvement in Korean politics, although incorrect, was nourished both by the government and by a large part of the opposition and dissident community, each for its own political ends. The United States paid for these misunderstandings from 1982 to the present with an unprecedented series of dissident-committed arsons and forcible occupations of its diplomatic and cultural facilities in South Korea. These events strengthened the resolve of U.S. leaders not to be misunderstood (or manipulated) in this way again. They also made it more unlikely than ever that the leverage supposedly available due to the U.S. military presence in South Korea could be used to shape the course of Korean politics or the government's human-rights practices.

As Cohen and Baker note, the United States continues to have influence in South Korea, even when it lacks leverage. Such influence is largely persuasive in nature. William Gleysteen was the U.S. Ambassador to South Korea during the last years of the Park regime through early 1980. Writing from retirement in 1987, he candidly described several instances in which the U.S. government, lacking leverage, exerted influence on the Seoul government to attain human-rights ends.[16] These included U.S. efforts to save Kim Dae Jung following his sedition trial and death sentence after the Kwangju Incident in 1980. The price for Kim's life, set in one of the very few instances of foreign-policy cooperation between the outgoing Carter Administration and the new Reagan Administration,[17] was an invitation to Chun Doo Hwan to visit the White House. (The timing of the visit, on the eve of the election that formally placed Chun in the presidency, was set by newly inaugurated President Reagan.)

Perhaps the most fruitful American approach to human-rights problems in the future will continue to be the unlikely and often mutually suspicious coalition between private-sector activists and watchdog organizations on the one hand and the professional diplomats and concerned members of Congress on the other. The former are able to keep abuses in the public eye and to keep pressure on the U.S. government, while the State Department also closely monitors problems and is often able to mitigate, if not always eliminate, particular abuses.

Several examples of U.S. government participation in such apparent coalition efforts may be cited. The United States government played an important role in saving the life of opposition political leader Kim Dae Jung on at least two occasions, in 1973 and 1980.[18] In 1985, official U.S. advice, coupled with publicity from international human-rights organizations, influenced the South Korean government's decision not to enact its controversial proposed Campus Stabilization Law.[19] Throughout the years of the Chun Government, the State Department continued to publish annual critiques of Seoul's human-rights practices and to criticize individual acts of torture and other abuses.[20]

Because human-rights organizations are usually not fully aware of unpublicized diplomatic activities, their calls for U.S. official action on human rights often amount to calls for public action. Asia Watch, a human-rights monitoring organization based in Washington, D.C., completed a study in early 1987 that characterized as "woefully inadequate" the U.S. official response to the worsening human-rights situation throughout 1986. Like similar organizations, the group had long called for the United States to take a more aggressive posture to encourage respect for human rights in South Korea. Asia Watch noted a change in the U.S. public stance in November 1986, however, when State Department spokesman Charles Redman responded to a question concerning the South Korean government's suppression of an opposition rally by pointedly noting the Korean government's obligation under its own Constitution to protect the freedom of association and speech. The group also noted with approval a December press interview with newly appointed U.S. Ambassador James Lilley in Seoul. In an amplification of Redman's remarks, Lilley told a Korean newspaper that "in a democratic country the government should permit a political rally and it is the government's obligation to make it safe." Asia Watch was also encouraged by a February speech in which Assistant Secretary of State Gaston Sigur called on

Koreans to "face the challenge of permanently 'civilianizing' their politics."[21] This series of public comments and speeches by U.S. officials marked the beginning of a remarkable period of relatively open diplomacy concerning human rights and the democratization process in South Korea.

Don Oberdorfer of the *Washington Post* interviewed numerous officials and policymakers in a careful study of the growth in public U.S. government statements and "carefully timed advice" to South Korea. In October 1986, according to Oberdorfer, U.S. officials in Washington began to reassess approaches towards human-rights issues in South Korea. The 1986 Asian Games in Seoul, pointing to the 1988 Seoul Olympics and the projected conclusion of Chun Doo Hwan's term in office the same year, inevitably prompted consideration of the course of political transition in Seoul. U.S. policymakers familiar with the Korean situation were aware of the weaknesses of the forms of "leverage" discussed above, and perhaps were stimulated by the combination of public and private diplomacy that had led to the peaceful departure of Ferdinand Marcos from the Philippines in February 1986. In any case, as Oberdorfer expressed it, they seem to have concluded that "talk, especially public speeches and statements, was a major instrument and perhaps *the* major instrument of persuasion and impact at the U.S. command."[22]

Whatever the reason, 1987 saw a series of unusually outspoken speeches, interviews, and other representations, both public and diplomatic, by senior U.S. officials. Sigur's speech in February urging the South Korean military to devote itself solely to the demanding tasks of national defense was reinforced by Secretary of State Shultz during his visit to Seoul in March. Other public statements and more direct representations continued through the political crisis in June, the subsequent referendum on a new constitution in October, and the presidential elections in December. The U.S. position emphasized compromise between the government and opposition forces, peaceful political transition, fair elections, and the avoidance of further military involvement in politics.[23] U.S. officials also strongly reacted to specific actions of the South Korean government, making public statements condemning South Korean government use of torture in the January 1987 death of student Pak Chong-ch'ol,[24] and issuing a demarche counseling against the storming of the Myongdong Cathedral in Seoul in June.[25]

Some official and private discussions were made public, either at the time or subsequently. For example, in an unusual press conference via a U.S. Information Agency telecommunications link with Korean journalists in Seoul in March, a senior State Department official acknowledged that the United States had raised with the Seoul government the question of restoration of civil rights to Kim Dae Jung and other opposition leaders.[26] U.S. officials also told journalists of the intensive U.S. efforts to discourage military intervention during the political turmoil in June. By early July it was disclosed in the *Washington Post* that President Reagan had sent a personal letter to Chun urging political rather than military settlement of the growing crisis, and that Sigur had emphasized the same point during his 23–25 June visit to Seoul.[27]

The United States gave abundant counsel in 1987 and 1988 to the South Korean government, both to mitigate human-rights abuses and to encourage the transition to more democratic institutions. This campaign was unusual in the degree to which it was carried out in the public eye, although important measures were taken in private as well. These efforts echoed the specific concerns of human-rights organizations, while also seeming to answer the longstanding call of the human-rights community for a stronger and more public stance.

U.S. public willingness to distance itself from the official South Korean government on human rights issues, reached a high point in June 1989, when the State Department released its report on the Kwangju Incident of May 1980.[28] Based on official records, the report dealt candidly and in some detail with U.S. actions and perceptions during the period from late 1979 through May 1980—the period during which Chun Doo Hwan had come to power. In important ways the report differed from the official South Korean government version of the same events, particularly with respect to the question of U.S. support for the emerging Chun regime. The report, forthcoming only in response to a 1988 query from South Korea's new, opposition-dominated National Assembly, appeared nine years too late to staunch the bitterness of some Koreans over the perceived U.S. role during the rise of Chun. However, it shed new light on the limits of U.S. influence on the human-rights situation in South Korea. In particular, the report made clear the special difficulty of conducting "quiet diplomacy" on democracy and human-rights issues in the absence of significant leverage and in a climate in which the United States lacked the means to overcome systematic disinformation on the part of the martial-law authorities.

In assessing the lessons of the past decade, several points suggest themselves. First, as the 1980 U.S. role in saving Kim Dae Jung's life illustrates, it is clear that "quiet diplomacy," although rarely satisfactory to extra-governmental human-rights advocates, can be effective. As the generally positive reaction of the major opposition parties to the State Department's belated statement on the Kwangju Incident shows, however, protracted public silence may mean sacrificing other U.S. goals, such as retaining the long-term trust and confidence of the Korean people.

Second, neither quiet diplomacy nor high-profile approaches are likely to be effective where the United States lacks strong policy goals, or where the host government is bent on pursuit of its own strongly felt goals. Major examples can be seen in the ineffective and poorly coordinated U.S. reactions to Park Chung Hee's coup d'état in May 1961 and during South Korean political changes in 1972 and 1980. In the latter two instances, presidential election campaigns in the United States, among other factors, deprived the U.S. foreign-policy apparatus of decisive and focused leadership concerning U.S.-South Korean relations. During the Chun regime, U.S. pressure against the 1985 draft Campus Stabilization Law may have temporarily deflected South Korean government goals, but did not deter Seoul from achieving the same purpose by alternative methods through "purification education," the following year.[29] In 1987, weak U.S. representations failed to forestall Chun Doo Hwan's ending discussion of constitutional reforms in April.[30] Similarly, the U.S. government was no more successful than human-rights advocacy groups in persuading the South Korean government to allow political prisoner Kim Kun-t'ae to travel to the United States to receive a human-rights award in October 1987.

Third, and most important, apparent successes or failures experienced by the U.S. government or private advocacy groups overseas in influencing South Korean human-rights practices should not be allowed to obscure the major role of Koreans themselves. In numerous instances, pressures within South Korea were combined with diplomatic and other external pressures to influence the course of events. In June 1987, these pressures included large-scale middle-class participation in demonstrations and undoubted reluctance among some elements within the South Korean military to see the army's popular reputation suffer again as it had after Kwangju. Chun's decision not to resort to martial law in late June, his acceptance of the Roh Tae

Woo formula for constitutional change, and the subsequent restoration of Kim Dae Jung to full political participation were influenced by all these pressures.

A final lesson drawn may be the realization that both the U.S. government—including both congress and the diplomatic establishment—and private-sector human-rights organizations have an important and mutually reinforcing role to play in furthering the cause of human rights in countries such as South Korea.

PROSPECTS

This survey of selected events in the development and experience of human-rights ideas and activities over the past century provides little sustenance for those on either side of Korean political issues who resort to "Korean culture" or "the Korean tradition" to support their side in current political struggles. The historicism of Hahm Pyong-Choon and numerous others—that for cultural and historic reasons Koreans can't understand concepts of "rights"—is seen to be far too simplistic and anti-historical. Against the universalizing language of modern liberal human rights, this is a blood-and-soil relativism weighted in favor of the past.

South Korean defenders of human rights, perhaps under challenge to prove their own nationalist credentials, and desiring to appropriate the Korean past for their own political goals, have also sometimes sought support for their viewpoint in examples from the Korean tradition. Thus, in the 1970s and 1980s, some members of the political opposition claimed to find democratic elements in Tangun mythology, the aristocratic *hwabaek* council of the Silla dynasty, or the anti-aristocratic mask plays of the Chosŏn period.[31] Apart from serious historical problems that it entails, this effort has struck many as ironic, because, for most of the past century, Korea's reform thinkers sought to reject Korean tradition—which was much more potent in the late-nineteenth century than it is today—as inimical to the development of rights.

Open to similar criticism is *minjung* or "populist" theology. This is an appreciation of the masses that speaks eloquently of unjust suffering. Like Anabaptist Christian political analysis, which in some respects it resembles, it identifies existing government with illegitimate, demonic power, and prophecy with political opposition. This movement exhibits a lively nativist delight in coining language said to be untranslatable into English, and rejects "the old theological formulas" learned from the West in favor of traditional religious and social concepts. For example, one such writer portrays the traditional Korean *mudang* (shaman) as a socially concerned, messianic role model, and reverses two hundred years of Korean Christian teaching to portray Jesus as "the supreme *mudang*" who exorcised social evil.[32]

This modern populism, which also is encountered in some contemporary literature and in student sloganeering, is another indication of growing political diversity in South Korea. It is a minority perspective, even among intellectuals, and it is not clear that it will succeed as a strategy for mass mobilization. In the end, it is how Koreans accept or reject this approach, and how they may utilize it, that matters. To an outsider, however, it is not clear that a populist triumph would mean a victory for human rights. Although rich in the traditional language of grievances, populism has yet to develop a philosophy of rights. Where it speaks of rights, it seems inevitably thrown back on the institutional and legal legacies of the natural-rights tradition and the Korean human-rights thinkers who, despite their various failings, have appropriated that tradition for the past hundred years.

The efforts being undertaken under the nativist banner to reawaken the old gods could backfire. There is support here for Albert Memmi's[33] observation, based on his reflection on the Tunisian and Algerian experiences, that the development of anti-colonial nationalism itself often is associated with a resurgent cultural chauvinism that is potentially inimical to liberal concepts of rights and the institutions needed to protect them. It seems at least as likely that the South Korean state might attempt to build an ultra-nationalistic cult around Tangun as that "Tangunism" could serve the cause of human rights or democracy. Shamanism has similar problems. During the last traditional dynasty it was philosophically heterodox and culturally subversive, but politically inert. (Shamanist iconography has its own statism in the form of bureaucrat-filled heavens and hells.) On its own, it has no particular social conscience, and maintains its traditional focus on spirits who may (or may not) bestow quite individual benefits to individual petitioners.

The first years of the Roh Tae Woo Administration (1988–1989) had mixed human-rights effects. Separation of powers, promised in the new Constitution, came to life in general elections (April 1988), which returned an opposition-dominated majority to the National Assembly, a first for South Korea. Freedom of the press advanced: The Basic Media

Act—a dead letter after the political compromise of June 1987—was abolished in 1988. By the end of 1988, reportage of formerly forbidden topics—politics in the military, the security agencies' domestic role, and dissident organizations—gave new flavor to print and broadcast journalism. A new anti-government newspaper published by dissident journalists reached nearly half a million circulation.

The legislature proceeded in 1988 and 1989 with hearings into corruption during the previous administration and the circumstances of Chon Doo Hwan's coup. The hearings, begun in late September 1988, drew a wider t.v. audience than the Seoul Olympics; they generated generally candid testimony by former officials about media suppression, punitive military induction of student dissidents, political extortion, and criminal actions by members of the Chun Administration and family, leading to criminal indictments and convictions. In November, the former President appeared on t.v. to accept general responsibility for the 1980 Kwangju incident, and to announce his retirement to a Buddhist monastery.

The effect of the elections upon judicial branch autonomy was soon felt. In mid-1988, a protest by one third of the judiciary forced the resignation of the Chief Justice. The new National Assembly rejected President Roh's first choice for the post. To appease them, Roh appointed Yi Il-kyu, a respected, independent-minded judge whose Supreme Court appointment Chun Doo Hwan had not renewed in 1986. The new Chief Justice reshuffled the judiciary and promised greater political independence. The courts proceeded to unprecedented rulings in human-rights and abuse-of-power cases. The new Constitution Court also began to function in late 1988, ruling in cases brought by individuals under the new constitutional right of constitutional petition.

Shortly after Roh's inauguration, the executive branch reduced the size and level of the Advisory Council of Elder Statesmen, a constitutional body many feared would permit continued political influence by Chun. In 1988, the Roh Administration directed national security agencies to be less active in domestic political issues, negotiating with opposition parties a bill to require the Agency for National Security Planning to remain politically neutral and to observe habeas corpus.

Despite these gains, less progress was made in other human-rights areas, such as the National Security Act and the Act Concerning Assembly and Demonstration. Political arrests during the first eighteen months of Roh's rule—even adjusted for increased arrests for violence—exceeded those for the Chun Doo Hwan years. Moreover, by early 1989, the Roh Administration had come under much criticism from elements in the military and its own right wing, some of whom were referring to Roh as "Water Tae Woo" because of his perceived tolerance for dissent and unrest. In February 1989, farmers demonstrated violently against agricultural trade liberalization. Labor unrest, sometimes violent, continued through the spring with strikes at the Seoul subway system and the Hyundai shipyards. The late-1988 Molotov-cocktail assaults by student radicals against government and ruling-party facilities also continued. Then came two final shocks to conservatives: the unauthorized visit of two well-known dissidents to Pyongyang in March; and a fire set by student demonstrators in Pusan in May that killed seven policeman.

As the State Department's report noted, the administration's human-rights performance declined in 1989. The National Security Law was applied more often, especially against unauthorized travelers to North Korea and those arrested for publishing or reading pro-North materials. The security agencies resumed their old levels of activity in political cases. Police used excessive force, for example, against teachers attempting to form an independent union. Lawyers for defendants in National Security Law cases were denied access to their clients during investigations; in September, the government proposed a law to make access even more difficult. These losses were tempered by abrogation of the Social Safety Act and by signs that some gains of 1988—particularly with respect to matters of judicial independence—remained intact.

The most ambiguous human-rights development was the early 1990 union of the government party with two of the three opposition parties. The new Democratic Liberal Party would restore control of the National Assembly to a single "government" party. Because the opposition parties had been the practical guarantors of the separation of powers theoretically provided by the Constitution, the new party was criticized by the remaining opposition party and viewed pessimistically in human-rights circles. As the 1990s began, careful official and unofficial monitoring and reporting concerning the South Korean government's actual practices seemed likely to provide the best continuing measure of human-rights performance.

PART ONE

The Late Nineteenth Century

Historian Vipan Chandra discusses the political ideas of Korea's Independence Club in the 1890s in the context of Korea's political tradition and modern liberal human-rights thought. He convincingly demonstrates that Korean debate on human-rights policy is not a recent development, but has a history of a hundred years. William Shaw's chapter examines traditional Korean legal theory and institutions to find reasons for the widespread contemporary appeal of the Independence Club.

Korean Human-Rights Consciousness in an Era of Transition: A Survey of Late-Nineteenth-Century Developments

VIPAN CHANDRA

In grappling with the question of human rights in late-nineteenth-century Korea, one must first come to grips with some general perspectives—the most important related to the question of defining the concept human rights. Should one choose a narrow, traditional definition that would restrict the concept to such rights as those of life, liberty, property, and the somewhat enigmatic "pursuit of happiness" (à la American Declaration of Independence), or should one broaden it to include those rights which, in more recent decades, have come to be extolled by thoughtful people, if not governments, everywhere? A broader list of human rights would include not only such obvious rights as freedom of expression, occupation, faith, movement, privacy, and assembly, and the right of equal protection under law, but also some that have barely entered human consciousness and are rather precariously established even in open, democratic societies such as the right to freedom from sexual and racial discrimination in educational and employment opportunities and in public interaction among individuals, and the rights to a decent, equitable wage, health care, perhaps even leisure. Access to functional literacy and control over the size of one's family have also entered the arena of human rights, the latter accompanied by a raging and still unresolved controversy.

In the strictly legal realm, almost all regimes today, except those with an avowedly theocratic and autocratic foundation,[1] pledge to honor most, if not all, of the following human rights even when some are violated in practice: the right to a prompt and fair trial, including the right to assemble and present evidence in one's defense and the right to have a counsel when accused of a violation of law; the right to appeal one's conviction; the right to be deemed innocent until proven guilty; freedom from physical and mental torture and exploitation, and the like. One could go on until the concept of human rights becomes a charter of all those ideal conditions that make life worth living and worth defending against all assaults.[2] Indeed, the ideal definition of human rights would be none other than the ideal definition of democracy, thus excluding both traditional despotisms and modern authoritarianisms, of both the right and the left. It could even be argued that all human rights are so organically linked that, in the absence of some, there is no true presence of the others.[3] On this measure even the most open societies of our world could be considered seriously flawed.

One is therefore left to settle for a more "realistic" approach to defining human rights—an approach that takes into account differences of age and culture and looks at human rights in each age and culture from an evolutionary perspective. Under this approach, one recognizes that, while the evolution of human rights is ultimately inseparable from the evolution of an open society, different eras and societies in human history lend their own color and variety to the concept of human rights by proceeding according to their own locally determined scheme of priorities and implementation.

In the West, the nineteenth century was known for a more or less universal acquiescence in, if not acceptance of, racial and sexual discrimination. Rare men or women would occasionally arise to question the notion, only to look around and find that their voices were cries in the wilderness. Thus, John Stuart Mill and Mary Wollstone-craft spoke eloquently of sexual equality but were treated largely with disdain, hostility, or "benign neglect." And Mill's Utilitarian colleagues certainly did not think Orientals were yet fit for the enjoyment of of democratic freedoms, for they were alleged to possess an undemocratic "character and temperament." To the Utilitarians, only the heirs to the legacy of Judeo-Christian ethics, Greco-Roman law, the Magna Carta, the works of Rousseau and Locke, the Cromwellian, French, and American Revolutions, and so forth, could presumably qualify for the exercise of "natural rights." Not until the Eastern character had been elevated to the level of the West could Orientals expect to enjoy such rights.[4] As students of East Asian history are well aware, many of the Christian missionaries who went East in the nineteenth century were imbued with the same spirit, even when they had charitable goals.[5]

Yet, looking back from today, or looking Westward from the East in the latter half of the nineteenth century, one could confidently argue that the West had made great strides in the advancement of human rights and was indeed a source of envy and inspiration in this regard to those in Asia who had cared to keep their intellectual windows open. Respect for the dignity and worth of the individual had in the West been given many laudable channels of expression and institutionalized means of defense.

A second perspective that one must keep in mind when discussing the question of human rights in late-nineteenth-century Korea is that there, as in China and Japan, the open-minded keepers of the social conscience examined this question less for its own sake and more for its role in what came to be seen as a larger universal trend called "progress," "advancement," "civilization and enlightenment," "national power and prosperity." (Today we would use for this trend the more prosaic terms *development* and *modernization.*) Debate on human rights in Korea, as in China and Japan, was often subsumed in the larger debate over national advancement or progress. At the very least, the large question provided an inextricable backdrop for the smaller.

A third perspective, especially useful for evaluating recent happenings in South Korea, stems from an argument used by both Korean and foreign defenders of authoritarianism in Korea. Tersely stated, it is this: There is nothing in Korea's remote or recent past that will make Western-type democratic values and institutions take root and flourish in the country. Concern for human rights makes sense in societies where the individual is the prime mover behind events. In Korea, as in other Asian societies, the group always prevails over the individual. It is in the country's age-old culture to stress the collective interest of the group over the individual's interest. The human-rights movement in this view smacks of selfishness and rests on a weak moral foundation.

Knowing the intrinsic weakness of this argument and that it might not be accepted in Western capitals, its proponents often present it as part of a larger package of reasoning.[6] This includes the argument that South Korea can ill afford the luxury of human rights when its survival is at stake—the "threat from the north" is a succinct expression of this argument—and it goes on to claim that restrictions on human freedoms are necessary at present for rapid economic development as well, and that eventually South Korea will move toward a truly democratic political and social order. Some modify the argument to suggest that South Korea must evolve its own form of democracy, in consonance with the spirit of its own culture and its national "genius." (I have deliberately ignored here the North Korean position, typical of the orthodox Marxist line in general, that its social and political order is indeed the finest expression of democracy—a position so obviously at variance with the conceptual framework of this study that any discussion of it belongs in the realm of political philosophy, not history.)[7]

A study of human rights in late-nineteenth-century Korea assumes some importance in the context of the argument cited above: that the Korean historical experience, even in recent decades, includes no concern for human rights. Some seem to have argued that the whole question is alien and irrelevant to the Korean psyche, except for a handful of the nation's Westernized intellectuals. If our study shows that Korea's recent history is utterly barren in this respect, then indeed serious questions arise about the future of the recently started democratic experiment in South Korea. If, on the contrary, we can demonstrate that Koreans in the immediate past have had an extended exposure to democratic ideals and that their consciousness has changed through this exposure, then the case for democracy in Korea becomes strengthened and the case against it rendered dubious, at least in terms of its claimed historicity.

I have chosen to start exploring these questions with late-nineteenth-century Korea because, with the opening of Korea in 1876, and especially with the signing of treaties with Western powers in the 1880s, one's frame of reference in discussing the country shifts from "traditional" to "modern," and certain common denominators, certain mutually comprehensible ideas, begin to mark the interaction between Korea and the Western world. Was late-nineteenth-century Korea then interested in human rights? If so, how deep was this interest and what were its wellsprings? Who were the leaders of this interest? What efforts did they launch to translate their interest into action? What success or failure attended their efforts and why?

To use words such as *traditional* and *modern* here is to assume, of course, that pre-1876-Korea was considerably, if not radically, different from the West in its ethical priorities, political and social ideology and institutions, and cultural foundations—an assumption that most students of Korea will agree is essentially correct. It is logical, thus, for us to consider first how traditional Korea viewed the relationship between the state and the individual and between any two individuals—the two relationships central to any discussion of human rights. The ethos determining these relationships often determines the entire structure of a nation's body politic. This was especially the case in traditional Korea.

THE TRADITIONAL KOREAN
BODY POLITIC AND ITS ETHOS

Chosŏn Korea's government and society were officially structured upon the tenets of Neo-Confucianism as enunciated by China's Chu Hsi.[8] These tenets, instilled through governmental edicts, laws, exhortations, and school texts, need scarcely be discussed in detail here, since all students of East Asian affairs are familiar with them. We all know why and how the five cardinal relationships, the five virtues, and the three special bonds were expected to shape everyone's public behavior.[9] Further, Chu Hsi, like most of the Confucianists, espoused, rather than attacked, inequality in all social relationships— between generations, between classes, and between sexes—as an expression of the cosmic order and as essential for peace and harmony in the social world. Equality stood for chaos, inequality for organization. Knowing one's station and fulfilling its attendant obligations, rather than freely seeking the fruition of one's own aspirations, was at the core of the Neo-Confucian ethic. Submission, not assertion, was the virtue most admired in a person who knew his or her place, for therein lay the key to the absence of discord or strife in society, and this stability was perceived as its overriding goal.

As Martina Deuchler has explained, no country seems to have taken Chu Hsi's teaching more seriously than Chosŏn Korea. The governing elite of Chosŏn Korea found in them an ideal ally for the purpose of maintaining its political sway. In particular, Chu Hsi's statements on maintaining class distinctions were embraced and propagated in Korea with a vehemence rare in China, though not so rare in Japan. The following teaching of Chu Hsi gave a special meaning to the clan-oriented loyalties of Koreans:

> In order to control the minds of the people, unify one's kin, and enrich customs so that people will not forget their origin, it is necessary to clarify genealogy, group members of the clan together, and institute a system of heads of descent.
>
> Since there are no heads of descent today, there are no ministers at Court who have come from families noted for generations. If the system of heads of descent is established, people will know how to honor their ancestors and take their origins seriously. As they take their origins seriously, the power of the Court will naturally be highly respected.[10]

Clarified lines of descent, established heads of lineages, and institutionalized ancestor reverence were thus proposed as the three "pillars" of social and political peace.[11] The cement that would hold the pillars firm was described as customs or *p'ungsok*. "*P'ung* means the civilizing or educational influence of the ruler whereas *sok* is the people's habits. *P'ungsok* is the basic moral energy of the state and if it deteriorates the state itself is in danger. *P'ungsok* must be nurtured by education." *P'ungsok* was presented as the practical side of "proper ritual behavior" or *ye* and it had a high moral status. The term *ye* came to be used as a word interchangeable with morality.

This does not mean that the state could be governed by *ye* alone. Criminal law or *pŏp* was presented as a necessary concomitant of rites. The explanation for relying on the supportive use of law was that outwardly not all men were good. Hence they were not all capable of understanding and obeying the rules of proper ritual behavior. Such men needed the sterner guidance and compulsion of law in order to draw out their "innate moral potential." The *Li Chi*'s statement that "the *ye* (Ch. *li*) do not go down to the common people; the punishments do not go up to the ministers"[12] was cited often to clinch the argument. *Ye* were perceived as preventing moral transgressions, and *pŏp* as punishing the offenders should they commit such violations. Moral teachings and legal sanctions against their violations thus jointly ensured social and political peace by ostensibly regulating two different, unequal segments of society.

The realms of both *ye* and *pŏp* did not recognize any logical distinction between public and private morality and conduct, which were related to each other like macrocosm and microcosm. Those who conducted themselves properly at home were bound to be good subjects as well. Theoretically, there was no distinction in Korea between what John Stuart Mill called "self-regarding" and "other-regarding" activities. It was, in theory at least, an "all-public, no-self" society. The law's reach could *in principle* extend to the innermost recesses of one's mind. Such a view recognized no limitations on the authority of the state, which had two mutually related dimensions: the educational and the penal, which reinforced each other. It was only natural for such a society to punish transgressions of filial piety severely, maintain extensive thought-control in order to prevent or penalize ideas held contrary to the state's orthodoxy, encourage through all its magisterial power and machinery the concept of a morally stern, parent-like government, and, in effect, loom as a totalitarian political system.

It is in this context that one should also view the widespread use of state-sponsored *hyangyak* or village contracts during the Chosŏn dynasty. "As embodiments of *ye*," these village contracts "became one of the most effective means to control the moral and, by extension, the political atmosphere" of areas away from the direct surveillance of authorities in Seoul. These social contracts, which spread all over the country in the sixteenth century, "essentially had four major parts: mutual encouragement to observe the rules of proper conduct; mutual correction of trespass; correct observance of rituals; and mutual assistance in times of disaster."[13]

Besides these contracts, which had a "binding force for a community beyond the radius of immediate lineage influence," Chosŏn dynasty Confucianists used another instrument for "social control and indoctrination." This consisted of lineage rules or *kahun*, whose aim was to smooth "intra-lineage relationships" and "spread [the] civilizing influence of Confucian teachings into the innermost chambers of a family, the women's quarters." They encouraged families to strive for moral perfection through "self-cultivation, economic austerity" and faithful observance of rituals. Thus, the "harmony of the domestic sphere" and the order and tranquility of the society at large were brought together, the latter issuing from the former.[14]

Obviously, in such a society the individual qua individual had only a muted role. The individual had to view himself or herself and had to be viewed by the society in terms of his or her status and role in the family and the larger social world. One always had to be either a parent or a child, a husband or a wife, an elder sibling or a younger sibling, a part of the ruling establishment or outside it.[15] One also had to establish one's identity through one's clan and one's occupation. How respectfully one was treated by the state and the society depended to a large degree upon whether or not one was viewed as enjoying a relationship of superiority with those one was dealing with. Individuals' asymmetrical relationships with one another and with the state were sanctioned and enforced by a system ordained by both ethics and law.[16] Language also reflected this asymmetry. Obsequious forms of address used toward those deemed to be above oneself and condescending forms of address reserved for those below were an integral part of the Korean language.[17] This was an important way to keep people conscious of their origin and status.

In this system, only the *yangban* elite exercised political rights. Others--commoners, and those belonging to the despised groups (slaves, butchers, prostitutes, shamans, acrobats, and the like)—were generally thought to be devoid of the capacity of enjoying such rights, though on occasion a meritorious deed by one from such strata might win him special consideration. The logic behind this was that such strata had no wisdom, and only wisdom, as demonstrated by a combination of high lineage and high educational attainments, could qualify one to participate in political matters. Any attempt by those outside this combination to express themselves in any organized fashion on political matters was considered at best bad form and at worse suspect as something akin to treason. Even when the law specifically did not forbid such a role for the masses at large, the ruling *yangban* elite exerted pressures to make sure that governmental functions remained its own exclusive preserve. The Chosŏn dynasty government could certainly be described as a government "*of* and *by* the *yangban* elite," though it managed to show enough occasional concern in both words and deeds for the well-being of the common man that it does not deserve the categorical characterization of *"for* the *yangban* elite."

In property transactions, where legally enforceable rights were less subject to class and sex distinctions, and free and equal transactions could conceivably take place, such rights were often rendered uncertain or weak for the common people by powerful extra-legal pressures exercised by the elite.[18] Within the family, both law and social practice prevented equal distribution of property among all children. Sex and age were important considerations in the application of inheritance law, with larger shares going to the elder son (or sons) and much smaller shares assigned to a daughter (or daughters).[19]

Between the individual and the state, rights for the control of private property were entirely unequal. Technically, all land was state land, and all wealth accruing from it could also be deemed state wealth. The state could, by merely issuing decrees, take over anyone's private property. One could appeal for mercy from the state, but one could not file a legal appeal for the recovery of one's ownership or for compensation for its loss. Decrees had the same force as statute law. In fact, distinction between the two was nonexistent. All commands of the sovereign were the law of the land.[20] All administrative provisions designed to redress any grievances on this score affirmed that the state was addressing not a case of legal wrong but of human distress. This system could not and did not countenance any struggle for rights.

Any kind of self-expression that questioned this order was frowned upon and, in extreme cases, was punishable with death. Alien ideas were extremely difficult to transplant into this kind of sociopolitical soil. Members of the elite—the beneficiaries of this system—saw to it that any such ideas were nipped in the bud. The bureaucracy of the state, manned by this elite, projected itself as the embodiment of rule by virtue and morality, indeed of royalty itself, since royalty was identified with virtue and morality. What was due to royalty—the people's unquestioning obedience—was also due by extension to the bureaucracy and its social nexus. This was the proper "way" of the loyal subject. Even loyal, constructive criticism of the court—remonstrance, that hallowed hallmark of good Confucian government—was, in Korea, for all practical purposes a preserve of the elite, the masses' participation in it suppressed or ignored more often than respected.[21]

In his 1967 book, *The Korean Political Tradition and Law*, the late Hahm Pyong-Choon, an eminent law scholar, has offered a lucid elaboration of this view of traditional Korean society. According to Hahm, since knowledge and wisdom were considered the exclusive possession of the ruler and his aides (that is, the government), it was logical for Chosŏn dynasty Korea to recognize only positive law as legitimate. Unless adopted and promulgated by the government, the local beliefs and customs of the people had no place in governing human affairs. It would otherwise be tantamount to institutionalizing popular ignorance and stupidity and offering it the same standing as knowledge and wisdom. This could not be permitted, because the populace at large was associated with the senses and instincts, whereas cool reason was the putative lubricant of government. Besides, the ruler had to be above the law, as its maker, not one of its wards. "Law as [the] accumulation of collective experience of the society never had any existence in [the] Korean political tradition."[22] It was

not even a product of the uses and wonts of the ignorant common man. It was an instrument of chastising the vicious and the depraved.

It was an unpleasant necessity prescribed by the failure of reason in politics. . . . It always signified a norm with physical force as a sanction behind it. It was therefore synonymous with punishment, no more, no less. . . . [Thus], the rulers were not only above the law in fact but they also believed they *ought to be* above the law.[23]

Law naturally was to be so severe that few would dare to break it. Only thus could it serve its avowed purpose as an aid to government. "Rule of law" to Koreans, according to Hahm, inevitably came to mean something dreadful, to be kept at bay, to escape from, rather than something to be used as an ally in the protection of one's claims and rights.

Hahm argued that judicial functions in such a society necessarily had entirely different connotations than in Western societies. Judicial officials and functionaries, who enjoyed the self-image of being a wise and virtuous ruling class acting under the name and authority of a "sage" king, need not be good judges in the modern sense, scrupulously examining the law and the evidence, fairly giving all parties to a dispute the chance to present their respective cases, interpreting the law and applying it without fear or favor. Their function, as of the rest of officialdom, was to prevent disharmony from occurring and spreading in the areas under their jurisdiction. At best, the judge might conciliate a dispute as a wise elder. At worst, he could impose a judgment, exercising his personal discretion for which there was ample room. The law was *designed* to leave much room for the exercise of such "wise discretion." In practice, such discretion seemed not infrequently to have been an item for quiet sale to the highest bidder or was dispensed in favor of friends or relatives.

Under a judicial system of this kind, the separation of political or executive functions from the judicial was scarcely conceivable. The last had to be subordinate to the first two. For judicial functions to acquire prominence signified a failure of virtuous government.

The Western concept of separation of powers could not emerge in this dispensation since there were no civil liberties sacrosanct or unassailable. Freedom and equality under law—a prime modern Western value—was not a political ideal in Korea. Whereas the West stressed the individuals's right to attain his full creative potential, both for its own sake and as a way of enhancing the richness of life for all in society, in Korea the idea stressed was conformity to the existing pattern of life. Or, in a crisis, the idea could be the offering of assistance to the state in rediscovering and reestablishing the worthy pattern of a "golden" past. Looking ahead—the idea of progress—was inimical to this way of life and was therefore discouraged. The idea of liberty and the idea of progress were not considered as "ethical goods or moral attributes of good life" in Confucian Korea. Specifically, when liberty was extolled at all, it was only as part of a larger virtue such as *chi* (wisdom) or *ye* (propriety, as defined by Confucianism), Hahm asserted. Liberation from the baser instincts of life was considered part of *in* or humaneheartedness. When a person's choice was determined by this kind of moral rationality, he was said to be free.

The notion of moral freedom, and, indeed, its implied right of alienation from the society, was thus not absent in the Korean or East Asian tradition; nor was it peculiar to East Asian Confucianists. The Taoists of East Asia and Buddhists everywhere in Asia, not to mention many Western philosophers, notably Plato, Rousseau, and Kant, and some modern anarchists, have spoken of this moral freedom. What is of concern to the average person in the modern West, however, is social and political liberty. The freedom of being oneself, of unfettered personal creativity and mobility was in Chosŏn Korea only a privilege bestowed by the state, not a right. Korea, like China, would have been more likely to have supported Hobbes's rather than Rousseau's or Locke's view of liberty. A man could conceivably be free in Korea in the moral sense but still subject to all kinds of political and legal restraints imposed from above. In modern Western law and politics, it is freedom from such fetters, from arbitrary arrest and punishment, and from arbitrary deprivation of one's life, property, and the like, that is of utmost consequence. This freedom in Chosŏn Korea was always stringently circumscribed and precarious.

Equality as a natural human right was even more unacceptable in Chosŏn Korea. According to Hahm, Koreans were always more impressed by the inequalities than the equality of human beings.[24] Hierarchy, the placement of some above and others below, the giving and receiving of commands were part of the natural, cosmic scheme of things. Monarchy and aristocracy, not democracy, were regarded by them as natural forms of government. As we have seen before, this acceptance of the intrinsic inequality of human beings in Korea governed even the relations between siblings. Even twin siblings were not considered equal.[25]

This "denial of the intrinsic equality" of all human beings meant that, even in purely commercial transactions, the low-born or the common folk were highly disadvantaged against the *yangban* elite. Exchange of goods and services was also based upon the superior-inferior equation, though perhaps less in practice than in law. All property laws were part of the highly discriminatory administrative and criminal codes. A separate private or civil law governing contracts, commercial transactions, torts, and so forth, did not exist in Chosŏn Korea, making it extremely difficult, as Hahm said, to institute a law suit, even when it was legally permissible to do so, against a social superior. It made a true adversary system of litigation virtually nonexistent, vitiating the whole concept of justice.[26]

A further implication of all this was, of course, what Hahm has called the "negation of free citizenship."[27] Since the masses were ignorant and devoid of wisdom, the "sacred" task of government could not be shared with them. Their well-being was talked about in much the same way as parents talk about the well-being of their children. The Chosŏn-dynasty elite could, on occasion, issue calls for respect to public opinion and even welcome memorials from all to rectify errors and reestablish virtue in government, but the idea of any institutionalized popular participation in government was anathema.

Since government was conceived less in terms of subjection to impartial laws and more in terms of obedience to paternalistic "wise" rulers, Chosŏn-dynasty Koreans had a very weak understanding of rule by an impersonal or abstract norm. They could understand the sovereignty of the king but not the sovereignty of law, much less the concept of popular sovereignty. The predictability associated with justice under law was unknown in Chosŏn Korea, the particular circumstances and "merit" of each case determining the judicial outcome, thus focusing attention not upon law but upon the "wisdom" of the person who administered it. "Humanistic particularism," not abstract universalism, might be a fitting label for this system. Cicero's famous enunciation of law—"for as the law governs the magistrate, so the magistrate governs the people, and it can truly be said that a magistrate is speaking law, and the law is a silent magistrate"—would have been a puzzling statement to Chosŏn-dynasty Koreans, according to Hahm.[28]

Since the function of law was mainly to serve as a stern deterrent to those ungovernable by moral suasion, its manifestations to the average public were always gruesome and grotesque. For serious crimes calling for capital punishment, decapitation, dismemberment of the criminal's body, and public display of his severed limbs were the ways the law showed its unforgiving power. Even for less severe crimes, the cangue, the switch, and the lash could be and were frequently used.

No doubt, everyone longed for, and many sought, entry into the ranks of the privileged who were either immune from the application of specific provisions of the law or whom the law treated more mildly than others. No doubt, those in power and privilege resisted such efforts from below, making Chosŏn-dynasty society far more rigid in restricting social mobility than the nation whence it drew its model—China. Only sons of *yangban* could normally become *yangban*. It was a uniquely structured, self-perpetuating class which clung to Chu Hsi's injunctions on the family and clan with a tenacity unknown in China.

As Hahm further pointed out, the Chosŏn dynasty in treason cases rigidly enforced the concept of guilt by association to keep the country under control. Responsibility in such cases was a concern of one's group and community, not just oneself. A family, a village, a town, a country, a whole province, could be held accountable for this crime—virtuous government had broken down there, the citation would read—and punished. A town with a "treasonous rebel" could thus be demoted to a village, causing it loss of "face" as well as many material benefits. No one coming from the tainted place could, for example, take the civil-service examination for a specified length of time. The criminal's family suffered an even worse fate. For such serious crimes one's whole family could be condemned to death, and the stigma of being the blood relatives of a criminal could go on the official records of future generations in the family as well, assuming there were survivors. The sins of one's parents or grandparents could literally visit their progeny. Misery and humiliation stayed with them until perhaps a highly meritorious deed won them the restoration of their good name. Similarly, a concubine's descendant's were forever discriminated against for being of her blood, even though concubinage was recognized by law and widely practiced by men of the *yangban* elite. All Koreans were obliged to carry at all times a kind of identification tablet called the *hop'ae*, bearing the carrier's name, date of birth, status, and address.[29]

A person was often believed to be guilty upon accusation, until proven otherwise. Chosŏn-dynasty Koreans seemed to believe that, if there was smoke, there was bound to be a fire of suspicious origin beneath it. (It is a pattern of thinking that Hahm believed still persists in Korea, as does the old thinking regarding guilt by association. It is hard for Koreans to believe that the immediate relatives of a Communist are not Communists.)[30]

For such reasons mainly, Koreans always tried to stay as clear of suspicion as possible and often attempted to curry favor with state officials through every available means at their command. Since suspicion could be aroused by a simple rumor started by a vengeful person, and since laws were often vague and, in any case, were believed to be applied arbitrarily, all common Koreans lived in a state of perpetual fear and insecurity. A well-known saying was: "No one's coat is truly dust-free, if you shake it hard enough."[31] Translated as practical advice, it meant an admonition not to incur any government official's grudge or displeasure. The vaguest suspicion of law-breaking or of unethical conduct in his mind against a civilian could jeopardize the latter's life or livelihood.

Several other factors contributed to the repressive political structure of Chosŏn Korea. Physical movement, especially across the country's borders, was severely restricted. Virtually no trade relations were conducted with any outsiders except the Chinese and Japanese. Diplomatic relations or contacts were likewise maintained only with China and, on a fitful basis, Japan, with the former as a suzerain. Travel to China, but not to Japan, was possible only for state-dispatched tribute missions and state-authorized traders. Any travel without such explicit authorization could be punished with death. The country and its people were thus in cocoonlike isolation from most of the world.[32]

TOWARD CHANGE: A TRADITION BEGINS TO ERODE

This isolation, stringent indoctrination, punitive laws, regimentation, and occasional gestures of genuine concern for the well-being of the common man ensured longevity if not unperturbed stability for the Chosŏn dynasty. The peninsula was from time to time shaken by peasant unrest and riots. None, however, was widespread and organized enough to threaten the dynasty's existence until very late in the nineteenth century. In Chosŏn Korea, even more than in Japan, isolation was a very effective policy in this regard. Koreans were not exposed to any alternative model of government. A highly stratified system of Confucian society and government came thus to be accepted both by the rulers and the ruled eventually as something axiomatic and preordained.

Occasional attempts to make a dent in the system met with hostility and repression. A few *yangban* intellectuals, for example, were exposed to Catholicism and the trickle of Western thought and technology that flowed into Korea from China during the seventeenth and eighteenth centuries, and they began to question the values of the existing sociopolitical system. Their ideas eventually sparked a minor intellectual movement known as *Sirhak* (Practical Learning), much as a similar movement called Han Learning was sparked in China. Korean savants like Hong Tae-yong, Yi Ik, Yu Hyŏng-wŏn, Yun Chung, Yi Su-kwang, Pak Se-tang, Yun Hyu, Chŏng Yag-yong, Pak Chi-wŏn, and others, not only learned a great deal about Catholicism and Western science and technology but also something of Western law, politics, and society. These men managed, often at great personal risk, to raise voices against class distinctions and the Confucian disdain for commerce, and argued for equality of opportunity to all for entry into government, the abolition of slavery, the teaching of Western scientific subjects in Korea, the encouragement of commerce and industry for both internal economic development and for exports, land reform, and other innovations. The government showed little toleration for such ideas. In 1785, Catholicism was officially banned and the import of all Western books from Peking was stopped. The *Sirhak* flame was practically extinguished, its embers barely kept alive by a handful of quiet scholars who continued, without public fanfare, their empirical studies in their private abodes.[33]

Another challenge to Korea's Confucian system arose in the early 1860s, in the form of a new, syncretic religion which styled itself *Tonghak* (Eastern Learning), as distinguished from *Sŏhak* (Western Learning or Catholicism). It was a curious mix of progressive and obscurantist modes of thought. Under its founder, an alienated *yangban* named Ch'oe Che-u, *Tonghak* drew elements from Confucianism, Taoism, Buddhism, and even Catholicism (which it otherwise attacked), and declared itself in favor of class equality as well as sexual equality, much as did the contemporary *Taiping* Movement in China. But, unlike the *Taiping* leadership, the *Tonghak* leaders were against the opening of Korea and opposed Western ideas and institutions. For this reason, the *Tonghak* Movement was tolerated by the government for a time, but ultimately the authorities saw the subversive potential of its ideas, arrested Ch'oe, and had him executed in 1864. By this time, however, Ch'oe had converted tens of thousands of Koreans all over the country. His simple, populist idiom, coupled with his evangelical zeal and his millenarianism, kept the movement alive under the underground leadership of his successor, Ch'oe Si-hyŏng.

Though couched in religious terms, the *Tonghak* ideology contained an unmistakable message of egalitarianism. Ch'oe Che-u encompassed this message in his famous phrase *si ch'ŏnju* meaning "divinity resides in human beings." Modified by later leaders of the movement to *in nae ch'ŏn* and *in si ch'ŏn* (man is God), these words have been explained in the following fashion by a Korean commentator:

Si ch'ŏnju means "bearing God" or "serving God." "Bearing God" implies divinity in man. [It] means that one has the Spirit within [oneself]. [It signifies] that this Spirit [ie. the "Totality of Life" of the universe] has gradually become individualized and complex and high, and has reached the most highly developed state in the human world after passing through the stages of the vegetable and animal worlds, and therefore man, having the most highly developed intellectual power, "has the Spirit within. . . . " Man is [merely] individualized life and God is the "Totality of Life. . . . " [In] this relationship there is no gap, no separation. [It is like the] relationship of part to the whole. . . . Man is [thus] necessarily dependent upon God, and bears and serves God.[34]

In its "fundamental monism," in its insistence that man in his essence is at one with God, the *Tonghak* ideology was clearly anthropocentric. "Outside God or Heaven there is no man; outside man there is no God or Heaven."

Since all human beings, of whatever birth, sex, or age, were believed in essence to be reflections of the divine, it was imperative that they all be accorded a treatment of utmost respect, equality, and concern. From the Chosŏn elite's point of view, this was a serious problem. If allowed to flourish, Ch'oe's doctrine would have struck at the very foundation of Chosŏn Korea's sociopolitical edifice. Like the *Sirhak* heterodoxy, it had the revolutionary potential of upsetting the cardinal principle of Korea's Confucian government—hierarchy as an immutable norm in all spheres of life. The ethical social formula of the *Tonghak*, "*sain yŏch'ŏn*" (Treat man as Heaven), threatened to introduce the chaos of democratic thought into Korea's feudal society. The threat became explicit to all when the *Tonghak* leaders called for the abolition of all discrimination between legitimate and non-legitimate children and elevation of the degraded status of women, especially by insisting that the ban on widow remarriage be lifted.[35] Under these circumstances, what is surprising is not that Ch'oe was executed but that he and his followers were not all destroyed the first time they spoke up in 1860.

During the late 1800s, Korean society received another challenge— this time from abroad. The Opium War and the resulting humiliation of China at the hands of Western powers, the forced opening of Japan, the imposition by the West of unequal treaties, especially their extra-territoriality clause, upon both China and Japan during the 1840s and 1850s, and the joint Anglo-French occupation of Peking, indicating a further weakening of China, were events of which the Korean intelligentsia were well aware. The Korean King during 1864–1873—the future Kojong—was a minor, and the events of the decade were controlled and directed in his name by his wily father, known by his official title Taewŏn'gun or Grand Prince. Though the son reigned, the Taewŏn'gun ruled.

Historian Han Woo-Keun has described this regent as "uncompromising" but "honest" and dedicated to recreating the Korean state and society upon the hoary prescriptions of the Confucian sages, subject to his own interpretations of course. He also embodied all the major defects of traditional Confucian thought: inflexibility of mind, obscurantism, and refusal to recognize realities that conflicted with his personal convictions. When Western ships appeared in Korean waters during 1866–1871 seeking trade relations, the Taewŏn'gun rebuffed them both in word and deed. The French, German, and American attempts to open Korea's doors to trade led to brief military encounters in which the Korean side scored victory each time and forced the outsiders to beat humiliating retreats. This was a matter of great rejoicing to the Koreans under the Taewŏn'gun, for it seemed to show that tiny Korea had succeeded where China and Japan had failed. But the Korean victories were illusory. As Han explains the situation, the Western powers had left Korea not because they lacked superior military might but because they were all occupied with urgent concerns elsewhere: The British in India; Russia in the Kuriles; the French in Indo-China; and the United States at home, addressing the aftermath of the Civil War. Korea was not a top priority to any of them at the time.[36]

Military defeats for the West at the hands of the Korean forces were accompanied by a new wave of violent persecution of Korean Catholics and the execution of foreign priests who had sneaked into Korea to minister to the small, cloistered community of native faithful. Nine French priests were put to death by decapitation. Koreans were forbidden to have any contact with foreigners upon pain of death. As historian James B. Palais has stated, the Taewŏn'gun's foreign policy was "simple": "no treaties and no trade with Westerners, no toleration of Catholic proselytization within Korea and no reordering of relations with Japan."[37] By 1871, Catholicism in Korea had been practically wiped out. Thus, the fragile attempts from within toward a progressive humanism and open society, and efforts from without for trade with the Western world, which could conceivably have led to the introduction of modern trends into Korea's intellectual and ethical life, had been firmly defeated.

Defeated, but not destroyed. Dealing with the Western powers that as yet lacked serious interest in Korea was one thing. Confronting Japan, a country vitally interested in Korea, was quite another, and it was Japan that proved to be the catalyst for changes, both tragic and salutory, that were to come to Korea soon. Taking its lessons from the West seriously, Japan decided to resort to both persistent diplomacy and force to pressure Korea to open its doors to trade and diplomatic relations. Japan had evinced great interest in Korea historically. Korea had been the subject of perennial concern as a dagger pointed at the heart of Japan or as a bridge for aggression against Japan, as had happened during two unsuccessful Mongol invasions in the thirteenth century. The peninsula had also been used by Toyotomi Hideyoshi in the late sixteenth century for his grandiose but unsuccessful plan of continental conquest and empire. In the nineteenth century, fear of Russian, and to some extent Chinese, expansionism had combined with the possible economic value of Korea to prompt Japan to cast a nervously covetous eye once again upon the peninsula.

Japan's attempts to open Korea succeeded after the fall of the Taewŏn'gun. Though enjoying wide literati support in his anti-foreign postures, the Taewŏn'gun had bitterly alienated many *yangban* by curtailing their power. His abolition of the *yangban*-run private academies (*sŏwŏn*), which had been hotbeds of factional dissidence and political intrigue; his subjection of the *yangban* to an unprecedented military tax; his debasement of the nation's currency; and his extravagant and expensive palace-construction project as a symbolic way of restoring the power of the Throne, which had been eroded by *yangban* assaults, were all unpopular. The last two reforms were resented not only by the elite but also by the populace at large. The Taewŏn'gun had to withdraw from power in December 1873 under a massive *yangban*-led protest movement spearheaded by such arch conservatives as Ch'oe Ik-hyŏn. The King, now an adult, was freed from the Taewŏn'gun's domination.[38]

This development did not lead to an immediate alteration of the policy of keeping Korea in hermit-like seclusion. The majority of literati were militantly against any such change. But a few of the more liberal and concerned scholars now began to speak with increasing boldness and vigor in favor of opening Korea to the world. The Court and some bureaucrats were also impressed by reports of Japan's progress since the Meiji Restoration. When Japan provoked a naval incident with Korea in Korean waters, the Korean Court became worried about a possible invasion by Japan and agreed to open its doors for limited trade and consular purposes.

In the treaty signed between the two parties on 27 February 1876, Korea was presented as an entity acting independently, without reference to its suzerain, China. Korea was thus detached from the apron strings of China, though China would not agree to this "sovereign" status for Korea until forced to do so after the Sino-Japanese War (1894–1895). Signed under duress, the treaty conferred many diplomatic and commercial advantages on Japan. Seoul and Tokyo were to exchange envoys and three Korean ports—Pusan, Inchŏn, and Wŏnsan—were to be opened to Japanese trade. Japanese merchants were to be "allowed to trade unhindered" in these ports and were to have the right to lease land and build commercial and residential property on it. Most important, Japanese nationals in Korea were to have the same extraterritoriality that Westerners exercised in China and Japan. Japanese offenders in Korea were to be tried not by Korean judicial authorities but by Japanese consuls. A further agreement between the two sides allowed Japanese diplomats the right to travel throughout Korea and to maintain residences in the open ports. Japanese and Korean currency could be freely brought in and taken out between the two countries. All items of trade between them were to be duty-free for several years. Korea was also to permit the free export of rice to Japan except in emergencies.[39]

The significance of this episode for human rights in Korea is not readily apparent, but the opening of Korea was bound to lead to further developments with a cumulative potential of inflicting serious damage on the country's traditional fabric, inaugurating what may be called the "transitional process"—a process that slowly but inevitably brings in fresh ideas and values and puts them against forces hitherto sacrosanct. This is precisely what happened in Korea after 1876. It is not that the treaty era opened up the floodgates of curiosity, freedom, equality, and innovation but rather that the traditional order of Korea became increasingly and hopelessly on the defensive. Koreans of all strata would now be gradually exposed to alternative modes of social and political behavior, would have a chance to compare them with their own, to reflect upon the eternal questions of what was good for the individual and society, and decide what was worth preserving and what was worth discarding in their nation's age-old legacy. The treaty of 1876, though humiliating for Korea, just as similar Western treaties had been humiliating for China and Japan, ushered in some salutary trends for Koreans, including the most deadly one for traditional thinkers—wider intellectual curiosity.

The proponents of the isolationist school were not, though, any less defiant after 1876. Many, styling themselves as champions of "righteousness" and opponents of "heterodoxy," continued to rail against the dangers of innovation, but others parted company with them and thought in terms of seeking a happy amalgam of Western technology and Eastern values. Much like the Chinese and Japanese nationalists of a generation or so before, who had talked of preserving Eastern morality and importing "Western techniques" in order to create a "strong and prosperous" nation, moderate Confucianists in Korea began to stir themselves and the King in favor of a selective program of modernization in order to strengthen the state. Martina Deuchler, a specialist on the history of Korea of this period has called them the "self-strengtheners" of the country, applying to them a term fashionable in contemporary China as well as in Korea: *tzu-chiang (K. chagang)*.[40] Their first chance to offer their advice to the Throne came in 1882 when the King invited suggestions from across the nation about the reforms to introduce.

The rallying call of these reformists, who included a small number of *Sirhak*-type Confucianists, was the concept of *iyong husaeng*, "Enrich the well-being of the people by taking advantage of the useful." Reformists sent a flood of memorials to Seoul in response to Kojong's call. These included proposals for the study of foreign lands and international law, the sending of students abroad, the eventual construction of steamships, cannons, and telegraph lines, the inviting of foreign instructors in science and technology, the setting up of a deliberative body, the founding of a chamber of commerce and a national bank, the restructuring of the tax system along modern lines, and the building of a navy. Ultimately, this led to the adoption of a limited concept of modernization: "Modern technology was to be grafted on to the body of traditional wisdom."[41]

The King and the Min clan leaders, then in powerful bureaucratic positions, gave full support to this approach, out of which also emerged the opening of Korea on a wider basis—the setting up of diplomatic or consular relations with Western powers. The 1880s saw the opening of such relations with the United States, France, Russia, Germany, Italy, and the United Kingdom. The government made plans to send envoys, observation missions, and official study panels as well as young students to Japan, the United States, and Europe. A study group also went to China to learn from the Chinese experience with "self-strengthening" through limited modernization.[42] This period also saw the arrival, at government invitation, of several missionary teachers to give instruction in English to a select group of Korean students at a state school, the opening of two private schools by missionaries (Paejae for boys and Ehwa for girls in Seoul), a missionary-run medical center, and the beginnings of Protestant Christian evangelical activity in Korea.[43]

THE ERA OF ENLIGHTENMENT:
A NEW IMPETUS FOR LIBERAL IDEAS

The cumulative effect of all these developments was an impetus to the further import of liberal ideas and values from abroad. A new movement emerged from this matrix. Called the *Kaehwa* or Enlightenment Movement, it sought to take Korea beyond a purely technological modernization. Though, in the choice of their means, some exponents of the movement were sharply different from others, their aim was a more general restructuring of the established order affecting all areas of life. Some of the enlightenment reformers opted for a course of violent overthrow of the government with foreign-government support in order to institute the changes they thought necessary for national revitalization; others chose the peaceful, gradualist approach of working within the system. Some believed in the total rejection of Confucianism and the wholesale adoption of Christianity; others believed that the freedom of faith, leading to the interplay of various religious ideas and a cross-fertilization of secular values, would best benefit the nation. On one thing all were of a unified mind: They all agreed that Korea's survival and prosperity were dependent upon urgent and fundamental changes in most aspects of life. Almost all were also of the *yangban* class.

The first stirrings of the Enlightenment Movement occurred very early in the 1880s. Its prominent leaders included a number of Korean *yangban*, some in their teens. All had been exposed to some knowledge about the West and Japan through their common study of a few elementary books imported into Korea clandestinely during the 1870s. All had also had some exposure to the scholarly works of the *Sirhak* School through their common association with a leading *Sirhak* teacher of the time, a *yangban* named Pak Kyu-su, and with O Kyŏng-sŏk, a scholarly Chinese-language interpreter employed by the government from the *chungin* class. (The *chungin* were a stratum between the *yangban* and the commoners—near the *yangban* class but not of it. Hence they were known for their acute dissatisfaction with the social system.)[44]

Among the noteworthy early leaders of the *Kaehwa* Movement were Pak Yŏng-hyo, O Yun-chung, Kim Ok-kyun, Hong Yŏng-sik, Sŏ Kwang-bŏm, Yu Kil-chun, Yun Ch'i-ho, and Sŏ Chae-p'il. All had been keen to see Japan and, if possible, the Western lands too.[45] Being sons of influential government personages, they found satisfaction of their desire in the early 1880s. At least three of them—Yu Kil-chun, Kim Ok-kyun, and Yun Ch'i-ho—during their visits to Japan were closely associated with Fukuzawa Yukichi and his private school, Keiō Gijuku, or were influenced by his writings.

Fukuzawa was not a towering intellect but was doubtlessly a major publicist of his time in Japan. A leader of the Japanese "Civilization and Enlightenment" (*bummei kaika*) Movement, a relentless critic of Confucianism and Buddhism, mentor to the activists of the People's Rights Movement (*jiyu minken undō*), a prolific writer of books on the West, educator, and press magnate, Fukuzawa was a multi-sided personality. His most famous statement, derived from his study of the American Declaration of Independence was "Heaven has not placed one individual above or below another." Fukuzawa's cardinal themes were equality, independence of mind, scientific inquiry, and a constant search for progress. All these he considered essential for making Japan strong and proud of itself and a true equal of any nation on earth. He was constantly looking at enlightenment from the angle of a Social Darwinist. "People's rights" (*minken*), he often argued, would strengthen "national rights" (*kokken*).[46]

Such in a nutshell was the man who exercised an important influence on Korea's enlightenment activists. In addition to Fukuzawa, Japan itself influenced the reformers. In Japan, these Koreans had seen the results of rapid modernization efforts undertaken by the government, which had abolished the class system and had built a formidable army and navy in a short period of time. Industrially and commercially, too, Japan had become what Kim Ok-kyun said was the "Great Britain of the Orient." Kim's ambition was to see Korea become at least the France of Asia.[47]

It was obvious to Kim and his fellow reformers that Japan's new status was due to its openness to the West and, like many Japanese at the time, Kim and his group in Korea attributed the advancement of the West to, among other things, Christianity. In a memorial addressed to the King in 1884, Kim stressed the importance of introducing Christianity into Korea:

Now that all the countries in the world are stressing commerce and competing with each other in [the] abundance of industrial occupations made available to their respective people's, it would be tantamount to waiting for the fall of the country not to make a strenuous effort to eliminate the *yangban* system and destroy the source of its evils. Your Majesty is asked to reconsider this point seriously; to expel ignorant and incompetent ministers who cling to the old system and are bigoted, as soon as possible; to abolish the practice of holding good lineage in esteem; to solidify the foundation of power centralization by appointing able persons; to win popular trust; to exploit human wisdom by establishing schools everywhere, and to enlighten the people by introducing a foreign religion [Christianity].[48]

This was indeed a far cry from Chu Hsi, the Taewŏn'gun, and even the *Tonghak*, for the last had from its inception shown a strong strain of anti-foreignism.

Kim and his colleagues did not wait too long to translate their ambition into reality. Knowing that their reformist ideas would be stoutly resisted by the ultra-conservative literati, they resorted to the radical step of a coup d'état in order to launch a bold, Meiji Revolution-style program. With the support of the Japanese legation in Seoul, the Kim group seized control of the palace and the government in a swift, bloody strike on 4 December 1884. The newly set up "reform" government promised—a first in Korean history—to work for the elimination of all class distinctions and the establishment of equal rights for all, and for the firm abolition of the tributary system, raising Korea's status to that of a truly sovereign state.[49] Other provisions were designed to reform the administrative and tax systems, all with a view to making the functions of palace and government efficient, fair, and free of corruption. The new government also intended to strengthen the Korean military and introduce a modern educational system. New forms of sanitation and health care and a transportation development plan were also in the offing.⁵⁰ In short, the reformers had proposed the rudiments of a modern nation-state.

The new government lasted barely three days. Supported by Chinese military intervention, the conservatives struck back, ousting the Kim group. The coup led only to street deaths for some of its members and an ignominious escape to exile in Japan for others. The new government fell so easily because it had been set up by a cabal from the top; it had no power base in the society at large. Kim Ok-kyun and his colleagues had not attempted to cultivate popular support. They had at best a shaky military support, and they had been limited by their reliance on a foreign power's legation. The general public did not pay much attention to the Kim group's ardent concern for popular well-being and to their patriotism. It focused its attention rather on the group's foreign connection and concluded that it was a treasonous faction. The fury of the public knew no bounds. Hong Yŏng-sik, a member of the Kim group, was set upon and killed. Kim Ok-kyun, Pak Yŏng-hyo, Sŏ Kwang-bŏm, and Sŏ Chae-p'il fled to Japan. Kim was hunted by agents of the Korean government for nearly a decade. He was finally assassinated in 1894. His dismembered body was brought into Korea and put on public display to warn others of the consequences of similar treason. Sŏ Chaep'il's entire family had to suffer death under the traditional practice of guilt by association.⁵¹

The failure of this attempt at radical reform did not mean that all progressive forces and figures were destroyed in Korea. Moderate progressives in the government under the encouragement of the King and the leadership of the powerful Min clan continued to work for national renovation in areas where they saw no danger to their own power or that of their class. Pak Yŏng-hyo, a radical reformist, did not accept his exile in Japan as a finality but rather honed his progressive ideas further by visiting the United States and studying Japan's modernization efforts in further detail. In 1888, he put his ideas together and sent them in the form of a long memorial to the Korean King, hoping the logic of his thinking might persuade the monarch to throw his weight behind a new, comprehensive program of national reconstruction. Pak also showed in his thinking much enthusiasm for Christianity. Though not a Christian himself, he had studied at Meiji Gakuin, a Protestant school. He once was reported to have told an American:

Our people need education and Christianity. Your missionaries and mission schools can educate and improve our people. . . . As the foundation of the existing religions is weak, the door is now wide open for the conversion of our people to Christianity. . . . It is necessary for our people to receive education and convert to Christianity before legislative reform. Through this process alone will our people be able to establish a constitutional government and create as free and enlightened a country as yours in the future.[52]

Pak's words show how much more ardent he was than Kim Ok-kyun in his feelings about Christianity. Pak's memorial also shows clearly that he had been influenced both by American missionaries and by the writings of Fukuzawa. The memorial contains two basic ideas. First, like Fukuzawa and the missionaries, Pak wrote of all human beings as equal in the eyes of the Creator; hence all have the same rights to life, liberty, and the pursuit of prosperity. These are inalienable endowments of all. Second, he said that it was the people who initially created all governments. Their aim was to seek ways in which to protect their rights. Government is thus nothing but a "trust" and, if the government fails to live up to its duty as a "trust," the people have a right to compel it to do so or alter it or replace it. The answerability of the government to the people is, after all, an integral aspect of inalienable individual rights.

Pak referred to the American Declaration of Independence specifically in the memorial, and many of his proposals merely spelled out its full implications.[53] For example, Pak wrote of the need for "a joint rule of government, shared by the monarch and the subjects," and suggested the setting up of a system of elected assemblies and elected officials at the local and regional levels as a concrete measure for popular participation in government. Knowing that such a proposal might be assailed by the conservatives, he cited the *Ta hsueh* (The great learning) in its support. *The Great Learning*, according to Pak, had said that all governments should respect public opinion; when the populace declares something good, it should be regarded as good by the ruler; when they determine something as bad, the ruler should likewise follow their judgment, for the people are the parents of the state. In this capacity the people should also have the full freedom of criticizing national affairs—for this, they should not be castigated and punished as traitors. In the same vein, Pak also called for the encouragement of newspapers and political parties as forums for the expression of public opinion.[54]

Pak's lengthy memorial was a comprehensive blueprint for national modernization. In addition to the above ideas, it contained a reasoned defense of the concept of equality of classes and between the sexes, and it proposed the banning of concubinage, freedom of choice in marriage, and the remarriage of widows. Pak also devoted a good part of the memorial to the role of law in a limited monarchy. The purpose of law according to Pak was to "regulate the interrelationships of human beings with a view to creating a just society and preventing evil."[55] Law should apply with equal force to all, "high and low, rich and poor." Pak also called for the abolition of the old tradition of guilt by association in treason cases; for open, fair and speedy trials; and for the right of all accused to have access to attorneys and to all evidence helpful to their case.

Pak drew the King's attention to the need to win the people's trust through such reforms and through abolishing torture, guaranteeing humane treatment of prisoners and convicts, and outlawing the private system of justice common in Korea under which powerful *yangban* would simply have those whom they did not like or those whom they considered their enemies locked up and physically punished in their private residences. Only when the law of the country and the law-enforcement activities of the state earned the trust of the people could Korea hope to "prevent disorder at home and danger abroad."[56] This kind of trustworthy government, compulsory schooling for all boys and girls after age 6, contacts of both trade and diplomacy with all "enlightened" foreign states, freedom of travel, and the like were some of the other means Pak thought Korea had to employ in order to enter the comity of civilized and advanced nations. Finally, of course, in this kind of rejuvenated nation there was to be no place for the traditional Korean policy of subservience toward China.[57]

There was, thus, a good deal of reference in the memorial to some of the human rights that are today taken for granted in democratic societies. Though Pak did not go into detail, he also advocated equal rights and equal education for women—an idea dear to both Fukuzawa and the missionaries. Here Fukuzawa and the West, but certainly not Japan, were Pak's inspiration.

The memorial had no immediate impact on the government in Seoul. According to Chŏn Pong-tŏk, a Korean specialist in the country's legal history, it cannot be ascertained whether the memorial was even allowed by the bureaucracy to reach the Throne.[58] Pak had to wait a while before his voice could have a hearing in Korea again. (This would occur in 1894–1895.)

Meanwhile, another eminent Korean, Yu Kil-chun, was engaged in quietly sharpening his own intellectual understanding of what was needed to make Korea a strong and prosperous nation. Kindred in spirit and inclination to Kim Ok-kyun and Pak Yŏng-hyo, but less radical, Yu had been associated with Fukuzawa's Keiō Gijuku in the early 1880s. In 1883, with the encouragement of Pak Yŏng-hyo and with the assistance of Yu, Yun Chi-ho, another young, progressive government official, had started the publication of *Hansŏng sunbo*, a newspaper, under the aegis of the newly created Foreign Ministry. Begun as a medium to enlighten both officials and the literate public about the outside world, *Hansŏng sunbo* was printed exclusively in *Hanmun* (Chinese characters). Both in this form and as a later version called *Hansŏng chubo*, which used both Chinese characters and the Korean script, this newspaper did much to spread progressive ideas among the people of Seoul and even outside, until its demise, due to financial reasons, in 1888.[59]

Yun Ch'i-ho and Yu Kil-chun were often the main writers in the early issues of this paper. Their essays showed much indirect influence of Fukuzawa Yukichi. The American Declaration of Independence and the human rights of life, liberty, and happiness were referred to and explained in editorials using the style and phraseology common to Fukuzawa's *Conditions in the West*, a popular book written for public enlightenment. As in Pak Yŏng-hyo's memorial, Yun and Yu argued that the state's main role was to protect such "Heaven-bestowed" rights: "A state that does not fulfill this role is not a state, and a government that betrays this responsibility is not a government." They further reasoned that, by rebelling against the English Throne, the thirteen colonies of America had expressed Heaven's own anger against oppression.[60] That Yun and Yu could write and publish such editorials under government auspices shows that the voices of progress in the bureaucracy were able, at least for a few years, to hold their own.

During 1883–1884, Yu was in the United States, studying, traveling, and polishing his insights about the world, much as Pak Yŏng-hyo was doing in Japan. On his way back, Yu also visited many European and Asian lands and further broadened his intellectual horizons. Upon his return to Seoul, Yu saw his mission much like that of Fukuzawa and decided to write a detailed and sophisticated book for public circulation on the meaning and uses of an enlightened spirit. Though this was not the only book he wrote, it was the most comprehensive of his works, modeled much after Fukuzawa's *Conditions in the West*. Even its title, "Observations from a Journey to the West," appears to have been inspired by Fukuzawa's title.

In the book, Yu projected himself as a teacher to his nation, covering everything in the Western world about which he believed his countrymen to be uninformed. The book contains much about political systems, international law, commerce, technology, education, and the like. There are significant portions devoted to theoretical matters like sovereignty and practical matters like human rights. Yu began his discussions of human rights by referring to that stock-in-trade of all human-rights advocates in East Asia—the American Declaration of Independence. He wrote of the essential God-given rights that he had already written about in the *Hansŏng sunbo* and, like Fukuzawa, rested his case for egalitarianism on the statement that Heaven had neither placed individuals above nor below others.[61] Like Fukuzawa, Yu used a good deal of space discussing the relationship between "people's rights" and "state's rights."

Like Fukuzawa, Yu held that the first condition for the proper exercise of human rights is a widespread awareness on the part of the people that they hold such rights in common. When this awareness is present, there will be a collective public determination to defend their rights whenever they perceive them to be in danger. People imbued with this determination will be equally determined to defend their political community or state. Yu was thus restating the theme common to the People's Rights Movement in Meiji Japan that, the stronger the "people's rights" (*minken*), the stronger would be the "state's rights" (*kokken*) in the world community; that the best way to forge a lasting solidarity between the populace and the government was to allow the former the fundamental freedoms to which they were naturally entitled; and that the freedom of a state was the direct consequence of the spirit of freedom cherished by its citizens.

Yu stressed, however, that the proper and responsible enjoyment of rights also necessitates a high level of "knowledge and enlightenment" on the part of the people and this of course requires a high degree of education for the entire citizenry. Unenlightened people are prone to violate each other's rights, and they contribute to the undermining of the strength of their nation, rendering it an easy target of foreigners' aggressive designs; for, unless each individual is assured that he will enjoy, in law as well as in actuality, the same rights as others, he will not feel a strong sense of indentification with the political community to which he belongs.[62] It is on the foundation of individual rights supported by public enlightenment that popular respect for a state's law and the security of its independence are based. Using almost a direct line from Fukuzawa's work *The Encouragement of Learning*, Yu also admonished his readers that rights carry with them the responsibility that the state is their commonwealth, which all of them—high and low, rich and poor, the lettered and the unlettered—must cherish and protect. It is much too precious a heritage to leave exclusively to management by government.[63]

Yu's discussion of people's rights in terms of "limited" and "absolute rights" is interesting enough to warrant elaboration here. "Absolute right" (*mugye ŭi t'ongŭi* or *kwŏlli*) are the rights, according to Yu, with which all individuals are born. Rights with limits are those conferred upon human beings by the state. Among the absolute rights are the classic rights to life, liberty, and property plus the following: the right to an occupation, the right to assembly, the right of faith or conscience, the right of free speech, and the right to protect one's honor or good name.[64]

This list shows a good awareness of the rights guaranteed to citizens of the contemporary Western societies, but, by not writing very clearly about what he means by "limited rights," Yu leaves the reader puzzled. The puzzle becomes compounded when, at the same time as describing the above rights as "absolute," he also proposed that they "do not conflict with the law of the land," that they "do not infringe the law," and that they "not be contrary to legislation."[65]

Those familiar with the Japanese Constitution of 1889, which limited most such rights through phrases such as "except as provided by law," will be familiar with the above expressions. Rights were described as both pre-state (or natural or Heaven-bestowed) and subject to the authority of the state. There could be several reasons for the apparent contradiction. Perhaps Yu's thinking was confused, or he was adding a formula of caution so as not to offend the authorities. It is also possible that he was so full of admiration for the Japanese Constitution, and wanted to recommend it to his countrymen so keenly, that he failed to see the logical contradiction in his writ-

ing. Finally his belief that Koreans were in a low state of enlightenment may have been another reason for Yu's taking away with his
left hand what he was offering with his right one.

This interpretation is supported by Yu's discussion of the meaning
and uses of the electoral process in Western democracies and constitutional monarchies. He greatly admired the process of electing public
officials and holding them accountable for all their deeds and omis-
sions. He severely criticized the Korean bureaucracy, wherein officials
were concerned only with private greed and thus daily undermined the
very fabric of the state, while the powerful got away with all violations
of law and the weak and those voiceless subjects were victims of such
exploitation and oppression that they were punished even when they
committed no crime.[66] Yu believed a Japanese-type "joint rule by the
monarch and the people" (*kunmin kongch'i chŏngch'e*) or constitutional
monarchy of some form was the best system of government. But he
maintained that, no matter how good an alien system of government
might be, it could not be transplanted and made to work in another
country's soil until the people had attained the right kind of education
and intellectual development. "An evil government can not be created
among a good people and a good government can not be created among
an evil people," Yu stressed.[67] Thus, enlightenment as a precondition of
peoples' rights is a theme to which Yu returned again and again.

Though cautious and self-contradictory in his discussion of
people's rights, Yu did feel that what Korea needed immediately, in
addition to modern education, was a system of modern laws. It was
possible for modern, progressive laws, according to him, to be introduced into the country's existing political structure. He admired, in
particular, the criminal and civil laws of the West and argued that, by
applying them in Korea, much of the corruption and inhumanity of
the country's judicial system could be eradicated. He unequivocally
denounced the Korean practice of ex post facto laws and called for all
trials and punishments to be conducted strictly according to published and open procedures. No official should be authorized to prosecute anyone's past offenses according to new laws. He also attacked
the Korean practice of judgment by analogy as unfair.[68] He advocated the Western practice of giving all the benefit of the doubt to the
accused. He considered this an eminently just and humane system;
he argued that punishment should always be meted out with extreme
caution, since any punishment strikes at the basic rights of the

accused as a human being. Yu praised Western habeas corpus and a swift release of anyone accused of a violation of law when no prima facie ground was found to proceed with a trial. Any detention of anyone after this determination, he argued, was unfair and inhumane.[69]

Yu also echoed Pak Yŏng-hyo's plea that all those accused of any crime, even the most heinous crimes, should have full and free access to an advocate and be allowed to assemble and present all evidence and argument in self-defense through their attorneys. A proper appeals procedure should be available to all those convicted of an offense, and punishments should be suspended until the procedure had been exhausted. Yu also explained how a bar association might serve as a guardian of the basic rights of all to a fair trial.[70]

Finally, Yu advocated a separate cadre of judicial officials whose sole function should be to interpret and apply the nation's law in judicial courts in a fair and impartial manner. They should not have any executive functions.[71] Yu did not advocate an independent judiciary of the American type but simply a separation of administrative from judicial functions. He was unquestionably influenced in this approach by the Japanese and English models of justice.

What was the impact on Korean society? Yu completed the book in 1889 but was not able to publish it until 1895. He had to spend his own money to have 1,000 copies printed in Japan. These he circulated free of charge among senior officials of the Korean government, obviously believing that enlightenment of his people should start from the top. Yu had to convert the bureaucracy before anyone else could be approached.[72]

Between 1889 and 1895, Yu's career, like the careers of many others, suffered vicissitudes; he found himself entangled in domestic factional squabbles as well as the intrigues of pro-Chinese and pro-Japanese elements in the bureaucracy. Until 1895, no pro-Japanese figure—and Yu was identified as such—could have much, if any, influence in Korea. China held sway over the country through its wily President Yuan Shikai, and Yuan's aggressive style led increasingly to a confrontation between China and Japan. The competing interests of China and Japan in Korea were, in any case, bound to come to a test of will between them. The two powers came to blows in 1894–1895. The background to the war was the *Tonghak* Rebellion of 1893–1894.

The *Tonghak* followers, as we have seen, had been quieted but not destroyed by the execution of their leader, Ch'oe Che-u, in 1864. The movement had continued to gain strength underground as more unhappy peasants and other disaffected elements of society swelled its ranks in the decades following the mid-1860s. The imposition of unequal treaties on Korea after 1876 compounded all the traditional ills of the society—the inequalities of the tax system, the rapacious behavior of the landlords and the traditional moneylenders, and the extortions and exactions of the petty and high bureaucrats. The opening of Korean waters to Japanese fishermen robbed many Korean fishermen of their means of livelihood. Japanese shipping services seriously hurt the Korean carrying trade; steam boats rendered many porters jobless and also increased the transportation cost and price of rice. Exports of rice to Japan increased not only the domestic price of rice, but the prices of other essential commodities as well. Textiles, kerosene, kitchen utensils—mostly imported items—became extremely expensive. Natural calamities like drought in 1876–1877 and again in 1888–1889 in Chŏlla province—the rice basket of Korea—caused even further misery to peasants. The resultant fall in government revenue caused more exactions by oppressive functionaries, making the plight of the peasants even more acute. Chŏlla province was at an explosive point. The situation was not dissimilar to the one prevailing in China after the Opium War and leading to the Taiping Rebellion of the 1850s.[73]

Those who belonged to the suffering strata described above gave the *Tonghak* Movement much of its support. In the early 1890s, their anti-foreignism did not stem from a conservative ideological outlook on life but from concrete hardships they attributed to the coming of foreign powers. Revolts spread in 1892–1893, often led by *yangban* fallen on hard times or by sons of concubines. Such revolts demanded the suppression of Christianity, the expulsion of Westerners and Japanese, and an end to all relations with foreigners. To those demands were added, of course, the ideas of the original *Tonghak* ideology. A 12-point document issued by *Tonghak* rebels under Chŏn Pong-chun in Chŏlla province called for, among other things, an end to oppression by officials and rich *yangban*, the burning of all slave registers, the abolition of the traditional class and status system altogether, permission for widows to remarry, equal distribution of farm land, and the like.[74]

As earlier, the state came down hard upon the rebels. Unable to control the situation with its own resources, the Korean government called upon China for help. Acting under the traditional obligation of an "elder brother," and to preserve its influence in Korea, China obliged by sending troops. On the grounds that its people and interests in Korea needed protection, Japan also sent forces of its own. Japan really intended to weed out the pro-Chinese, conservative forces and thus China's hegemony from Korea for good.[75] Armed engagements between Japanese and Chinese troops began in July 1894, leading to one victory after another for the Japanese. The Chinese and the *Tonghak* rebels were dealt with summarily, the latter executed or jailed. The rebellion was crushed and the Chinese were forced to sue for peace. Japan seemed at a single stroke to have wiped out two obstacles to its expansionist aims in Korea.

The Sino-Japanese peace treaty signed on 17 April 1895 gave Japan a free hand to do what it wished in Korea. The Korean King was now a virtual captive of the Japanese Minister in Seoul, and the Japanese decided to use their control over the monarch to begin a whirlwind course of "renovation" in the peninsula. Even before the conclusion of the war, pro-Japanese officials had been given key positions. A Reform Council had been set up to suggest, formulate, and promulgate comprehensive changes in the government and in the social structure. Decree after decree was issued in the name of the King against what the pro-Japanese Korean ministers considered improper and unhealthy social and administrative practices. Class distinctions for civil service examinations—surely the object of long-needed reform—were done away with and private slavery was abolished. (Government slaves had been freed in 1801, and hereditary slave status had been ordered removed from the books in 1886 but, as Homer B. Hulbert, a contemporary observer of Korean affairs, suggests, issuing orders and having them obeyed were not always the same in late Chosŏn Korea.) All subjects were declared equal before the law, discrimination against "illegitimate" children was outlawed, and all Koreans were given the freedom to choose their occupations. Early marriage was forbidden, and the legal age for marriage was set at 16 for women and 20 for men. Widows were given the right to remarry, and the notorious practices of guilt by association and collective punishment were outlawed.[76]

The special privileges enjoyed by officials for centuries were also outlawed. They could not claim deference on the street from commomers, and, except at the highest levels of the bureaucracy, the use of palanquins was forbidden. Official dress was also simplified in order to help erode the extreme rank and status-consciousness within the bureaucracy. Anyone could send reformist ideas or appeal for the redress of personal grievances to the Reform Council. Progressives like Pak Yŏng-hyo, Sŏ Kwang-bŏm, and Yu Kil-chun were invited to become ministers in a cabinet-style government. Already, on 7 January 1895, the King had proclaimed a 14-point "Constitution" as the new fundamental law of the land. Patterned somewhat after the Charter Oath of the Meiji Emperor and the Japanese Constitutions of 1868 and 1889, this Korean document put the Throne's seal of approval on the reforms described above, all designed to make the Korean government a progressive, efficient, and public-interest-oriented body. A royal statement incorporated into the Constitution also promised comprehensive reforms in civil and criminal laws. Under these reforms, a new judiciary and an appeals system were introduced, a high court in Seoul and district courts in provinces were provided for, and special courts were to be set up for port cities and for the royal family. Many new schools were set up or planned.[77]

All these were progressive changes and no doubt showed the hard work of men like Pak Yŏng-hyo, Yu Kil-chun, and others. But, as with many changes introduced from above elsewhere in history, these reforms included no provision for an institutional means for popular participation in government, nor was any promise made toward that end. The Japanese were in control, and they did not intend to allow any "radical" reforms. They did not envision for Koreans even the extremely restricted "popular" participation in government the Meiji Constitution of 1889 had granted Japanese subjects. Possibly their Korean collaborators did not consider it desirable either. It certainly was not in Japan's interest to encourage the Korean public to think that the government should be accountable to it. In order to accomplish their own designs in Korea, the Japanese wanted to make the Korean officials accountable to them instead.

Even this limited progress toward a more human-rights-oriented government was not easy to realize. The Japanese and their Korean supporters found Queen Min an intractably anti-Japanese and crafty woman who would do everything to foil not only Japan's expansionist designs but also domestic reforms. In attempting to deal with this obstacle, the Japanese Minister in Seoul, Miura Gorō, committed what was both a highly criminal act and a grave tactical error. Under Miura's instigation conspirators murdered the Queen. This, coupled with another "reform" decree ordering all Korean men to cut off their topknots, created such an anti-Japanese backlash throughout Korea that all the reform decrees fell like a house of cards. Confucianists saw the anti-topknot order as an assault on the very fabric of their society. Ch'oe Ik-hyŏn, a veteran fighter against modernity, declared that he "would sooner have his head cut off than his hair."[78] Armed anti-Japanese and anti-progressive uprisings occurred all over Korea in early 1896. The King, uneasy under Japanese hegemony, escaped to the Russian Legation in Seoul in February 1896 and the pro-Japanese Cabinet fell. Its members became targets of mob wrath. Some lost their lives. Pak Yŏng-hyo and Yu Kil-chun escaped once again to Japan, living in exile with the stigma of traitors.

Russia now replaced Japan for the next few years as Korea's hegemon. Most of the reforms proclaimed during 1894–1895 remained intact, however. The pro-Russians in the Korean government were also progressive in their inclinations and they did not want the reforms scrapped.

The cumulative impact of the *Tonghak* Rebellion and the 1894–1895 reforms was negligible. The Rebellion was crushed ruthlessly, as we have seen, and the reforms suffered from the same weakness that had troubled the 1884 coup. Both were devoid of any popular base and both were attempts by people who were too closely identified with the interests of a foreign power. The label "traitor" could be easily hung around the reformers' necks by all those opposed to reform if they managed to gain control of access to the monarch—the source of finality for all state actions.

BOLD THRUSTS FOR REFORM: THE MOVEMENT OF THE INDEPENDENCE CLUB

Korea's new patron, Russia, through its envoy in Seoul, Karl Waeber, showed much prudence in handling relations with Korea in the early stages. There was no attempt on Russia's part to browbeat Korea into abject subservience. The King and his entourage enjoyed much freedom in appointing and promoting officials and making policy from their refuge in the Russian Legation. This encouraged Sŏ Chae-p'il and Yun Ch'i-ho, independent-minded progressives who were neither pro-Japanese nor pro-Russian, to launch a new movement for comprehensive reform entirely unaided by any foreign power for the first time since 1876. A significant feature of this movement was that its two leading spokesmen made a more frontal assault on Confucianism than any reformists of the past. The two men likewise expressed a far more ardent support for Christianity than any earlier reformists.

The approach of Sŏ and Yun was considerably more analytical than that of previous reformists, perhaps because both had had a considerably longer and deeper education in the West. In consequence, their approach to human rights was considerably more systematic than that of Pak Yŏng-hyo or Yu Kil-chun.

Sŏ and Yun had both had the necessary Confucian education at home, but they had come to look at it from a fresh vantage point after their long stay and studies in the United States. Though they had also had a good deal of experience in Japan, it was their American education more than anything else that shaped their views about reform. Sŏ had spent about ten years in the United States, acquiring a medical degree, an American wife, and an Anglicized name—Philip Jaisohn—and becoming a convert to Protestant Christianity. Yun had spent a total of about six years in the West, studying at Vanderbilt University and eventually getting a degree in theology from Methodist Emory College.[79] From February 1896 to December 1898, these two men worked in unison, publishing a newspaper for public education in both vernacular Korean and English (called the *Tongnip sinmun* and *The Independent*, respectively), organizing a body of citizens of all strata called the Independence Club, and putting pressure on the government through constant petitions to move toward making Korea a progressive, modern state. Supported by people who did not necessarily share their enthusiasm for Christianity but who nevertheless had progressive instincts, Sŏ and Yun provided what were unquestionably the most trenchant criticisms of Korean society's ills and proposed solutions that certainly were the most articulate, if not the most realistic, of all reforms proposed during the first three decades after 1876.

To both Sŏ and Yun, Western civilization meant Christian civilization. Their premise was that the salvation of Korea as a nation and that of its individual subjects lay in throwing away the weight of the Confucian culture and adopting Christianity and Christian civilization as rapidly as possible. The Korean body politic had become so deeply afflicted with all the worst aspects of Confucianism that this was the only way to raise Korean subjects from their abject state of submission to government and give them a genuine feeling of autonomy and self-respect. Describing his feelings about the way the "law" functioned in Korea, Yun once wrote in his diary:

> The parents and children of the English rebels in 1685 [a reference to the unsuccessful rebellion of Monmouth and Argyll] were not butchered on such a light reason that they were the relatives of the rebels. But in Korea no relatives are spared. Age or sex or innocence or any cause whatsoever cannot protect a rebel's relatives or friends from the execrable laws of the accursed government. No wonder that [the] God of vengeance lays His hand heavily on the abominable gang of cutthroats which constitutes the Korean government.[80]

In an essay published in 1895 in the English language monthly, *The Korean Repository*, Yun enlarged his critique of Korean society specifically in terms of the stranglehold of Confucianism. "What has Confucianism done for Korea?" Yun asked, and then answered his own question:

> With diffidence yet conviction I dare say that it has done very little, if anything for Korea. What Korea may have been without Confucian teachings, nobody can tell. But what Korea is with them we too well know. Behold Korea, with her oppressed masses, her general poverty, her treacherous and cruel officers, her dirt and filth, her degraded women, her blighted families—behold all this and judge for yourselves what Confucianism has done for Korea.[81]

Yun saw his own role in terms of an evangelical mission, of spreading the Christian "Gospel and giving education to his people." What Korea needed in his view was the Christian ideal of putting man in the context of the divine, replacing Confucianism which he saw as focused entirely on man. It was this Confucian humanism with its lack of accountability to a transcendent power that, he concluded ironically, was at the root of all the exploitation and degradation to which Koreans had been subjected for so long.[82]

Sŏ was just as critical of Confucianism and laudatory of Christianity. *The Independent* frequently praised the evangelical and educational endeavors of the missionaries in Korea and expressed the hope that, due to their efforts, the country would be raised to "civilization." For example, *The Independent* once wrote that "the sooner the teaching of Chinese classics and the doctrine of the Chinese sages in the Korean schools is abolished the better for the country and the people."[83] In its place Sŏ recommended the teaching of Western civilization:

History tells us that, wherever Western civilization has made its appearance, the place was transformed into a new country altogether. We hope the time will soon come when Western civilization will penetrate every corner of the continent of Asia and make use of the Creator's beautiful soil for the good of his people the world over.[84]

Employing a more fulsome idiom Yun echoed this theme in a later editorial:

What we want is the rich, renovating, nay, revolutionizing ideas of the West introduced and naturalized, as it were, in Korea. . . . [We need] the epoch-making and world-moving thoughts of the Occidental races.[85]

To Sŏ and Yun, as to other reformists before them, it was perhaps the American Declaration of Independence that best embodied the distilled wisdom and the quintessential message of the West's accumulated political heritage. The ideas of popular sovereignty, the rule of law, equality, inalienable individual rights, social contract, limited government, governmental accountability—all the hallowed principles of modern political democracy—are either stated or implied in the Declaration. And, in their inimitable editorials, Sŏ and Yun sought to spread variants of these principles far and wide in Korea.

To both Sŏ and Yun, a major problem of Korean society was that the average subject was in a state of mental torpor as a result of centuries-long subjection to injustice and oppression. That individuals had any political rights, as distinct from family and property rights, was an idea alien to their sensibilities. In times of extreme suffering they might ask for relief as supplicants or might even stage rebellious—often disorganized—protests, but they had no legal, institutional means to compel the government to bow to their demands. Concepts like "civil rights" (*minkwŏn*) or "human rights" (*inkwŏn*) were not part of the Confucian tradition. If the officials deemed it their inherent right to demand absolute obedience from the masses, the latter by and large were resigned to offering such obedience just as unquestioningly. As Sŏ wrote:

Koreans have been under the suppression of their own compatriots for so many centuries that they have never possessed any people's rights (*paeksŏng ŭi kwŏlli*); they have never known what their meaning is.[86]

Or, as he wrote in *The Independent*, using a more Western idiom, "The slavery of feeling among the masses is due to the ignorance of their rights as citizens of this commonwealth."[87]

The masses had to be awakened to the notion that they were "masters of the nation," and, if they were to enjoy security of their lives and property, they had to act as such. They needed to strive to assign government officials to their proper station as salaried employees commissioned to work for the people's well-being.[88] Without organized resolution on the part of the people to recover their inherent power as the ultimate employers of government officials, attacking their illegalities and irregularities and demanding corrective action, the illogical situation of servants behaving as masters would continue.[89]

The idea that the people are masters of the state and government officials are their servants is, of course, the essence of the concept of popular sovereignty, and converting the people at large to this new idea was the major theme of the Sŏ-Yun editorials. In these editorials, Sŏ and Yun emerge as schoolteachers giving elementary civics lessons to a national audience. Though the editorials often use such familiar expressions from Western political philosophy as "rights that Heaven had endowed the people with," "rights bestowed by God," "liberties that inhere in every person," "Heaven-ordained rights,"[90] and the like, their overall idiom exhibits a rather simple, almost schoolroom quality. Discussing, for example, the origin of the state, *Tongnip sinmun* said:

What is called a country (*nara*) is that on a big or small land many people gather together and, recognizing that, since without a government they can not live together, they establish one, and entrust the functioning of commanding both the government and the people to a ruler and regard him as their head.[91]

The editorial elaborated by adding that the original purpose of establishing a state was to have many people discuss and plan their society's variegated tasks on a common, shared basis, since it was in their own interest to do so, and thus the decision to have officials and pay taxes was also theirs, "for their own sake."[92] This theme was reiterated or embellished through many other editorials. It is not uncommon for a reader to encounter in them such expressions as "the entity called state or nation resulted from the joint efforts and united minds of the king, the government, and the people," or "a country has its foundation in the people," or "the ruler derives his authority from the people," or "the government exists for the people, not the people for the government," or "a nation cannot be said to be a nation" unless it is embedded in the "trust of its people."[93]

These editorials were restating the idea of social contract in language intelligible to the average literate reader. Even more obvious is their message on the position of the monarch: that he is subject to the sovereign authority of the people in the same way his officials are, and that he is merely the head of the polity with the specific function of ensuring that the government maintains conditions for the people to live together in peace and security. The people have commanded the ruler to direct both the government and themselves for this purpose. Operational power thus lies with the monarch, but his authority represents not total surrender, only a conditional transfer, of sovereignty by the people.

Western exponents of the social-contract theory, such as Rousseau, Locke, and Hobbes, left some of its serious problems of logic and history unresolved, with the result that it was subsequently interpreted as an argument for both democracy and absolutism.[94] In the hands of Sŏ and Yun, its internal inconsistencies were less apparent because they stated it so tersely and chose not to dwell on its intricacies. In their writings, the social contract is unequivocally on the side of popular sovereignty, even within the monarchical framework.

From this basic premise follow many themes and sub-themes. Though these themes were enunciated over a period of many months on a scattered basis, they have an underlying unity, an ideological coherence. From this premise it is natural for Sŏ and Yun to argue that the people should be loyal to the ruler and obey the commands of his government but that such obedience should be conditional upon how well the ruler and the government look after the people's interests.[95] If the people, exercising their right of overseeing the government, find that government officials, who "earn their livelihood from the people's money," are not performing their duties honestly and competently, they may conclude that the officials are nothing but "bandits" who should be thrown out and replaced with those worthy of the popular trust.[96]

The ideology of Sŏ and Yun stressed that a polity organized around the concept of popular sovereignty must be a polity of laws, not men. Law, as Sŏ wrote in *The Independent*, was—and we may forgive here Sŏ's mixed metaphor—the "keystone of the political fabric."[97] Early Western liberalism viewed government as a necessary evil but law as a positive force in society making for order out of chaos and acting as a restraint on the human tendency toward excesses of power. By furnishing the society with the right and power to curb the freedom of its more recalcitrant members, law guaranteed the freedom of the rest. To achieve this objective, law must be administered on the principles of equality, impartiality, and openness. It should be universalistic, not particularistic, in content and application. It was this kind of law that Sŏ and Yun admired.

As they looked around, they saw abundant examples of perversion of justice in the Korean government. The lives and properties of innocent subjects were daily subject to the whims and the sufferance of the ruling class. Courts were a "farce in the true sense of the word." Influential men could arrest any citizen without a trial, and, where trials took place, it was not uncommon to see "the consanguinity of the judge and the plaintiff . . . over-riding . . . points of law."[98]

It was only when an American, General C. R. Greathouse, took over as adviser to the Law Department in early 1896 that a dent began to be made in the maladministration of justice. To the extent that he was personally able to supervise the functioning of the court system in the capital, he introduced modern procedures to ensure that trials would be open and fair and there would be no torture. It was only natural for Sŏ and Yun to extol these reforms and demand their full-scale introduction into Korea.[99] Korea's foremost need, Sŏ wrote, was for courts where the people "can lay charges against any man who has wronged them, whether it is a sneak thief who has stolen a pipe or a magistrate who has stolen a wife."[100] Elaborating this theme in August 1898, Yun urged the Independence Club to consider demanding from the government the following 5-point pledge:

(1) That it would protect people's lives and properties to the utmost.
(2) That no one should be arrested without good reason. If a person is to be detained, his indictment should be made clear and issued officially and only then should he be carted away for detention.

(3) That, after the arrest, until the indictment has been upheld in a court of law, no accused should be treated as a criminal.

(4) That, within twenty-four hours of his arrest, an accused should be presented before a court of law for trial.

(5) That an arrested person, his relatives, or friends should have the right to demand such a prompt trial from the magistrate in charge.[101]

Nothing sums up better the views of Sŏ and Yun on the role of law in society than the following words written by Sŏ—words that could have come from the pen of Jeremy Bentham or Thomas Macaulay:

The more perfect the law the greater will be the liberty. The law that makes it possible for a man to do the best thing that he was made for, is the perfect law, and the man who most perfectly obeys that law is the most nearly free. Freedom then, or liberty, is the most perfect obedience to perfect law . . . Korea will never be free till she has good laws, laws that open up the way for every citizen to most readily earn his bread, educate himself and his children and provide for the moral training of himself and his family.[102]

When one adds to these words the quantitative fact that the combined number of editorials on law or law-related subjects in *Tongnip sinmun* and *The Independent* during April 1896–December 1898 was 128, one can readily see the importance that Sŏ and Yun attached to the supremacy of law. With law set on so high a pedestal, it also seems logical that Sŏ and Yun described compliance with law as the highest form of loyalty and its violation as the worst form of treason. To Sŏ, any official who was in charge of the implementation of laws and yet himself violated them was an "enemy of the nation" and "the lowest kind of human being" (*cheil ch'ŏnhan saram*).[103] The people must direct their full fury against such persons and force them to relinquish their offices.[104]

Clearly, the ideology of Sŏ and Yun was an elaboration and a more articulate reaffirmation of the views of Yu Kil-chun and Pak Yŏng-hyo. But more important is the connection that Sŏ and Yun sought to establish between the enjoyment of liberty and obedience to law. When laws were grounded in the concept of popular sovereignty and were thus people-oriented, compliance with them would become an expression of freedom, not of constraint. Yet, neither Sŏ nor Yun advocated a direct role by the masses in the function of lawmaking. They remained, without saying so, skeptical of the value of such a role in the absence of an enlightened citizenry. As with Yu Kil-chun, the idea that the masses should be led by an educated elite stayed yet unquestioned. Though considerably more sophisticated than the views of Yu and Pak in general, the frame of thinking of Sŏ and Yun in this respect remained very Confucian. Law was definitely to be *for* the people and it was, in its ultimate logical implications, also *of* the people, but it was not yet to be *by* the people.

Only an informed public, of course, could be expected to have the ability to detect violations of laws. Unless the people knew what the statutes of the nation were and what objectives they sought to serve, it would be impossible to enforce compliance with them. Even a small step in the direction of making the public eager to study the laws of the nation would be better than no step at all. Two months before Sŏ left Korea, he encouraged the Independence Club to take precisely such a step. In March 1898, the Club appointed a committee of three to read up on chosen sections of Korean laws each week and explain to members' weekly gatherings the "exact purpose and spirit" behind their enactment. Activities of this kind, Sŏ commented, would not only encourage the people "to take more interest in national affairs" but were among "the best means by which the people can be brought closer to the government."[105]

Popular "interest in national affairs" and solidarity between the government and the people were treated by Sŏ and Yun as mutually related themes, and they viewed them as the sine qua non of an advanced nation. In their view, much of the strength and prosperity of the Western nations was due to the feeling of solidarity between the government and the people, and this solidarity was the direct outcome of the freedom with which the man-in-the-street was able to express his views and opinions on the actions of his government. That the people criticize their government and demand rectification of its errors should not thus be regarded as a sign of disaffection on their part but a sure indication of their sense of identification with it.[106] Yun called such opposition "the root of progress" and wrote: "The more enlightened a nation, the more room for public discussion of right and wrong, and [the more debate there is] of right and wrong, the better the enlightenment of the people."[107] To those who might be skeptical of such a view, he pointed out the example of England and said that, according to an "English scholar," that nation's top position in the world was due to its people's propensity for "complaining [about] and discussing [things]."[108]

Before we reject the unnamed English scholar's analysis of the basis of Great Britain's world power, together with Yun's acceptance of it, as too simplistic, we should remember that in the late-nineteenth-century world, and especially in colonial lands, it was fashionable to stress a cause-and-effect relationship between democracy and national power. Indeed, such a view had become almost axiomatic. The importance attached to "complaining [about] and discussing [things]" merely reflected the age-old wisdom: that a restless quest for truth lay at the root of all advancement and that dissent—we may here safely use the word *dissent* as being interchangeable with *democracy*—not conformity could best foster that quest. In this belief, Yun could have found eloquent support in the oft-quoted words of John Stuart Mill. "The peculiar evil of silencing an opinion," Mill had written in *On Liberty*,

is that it is robbing the human race; posterity as well as the existing generation; those who dissent from the opinion still more than those who hold it. If the opinion is right they are deprived of the opportunity of exchanging error for truth; if wrong they lose, what is almost as great a benefit, the clearer perception and livelier impression of truth, produced by its collision with error.[109]

In consonance with this line of reasoning, Sŏ and Yun strongly called for freedom of association, encouragement of newspapers, and the establishment of public discussion forums in every neighborhood in the country.[110] It is not surprising, also, that they should have called for the introduction and legitimization of party politics in Korea, for, if dissent is the core around which public opinion is formed, parties are the structures that lend rational organization to public opinion and make its weight felt in the polity. Sŏ and Yun stressed that the new parties, unlike the traditional factions of Korea which were centered around powerful individuals or clans, should crystallize around principles and platforms. Confronting each other with ideologies, the new parties should try to gain political power by winning public support and use this power to work for the "nation and the public." Let all conservatives, Sŏ urged, be organized as one party and let all the progressives be united as another party and contest each other's appeal to the public with their "policies" and "true purposes," and let the winning party run the government with these "policies and true purposes" as a firm and inviolable "pledge."[111] The words were Sŏ's but might just as well have been penned by Edmund Burke. In his pamphlet "Thoughts on the Cause of the Present Discontents," Burke had defined a party as a "body of men united for promoting by their joint endeavors the national interest upon some particular principle on which they all agreed."[112]

We also find Sŏ broaching as early as April 1896, the idea of electing public officials on a limited scale. Since nowhere was there more maladministration, corruption, and disorder than in the provinces, Sŏ wondered if the introduction of elected magistrates would not help improve the situation. He expounded all the traditional theoretical advantages of the elective principle. He argued that elected officials were certain to enjoy the trust and affection of their constituents; that they would be competent, honest, and conscientious in the performance of their duties; that, in order to retain the trust of their electors, they would look after the latter's interests more keenly; and that only those well-versed in local affairs would be likely to be elected. He added that another advantage of this system would be the forging of solidarity between the government and the people. If an elected magistrate turned out to be bad, the people were not likely to feel disaffection towards the government as a whole but would blame only themselves and would try to choose better men in subsequent elections. Thus, people's participation in public affairs would be an educative and responsible participation.[113]

In retrospect, Sŏ's unqualified championship of the elective principle may seem somewhat naive. At the time, however, he believed his conviction was vindicated by the example of the self-governing Korean émigré settlements in Russian Manchuria (Siberia). After visiting them and observing their daily activities, British geographer Isabella B. Bishop had praised their contented lives and attributed this situation to the good leadership of their elected headmen.[114] On learning this, Sŏ wrote:

If the magistrates of the various districts obtain their offices by the vote of the people they will serve the people as their masters instead of some high official in Seoul through whom everybody now procures official positions. This will also teach the ambitious men of the country to obtain good reputations and it will restrain them from giving or taking bribes. Another important point in favor of the inauguration of this system is that the people will consider themselves as [a] political fabric because they have a voice in the management of public affairs in their districts by means of their votes. This will give them a free and independent spirit and they will be ambitious to be thrifty and prosperous, because they will know their lives and property will be safe as far as their magistrates are concerned.[115]

Nevertheless, there was no room in the Sŏ–Yun ideology for republicanism. Yun, who wrote more often on this question than Sŏ, stressed that politicians must be attuned to the times and conditions of their societies and move accordingly. Korea's prime need of the hour was national unity; and the retention of monarchy within a combined framework of popular rights and a rigorous system of laws were the best means of achieving it. The transformation of Korea from an "absolutist polity" into a "constitutional polity" was necessary. "Only when absolutist government had been abolished," Yun pointed out, "constitutional government established, and the people given freedom did Italy become united."[116] Thus, while the idea of popular sovereignty needed to be introduced to Koreans so that they could begin to stand up for their rights, it need not mean instantly transforming Korea into a republic. Monarchy was perfectly compatible with the idea of popular sovereignty, as long as the concept of social contract and the limited nature of the monarch's position were understood. Moreover, Yun argued that the Korean people were not yet ready to assume the full responsibilities of citizenship. Until, through a gradual process of "knowledge and scholarship," they had learned "to appreciate not only their own rights but respect those of others," "place public affairs above private affairs," and uphold "not narrow visions but large moral principles," entrusting all political power to the people could only undermine the solidity of the state, "as is well illustrated by both ancient and modern history and by the present state of affairs in the Euro-American world."[117]

What Yun seems to have had in mind was the continued existence of the monarchy as a symbol of the state, as the final repository of legitimacy, and as an instrument for the ultimate registration of the popular will. Yun seems to have believed that gradually transmuting the monarchy into a British-style institution which "reigns but does not rule" was an appropriate political course for Korea. Sŏ and Yun frequently admonished their readers that the institution of monarchy was a valuable part of the Korean tradition and therefore always deserving of their affection and loyalty.[118]

Through *The Independent*, Sŏ and Yun also gave strong support to the uplift of Korea's women. They called the exploitation and oppression of women in Korea most "heart-rending" and the society that permitted such treatment most "barbaric." They called for equal, modern education for men and women with a view to transforming their status to one of mutual equality, decency, and propriety.[119]

The immediate impact of the two leaders' enlightenment campaign, which included the publication of *The Independent* and lectures at public meetings as well as at the newly-opened mission schools, was considerable. Thousands of people of all strata of the society joined the public meetings organized by the Independence Club, and the newspaper was distributed all over Korea. Sometimes a single copy was read by as many as 85 people.[120] When Sŏ decided to leave Korea and return to the United States, Yun paid him the following editorial tribute:

Through the columns of this vernacular paper he taught the oppressed that all men are born equal—a doctrine true not only because it is Anglo-Saxon or Latin but because it is divine and universal, that they are not so many cows or oxen to be used as beasts of burden for kings and *yangbans*, that the inalienable rights and prosperity which they envy in their foreign neighbor[s] were not picked up in the street . . . but were attained after ages of labor, of study, and of struggle and that if Koreans want to enjoy these rights and prosperity they must work, nay struggle, nay fight for them.[121]

Outsiders' assessments of *The Independent*'s role were no less flattering. *The Korean Repository*, referring to Sŏ's editorial role, said that "the common people were not slow in recognizing a friend of their rights in the editor. He spoke to them and for them."[122] Isabella B. Bishop applauded the paper for "creating a public opinion which shall sit in judgment on regal and official misdeeds," for "unearthing abuses and dragging them into daylight . . . and [for] becoming something of a terror to evil doers."[123]

These activities warrant some discussion. After 1895, though enactment of progressive legislation was to remain a matter of ongoing concern, the more immediate objective of all those trying to introduce modern concepts of liberty and law into Korea was to ensure that progressive laws already enacted and promulgated were faithfully implemented. Under the leadership of Sŏ and Yun, the Independence Club waged a running battle to win respect for new laws from those in charge of enforcing them. It is pertinent to note here that

much of the credit for the open and fair trial of those Koreans implicated in the murder of Queen Min belongs as much to the watchful
eyes of the Independence Club as to the direction of the court by
General Greathouse. The two persons who actually conducted the
proceedings were General Han Kyu-sŏl, the Minister of Justice, and
Kwŏn Chae-hyŏng, his deputy. Both were members of the Independence Club. Hulbert commented on the proceedings as "dispassionate" and "without torture and with every privilege of a fair trial," and
noted that they "pointed toward a new and enlightened era in Korean
political history."[124]

Hulbert was too optimistic, however, for the probability of reactionary men being reappointed to high positions was always high in
the volatile world of Korean politics in the later 1890s. For example,
despite the Independence Club's objections, Sin Ki-sŏn, widely perceived as a reactionary, was appointed Law Minister in 1898. Sin
declared soon after assumption of office that a more "liberal use of torture" should be reinstated as a supplementary punishment for
crimes, according to the old law codes. In general, he was an advocate
of the restoration of the *ancien régime*, including the tributary relationship with China.[125] Earlier, a violently anti-reform man had
been appointed Seoul's Chief of Police. The assassin of Kim Ok-kyun
and the man who had attempted once to murder Pak Yŏng-hyo had
also been elevated to high positions, including the headship of the Justice Ministry before Sin Ki-sŏn was appointed to it. As long as such
individuals were to remain in high offices the Club would have to
wage an uphill battle.

The issue between the progressive forces and the conservative
forces came to a head several times in 1898. In the summer of that
year, rumors circulated in the capital that An Kyŏng-su, a former
President of the Club, had conspired with some other Koreans, presumably disgruntled members of the bureaucracy, to force the abdi-
cation of the King and replace him with the Crown Prince, ushering
in "a new era in Korean history." Knowing what such rumors could
mean to one's life, An promptly decamped to Japan for safety. From
there, he protested his innocence and later even agreed to stand trial
if fairness of proceedings could be assured. In the year 1900, accepting the Korean government's assurances on this score and those of the
Japanese government regarding his safety, he and a fellow accused
returned to Seoul. On the night of 27 May, however, both were

secretly strangled to death just before the trial was to open. An outraged Hulbert wrote that "no more dastardly crime ever stained the annals of this or any other government."[126]

Meanwhile, the Club itself had fallen victim to rumors. In late 1898, its leadership was first accused by its enemies of preparing to stage a republican revolution and then charged with inviting Pak Yŏng-hyo back to Korea to become the country's king. The charge of republicanism stemmed from the fact that the Club had fought for and won the King's approval for its proposal to convert the Privy Council, an advisory body, into a rudimentary elected legislative assembly with the right of exercising substantial control over lawmaking and holding government ministers accountable to itself. The credulous King Kojong, alarmed over the rumors, ordered the Club disbanded and its leaders arrested. Thus, a popular, progressive movement came to an abrupt end.[127] The conservatives were to preside over Korea more or less unchallenged from then on, for, while progressive voices were not all silenced, there was to be no organized forum of the size and strength of the Independence Club any longer to sustain them.

LAW REFORM: THE UPS AND DOWNS

The topsy-turvy course of law reform during and after 1894 should also be viewed in the light of these changes. It was a course that began with much hopeful activity for the modernization of law but ended with the reascendance of the traditionalists.

One of the many structural reforms begun under the short-lived (1894–1895) hegemony of the Japanese was the setting up of a Supreme Court in place of the traditional State Tribunal (Ŭigŭmbu). The later had always tried, at the command of the King, "high state crimes, private crimes of officials, and serious crimes committed by *yangban*." The new Supreme Court was to hear appeals from the Seoul and Chemulpo courts as well as criminal charges against members of the two highest ranks in the civil service. The Supreme Court did not, however, function as a general court of last appeal, although it conceivably would have taken over that function eventually.[128]

A law institute was also set up, designed to train officials in modern civil and criminal law and to qualify them for appointment to prosecutorial and judicial positions. In April 1895, a revised court system was inaugurated under the Ministry of Justice. It provided for three types of courts under the Supreme Court. District courts were to be established in important localities around the country. The Ministry of Justice could also set up branch courts of the district courts at its discretion. District courts were empowered to hear, with some exceptions, both civil and criminal cases. Circuit courts were also provided for. Convened for six months at a time, they were to be itinerant bodies with the principal function of hearing appeals against their own previous judgments. They were also empowered to supervise the conduct of all lower courts, "correcting misinterpretation or misapplication of the law or procedure, regardless of the absence of an appeal." The system encountered many difficulties, since qualified people to staff it were scarce. Appellate functions of the circuit courts were therefore left in the hands of a General High Court in Seoul.

New government resolutions in 1894–1895 forbade punishment without trial, required warrants for the arrest of persons suspected of non-military crimes, and at the same time prohibited their arrest by military officials. The private "requisitioning of police" by civil officials was also forbidden in order to prevent magistrates from meting out extra-legal punishments to anyone. Edicts also limited to paddling the use of torture during the interrogation of suspects. In January 1895, all torture was abolished except for capital crimes, paddling was proscribed as a punishment, and only the light whip was allowed "as punishment and for extracting confessions." Executions were "to be carried out only by hanging (for civil offenses) and shooting (for military offenses)." Decapitation, public display of dismembered bodies, and the use of poison (arsenic, mercury, gold) in *yangban* executions were all outlawed. Penal servitude and "monetary commutation" of sentences were also later standardized. Such commutation was not available, however, to those convicted of capital crimes or crimes against "public or private morals." The use of the cangue, the stock and the switch was placed under careful restrictions. Women, youths, the old, and the feeble were not to be subjected to such punishment at all. Only those guilty of violent crimes or suspected of contemplating escape could be fixed to the cangue or the stock. The penalty of beating was also restricted to certain carefully specified serious crimes.

Guilt by association was forbidden, though the notion was so well established in the nation's consciousness that it became necessary to reissue the prohibitory edict many times, reminding job-appointing officials in particular that relatives of criminals were not to be "barred" from public office. Another important piece of legislation abolished the distinction between the "private" crimes of officials and their public ones.[129] The later were defined as offenses committed in the line of official duty. Reprimand, fine, dismissal, imprisonment, and banishment were now to be applied as punishments to both categories of offenses.

While these reforms still needed much further refinement, they were a significant departure from the traditional system. When foreign advisers like General Greathouse and progressive figures like Han Kyu-sŏl or Kwŏn Chae-hyŏng were involved in their enforcement, they were honored, as we have seen, in both letter and spirit. But, in the kaleidoscopic world of Korean politics, men were frequently in office one day and gone the next. When conservatives and reactionaries replaced the progressives it did not matter how progressive the statutes were. If it served their interests or whims, they flagrantly flouted the laws. Foreigners in Seoul often observed that "political inquisitions" and "non-statutory torture" continued unabated, the law courts administered not justice but injustice, and bribery was rampant.[130] As long as progressive laws were on the books, there was some hope, nevertheless, that some day they would begin to acquire some sanctity and thus begin to be enforced with increasing seriousness. But this hope was precisely what the anti-reform forces were determined to thwart, and retrogressive legislation was thus almost inevitable. Subversion of reform by the more familiar practices of bribery and personal connections was even more common. Illegal exactions and oppression of average subjects by lawless officials reached such proportions that the King himself had to issue two edicts lamenting this state of affairs and hoping that ministers would respond to his trust in them and rectify the situation.[131] The same King, however, continued to appoint the most corrupt officials to positions of trust. Late-nineteenth-century Korean bureaucracy, with some honorable exceptions, had become so mired in inefficiency and graft that the law-enforcement machinery seldom enjoyed the public's confidence.

To this worsening situation was added the more ominous development of retrogressive statutory action. In mid-1899, the State Council was seriously considering reenacting the principle of punishing families of those convicted of grave crimes. The proposal was finally dropped because of the protest of Western envoys. In September 1900, the government reinstated decapitation for crimes against the state and the royal household. This penalty was to be supplemented by the total confiscation of the convict's property, which served, in effect, to punish his family as well.[132]

Soon after the suppression of the Independence Club, the King also reinstituted the pre-1894–1895 system of government through the promulgation of a "quasi-constitution." In effect, this meant giving back untrammeled law-making authority to the civil bureaucrats acting in his name, and it nullified all the provisions limiting his authority promulgated under the 1894–1895 reforms.[133]

With the eclipse of Russian power in the peninsula and the reemergence of Japan as a power to reckon with in Korea at the turn of the century, there were some renewed steps toward progressive legislation. The details of this new phase are well covered by Edward J. Baker's 1979 study of the subject. He demonstrates that legal reforms in Korea during 1905–1919 were designed to facilitate Japan's takeover and firm control of Korea.[134] Whatever good was associated with those reforms must therefore be evaluated in the context of this overall darkness.

CONCLUDING OBSERVATIONS

It is clear from the foregoing account that modern human-rights concepts had gradually but increasingly penetrated Korea slowly during the period 1876–1900. At the start of the period, the understanding of these concepts by literate Koreans was naturally incomplete and hazy, but, with time, it grew into a fairly reasoned comprehension, as evidenced especially in the writings of Sŏ Chae-pil and Yun Ch'i-ho. It is also clear that, for a time, leaders like Sŏ and Yun were able to reach the lowest strata of the society and stir them with their new message, demonstrating that many ordinary Koreans understood that these two men and their associates were speaking and working for their best interests. The understanding of and desire for human rights would certainly have grown if progressive ideas had been allowed to flourish. The Korean government, largely a conservative, Confucian body with only a sprinkling of progressives precariously holding on to their tenuous positions, tolerated progressive ideas only as long as they were backed by a strong foreign power. The government was, however, quick to react against such ideas whenever it perceived in them even the slightest danger to its existence. As long as the diffusion of human-rights concepts rested on the sufferance of a conservative bureaucracy presided over by a weak, credulous, and often indecisive monarch, there was little hope that the masses of Korea would come to enjoy human rights on an enduring basis. Only a revolution, sweeping away the old and establishing a new era of republican government, or constitutional monarchy, could possibly have held such a promise. But there was no one in Korea to call publicly for a revolution. All the reformers hoped for piecemeal creativity within a system that stressed conformity. Such a system, the progressives seem to have reasoned, would ultimately collapse of its own accord. In this reasoning, they were, sadly, mistaken.

Koreans were psychologically ready to enjoy human rights at the turn of the century. What was lacking was the willingness of the government to accept this readiness and the willingness or ability of human-rights advocates to take actions commensurate with their dreams.

Why, then, were the progressives unwilling or unable to launch a more militant, better-organized, and sustained campaign on behalf of human rights? To be sure, concern for personal safety provides a partial explanation for their caution. But this is not a complete answer, for it seems to suggest that they all lacked the courage of their convictions, a charge that does not hold up well under scrutiny. There is much evidence to substantiate considerable, even reckless, bravery on the part of many Korean progressives. Some, as we have seen, died in their quest for reform, and others suffered various kinds of privation.

The problem, in my view, lay in the temporal context and cultural conditioning of these dedicated men. They tended to view the value of human rights always from the perspective of the crisis affecting Korea's survival as a nation. The issue of human rights was always presented in terms of its presumed connection with the power and prosperity of the state. The nation's Confucian heritage, which many of the progressives publicly attacked as worthless, was nevertheless implicitly reaffirmed by them in their paradoxical emphasis on the primacy of the state. The state remained the end, and the individual remained the means. Even the most radical of the progressives could not throw off this aspect of their Confucian heritage. This prevented the emergence of that vibrant, creative tension between the individual and the state that has historically been the engine of the development of human rights in Western societies. There was clearly a built-in weakness in the Korean progressives' perception of the role of the individual in the state.

It is difficult to subscribe to a theory of cultural determinism that postulates the virtual impossibility of cross-cultural borrowing. I do believe, however, that a refined concept of cultural relativism does apply to the Korean story. Cultural relativism stresses that, when ideas, institutions, and values are divorced from their original milieu and planted in another cultural soil, they inevitably get transformed, both in content and application, and even acquire a brand new texture and meaning as a result of new synthesis. If this is the meaning of those who suggest that the Korean version of democratic values must inexorably reflect the nation's own "genius," then they seem to be on solid ground. But this surely does not suggest that the Koreans have been historically unable to appreciate the concept of human rights. It simply means that the Korean people's understanding of human rights rests on a mix of tentativeness and ambivalence uniquely their own. Other cultures have shown in history their own brand of this tentativeness and ambivalence. Some of them have moved forward to a stage of greater clarity. Others are still struggling to find that clarity. The history of modern Korea can be seen as an expression of this unfinished, continuing pursuit of what constitutes a satisfactory role for the individual and the society in human life. The events of 1987–1990 in South Korea show that considerable progress has already been made toward a resolution of this question, although no doubt much further movement still lies ahead.

CHAPTER TWO

Korea Before Rights

WILLIAM SHAW

Was the late-nineteenth-century call for reform and justice not only politically doomed, as Vipan Chandra has demonstrated, but conceptually flawed as well? Did the reformers naively fail to understand Korean legal and political culture and values? Were those values hostile to the reformers' notions of "rights" and the rule of law? The relationship among official ideology, popular consciousness, and legal institutions in traditional Korea is worth further examination if we are to understand the successes as well as the failures of Sŏ Chae-p'il, Pak Yŏng-hyo, and other late-nineteenth-century reform thinkers.

OFFICIAL IDEOLOGY

There was a closer conceptual relationship between law and justice in the Confucian state of Chosŏn-dynasty Korea than is sometimes argued. The theoretical link between law and justice was provided by Chinese ideas, which taught that Heaven held government responsible for maladministration. Heaven heard cries of grievance from victims of injustice and repaid failure to redress their grievances with portents and natural or political disasters.

Korea adopted the Neo-Confucian version of this political philosophy during the fifteenth century.[1] Chŏng To-chŏn, one of the most systematic early writers on the subject, noted:

The sagely ruler . . . delays his penalties to allow the fullest leeway for compassionate benevolence and his natural desire to fully uncover the situation. Truly, if the sovereign fails to win the affections of the people, latter-day evils will increase and brutality and disturbance are sure to follow. Nor will it be the people alone who suffer; their grievances will eventually reach Heaven, shattering the harmony of yin and yang and inviting disasters of flood and famine, and thus will the state too be put in jeopardy.[2]

An eighteenth-century commentator used essentially similar language in underlining the need for legally competent local magistrates:

Some of the worst do not even investigate those who injure others, nor do they punish murderers, thereby causing a spirit of resentment to stretch to the heavens. It is said that "the grievance of a woman can bring on three years' drought," and that "the sad heart of a [wrongfully] bereaved father can bring a late spring frost."[3]

Chosŏn-dynasty fiction shares the same moral universe. In the eighteenth-century novel *Tale of Queen Inhyŏn*, the righteous official Pak T'ae-po is put on trial for criticizing King Sukchong when the King deposes Queen Min. During his trial, Pak confronts the King with these words: "Your actions that violate the moral law—unjust persecution of a good person—will be subject to censure." Later, while undergoing gruesome tortures, Pak warns the Chief Justice: "If I die, my soul will join the just in heaven. You are the enemy of the state; bear in mind the law of retribution. A lasting curse will prevail upon your descendants."[4] Official ideology thus emphasized the duty of the state benevolently to ease the grievances of the victims of injustice. An important mechanism for this was the legal process, including strict standards for both investigation and review of serious criminal cases.[5] In principle, both laws and Confucian social ethics existed to prevent and to remedy injustice. In practice, both legal mechanisms and Confucian values were sometimes unequal to the task.

POPULAR CONSCIOUSNESS

What was the nature of popular legal consciousness during the Chosŏn dynasty? Did the Korean populace expect the law and the government to right wrongs? The key to understanding this question is to be found in the interaction of legal institutions and the sense of injustice or grievance (*won*) so often cited in contemporary legal cases and other records. Criminal case records from the Chosŏn dynasty show that the sense of grievance—whether directed at ordinary individuals or officials—provided much of the raw motivational and emotional material with which ideology and law each had to come to terms:

Ch'i-hung had bad feelings against Ch'oe Kwi-man for revealing his sister's debauchery, and threw him down and kicked him . . .[6]

Kim Kwang-ji resented being placed on the roster of able-bodied men for labor service by the village head, Chŏng Ch'am-san. Together with Kim Kwan-t'aek and others he beat and strangled Chŏng.[7]

Se-un suspected Pak P'il-gi of wanting to have illicit relations with his wife . . . and together with Kim Kŭm-gŭm beat him with sticks.[8]

Pak Hyŏng-do had a falling out with Yu Un-sam. Seeking revenge on his enemy, Un-sam strangled himself in Hyŏng-do's house.[9]

A sense of being wronged is a precondition for rights consciousness. However, there can be no rights consciousness in the modern sense unless the person with the grievance has a reliable claim to an institutional remedy. Those with grievances in traditional Korea could claim institutional remedies, but these remedies were not always reliable.

REMEDIES WITHOUT RIGHTS

Legal Mechanisms

Violence or other criminal or suicidal conduct was not the only recourse open to someone with a legally valid grievance. It was also possible to petition the government for relief. Korea established the petition drum, a Chinese institution, in the early fifteenth century. This permitted appeal from legal decisions of lower officials in civil cases after all formal appeals had been exhausted. A less formal system, "striking the gong," brought grievances immediately to the attention of the king. It proved immensely popular in the late Chosŏn period despite repeated bureaucratic attempts to curb and restrict its use. In harmony with the Neo-Confucian ideology of the state, both institutions were administered as acts of official grace, and not in terms of rights of the populace. Yet, petitioning and striking the gong both remained highly popular means of "crying grievance" (ch'ingwŏn).[10]

The Quality of Mercy

The protection available to the populace against certain forms of official and unofficial abuse of power, though doubtless uneven and paternalistically administered, should not be discounted entirely. The formal benevolence exercised by the king was especially concerned with serious injustices arising from the extortionate acts of local bullies and their "private punishments"; with the illegal actions of corrupt local officials and yamen underlings; and even with grievances arising within the criminal review process itself. For example, petitions by the relative of a defendant in a death-penalty case were especially effective and often resulted in a reinvestigation that exonerated the defendant or mitigated his guilt.

In less serious matters, however, the system of petitioning suffered from official ambivalence and even hostility, especially at the lower levels of government. As a practical matter, the magistrate was little concerned with one villager's grievance against another, or even against a kinsman, unless it resulted in a criminal act. Constantly shifting rules also lessened the effectiveness of petitioning. Nonetheless, the continuing popularity of the institution with the general populace often exceeded the tolerance of officials for the kinds of grievances most petitioners brought forward. As one eighteenth-century official complained:

In the provinces, the functionaries and people hold resentments against the local official and file false accusations with the provincial governor. Moreover, there are repeated appeal petitions and beatings of the petition gong.[11]

The Ambiguity of Confucianism

One reason for official discomfort with the petitioning system can be traced to a tension within Neo-Confucian thought. The petition system, like the system of careful review of criminal cases, existed to implement the Confucian obligation of the state to rectify injustice. To many officials, however, it often seemed that petitions threatened to undermine the hierarchical social structure also supported by Confucian doctrines, in which they had a considerable interest.

Since there were no legal barriers to prevent petitions against social superiors or even officials, such perceptions were sometimes justified. The problem was made worse from the seventeenth century onward as some members of the *yangban* class drifted into genteel poverty while upstart commoners, using new farming methods to accumulate wealth, began to purchase and flaunt some of the symbols of *yangban* status. Tensions grew as here and there the older patterns of deference began to erode.

The legal system became the setting for the resolution of these tensions, sometimes supporting claims for justice even against the social hierarchy and at other times buttressing the social order, and yet generally failing to resolve the underlying ideological ambiguity. The result was a legal system that had many "rational" aspects and that produced justice in disputes across class lines surprisingly often, yet failed in the end to establish a consistent pattern of justiciable remedies—rights in the modern sense—through which grievances and complaints could be heard and assessed.

Weak Institutions of Mediation

Less formal institutions for conflict mediation also seem to have been too weak to handle the demands upon them. One example is conflict among family members. Confucian thought encouraged a spirit of grievance and revenge against the assailant of one's father, for example, but gave no legitimacy to the emotion of revenge within the family bond. The legal code also generally upheld the position of the husband versus the wife or the parent versus the child. Resort to violence against kin, though contrary to Confucian teachings, sometimes resulted when frictions within families reached the breaking point.

Village-level institutions for conflict resolution may also have been weak. Serious criminal cases in eighteenth-century records often originated in minor disputes, such as irrigation problems, disagreements over farm tools or animals, and the like. Many such cases probably represent instances where mediation failed or was simply not available.

CONCLUSION

There seems to have been a considerable and unsatisfied popular appetite in the late Chosŏn period for institutional remedies. Many methods for the alleviation of injustice or grievance available in the late Chosŏn period were extra-legal and hazardous at best. Legal approaches varied in effectiveness and were essentially paternalistic in nature. To rephrase the lawyer's dictum that there is "no right without a remedy," approaches to the problem of injustice in the Chosŏn dynasty were remedies without rights. Most forms of self-help risked serious criminal charges or death through suicide, an indication of how desperately felt such unalleviated grievances could become.

Late-nineteenth-century reformers were pioneers in the development of modern Korean human-rights thought. Many had returned from years of sojourn in the United States, and were steeped in the natural law thought of the U.S. Constitution and the Declaration of Independence. Others had encountered the same ideas under the influence of nationalist Japanese reformers like Fukuzawa Yukichi and had been inspired with Japanese efforts at modernization and self-strengthening. Impatient with the injustice, despotism, and maladministration of their native country, the Korean reformers were quick to emphasize the shortcomings of the legal system and the absence of justiciable rights.

For a time, while they stayed clear of politics and confined their efforts to raising the general level of public consciousness, they were successful. Even after beginning a rudimentary political program in 1897, The Independence Club and its newspaper, *The Independent*, acquired a sizeable public following until overcome by the desertion of influential allies, a crisis-torn international political climate, the shortage of time, and the ever-present chasm between their ideas and aspirations and those of important segments of Korean officialdom. The remarkable degree to which the reformers were able to move public sentiment at several levels of society, despite the impracticability and seeming foreignness of some of their ideas, was due to the resonance of those ideas with deeply held traditional popular Korean values, and even with some themes within the official state ideology itself.

PART TWO

Japanese Colonial Rule

Historians William Shaw and Michael Robinson examine the tension between anti-colonial nationalism and one Korean human-rights movement during the period of Japanese colonial rule, 1910–1945. This was the movement for social emancipation among Korea's *paekchŏng* population, which had long suffered from social prejudice and discrimination. The *paekchŏng* equalization movement (*hyŏng-p'yŏng undong*) attempted to put into practice some of the ideals that had been expressed by Korea's human-rights reformers at the turn of the century. It received modest support from elements of the majority population who were interested in the principle of human equality. However, the movement was an embarrassment to many politically active Koreans, in part because it underscored a social problem of purely Korean origin at a time when, for many Korean nationalists, the urgency of the struggle against Japan dictated a submerging of internal conflicts among Koreans. Korean Marxists had room for economic conflict in their understanding of Korea's colonial predicament, but little tolerance for liberal conceptions of rights apart from the class struggle. In postwar Korea, the movement has remained an embarrassment to historians, probably because its simple focus on rights lacks the qualities that state-sponsored racialism or Marxism have sought to foster in pursuit of rival priorities and ideologies.

CHAPTER THREE

Between Class and Nation: The Equalization Society of the 1920s

WILLIAM SHAW

Discussion of Korean social and political movements of the 1920s has largely overlooked the movement for social equality among *paekchŏng* groups which took place during that decade.[1] A wide variety of other social movements—from the reformist "village enlightenment" activities of the YMCA and YWCA and the self-help movements to the labor movement and more militant forms of leftist struggle against Japanese domination—seem to have taken over the center of the historiographical stage.

Neglect of the *paekchŏng* movement for equality (*hyŏngp'yŏng*) may have come about because of the sensitivity of the questions of historical interpretation that it raises, especially in the context of contemporary Korean nationalism of every political hue. Neither the origins of the movement nor its subsequent development can be satisfactorily accommodated within the major established frameworks of interpretation of the colonial period. At the risk of oversimplification, I would suggest that three interpretive tendencies (not necessarily incompatible with each other) shape our understanding of the period of Japanese colonial rule in general and of Korean social movements in particular.

First, there is a tendency to treat such social movements in terms of their value as evidence of opposition to Japanese domination, to demonstrate that the Korean people did not supinely accept Japanese rule, but used a variety of creative cultural, economic, and political tactics to attempt the preservation of racial and cultural autonomy. Historically, of course, these movements exerted a critical formative influence on both the experience and iconography of Korean nationalism. For an intellectual writing for *Kaebyŏk*, a student making his sacrificial pilgrimage of service "to the villages," or a rank-and-file worker organizing a strike, the experience of intellectual and physical resistance to Japanese definitions of Korean-ness must have played a salient role in the establishment of personal and national identity. After Liberation, the symbolic value of this formative experience continued to be quite high—though it could be politically hazardous to attempt to repeat such experiences in the context of native Korean rule, whether of left or right: "We are the nation which successfully resisted Japanese attempts to oppress us. Our identity as a people has been shaped by our refusal to submit to (foreign) oppression." It is no accident that this interpretive theme is firmly entrenched in elementary and middle-school language and civics textbooks.[2] But it cannot be denied that it influences scholarship on the colonial period as well.

A second theme, particularly evident in South Korea scholarship, may be seen in the tendency to treat all social movements as "leftist." Kim Chun-yŏp and Kim Ch'ang-sun devote a large portion of Volume II of their history of Korean communism to the "leftist movements" which followed the March First Movement and which covered—if the list can be credited—every form of intellectual and social activism of the period, including the *paekchŏng* emancipation movement.[3] Finally, from the left, there is sometimes a tendency to treat all non-leftist movements and personages of this period as tainted with collaboration, or futility, or both.[4]

All these interpretive tendencies threaten to distort our understanding of the nature and meaning of the Korean experience under

Japanese colonial rule. Our understanding of Korea and of colonialism and its effects may become correspondingly impoverished, not just through distortion, but through our choice of what is studied as well. And here may be found a few reasons for historians' neglect of the *paekchŏng* emancipation movement.

The *Hyŏngp'yŏng* Movement intractably resists, for example, the search for evidence of Korean resistance to Japanese oppression and injustice. The problems the movement attempted to redress antedated by centuries the period of Japanese colonial rule and represented a specifically (though not uniquely) Korean pattern of injustice and oppression. Unlike so many other problems facing Korean society during the colonial period, this one could not plausibly be laid at the feet of the foreign oppressor.

On the other hand, it seems strange indeed that this movement could ever be seen as leftist. Despite their interest in the movement, Korean leftists were certainly under no such impression. Kim Tŏk-han, for example, was present at the ceremonies in commemoration of the first anniversary of the founding of the Equalization Society (Hyŏngp'yŏngsa), held in Seoul on 25 April 1924. His reactions to the movement were published several months later in an article he wrote for *Kaebyŏk* magazine, titled "Internal Strife within the Equalization Movement: a Critique."[5] Kim was sympathetic to the movement and had a high view of its potential impact on Korean society:

... they have experienced every kind of cruelty and sorrow and have only now had the opportunity to barely raise the flag of revolt. Under these new circumstances they must firm up their unity and strike for victory against their antagonists ... fully united and making a firm front, they are capable of becoming a great force which no one will be able to despise.

Nonetheless, he had harsh words for the movement's "theistic tendencies" (as evidenced in such slogans as "God created all men equal") and worried whether they were naively depending on incurring the good will of others rather than preparing for resolute struggle. Kim also advanced a Marxist critique against what he felt was a too narrow preoccupation with human rights:

... originally the *paekchŏng* class suffered more from oppression of human rights than from economic oppression. As a result, they have devoted their efforts more to recovery of human rights than to economic matters. The Equalization Movement of today thus signifies, not economic equalization, but simply the equaliza-tion of human rights. Thus the movement is not a mass movement and cannot escape its character as a movement of one segment of the population only.

Without a change in philosophy, Kim felt, the fate of the *Paekchŏng* Movement could be no different from that of the theories of Ferdi-nand Lassalle[6] or the Mensheviks:

Love for humanity, a philosophy of cooperation, policies of reconciliation; these kinds of lukewarm measures are completely without value . . . for the attainment of human rights in the truest sense, there must be clear and distinctive class-consciousness—the consciousness of the proletarian class—and there must be striving to acquire such class-consciousness.

Perhaps Kim Tŏk-han is a poor example, since there are indica-tions that he may have been theoretically shallow and tactically inflexible. His call for a proletarian base for the human-rights con-cerns of the Equalization Movement, for example, reveals a striking naiveté with respect to the actual composition of Korean society at this time and suggests that Kim's Marxism was more closely attuned to issues espoused by Japanese Marxist circles than to Korean reali-ties. It was about this time, for example, that Yamakawa Hitoshi was arguing for a proletarian political party;[7] but industrial workers in Korea numbered about 55,000 in 1920 as compared with nearly 2 mil-lion in Japan at about the same time.[8] Kim is also known to have unsuccessfully opposed the merger of his nascent Korean Labor Party with several other minor leftist organizations and study groups in the summer of 1925. The history of Korean Marxism knows little of his activities after that point.[9]

More successful Korean Marxists also took an interest in the Equal-ization Movement and tried, with some success in the late 1920s, to infiltrate and influence it. But, as a 1926 Communist Party report indicates, the operating philosophy of the movement remained essen-tially uninfluenced by Marxist insights:

The people of this class do not have much class-consciousness, and even their lead-ers, Chang Chi-p'il and O Sŏng-hwan, do not have a thorough, class-conscious understanding of social revolution. Therefore a healthy movement here is yet to be constructed.[10]

It would seem, then, that the Equalization Movement does not readily fall within any of the three types of interpretation we have mentioned. Though the movement faced pressures to concern itself with nationalist and anti-Japanese issues, it originated and developed in resistance to Korean, not Japanese, patterns of injustice. Though it was under pressure to adopt a Marxist class-conflict model of social change and an "economic-rights" rather than a "human-rights" outlook, it remained essentially distinct from those social movements of the 1920s which were more directly influenced by the Marxist vision. Finally, though it sought to work within the political framework of Japanese colonial rule, the Equalization Movement cannot be convincingly portrayed as collaborationist. The remainder of this chapter discusses this movement in some detail, beginning briefly with the extended and immediate historical background to the *paekchŏng* problem and continuing with the development and character of the Equalization Movement during the 1920s. It concludes with some reflections on the meaning of this movement in terms of human rights in Korea.

HISTORICAL BACKGROUND

Paekchŏng *in Traditional Korea*

In discussion of the origins of social prejudice against the *eta* or *burakumin* people of Japan, a large place is usually given to the role of Buddhist prohibitions against the taking of life and Japanese conceptions of ritual cleanliness (and pollution) which predate Buddhist influence. Such influences may have played a role in Korea as well, but the full story is more complicated. The modern term for butchers and certain other disdained groups, *paekchŏng*, did not acquire its negative connotations until the fifteenth century. Koryŏ dynasty *paekchŏng* seem to have been a group with no fixed occupational duties or family registration, used at times by the government to fill military quotas or as station employees (*yŏkchŏng*), in which cases state-land allotments were provided. In social standing, Koryŏ *paekchŏng* seem to have occupied an intermediate position between commoners and low-born persons (*ch'ŏnin*).[11]

In the early Chosŏn period, the term *paekchŏng* was first applied to the *hwach'ŏk* people, a disparate social group made up of vagabonds (*mujari*) and others believed to have originated among Jurchen and other non-Korean nomadic groups from outside the peninsula. These groups lived a gypsy-like existence, wandering freely from place to place, supporting themselves by hunting or in other informal ways, and from time to time even raiding villages or government outposts in the guise of Japanese pirates. In the early Chosŏn period, the *hwach'ŏk* came under increasingly strict government control, but were still unable to mix freely with the general population and took on disesteemed tasks such as butchering. In 1423, King Sejong attempted to integrate them into Korean society (and military service in particular) by registering them as "new *paekchŏng*," but the result was to downgrade the term *paekchŏng* rather than to upgrade the social standing of the *hwach'ŏk*. The *Kyŏngguk taejŏn* Code of 1485 required *paekchŏng* to be quartered separately in each community and prevented them from leaving their assigned location.[12]

The early Chosŏn sequestering of *paekchŏng* groups was not intended to segregate them as much as to forcibly assimilate them into the political economy of sedentary agricultural life.[13] Thus, allegations of non-Korean origins of the Chosŏn dynasty *paekchŏng* may have a basis in cultural fact. Slaughtering of animals may indeed have been disesteemed in the Koryŏ period, but it also seems to have been a natural occupational choice for those like the *hwach'ŏk* who were already excluded from sedentary Korean society and skilled in the use and preparation of animal products and hides as part of the ecology of their nomadic origins. It may also be that slaughtering of animals came to be disesteemed through its association with such disesteemed groups as much as through Buddhist sensitivities.

Chosŏn-dynasty *paekchŏng* were at the absolute bottom of the social scale. Prohibited by custom from wearing the same clothing, hats, or even straw shoes worn by commoners, they had to yield the road to all passersby, including slaves.[14] Whether they could be cut down with impunity by any offended person as is sometimes claimed, they do not seem to have been given more than the minimal legal protection from violence. Legal records demonstrate that violence could erupt easily against such persons in a society where language as well as clothing could carry socially significant nuances. A late-eighteenth-century criminal case book contains the following illustrative cases:[15]

Ch'il-gŭm, a palace slave, mistook Kim Tŭk-kyŏng for a butcher and called him over. When he refused to come, Ch'il-gŭm stabbed him, and he died on the spot. (*Simnirok* [*SR*], I, 30)

Mok-ch'im, a local magnate, was quarreling with Mun Tŭk-kyŏng and struck him with a stick. The victim died the following day . . . [Board of Punishments comment:] Mok-ch'im is a local magnate, while Tŭk-kyŏng was an entertainer of low status, naturally held in contempt. [He] did not consider it difficult to deliver a lethal blow. (*SR*, I, 42)

Sam-jing is a traveling entertainer (*ch'angdae*); while walking with Hwang Sŏng-jae to a village meeting, Sam-jing became angry at the other's over-familiarity and struck and kicked him. The victim died three days later. (*SR*, I, 205)

T'aek-su, seeing Pak Ch'u (a dog butcher), quarreling over the price of meat with a government female slave, Chae-ran, beat Ch'u. On the nineteenth day Ch'u died . . . [Governor's memorial:] It is a common practice for dog butchers to quarrel over prices; this rough fellow was drunk and became quite angry without warning. [Royal comment:] People naturally despise these dog butchers; when he suddenly raised the price and then began to speak in a disrespectful manner, then in addition to being drunk became angry, it is not strange that [the defendant] would hit him a few times . . . (*SR*, I, 381–382)

Social Position of Paekchŏng *in the Early-Twentieth Century*

When a small group of Korean reformers gained brief control of the Korean government under Japanese sponsorship in the summer of 1894 and promulgated a series of paper reforms, one of the new policies of the government was to end discriminatory treatment of "despised persons" such as station workers, entertainers, and leather-workers.[16] Though this reform may have reflected Japanese hopes of claiming a tutorial role in assisting Koreans to enter the ranks of modern nations, the discriminatory treatment of butchers (*paekchŏng*) and others of similar status had already aroused criticism and proposals for reform within Korea, most recently in the demands of the insurgent *Tonghak* forces that the treatment of the "seven despised groups" (*ch'ilban ch'ŏnin*) be reformed and that butchers no longer be forced to wear the straw "*p'yŏngyang* hat" betraying their occupation and social status.[17] These aspirations remained unfulfilled; the *Tonghak* armies were defeated and the reforms of 1894 also proved unable to outlast the short-lived Japanese intervention into Korean politics. Later attempts by the Japanese to legislate change after seizing first protectorate and then colonial control over Korea in 1905 and 1910 also remained ineffective. As one Japanese writer commented in 1911, "Even though the rules forbidding them to wear the long clothes and the hat have been withdrawn and they enjoy many advantages, including sending their children to schools, still people cannot accept them on a level of equality and associate with them.[18] The Government General itself was not fully free from such prejudice; well into the 1920s, census and other official forms required that *paekchŏng*, whatever their occupation, be denoted with the term *tohan*, "butcher."[19]

An irony of Japanese reforms in Korea lay in the inability of the Japanese government to improve the social position of its own *burakumin* population.[20] Though an Imperial Edict of Emancipation had purportedly equalized the status of *burakumin* and proclaimed them "new commoners" (*shin heimin*) as early as 1871, pervasive and sometimes violent prejudice remained firmly entrenched. "*Eta*-hunting" (*eta-gari*) or "chastisement" drives (*eta-seibatsu*) sometimes occurred in the 1870s as the general populace sought scapegoats for the trying uncertainties of the period. The attitude of the government following the 1871 proclamation remained summed up in the statement of an 1880 handbook of the Ministry of Justice that the *eta* were "almost like animals." By the early 1900s, various self-help organizations had come into existence to improve the social standing of the *burakumin* and to press their cause in legal and other encounters. Some progress against overt public discrimination and harassment was made during the 1920s through an aggressive program of protests and demonstrations under the leadership of the Suiheisha, or Levelers' Society. It is not surprising that social prejudice against members of these groups remained strong in Korea well into the twentieth century.

Such prejudice and discrimination against *paekchŏng* in Korea went far beyond the reluctance of majority persons to associate with them and the routine use of derogatory and humiliating language both to and about them. During the Chosŏn period, *paekchŏng* had served the legal system as body-handlers in autopsies and as execution-ground attendants. In most communities into the twentieth century, it fell to the *paekchŏng* to do the jobs no one else would do, such as removal and burial of corpses. Even more offensive from the *paekchŏng* point of view was the popular association of *paekchŏng* and dogs. Judging from the remarks of an informant who grew up in Ulsan in the 1920s, *paekchŏng* were commonly suspected as the ones who "would catch your favorite pet dog if you weren't careful and cut him up."[21] *Paekchŏng* were often required by the police to kill stray or rabid dogs, a task not only intrinsically unpleasant but one that increased the contempt in which they were held by the majority population.[22] One informant expressed majority sentiment well: "I still cannot get over the feeling that a man who kills dogs is the worst kind of human being there is."[23]

Local communities often added their own customs, language, and practices to the standard list of stereotypes and prejudicial treatment. In some communities, private schools denied admission to students of *paekchŏng* origin, while, in others, *paekchŏng* students were daily required to brave jeers and bodily assault. In Yech'on, majority citizens traditionally held a celebration each July in which *paekchŏng* women were seized and roughed up until the *paekchŏng* community provided meat or eggs as a ransom. The festivities then continued with the extorted food.[24]

Notwithstanding such problems, it seems clear that, for a variety of reasons, including the rising influence of Christian and Ch'ŏndogyo religious values and the demise of certain formal occupational and residential restrictions, some *paekchŏng* were able to move away from communities where they were known and to engage in farming or other majority occupations.[25] These factors, coupled with the relative anonymity provided by modernization under the aegis of Japanese colonial rule, may have brought about the substantial drop in the number of people identifying themselves as *paekchŏng*, in a Government-General survey of 1923, for example.[26] In contrast to a numerical strength of some 400,000 estimated by Equalization Society leaders, the number of *paekchŏng* in the survey amounted to fewer than 33,000, a majority congregated in the southern provinces.

THE EQUALIZATION MOVEMENT

Origins

It is perhaps a measure of the residual strength of traditional social sentiment in Ch'ungch'ŏng, Chŏlla, and Kyŏngsang that most of those unable to avoid identification as *paekchŏng* at the time of the 1923 survey lived in those provinces.[27] It was also in the southern part of the peninsula that the movement for the improvement of *paekchŏng* social standing both took root and remained most active.[28] The founder of the *Hyŏngp'yŏng* or Equalization Movement was Yi Hak-ch'an, a prosperous individual from the large *paekchŏng* community in the vicinity of Chinju in South Kyŏngsang province. Yi had tried in the early 1920s to enroll his son in various public and private schools, repeatedly encountering rejection because of his social origin. In 1922, a local night school had accepted a large sum of money (¥ 100) to admit his son, but the reaction of neighborhood residents and the other students led to the boy's withdrawal shortly thereafter. An attempt to place him in a school in Seoul met with similar failure.

The following year, however, groundbreaking was begun for a new private school in Chinju, and *paekchŏng* families were among those to receive notices recruiting workers. About 70 men (from a community of 350 persons) reported for work in the hopes that finally school admission would become a possibility. When these hopes became clear, however, the school committee informed them that their services would no longer be required and that *paekchŏng* would not be granted enrollment in the new school. At this point, Yi Hak-ch'an took his story to a local sympathizer of majority status, Kang Sang-ho, and together they sought out the head of the Chinju branch of the *Chosŏn ilbo*, Sin Hyŏn-su. Within a few weeks, these men and three others had agreed to establish a society to improve the social position of the *paekchŏng*. Following a planning session in April, an inaugural meeting of the new society was held on 13 May, with more than 150 persons from three provinces in attendance. The meeting had been well publicized in advance, and several tens of congratulatory messages from various other social organizations were received. The Statement of Purpose of the new organization included the following points:

(1) Equality and fairness are [should be] the basis of society; kindness is [should be] a basic attribute of human nature.
(2) The basic purpose of our society is to smash down social ranks, do away with contemptuous labels, and encourage education so that we too may truly have standing as persons.

The declaration concluded with reference to the "400,000" compatriots for which the Equalization Society claimed to speak.

A constitution and by-laws passed in the same meeting demonstrated the essentially ameliorative or integrationist orientation of the organization, affirming the society's commitment to lawful methods and displaying a familiarity with parliamentary procedure. Self-improvement was the dominant theme. An "equalization school" was to be established, together with a society journal, and day and night programs to raise the educational level of the members. There were also provisions for mutual aid in case of natural disasters and plans to extend the activities of the society through additional chapters.

The Politics of Confrontation

By the end of 1923, the Equalization Society had established 12 branches and more than 60 local chapters.[29] In most locations, public reaction was divided. Local representatives of previously established social-reform groups sometimes joined the new society or demonstrated sympathy in other ways. Seoul newspapers such as *Tonga ilbo* were openly sympathetic and followed Equalization Society activities closely.[30] In May 1923, for example, the *Tonga ilbo* ran more than a dozen articles and editorials on the subject, covering the establishment of the new organization, the public reaction to it, and on one occasion printing an extended essay by society co-founder Chang Chi-p'il, in which he described his personal experiences as a *paekchŏng* and explained the character of the movement.[31] Members of the traditionalistic farm workers' associations (*nongch'ong*) on the other hand, sometimes reacted with criticism, even violence. Violent incidents resulting in personal injury averaged more than one a month over the first two and one-half years following the establishment of the Equalization Society. Examination of several of these incidents will clarify the nature of the society's impact on Korean society and the range of reactions to the Equalization Movement as a whole.

The reaction of these traditionalistic elements of the majority population of Chinju to the establishment of the Equalization Society clearly illustrates the disesteem in which *paekchŏng* were held and the tension which would accompany efforts at organization and amelioration. An initial sign of community reaction had been the refusal of *kisaeng* entertainers to serve at the inaugural celebration of the new society.[32] Within days after the inaugural meeting, some 2,000 *nonch'ong* members convened a mass meeting, called for a boycott on meat, and then marched on the Equalization Society headquarters to demand that the organization disband. Society members, perhaps aware of similar tactics by the Japanese Levelers' Society, quickly organized a "dare-to-die" self-defense force of some 40 men.[33] Later in the month, another mass meeting took place, and the police mobilized to prevent violence. The meeting urged another boycott of meat and passed resolutions against the new organization and against supporting groups such as the Labor Fraternal Association (Chosŏn Nodong Kongjehoe). The latter organization had a local branch in Chinju since February of 1922 and had come out in support of the Equalization Society.[34] Most of the resolutions contained abusive language directed against *paekchŏng* and their supporters from among the majority population. For example, the Youth Association hall, where the initial meeting had taken place, was contemptuously renamed "the slaughtering ground." The *Tonga ilbo* reported a tense and near-violent atmosphere.[35]

Under the stimulation of the new organization and its activities, many *paekchŏng* grew more assertive and unwilling to tolerate without outward complaint the traditional treatment they had previously received. The new organization often responded quickly to even minor incidents felt to impair the dignity or equality of the *paekchŏng*. In Pohang in the spring of 1924, for example, an elderly member of the society was slapped in the face by a Japanese policeman. The Equalization Society promptly held a mass meeting to protest the policeman's conduct, and a representative of the headquarters branch in Chinju was sent to present several demands to the police, including the resignation of the police chief and the firing of the individual officer involved. The demands were accepted and the police chief was brought to a meeting and publicly slapped in retribution.[36]

The Equalization Society quickly came to provide not just a rallying point for discontented members of the *paekchŏng* population but a visible target for those in the majority population who felt that the despised *paekchŏng* were losing their sense of station. In Taegu in July 1924, for example, a *paekchŏng* became involved in a complicated land transaction involving a middleman of majority status. When the deal did not work out as expected, a fight occurred in which both were injured and numerous friends of the *paekchŏng* participant took part. Two days later, a group of about 30 friends of the middleman invaded the offices of the local Equalization Society and attacked the chairman. The next day, *paekchŏng* houses were ransacked; when a number of cudgels were discovered in one of the houses, the crowd seized the owner and was about to administer the traditional "private punishment" (*sahyŏng*, beating) when the police intervened.[37] Further examples may be given to show that the Equalization Society was often the center of controversy and violence. In 1925, for example, a riot broke out on the occasion of the second anniversary of the founding of the Yech'ŏn branch of the society.[38] The celebrations were marked by flying flags, a prominent arch erected for the occasion, and the presence of national officers of the society. Perhaps the celebrants also followed Equalization Society practice of saturation publicity, involving loudspeaker cars and the distribution of thousands of fliers for several days prior to a large meeting.[39] In any event, subsequent events clearly demonstrated that townspeople were aware that the meeting was taking place. A number of strong speeches, stressing the oppression suffered by the *paekchŏng* and the need for determined resistance, were followed by a speech of a different character, given not by one of the visiting society dignitaries but the head of the local Youth Association, a sympathizer of *yangban* origin. His speech suggested that organizational activities were "behind the times" and that more practical efforts at self-improvement should take precedence. The assembly strongly criticized his remarks as paternalistic. By nightfall word somehow reached the townspeople that a local *yangban* had been verbally insulted. Citizens collected into an ugly crowd outside the meeting place. Representatives of the mob were sent in to demand a return to the self-effacing language and demeanor of pre-movement days. The representatives were set upon by angry members of the Equalization Society, and the ensuing melee lasted until 10 p.m. Over the next three days, the confrontation escalated as both sides received reinforcements. The Equalization Society was backed by local representatives of other social organizations and by the arrival of more national officers, who chided the local chairman for seeking personal protection from the police and at times became personally involved themselves in the street fighting. Angry townspeople were emboldened by the arrival of laborers for market day. Within a few days of the initial outburst, numbers of injured on both sides had been admitted to the hospital in Andong.

Prominent members of the national Equalization Society organization tenaciously continued the struggle in Yech'ŏn, stating that the incident was not merely a local matter but represented an attack on the organization as a whole. A week after the outbreak (19 August), the Seoul headquarters of the society released a resolution calling for the recruitment and dispatching of "righteous defense units" (*chŏngwidan*) and "do-or-die" squads (*kyŏlsadae*). Japanese authorities censored the papers in which these resolutions were published, however, and the incident gradually came to an end.[40]

Relations between *paekchŏng* and members of the majority populace were not uniformly disastrous. In Ch'ŏnan, for example, a serious attempt at integration was being made in the mid-1920s in a private school.[41] Tensions persisted under the surface, however, for majority students staged a walkout in July 1924 following a dispute with *paekchŏng* students over a tennis match. School officials, one of whom was also the sub-county chief, attempted to reconcile the two sides with a lecture aimed at both groups. Majority students were told of the history of discrimination against the *paekchŏng* and reminded that they were now to be treated as ordinary citizens. Students of *paekchŏng* origin were reminded that their social position had improved. The Equalization Society came in for some criticism, however, when it was noted that, since its formation, some individuals had evidently been inspired to unwarranted arrogance and insubordination. *Paekchŏng* students were told to be grateful for the progress that had been made and were warned not to be used by the society and thus incur the greater displeasure of the majority population.

Whatever the motives of the sub-county chief's speech, it does seem that the tactics of the Equalization Society had rapidly broadened from those of accommodation and self-improvement to include aggressive confrontation. Instances of reported *paekchŏng*–majority violence correlate strongly with the number of society branches in each province. Of course, the mere articulation of *paekchŏng* aspirations for equality was often enough to irritate many members of the majority populations, and to enrage those at the lower socioeconomic edge of that population. Yet, society officials often seem to have played a role in expanding confrontations once they had begun rather than trying to resolve them quietly, seeming at times to have been almost more sensitive to criticism of the society than to accomplishing the ameliorative and integrationist goals with which it had begun. The Ch'ŏnan school incident, for example, was on the verge of settlement when a society member overheard the criticism of the sub-county head directed at the society. He rushed into the class-room and argued with the man until forcibly ejected from the room. The result was a series of telegrams to the Seoul headquarters for assis-tance, the arrival shortly of some 60 actives from various society branches, further demonstrations and mass meetings by both *paek-chŏng* and majority populations, and a debilitating meat boycott which eventually broke the back of *paekchŏng* resistance and forced them to sign a formal statement of apology.[42]

The reasons for this change in tactics—if indeed it represented a change in the original approach of the organization—are not immed-iately clear. A contributing factor may have been the increase in num-ber and scale of violent tenant-and-labor disputes during the mid-and late-1920s.[43] Many of the social movements and organizations that had come into open existence under the "cultural policy" of the Jap-anese Government General during this period became increasingly skilled in the techniques of protest as the decade progressed, both through direct experience and under the influence of increasingly left-ist leadership. Possibly the Equalization Society itself was influenced by the leftward trend of the middle and late 1920s as well. Members of the society were among those arrested in the large-scale July 1926 round-up of Communists, for example, and, by 1928, the organiza-tion had voted to make democratic centralism its guiding principle of organization, revealing at least some Communist infiltration of the leadership.[44] In Japan, the corresponding organization, the Suiheisha, had demonstrated some Marxist orientation from the first and rather rapidly moved to the use of violence, including the formation of "do-or-die" commandos and other tactics of militant confrontation. The effect of this and of social movements within Korea remains to be studied, as do the ties between the Equalization Society and the Korean labor movement during this period. All these considerations notwithstanding, it is possible that another factor in the increasing militance of the Equalization Society may have been the existence within the society from about 1924 of more and less militant ele-ments, and the ensuing contest for control of the society.

"Militancy and "Conservatism" in the Equalization Movement

A difference in orientation among various members of the Equalization Society leadership appeared within the first year of the new organization's existence. The split seems first to have become publicized in February 1924 at the society's national convention in Pusan when one group within the leadership failed to secure passage of a motion to move the national headquarters to Seoul. This group promptly held its own meetings and resolved to move to Seoul. Neither group seems at this point to have been numerically strong enough to completely subdue the other.[45]

At the time of the first anniversary of the founding of the Equalization Society in April, the two groups met separately. The Chinju leadership and their supporters, including Yi Hak-ch'an, Kang Sang-ho, and Sin Hyŏn-su, issued a declaration attributing the split to a simple difference of opinion over the location of the headquarters and calling for immediate reunification of the organization. The Seoul group, centering around Chang Chi-p'il, held its own commemorative celebrations under the name of the General Headquarters of the Equalization Society Reform Alliance.[46] This was the meeting attended and commented upon by Kim Tŏk-han.

During the summer, efforts were made to reunify the two factions, and a compromise settlement was announced in August.[47] As part of the agreement, it was announced that Kang Sang-ho (of the Chinju group) and Chang Chi-p'il (of the Seoul group) would resign their positions in the organization. Kang's departure was actually engineered on the newly accepted premise that the organization leadership should be open only to persons of paekchŏng background. Chang Chi-p'il thus remained an ordinary member for a short time, since he was of paekchŏng origin, but eventually he was forced to leave the organization altogether due to pressure from the Chinju group. It seems that the Chinju group was under the discipline of the Seoul headquarters from that time on.[48]

The reasons for the split remain unclear. According to Kim Chun-yŏp and Kim Ch'ang-sun, the Chinju group represented a "conservative" wing of the movement which had genuine differences of philosophy and method with the other, "reform" faction, but attempted to bury this fact in the controversy surrounding the location of the headquarters.[49] It would be tempting to portray the Chinju group in terms of the gradualist and assimilationist goals and tactics of the early-twentieth-century *yūwa* (reconciliation) organizations among *burakumin* in Japan. According to one study of such movements, such organizations represented the efforts of relatively prosperous members of the *burakumin* community to channel the energies of the *burakumin* into "self-help" and "self-improvement" kinds of activity rather than into forms of direct action favored by poorer, more radical *burakumin*. After World War I, *burakumin* interest in Marxism increased, and such organizations gradually lost ground against the confrontationist tactics of newer organizations such as the Suiheisha.[50]

To pursue the analogy with the Japanese case, the "reform" faction of the Equalization Movement might be seen as standing for the tougher, more self-reliant, and militant approach. Chang Chi-p'il might have contributed to the new radicalism of the reform faction, it might be argued, because of his exposure to student activism during his years at Meiji University.[51] Though little is known of Chang's political views, there does exist one statement made during the earliest days of the *Hyŏngp'yŏng* Movement, in May 1923. After describing his own personal experience and detailing the reasons for the movement, he commented briefly on the methods the new organization would use:

Our movement is petitionary in nature, not a movement of forcible antagonism. However, if society at any time should fail to treat us as human beings, there will be no recourse; we are resolved to resist.[52]

There would seem to be in this statement the promise of subsequent activism.

Interestingly, this view of the evolution of the *Hyŏngp'yŏng* Society is also the one taken by Hirano Shoken, one of the few Suiheisha members to visit Korea who is known to have left a record of his impressions of the *Hyŏngp'yŏng* Movement.[53] Hirano listed the goals of the original *Hyŏngp'yŏng* Movement: elimination of class distinctions; abolition of abusive names; the encouragement of education and mutual kindness; the publication of papers and magazines and the establishment of lectures; prohibitions against drunkenness and immorality; and exhortations to thrift. "This is the same list as that made by the Yūwakai (Conciliation Society) in Japan, which was simply a bureaucratic and government-serving organ. In response to the continuous oppression and obstruction visited upon their movement by the *yangban* and majority population, the leaders of this early Equalization Society could do nothing more than devote themselves to public relations.[54]

Hirano continues with an account of the dispute of the spring and summer of 1924. Several non-*paekchŏng* among the top leadership were misusing funds and leading the movement in a bad direction. A group of *paekchŏng* among the leadership saw what was happening and, after some effort, were able to gain control of the movement, under the new slogan: "The emancipation of the *paekchŏng* will come on the basis of the strength of the *paekchŏng* alone." Under the new "reform" leadership, the movement went on to organize counter-vigilante groups (the *chŏngwidan*, or righteous defense units) and collateral student organizations and to take a more militant posture.[55]

It would be tempting to accept this line of interpretation. It would put the Equalization Movement of Korea squarely within the pattern of development evinced by the *burakumin* movements of Japan during the 1910s and 1920s and would also produce some striking parallels with the American civil-rights movement of the 1950s and 1960s.[56] However, there are several reasons why the nature of the movement may have been less clear-cut than Hirano's comments would indicate.

First, it is not certain that increased militance *followed* the resolution of the leadership crises of the Hyŏngp'yŏngsa in the late summer and fall of 1924. It is true that organization activities did increase— especially through the establishment of collateral organizations—as Hirano pointed out. This would have naturally followed, however, a year of grass-roots organizing and expansion in any case. There is no indication that the "reform" leaders were more disposed to expanding the scope or number of branches of the Hyŏngp'yŏngsa than were the leaders of the "Chinju" group; expansion seems to have been on the common agenda. (The errors of view of the "Chinju" group—apart from their handling of the organization's finances—are not mentioned specifically in any of the materials available.)

Moreover, the counter-vigilante defense units were likewise a natural outgrowth of the *kyŏlsadae* (do-or-die brigades) and similar groups organized during the uproar that often accompanied articulation of *paekchŏng* grievances. Such organizations existed from as early as June 1923;[57] more evidence is needed before it can be determined whether such counter-vigilante tactics represented any systematic tactical philosophy or were simply spontaneous responses to specific situations. There is no clear record of opposition to such tactics on the part of "Chinju" faction leaders.

An unusual view of the thought of the "reform" faction may be gained from the observations of the Marxist Kim Tŏk-han, who was present at the commemorative celebrations in Seoul in April 1924. His account provides strong evidence that the "reform" leadership shared many of the attitudes scornfully dismissed by Hirano as typical of the ineffectual, "conciliationist" Chinju faction. Kim, as we have noted, took the movement to task for its non-proletarian character and its preoccupation with "human rights" rather than "economic oppression." He also was irritated that among those invited to the ceremonies (and to a banquet afterward) were various "persons of repute" who supported the aims of the society. Kim could not understand why the *Hyŏngp'yŏng* Movement would cultivate relationships with elements of society toward whom they should (on his view) feel nothing but antagonism:

One part of the opening address "hoped that everyone will give their sympathy to the Equalization Society." Someone else's observations concluded with "the success of our Equalization Society depends on the sympathy of all men." In other words, the fate of the Equalization Society does not depend on the struggle of the society members themselves, but rather on the sympathy of those in the world around them. Those who have embarked on the path of activism should simply press onward toward their objective regardless of whether others may sympathize or not. Once the irrationality or the evil have been recognized for what they are, all that remains is to select the means by which they are to be demolished. There is no room [in this process] for "sympathy" or "lack of sympathy" . . . there is no room for compromise, no room for anything but smashing the enemy."[58]

These reactions would seem to illustrate not only that the "reform" element were not receptive to a Marxist approach to their problems, but that they seem to have shared some attitudes with the "conservative" Chinju wing of the Equalization Society.

With this awareness that philosophical or tactical differences within the leadership of the Hyŏngp'yŏngsa may have been less sharply defined than Hirano and others have asserted, it still might be possible to go back over the demonstrations and counter-demonstrations of the first year of the society's existence to probe the roots of the increasing militancy of the movement at this time and subsequently. One possibility might be the use of militant tactics by those engaged in a leadership struggle which had its basis in other issues, as a means of gaining prominence among the rank-and-file of the movement. This might account for the apparent role of some Hyŏngp'yŏngsa leaders, notably Chang Chi-p'il, in exacerbating or escalating violent conflict once they had arrived on the scene of a confrontation. Whether this hypothesis is correct or not, the question will help us in our understanding of the nature and development of the Equalization Movement. At this point, a few thoughts on the meaning of this movement in the context of modern Korean history and in the context of the topic of human rights may be in order.

CONCLUSIONS

It seems clear that the Equalization Movement, from its inception and for a good part of its history in the 1920s, provides an example of a relatively unalloyed concern with human rights. Whatever one may think of Kim Tŏk-han's critique as a whole, he was certainly correct in pointing out that economic grievances were not a major part of *paekchŏng* motivation. It is this that must explain the relatively weak response made by the movement to the theoretical blandishments of the Korean left, with the result that hatred and antagonism based on class (however defined) does not seem to have become a part of the Equalization Society program. Desire for equality and the experience of discrimination provided more fuel for this movement than did principled animosity.

It is also apparent that the Equalization Movement was not complicated by the racialist ideas that informed the thought of so many movements that had as their objective the struggle to define and preserve *Korean* identity against Japanese oppression. Equalization Movement literature does, at times, refer to the Korean race, but then only in the spirit of slogans such as "There should be no discrimination among members of the same race"; the real target of this is clearly the popular idea that the *paekchŏng* were not really Korean, not the distortions of Koreanness being fostered by Japanese policies.

Albert Memmi, reflecting on the Tunisian and Algerian colonial experience in *The Colonizer and the Colonized*, has touched on that paradoxical quality of resistance to colonialism, which is that such resistance often awakens and then harnesses ideas—like nationalism, or the class struggle—that seem essential to the overthrow of colonial oppression but themselves contain many elements inimical to justice if allowed to hold power autonomously. In the light of this, the fail-ure of the Equalization Movement to fit either the ultra-nationalist or Marxist mold during this period is highly significant.

The nationalism of the Equalization Movement is, as the *Tonga ilbo* editorialist pointed out, a source of repentance or reflection (*pansŏng*);[59] there can be no basis here for the symbolic assertion of the nation or race over against the individual or deviant group. Likewise *paekchŏng* grievances uniquely undermine the other potent myth of modern nationalism—that the principle origin of evil or injustice in society is to be found outside the national or racial bond. Under the spell of such a myth, injustice and oppression are foreign by definition; resistance to oppression can thus only be resistance to foreign oppression.

The same critique might be leveled at Marxism as a tool for anti-colonial struggle; it is intellectually and historically the twin of nationalism, in which a chosen class replaces a chosen people. Like the national struggle, the class struggle is one in which no forgiveness is possible or necessary, since the enemy is outside the circle of mean-ingful humanity. It is this that underlies the permanent stigmatiza-tion of some 10 percent of the population in North Korea today"[60] just as it is the counter-myth of the nation that produced a "Korean-style democracy" in South Korea and stigmatized notions of human rights as impure or alien.

Whatever the shortcomings of the Equalization Movement—and these would have to include its ultimate failure to break the circle of violence—it did, during its brief existence, articulate and hold to con-ceptions of human dignity couched in terms that transcended the nation. Since it is the preeminence of particularistic (and hence lim-ited) conceptions of human dignity—grounded in the alternative con-ceptions of *minjok* and *immin*—which seem to characterize post-Liberation Korea, perhaps it is time not only to reconsider the Equalization Movement, but to reassess other social movements of the 1920s (and of the present) in the light of the question of whether they may contribute to the development of non-racial, non-class struggle conceptions of human rights.

CHAPTER FOUR

Nationalism and Human-Rights
Thought in Korea under Colonial Rule

MICHAEL E. ROBINSON

Colonial societies are seldom used as models of social justice. The crushing indignity of loss of sovereignty, dual legal standards, racism, economic discrimination, and political oppression perpetuated by colonialists upon the colonized has provided a singular example in history of human-rights abuse. Such a situation faced Koreans between 1910–1945 as they suffered the yoke of Japanese rule. Resentment toward Japanese rule was the strongest single motivator of political solidarity for Korean nationalists of all political persuasions within the broad movement for liberation from colonial rule. The economic and legal structure of the colony, however, created deep divisions in Korean society that separated leaders, mostly urban intellectuals, from the peasant masses. Moreover, political leaders found it difficult to agree upon a unified program of independence. Ultimately, it was

Japan's defeat in 1945, not nationalism, that liberated Korea; and this fact contributes to the bitter postwar legacy of the Japanese occupation.

Thus, the record of the Korean nationalist movement demonstrated that the simple desire for independence or anti-Japanese solidarity did not lead to Liberation. After 1919, it was clear that Korean independence would not be achieved with the aid of outside powers (a hope of the pacifistic March First Movement). In addition, the contemporary popularity of social revolutionary thought drove a wedge between Korean nationalists by offering an alternative mode of analysis for Korea's political situation as well as different tactics for the achievement of independence. Even though the March First Movement of 1919 had marked the arrival of mass nationalism in Korea, the history of the nationalist movement in the 1920s shows that the complex array of social and political problems facing the Korean nationalists would not be solved easily. Indeed, by the mid-1920s the vernacular journals and newspapers of the colony (one of the hard-won concessions of the March First era) were replete with virulent polemical attacks hurled between nationalist leaders.[1]

In short, the nationalist movement was in disarray in the mid-1920s. Although anti-Japanese sentiment was strong and growing stronger, nationalist leaders could not mobilize significant grass-roots power to challenge Japanese rule. Concurrently, the Japanese, having been surprised by the unexpected size and power of the 1919 demonstrations, strove to tighten and rationalize their grip on Korean society. They bolstered their efficient repressive mechanism with a calculated and effective policy of co-option designed to capitalize on dissension within the nationalist ranks.[2] This policy was effective in playing Korean against Korean to the detriment of the anti-Japanese struggle before 1945, and it has left an enduring legacy of enmity in postwar Korean politics as well.

Close examination of Korean nationalists' essays on politics and society, particularly those of the moderate nationalists, reveals a singular obsession for solidarity and unity. They were often willing to overlook problematical aspects of Korean society because they were convinced nothing should override the cause of independence. Coincidentally, post-Liberation histories of this period also exhibit this tendency. In this literature, one finds a rather single-minded portrayal of the nationalist movement as unified and active yet thwarted by the modern technology of Japanese political and economic repression.

Thus, in histories published in anti-Communist South Korea, leftist opposition to moderate nationalist programs has often been portrayed as a betrayal of national solidarity, even "anti-nationalist" in character.[3] This concern mirrors the frustration and concern of nationalists in the 1920s as they attempted to counter the growing popularity of socialist thought among a younger generation of intellectuals.

The Korean left of the 1920s faced the opposition of moderate nationalists and the unremitting repression of the Japanese police. Moderate nationalists believed that social revolutionary appeals weakened national solidarity, and, further, that leftist talk of international class ties undermined the important task of national-identity formation. This attack, however, was insufficient to deter leftist enthusiasm for the importance of the masses to the political process and the centrality of class divisions in colonial society to the goal of Liberation. The Japanese police, for their part, worried endlessly that a leftist movement might fuse social and class inequities to the cause of national liberation. They correctly interpreted the danger and attractiveness of an appeal to the masses that emphasized class oppression and the social abuses of colonial society writ large.

The left and right wings of the nationalist movement myopically pursued their own interests and were unable fully to comprehend each other's political positions. Interestingly enough, a similar myopia in post-Liberation Korean society prevails in writing about the colonial period. The difficulties in creating a coherent and comfortable "memory" of the colonial period lie in the division of postwar Korean society. Liberation in 1945 did not resolve the problem of solidarity and unity within the nationalist movement, nor did it even establish a single political system to represent the nation. The existence of two states on the peninsula, each vying for the mantle of legitimate national leader, has led to a tendency for each to skew the history of what happened in Korea before 1945 in an attempt to further legitimize its own political systems.

Accordingly, North Korean histories emphasize the development of class-related movements such as peasant unions and labor groups that fought against Japanese imperialism as well as their bourgeois Korean allies. In this scheme of interpretation, bourgeois nationalists were part of a socially and politically repressive colonial class structure; any appeal by bourgeois nationalists for solidarity based on pure nationalism or anti-Japanese sentiments was seen simply as a cynical device to maintain their privileged position in colonial society. The North Korean Marxist interpretation of the period of Japanese occupation has a predictably dogmatic approach, but, by focusing on class divisions, it does give us certain insights into the social condition of colonial Korea. Worse than the dogmatism of Marxist historiography is the tendency to further obscure the record by rewriting events in order to heighten the role of Kim Il Sung and his family in the anti-Japanese struggle. Here, Kim Il Sung's growing personality cult does little justice to the true record of the political and social movements of the era of Japanese occupation.

South Korean histories of the Japanese occupation are not as unified in their ideological approach. There is, however, up to the mid-1970s a trend in this literature emphasizing anti-Japanese resistance and the nurturing of national consciousness by moderate nationalist leaders. Many histories of this period paint a portrait of staunch anti-Japanese solidarity in the face of overwhelming Japanese power. This line is upheld even when, upon closer scrutiny of the record, it is clear that no such solidarity existed. In many of these histories, social movements that sought redress of specific grievances such as the *paekchŏng* emancipation movement or labor and peasant unions organized by leftists are interpreted as part of a grander nationalist front; their original motivations based in economic and social discrimination is glossed over.

There is a tone of longing in these histories, a longing for the discovery of something to celebrate in an otherwise dismal period. Why else would such disproportionate attention be given the March First Movement of 1919? After all, Liberation came as a gift with the defeat of Japan by the Allies, and Liberation was followed by a humiliating occupation and the eventual partitioning of the nation. Worse yet, the Republic of Korea was created in a rancorous climate of charge and countercharge hurled amongst the founding fathers of the republic and their critics.[4] Subsequent historical analysis of the pre-Liberation era under Japanese rule, therefore, has suffered the consequences of keen personal and political interest in how the record of the Japanese occupation should be read.

The politicians and writers of the 1920s were more than willing to overlook "social problems" because of their interest in forging nationalist unity. Similarly, historians of the post-Liberation era have had to tread lightly on this "sensitive" subject because of intense political interest in the genealogy of various politicians' nationalist credentials. Therefore, it comes as no surprise that both the nationalists of the 1920s and postwar historians have had difficulty accepting or interpreting the existence and consequences of the *paekchŏng* emancipation movement (*paekchŏng hyŏngp'yŏng undong*). Such a social movement posed a dilemma to nationalist organizers at the time. A movement with pure motives and legitimate social aims was viewed by many at the time as detracting from national unity. Furthermore, general reaction in the community to this movement was less than enthusiastic. Opposition to the activities of the *paekchŏng* emancipation movement was based on traditional attitudes of separatism and hostility to the *paekchŏng*. In a society marked by gross discrimination against Koreans by the Japanese colonial overlords, such traditional modes of social ostracism seemed scarcely relevant.

The *paekchŏng* emancipation movement highlighted a specific social inequity in traditional Korean society that had existed for centuries. At issue was full social acceptance for a group within society irrespective of whether the Japanese ruled or not. This fact distinguished the emancipation movement from other nationalist-inspired mass movements such as the Buy Korean Movement (*Mulsan changnyŏ undong*), The National University Movement (*Millip taehak kisŏng undong*), and the Peasant Literacy Movement (*Nongmin munja pogŭp undong*). Each of these larger nationalist projects represented an attempt to redress discrimination in economic matters and education. Such discrimination was based on Japanese political dominance in Korea. As such, these movements each addressed indirectly a fundamental problem in colonial society, without confronting the fact of Japanese sovereignty. Each movement was aimed at ameliorating discrimination within the colonial system so that Koreans could achieve the full potential of their second-class status in Japanese imperial society.

In the case of the Buy Korean Movement, the idea was to strengthen Korean entrepreneurship and capitalism in competition with more developed Japanese companies.[5] The naive assumption was that national capital developed in isolation from Japanese capitalism; critics of the movement pointed out how it only further heightened class divisions by enriching Korean capitalists.[6] The National University Movement sought to raise money for a Korean-administered private university to fill the void of opportunity for higher education for Koreans in the colony. Yet, few Koreans were able to afford a university education, irrespective of who administered the university. The literacy campaigns were broad-based attempts to redress the inadequacies of the colonial education system. Of the several movements mounted by the moderate nationalists, this movement was the most successful because it appealed to a mass base, and its goals coincided with those of the left.[7]

The largest movements failed for a variety of complex reasons; but perhaps foremost among them was the growing rift among nationalist leaders themselves over ideology and tactics. The problem that faced Korean nationalists was a choice between overtly confronting Japanese rule and risking the consequences of further repression or working within the structure of colonial society to strengthen Korean cultural identity and develop internally the requisite economic and political power upon which to base future independence.

The latter strategy was the hallmark of moderate nationalists, often referred to as the cultural faction (*munhwap'a*). They believed that cultural solidarity, the development of Korean capitalism, and mass education were necessary before Korea would be in a position to demand nationhood.[8] The projects to strengthen Korean capitalism, establish educational institutions, and spread literacy mentioned above were important causes for this group. Behind these efforts lay the assumption that internal strength must first be nurtured before confronting directly the inequity and injustice of Japanese rule. This approach tacitly accepted the main features of colonial society, including the fact of Japanese sovereignty, and projected a drive for political independence in the distant future. Indeed, moderate nationalists of the 1920s, like many intellectuals of the earlier enlightenment period before 1910, believed Korea should develop along the lines of the modern Western nation-states. What moderates wanted to see was the growth of the Korean middle class, an educated and "socially responsible" core class capable of leading Korea to nationhood.[9] The implicit assumption behind this thinking was that Korean society in the 1920s was not ready to assume control of its own destiny, even if independence were possible.

Such a gradualist posture certainly ignored the central political problem of the period—Japanese rule. And, in arguing for what was in effect a bourgeois revolution within colonial society, moderate nationalists compromised themselves in the face of more radical thinkers as well as the repressed Korean masses. Later experience of the Chinese and Vietnamese nationalist movements proved that nationalism wedded to social revolution was a powerful political mobilizer. In Korea under Japanese occupation, however, a significant portion of the nationalist leadership was willing to work within the confines of colonial society, and, more important, they were uncomfortable with social revolutionary demands that might endanger their own position as a privileged middle class in colonial society.

This posture angered more radical nationalists. The gradualism and elitist approach offered by the cultural nationalists as a solution to the national crisis appeared to radicals as a denial of the growing social problems within Korean society as well as implicit acceptance of Japanese rule. Socialism informed the radicals' view of what should be done and radicalized their choice of political tactics. Breaking from the worship of the democratic nation-state model that had evolved in the West, radicals attacked the capitalist social and economic system that lay at the root of this model as the core problem. According to this view, further development within the framework of colonial society would simply intensify class oppression perpetrated by Japanese imperialists with the aid of their Korean bourgeois allies.

The radicals rose to prominence in the years following the March First demonstrations of 1919, when avowedly leftist and socialist journals and organizations first appeared in the relatively relaxed censorship and organizational atmosphere of these years.[10] From this base, radicals began to attack the moderate-nationalist line in editorials and feature articles in the Korean-language press. The radicals' attack focused on the social inequities of Korean colonial society, and they excoriated the gradualist program of the moderates as an approach that would only perpetuate social inequity. The Buy Korean Movement was particularly attacked as a transparent device to strengthen the hand of the Korean bourgeoisie by appealing to poor Koreans to buy more expensive and lower-quality Korean-made goods on the basis of patriotic appeals.[11] Similarly, radicals attacked the National University Movement as a cause that would serve only a narrow range of Korean interests, namely the well-to-do who could afford higher education.[12] Radicals supported literacy campaigns, but they disliked the tutorial approach of moderates who felt literacy and education were prerequisites to citizenship in a nation-state.

The radical critique held that the benefits of colonial economic development were monopolized by a small minority. Radicals combined their loathing for the Japanese with a healthy distaste for the inequities of capitalism in which some Koreans prospered while the majority languished in misery. In this period, however, the radical leadership was very elitist and adhered dogmatically to social revolutionary ideology.[13] Their sensitivity to class conflict heightened their sense of social justice; and they clung to a rigid view of historical materialism which focused their organizing energies on the then-nascent Korean proletariat. The absence of a large proletariat and their own overly intellectual and elitist approach to organization hindered their ability to work within Korean society at the grass-roots level.

Leftist attitudes toward the *paekchŏng* emancipation movement provide a fine example of this problem. Korean Marxists attempted to use the Equalization Society, but they worried that the Movement had insufficient class-consciousness, and that its demands ignored "economic rights" for purely "human-rights" considerations.[14] Thus, Korean Marxists missed an opportunity to encourage an important grass-roots movement in colonial society. This pattern of failure to organize at lower levels of Korean society continued to trouble the Korean Marxists throughout the 1920s.

In the 1930s, as a political movement Korean nationalism was moribund; the locus of activity had shifted to the exile movement which was divided between Communist and nationalist groups. Within Korea, however, the brutality and inequities of colonial society developed unchecked. Only small Korean middle and upper classes formed of rural and absentee landlords and urban white-collar and intellectual elements had any chance of avoiding the economic and political inequities of colonial society. And, after 1937, Korea was transformed into a base camp for the Japanese war effort against the Chinese. The forced mobilization and assimilation campaigns of the last eight years of colonial rule in Korea brought society to the breaking point. Tragically, the postwar occupation and division of Korea negated the potential unifying force of national consolidation because, after 1948, two states began to compete as rival claimants for the mantle of nationalist legitimacy.

This cursory glimpse into the nationalist movement of Korea under Japanese occupation makes clear that the nationalist cause was never resolutely linked to human rights. Although national liberation movements are generally seen as progressive, their first object, whether led by social revolutionaries or bourgeois nationalists, is the creation of a state to represent the political interests of the nation. To that end, solidarity in the overriding issue of national independence must precede issues of economic or social discrimination. While the Korean left came close to linking social and economic equity to the national cause, they failed in the end to gain decisive control of the nationalist movement. With the division and ultimate creation of separate states representing the Korean people, state interests have continued to ride roughshod over social and economic issues.

The efforts to legitimate their separate political systems as the true representative of the Korean nation have perpetuated a mentality that stresses collective nationalist goals over issues of human rights. In South Korea, the state demands social "discipline" in the name of national security and for the advancement of economic-development goals. Thus, labor organization is inhibited in the name of development, and political opposition, until recently, has been repressed as deleterious to national unity. The imperatives of national unity, for whatever reason, certainly guided the thinking of prewar nationalist leaders just as they have colored the historical analysis of postwar historians in both North and South Korea. Solidarity and unity against a greater common enemy diluted the objectivity of moderates and radicals alike. Much worse, they obscured the reality of colonial society from both. How often in postwar Korea, North and South, have legitimate human-rights questions been obscured by calls for unity in the face of graver or immediate concerns? Similarly, how often are historians or social analysts pressured to overlook reality when a faithful rendering of the record threatens the ideological legitimacy of a political regime? All too often, unfortunately, is the answer to both questions.

Korea, like many post-colonial societies, has spent much of the last generation playing the game of economic and political catch-up. Compounding the Korean situation is the fact that the two states dividing the nation both claim to be the rightful and legitimate heir to the pre-Liberation anti-colonial struggle. Furthermore, each state continues to demand political and social unity for reasons of security and economic performance. Small wonder, then, that human-rights considerations for individuals or groups within their societies remain an ideal goal rather than a fundamental basis of policy in both Koreas.

One has only to read the statements of pre-Liberation nationalists of both moderate and leftist leanings to realize that there was no lack of interest in a just and equitable society. The great injustice of Japanese rule, however, often blinded these patriots to the everyday problems and inequities of colonial society. Similarly, the political uncertainties produced by the postwar division provided competing states with a rationale for continuing to demand social and political discipline to the detriment of social equity. Until the problem of ideological schism and political division within the nationalist movement as a whole is resolved, or a political mechanism for defusing these differences is constructed, serious consideration of the human-rights problem in both North and South Korea will continue to be postponed in the name of social and political discipline.

This is not to say there is no hope on the Korean peninsula. As the events of the 1987 summer of "democratization" in South Korea show, the political situation is quite fluid. Optimists view the events of 1987 as an indication that structural change in South Korea has combined with increased economic and social internationalization to create a new consensus for political change. But the simple consensus for a return to civilian rule and direct elections will not magically solve the myriad problems facing South Korean political leaders. In a sense, the "democratization" consensus of 1987 is like the heady unity of the March First Movement of 1919. At that time, many Koreans felt the problems of the nationalist movement had been solved. But the consensus and grass-roots support that had been mobilized around the simple and idealistic demand for self-determination were unable to bridge the serious differences that plagued the nationalist leadership. Similarly, the victory embodied in government concessions in June 1987 to revamp the presidential-election law temporarily obscured the deeper divisions within the opposition camp. Nevertheless, recent events show that the political culture, of South Korea at least, is not as ossified as recent political history might suggest. This bodes well for political change and the cause of human rights on the peninsula.

PART THREE

The Postwar Period

In his chapter, Gregory Henderson discusses the important linkage period between the end of Japanese colonial rule and the post-Korean War era. This period carried great significance, not just for Korean liberation but for the form to be taken by an independent Korean government. The United States Army Military Government in Korea, which ruled in the south until 1948, possessed more sweeping powers than those of the Supreme Commander for Allied Powers (SCAP) in occupied Japan. Ironically, however, the Americans were able to accomplish less in Korea than in Japan in preparation for transition to democratic rule. Henderson shows that the military government often found itself retaining and buttressing the old colonial legal and police apparatus, whereas American legal reforms, such as an effort to institute habeas corpus in 1946, often were weakly asserted and failed to reach widely throughout the judicial and police system. Following establishment of a South Korean government in 1948, President Syngman Rhee continued in the prewar pattern to use law and the police for political purposes, including intimidation of the judiciary, arrest of journalists, control of the teaching profession, and pressure on the new National Assembly. Gregory Henderson served as a Foreign Service Officer in Korea in the 1940s and 1950s.

Edward J. Baker and Jerome Alan Cohen, both lawyers with many years of experience in Asian affairs, provide a catalog of serious and systemic violations of civil and political rights under the governments of Park Chung Hee (1961–1979) and Chun Doo Hwan (1980–1987), and argue on historical grounds that the United States bears a "special responsibility" to prevent human rights abuses in South Korea. In reply, Professor Donald MacDonald agrees that the South Korean record has been a poor one, and that U.S. efforts at amelioration have often been unsuccessful; but he argues that there are limits to what the United States can or should do in South Korea to advance political and human rights development. MacDonald has served both as Political Counselor at the U.S. Embassy in Seoul and as the Korea desk officer at the Department of State. The two essays illuminate the differing perceptions of U.S. policy in the area of human rights held by human rights activists and practicing diplomats.

James M. West, a specialist in jurisprudence with a longstanding interest in Korean affairs, joins with Edward J. Baker to explore constitutional, electoral, and judicial implications of the 1987 transition to the administration of President Roh Tae Woo.

Human Rights in South Korea 1945–1953

GREGORY HENDERSON

THE SETTING

On 15 August, 1945, Japan surrendered. American military and civilian planners, left without a firm agreement on the occupation of Korea, had proposed on 11–13 August (Truman approving on the latter date) that Soviet troops accept surrender and control from the Japanese north of the 38th parallel, U.S. troops implementing surrender and control south thereof. The Soviets, accepting the proposal without comment, had already started to fight their way into and occupy Korea, but pulled up short, with conscientious scrupulousness, when they reached this line. The Americans, landing later on 8 September, immediately received the Japanese surrender and occupied the south. With minor exceptions, all Japanese soldiers, administrators, and residents throughout the peninsula were repatriated to Japan by the next spring, and the peninsula was left divided under two increasingly hostile, non-communicating, alien military governments. The abrupt end of all Japanese presence and control led to sharply different developments in legal process and human rights in what were to become the two Koreas.

Establishment of New Communist System in the North

In the north, the imposition of a Soviet Communist occupation forced property confiscation and sometimes the arrest of those who had served the Japanese government or acquired substantial wealth during its course. Almost all those in this class—as well as many not in it—chose flight to South Korea, usually with their families. Their places were taken by people of little property who had not served the Japanese. When possible, the Soviets chose those who, as Communists or other opponents of Japan, had struggled against colonial control. Key officials such as the vice-ministers were often ethnic Korean Soviet citizens trained in the Soviet system.

The Soviets in their zone thereby rapidly emplaced an elite totally new to Korea's political or administrative experience. Organized opposition was rarely possible and, as at Sinŭiju in November 1945, occurred only occasionally. Those elements who had been repressed now tended to assume leadership; they were opposed to existing vested interests and often accepting of sweeping new change. A new Communist system was rapidly instituted. In the legal field, there came to be established in North Korea a Korean system of justice and judicial process closely modeled on that of the Soviet Union. Koreans, headed by the Soviet-sponsored Kim Il Sung, began to function as a government under the Soviet occupation sooner than in South Korea. Political, social, legal and enforcement activity was soon dominated by the Communist North Korean Workers Party under Kim which, uniting with the remnants of the South Korean Labor Party, became the Korean Workers Party in 1949. By then, the governmental structure had, on 1 September 1948, become an "independent" Communist satellite under Kim Il Sung, the Democratic People's Republic of Korea.

North Korea's transition from an anti-Communist state under stern colonial control to a rigidly Communist state is one of the smoothest on record. Despite four fairly major purges from 1946–1960, the political stability of the D.P.R.K. under Kim Il Sung has been perhaps the greatest of any state in the world. Today Kim Il Sung, next to Hoxha of Albania, is the world's most enduring political leader. Rigid controls, the occasional use of force before 1960, and the absolute proscription of any opposition or its expression characterized and still stamp this regime. Civil liberty—even the concept thereof—is not and never has been known in the political system of North Korea. Perhaps largely for that reason, the surfacing of incidents of violations of human rights is far less frequent than in the south—not because they do no occur but because indoctrination, social discipline, and controls have been so pervasive for so long that personal expression of any kind, including any concerning individual human rights, is minimal and because North Korea's control of the media and lack of human contact with the outside suppress almost all exposure of incidents of repression.[1]

On 5 March 1946, the Cabinet of the new North Korean Provisional People's Committee, the third in succession of the bodies to which the Soviet authorities had transferred administrative powers in the north, promulgated a law expropriating all lands, public or private, in excess of 12.25 acres, these being redistributed to landless peasants. On 10 August 1946, a law for the nationalization of basic industries, transport and communication facilities, and banks was announced, whereby all but 10 percent of the industrial and financial sectors came under state control. Meanwhile, the North Korean Democratic National United Front, which included the Communist Party, enforced compliance with these measures and forestalled the development of any autonomous center of power.[2] Even before these measures, all Korean social elements that might either have sought the perpetuation of the old or the obstruction of the new system had responded to pressure or threat and fled to South Korea. Some 1,800,000 strong by 1948, such refugees outnumbered many times all former major land or industrial property holders in the north.

Responsible service or appointment has continually been similarly controlled. The Constitution specifically states that those who served as judges or procurators under Japanese rule are ineligible for those offices in the D.P.R.K. Local courts are elected by People's Assemblies at the various levels and may be removed only by them. Every citizen with the vote can become a judge or people's assessor. A

Supreme Court, elected in theory by the Supreme People's Assembly but in fact appointed by the Party, reviews cases appealed from provincial courts. The Ministry of Justice was abolished in 1959. Political reliability, not technical expertise, appears to determine appointments at all levels.[3]

One system with scant regard for human rights and legal process was thus substituted for another, without any intervening period in which consciousness of the rule of law could be developed. It was, however, a new system staffed by a new elite—or new recruits—who had never served Japan and was committed to an ideology opposed to its colonialism. Uncommitted either to human rights or the rule of law, the new elite enjoyed some initial basis for legitimacy in the anti-colonial sentiment of the newly liberated colony.

Formation of South Korean Government: Partial Continuity in South Korea

South Korea's break with Japanese rule and with those supportive of it was far less abrupt and extreme than the north's. Failure to distance the society from older administrative outlooks and practices was acute and caused prolonged dislocation and violence. Incoming Americans were under instructions to build and encourage democracy but, unlike MacArthur in Japan, they found no Korean government which seemed to General Hodge and many—not all—of his officers operative and legitimate. Ironically, in "liberated" Korea they felt forced to establish their own military government, rather than to operate through an indigenous one as they proceeded to do across the straits in "conquered" Japan.

After briefly and traumatically leaving the Japanese Government General in place from 9–12 September, Hodge swept with characteristic volte-face swiftness to the uprooting of almost all Japanese officials. These were repatriated so abruptly and on so large a scale as to allow for no orderly transition of power nor any systematic documentation, safeguarding, and orderly disposition of their property!

The United States Military Government in Korea (USAMGIK) thus had disposition over more immediate organizational means and a far more radical framework of personnel changes in law, legal administration, and legal process which such aims called for than SCAP presided over in Tokyo. Yet, in Japan, the requisite changes were effected; in Korea, they were not. USAMGIK personnel were inadequate, more inadequate in quality and continuity than in numbers. There were almost no Americans trained for Korea and no Americans or Koreans organized to provide guidance and continuity in effecting change. Personnel typically changed every three to six months. During the first year, U.S. civil-affairs teams were allowed considerable leeway in establishing local government which, at best (which it rarely was), gave some impression of newness to and caring for local conditions and offered hope for a framework of home rule in which democratic indoctrination was–or might become–possible.[4] Unfortunately, once initial confusion and the impact of inadequate communication had passed, U.S. Military Government reimposed the rigid centralization of the Japanese. With this, the chance for a semi-democratic local administration went aglimmering. The new approach–centralization, distance from local concerns and people, the increased use of Koreans inured to Japanese colonial practices, an emphasis on national administrative conformity rather than responsiveness–provided a poor matrix for human rights.

Centralization and the undue predominance of central government in every sphere were, in fact, assured from the beginning by Military Government Ordinance 2, 25 September 1945, which, in effect, forbade any transactions in private or public Japanese property; and by Ordinance 33 of 6 December 1945, which vested in Military Government all property owned or controlled by the Japanese government or any of its nationals, corporations, societies, associations, and so forth.[5]

Such ordinances swept into the hands of central government between 90–94 percent of all industry; 12 percent of all agricultural holdings; vast proportions and quantities of commercial and private properties including housing; and seas of personal and artistic property collected by an acquisitive and prosperous Japanese colonial population which, for several decades, brought valuable objects with it and collected more from Korea and China. Very little of this property could be controlled by the American forces available, especially since hundreds of thousands of Japanese were "repatriated" before the property they were forced to leave behind could be catalogued or stored.

The consequences proved uncontainable and probably more extreme for "liberated" Korea than for "enemy" Japan and Germany. The central government expanded overnight to control almost all economic activity and trade which could be controlled as well as a vast amount which could not. The controls were not only over the "means of production" but over almost everything else, creating in effect an extreme socialist state without ideology, intention, or infrastructure to justify it or make it work. Concepts of legitimate private property claims maintainable against public and state were eroded. The vastness of the areas of uncontrolled property magnified its illegitimacy, creating menacing extra-legal fiefdoms of black markets, gangsterism, and quiet evasion seeking tacit government protection. The illegitimate, the illegal, the insecure displaced any sense of pride of property or vested interest. An ambience was hence created which, from the beginning, mocked the concept of rights. Crime and disrespect for property, order, or government were inadvertently but systemically encouraged. What order there was tended to build itself on force; rule of law was beaten back into redoubts still smaller than those it had occupied in the Japanese and Chosŏn periods; legal process retreated still farther.

Extreme gaps opened between rule and ruled. The demands upon rule exploded at the very time that the capacities for rule drastically contracted. The result was often an increased use of rising police, army, and control instruments and drives for "enforcement" and "security" conducted more with an emotional defensiveness, sometimes brutality, than with caution or a sense of justice.

U.S. MILITARY GOVERNMENT REACTION TO LEFTIST POLITICS. Japan's extraordinarily intensive colonialism in Chōsen—repressive and developmental—had ruled not only directly through excessively large property ownership but far more indirectly through taxation and regulations as also through agricultural, irrigation, and other official associations which controlled prices, norms and means of production, processings, and transportation.

Institutional and higher-educational life had been heavily Japanese-dominated; in the cities, commercial, industrial, transportation, and residential property reflected this Japanese dominance intensively, but the pattern could be seen even in small towns. Korean life and values had largely been beaten back to the villages where modernists tarred it as naive or exotic. Koreans felt repressed and dispossessed. Post-Liberation reaction was strong—almost in proportion to the intensity and ubiquitousness of the preceding colonial control.

Politics in the wake of Japan's overthrow reacted not only against Japan but against the instruments of its domination: vested interests, capitalism, and even, to some extent, property holding. Propertied Koreans were suspect either as having served the Japanese or has having improperly benefited from their rule. Conservatism and conservatives were—temporarily, as time proved—weakened. The dominant political atmosphere throughout the peninsula immediately after Liberation was leftist, vocal, and aroused, perhaps especially so in the more thickly settled south and in the capital, Seoul. This political activity coalesced in the rapid establishment of some 142 People's Committees which were taking over functions from the Japanese throughout most of the peninsula, especially in the south. Independence leaders to whom the Japanese had turned in their anxiety to protect Japanese lives and property had, on 6 September, two days before Hodge's landing and in anticipation thereof, rushed to form out of these committees a "government" which was, with small regard for the probable prejudices of the future occupiers, named the Korean People's Republic (K.P.R.). Too hasty to be formally representative, it nevertheless had much evident support among workers, the press, urban residents, and even, in several areas, farmers. Hodge understood from its name and what he could learn from English-speaking Koreans of its composition and aims that this incipient "republic" was leftist. Feeling instructed to recognize no preestablished government, he distanced himself from the K.P.R. and, after months of acrimony and inadequate communication, on 12 December 1945, outlawed it.[6]

In pursuing this path, Hodge placed American Military Government on a collision course with most of those who, within Korea, had committed themselves to active struggle against Japan's colonial regime. The United States, having refused to work closely with the Korean independence movement abroad, now found itself with little or no political base within South Korea. Without such a base—presumably conservative, anti-Communist, and pro-American—American Military Government control of South Korea would rest on force alone.

Added to this political exigency were the critical technical requirements of running a highly centralized administrative system keyed to detailed control of all aspects of social, political, religious, and economic life. Factories, banks, and private businesses, some 90 percent owned and manned by some 70,000 Japanese, required substitute management far beyond the capacity of Hodge's soldiers, even when presently supplemented by better-qualified civilians.

THE ESTABLISHMENT OF A CONSERVATIVE KOREAN REACTION. Hodge's lack of political base and his destruction of such organized politics as existed unavoidably pointed him in the direction of utilizing those who had worked with the Japanese; for these were anti-Communist preservers of vested interest, recipients of the country's best Japanese institutional education, and repositories of the only administrative experience available. Though many had from 1941–1945 fought or spoken out against the American and democratic threat, most were pliant suppliants now of the new conqueror's will. Hodge's tactical predilection toward the collaborators was shown in its greatest strength by his special reliance on the law-and-order personnel trained by Japan. For in them lay his resort for mastery of crisis and disorder in South Korea during the fifteen tumultuous months following Japan's surrender.

Only seventy years before a land of, on the whole, internal exemplary tractability, Korea now seethed with dislocation, change, and impatience. Population in South Korea exploded. Between 1945 and 1950, 1,108,047 Koreans, mostly war workers, returned from Japan, 120,000 from China and Manchuria, 1,800,000 from North Korea; the increase of births over deaths ran at more than 3 percent. Most returnees went to already explosively growing cities, one-third to Seoul. Administration buckled and broke under their sudden weight.

The economy collapsed. Japan, which had taken 99 percent of Korea's exports by 1944, now took almost none. Raw materials and repair for Korea's overworked industrial plant were suddenly cut off. Ninety percent of industry was unowned and unmanned in the wake of the Japanese departure. Production fell 85 to 90 percent, industrial employment by 60 percent, while unemployment, almost nonexistent before Liberation, rose to some half the working population. Retail prices rose 10 times between August 1945 and December 1946, wholesale prices 28 times, the cost of food 100 times. In such conditions, strikes, demonstration, and angry demands proliferated.[7]

There were spates of urban crime, stealing, black-marketing, pimping, house-grabbing, squatting, rifling, and machinery cannibalization. Offices were awash with corruption, since salaries kept no pace with inflation. As crime rose, so did gangs; youth organizations, both leftist and rightist, threatened to dominate society, often with terror, always with force and illegal methods. Such gangs depended on "contributions" verbally masquerading as "voluntary" because they were in fact so forced; these in various forms were estimated by the U.S. Embassy to constitute, by 1949, half the government's actual revenues. Fear, uncertainty, distrust preempted the mind of society. Thoughts of security, suppression, discipline, and police protection dominated all other civic desires.[8]

These conditions, rampaging beyond remedy by law but calling out for whatever order could be mustered, determined Hodge's political response. An intensely anti-Communist, decisive officer, Hodge felt obliged to support—almost to form—a conservative Korean opposition to the dominant leftist trend of Korean society. He did this from among those who had worked, with greater or lesser degrees of closeness or profit, with or within the Japanese colonial framework. Moreover, in his need to contain violence, Hodge saw himself forced to retain and strengthen the Koreans who had served the security interests of the colonial regime—initially the police, the judges, and prosecutors—somewhat later, the Japanese-trained military officers.

In this way, it came about that, unlike the north, no clear break occurred in the systems of security, arrest, imprisonment, torture, and legal process in South Korea despite the complete departure of the Japanese.[9] Territorial division, the rise of organized force in the north and of unions, gangs, resurgent politics, and chaos in the south provided a milieu far more tumultuous than at any time in Korean memory. The post-1945 police and judiciary were thus tempted toward an even more brutal repressiveness than the more secure colonial era had usually found necessary. Yet the cloth of which the system was cut remained the old, colonial cloth, the methods also the same. Hence it was the character of the Japanese colonial system and attitude toward human rights that dominated the situation, not the old, indigenous Korean system, not the aims of the independence movement or the ideas or reforms of the incoming Americans.

THE POLICY OF CONTAINMENT

The Materials Available from the Colonial Regime

The Japanese colonial period in its last ten years had greatly concerted its control over the experiences and its influence over the attitudes of ambitious, educated Koreans who aspired to power and government service. These last years from 1932—especially from 1936—to 1945 saw mounting totalitarian military controls over Japan's Chōsen. Military coups and direct access of the military Cabinet ministers to the Emperor had largely eviscerated civilian rule in Japan. The military was especially committed to the control and development of Manchuria and Korea as military fiefdoms as a base for further expansion against China and into Asia. In pursuit of these policies, tough top generals of the Manchurian clique, General Minami Jirō (1936–1942), General Koiso Kuniaki (1942–1944), and General Abe Nobuyuki (1944–1945), were successively sent as Governors General to Seoul. There they directed the transformation of Chōsen into a minutely controlled and increasingly militarized totalitarian state, ever more obediently laced into Japan's own war-directed system. From the end of 1936 on, the Japanese were increasingly obsessed with thought control, which played a mounting role in police activities. Between 1935 and 1937, the Japanese dissolved all indigenous Korean social and political organizations and all that was left of political activity. The Korean press was forced to close down by 1940, and any remaining media freedom or criticism was stamped out. Radio, introduced into Korea during this era, was from the beginning a propaganda instrument.

Oppression intensified. In 1938 alone, 126,626 persons were arrested. All Christian leaders of anti-Japanese tinge were forced to resign and, in 1944, all those under 45 were subject to conscription. All intermediary organizations capable of mediating the naked repression of government on Koreans were neutralized or removed. In their place, instruments of mass mobilization were formed: the Spiritual Mobilization League; the Patriotic Workers Group of Roving Asian Youth; the All-Chōsen Patriotic League; the Chōsen Youth Alliance; the Voluntary Pioneers' Training Camp; in 1940, the Chōsen branch of the Imperial Rule Assistance Movement, one of whose heads was to be the last Governor General; finally the Asia National Total Mobilization League.[10]

Koreans, increasingly integrated into Japanese totalitarian colonial Chōsen, were forced to participate in Chōsen's ubiquitous social mobilization. Conscription needs began to blur the formerly strict distinctions between Koreans and Japanese. Japanese males were conscripted into the armed forces, and Koreans, in an industrially expanding milieu, took their places. Koreans, for example, had constituted 40 percent of the employees of the Shokusan (Siksan) Bank in 1928 and 15 percent of the Chōsen Ginkō (Bank of Korea) in 1929. By the end of the war, these percentages had risen to 70 percent and 50 percent respectively, and Koreans had begun, since 1938, to penetrate upper-level management.[11] Much the same was true in private business. Swift, even hectic, on-the-job training took place, much of it neither long planned nor even intended.

Finally, Koreans followed Japanese into the once-exclusivist Japanese armed forces. In 1938, only 406 Koreans were in Japanese military service; in 1940, 3,208; in 1943, 6,300 Army and 3,000 Navy. In January 1944, a Korean conscription bill passed and, by the year's end, 186,980 Koreans were in the Army and 82,290 in the Navy, even more entering, briefly, in 1945.[12] In 1942, 13,000 Korean youths were studying in Japanese colleges and universities. Ten percent of these enlisted in 1943 as special military volunteer service recruits. The others were compelled to do forced labor.[13]

Police, including both regular forces and the military and thought police, were also increased, and the proportion of Koreans within them, though level or slightly declining for many years until 1943, apparently mounted in the last two years of Japanese control to one-fifth of patrolmen and one-tenth of officers.[14] Some 10,000 civilian and military police were Korean by the end of Japan's control. These policemen constituted the largest group of trained, dedicated, and reasonably cohesive Korean functionaries within the Japanese world.[15]

The legal world integrated closely with these developments. In 1930, the first modern law college class in Korea graduated, a few Koreans among its members. Through years of educational discrimination, Koreans increased slowly in numbers but decreased slightly in proportion of law-school graduates and also in the legal professions until the colonial era's end. In 1940, no Koreans sat on the Supreme Court, and only 4 judges out of 35 on courts of review were Korean. In 1945, only 8 out of 120 prosecutors, 46 out of 235 judges, and an estimated 195 qualified lawyers in the south were Korean. Only one of the lawyers had non-Japanese training.[16]

In Japanese practice, judges and especially prosecutors, worked closely with the police, sharing many of their suspicions and attitudes. Judges awarded warrants almost automatically at police request, and police were the close accomplices of prosecutors in the extracting of confessions used by the prosecutor as the basis of his prosecution statements, a process that institutionalized torture. This complicity was hardly ever broken during the 1945–1953 period; it has continued in political trials up through the present time.[17]

Use of the Japanese Inheritance

Instead of fleeing, as in the north, the police in the south remained and were augmented by the great majority of the police from the north who had been opposed and uprooted by leftists and Communists. These augmented "southern" police were the first shock troops against urban crime and political threat. The security-conscious USAMGIK assigned 63 U.S. advisers to the South Korean police— more than to any other part of the Military Government. By the beginning of 1946, some 14,000 repatriated Japanese-trained police, 85 percent of whom stayed in police service, constituted almost all the higher ranks. With their greater experience and cohesiveness, they effectively controlled the force. By July 1946, the police numbered 25,000, their swords and clubs replaced by rifles and machine guns which, for almost two years, they alone could bear and man within South Korea. They also were the chief practitioners in Korea of judo and karate, which in those years were far from being associated with Korean nationalism.

By 1948, the force had increased to at least 34,000. To maintain law and order during the election period, the American Military Government also authorized the police to deputize large bands of "loyal citizens" known as the Community Protective Association. These "loyal citizens" were drawn from rightists, and often terrorists, especially right-wing youth organizations. With such additions, police forces may have totaled 60,000.[18] During the Korean War, police strength increased to 75,000, only thereafter gradually ebbing to 47,000 in 1956,[19] by which time the long-dominant police role was passing to an enormously augmented army.

Until the reestablishment and growth of the Korean Army from 1951 on, the police in South Korea constituted the largest trained and armed force with an esprit de corps and a sense of continuity. It ruled, in essence, a police state. This esprit maintained much of the feeling of contempt for the Korean public and its "unruliness" that Japan's colonial police had held for Koreans. Lacking a broad political base, the USAMGIK, with few interpreters and skilled bureaucrats, relied on the police for much political action and information. Unlike the military, which had, from the beginning, substantial training in the United States, next to no police were sent for training in the United States. The first one so selected in 1949 resigned shortly after his return to become a politician. America and its values, he confessed, mixed poorly with Korean police esprit de corps.

Blanket instructions to arrest all leftist leaders and agitators were known to have been issued in the 1946–1947 period.[20] Police work was active and fruitful. By mid-1947, there were almost 22,000 people in jail, 50–100 percent more than the Japanese had jailed in South Korea.[21] Syngman Rhee had incontestable anti-Japanese credentials, but he needed the police as protection against leftist foes and as support for his regime. Arrests and prisoners therefore mounted dramatically. It was reported to the U.N. Commission that 89,710 people had been arrested between 4 September 1948, and 30 April 1949, of whom 28,404 were released; 21,606 turned over to the prosecutor's office; 29,284 transferred to a "security office"; 6,985 transferred to the MP's; and 1,187 were pending disposition. Of those turned over to the prosecutors, over 80 percent were declared guilty.[22] Figures of those jailed were not separately announced but the Minister of Justice stated, on 27 December 1948, that "jails can accommodate 15,000 but have 40,000 now."[23] The rice-rationing plans of the Ministry of Finance in the spring of 1950 listed the population of South Korea's 21 prisons at 58,000 persons. Inspections of the National Assembly revealed that 50–80 percent of the prisoners were charged with National Security Law violations. An earlier ration plan of November 1949 had called for the feeding of 75,000 prisoners. Figures differ, and both latter figures were doubtless swollen to allow the police side income from the sale of food rations. Yet, compared to the 30,000 or less in both North and South Korea held by the Japanese, an enormous population of detained and sentenced persons drifted in and out of jails in the first decade of liberation.

The police were *imperium in imperio*; no effective controls curbed them. Despite Hodge's attempt, from the spring of 1946 on, to set up a Korean governmental hierarchy under his command with Americans becoming, from 11 September on, only "advisers" to the Korean department heads, the Korean Chief Civil Administrator admitted before the Korean Interim Legislative Assembly that he had no control over police acts, nor could he fire police chiefs.[24] Promulgation of rules for the organization and administration of the Korean Civil Service on 13 June 1946 also made no dent on the independent powers of the Korean police. The police command had direct access to Hodge and was backed up by its chief U.S. advisers. When Rhee became President of the Republic of Korea on 15 August 1948, he retained Hodge's system, expanding the police and protecting them from press and National Assembly criticism.

All major South Korean organizations were undermined by these arrests and threats of arrest except the police themselves. This trend was heightened after the transfer of power to the Rhee Government. Even the Army was subjected to radical purging following the Yŏsu-Sunch'ŏn Rebellion of 19–27 October 1948: Over 1,500 officers and men (most of the latter NCOs) were dismissed; many of them were arrested and tortured.[25] Included among them was the future South Korean Chief of State, Park Chung Hee. Senior constabulary officers estimated that upwards of one-third of the original NCO corps were in this way either executed, jailed, or discharged. Thus, the power of the police continued to grow not only because of augmentation and support from the top but because all other organizations and sources of power beside the President were undermined by arrest or its threat.

LAW UNDER U.S. MILITARY GOVERNMENT

The Weight of the Japanese Legacy

The rulers of South Korea, their administrators, and the existence of informal organizations like youth groups, as well as the assumptions under which society operated, all combined to place South Korea largely outside the reach of law and formal legal process. Under U.S. Military Government, law and its processes were ambiguous in both intention and effect. USAMGIK had been directed from Washington in 1946 to institute broad programs of economic and educational reforms, looking to the creation of conditions favorable to the development of a strong and lasting democracy in Korea. U.S. Military Government in Seoul, however, was too poorly staffed, too unaware of the background of Japanese colonial control and of the needs for reform it had engendered, too inhibited by conservative colonels interested chiefly in rotation to initiate changes of the kind then being effected by more competent and zealous staffs in Japan. Though the Civil Service System was alien and imposed, the Military Government stated that it "expect[ed] to make no basic change in the Civil Service System established by the Japanese."[26] Ironically, the many reforms carried out under SCAP in Japan were not implemented nor applied in Korea because Korea was a "liberated" not an enemy country and therefore should make its own reforms.

It was the same with law. Korea had had a large, complex, Sinic legal system. The Japanese had instituted, largely in its place, a greatly expanded, codified, and systematized corpus of law and directed it toward modern needs for commerce, for property holding, and for business as it saw these needs. Law became more than ever an effective instrument for central-government control; its place within society expanded, and criminal law became a primary tool for political repression.

This vast, repressive, and anti-democratic corpus of Japanese law was taken over en masse. In Ordinance 21, 2 November 1945, USAMGIK specified that, "until further ordered and except as previously repealed or abolished, all laws which were in force, regulations, orders, notices, or other documents issued by any government of Korea having the force of law as of August 9, 1945, will continue in force until repealed by competent authority." In addition, "the provisions of law with respect to the organization of the Government General of Korea . . . are continued in force until abolished . . ." and the (Japanese-constituted) courts of Korea are "hereby constituted Military Occupation Courts."[27]

Changing the Legacy

There were exceptions of some importance. USAMGIK did repeal a good many Japanese laws, some specifically, others more ambiguously, by general category of their provisions. Americans also issued, first in Orders of the Supreme Commander for the Allied Powers in late August and early September 1945, orders regarded as legally binding on South Korea. As soon as USAMGIK was set up on 7 September 1945, it also started issuing its own legislation in the form of ordinances, 141 of which were issued before 17 May 1947, at which time the South Korean Interim Government was established and the Korean Interim Legislative Assembly (KILA) given the legislative function, subject to USAMGIK veto. This body, however, succeeded in its year and a half of existence in passing only 12 pieces of legislation, most of them routine. USAMGIK Ordinances continued to appear, 211 being issued by the end of Military Government.[28] Were these important for human rights?

USAMGIK Ordinance 11 of 9 October 1945 repealed laws and clauses relating to the Japanese Emperor; the control of Korea by Japan and its agencies; and religious provisions relating to Shinto; certain laws, especially from 1936 on, governing political punishment, preliminary imprisonment, preserving public order, publication, political convicts, and the judicial powers of the police. There was also a rather vague and sweeping repeal of "all other laws, decrees or orders having the force of law . . . the Judicial or Administrative enforcement of which would cause discrimination on grounds of race, nationality, creed or political opinion." (Section II).

Likewise, Section III attempted to establish the principle of habeas corpus by providing that "no charge shall be preferred or sentence imposed or punishment inflicted against any person for an act, unless such act is expressly made punishable by law in force at the time of its commission . . . The detention of any person not charged with a specific crime or offense and the punishment of any person without lawful trial and conviction are prohibited." The effective improvement of these attempted changes on human rights was extremely limited. Most laws abolished had been made dead letters by liberation from Japan. The effect of others was soon replaced by new Korean legislation. Others, like habeas corpus, were vitiated by lack of supervision or newly trained personnel to implement them. Perhaps the abolition of the judicial powers of the police (of the deck court martial ilk) alone approached effectiveness.

HABEAS CORPUS. The question of habeas corpus in Code or Criminal Procedure during this period was complex and sufficiently ambiguous so that, in February 1946, the Bureau of Police in Seoul requested an opinion of the USAMGIK advisers to the then Bureau of Justice. The opinion, Number 19, 7 March 1946, by Captain Stanley N. Ohlbaum,[29] makes clear that, though suspects should be released to the prosecutor within 48 hours, they might in practice be held up to 30 days with no legal remedy by recourse to the courts. This was the period in which, in fact, there was much torture. Similarly, legal remedy was lacking to the suspect who had to be served with a warrant 24 hours after being turned over to the prosecutor but instead was kept for 30 days. Only after that time, in both cases, could the suspect petition the Director of the Department of Justice (later Minister of Justice). In practice, however, few suspects knew of such a right or would, from their prison cells, have dared to seek it, even on the assumption that those between the prison cell and the top legal office would have fairly processed such petitions. In addition, many exceptions to the swift processing of the suspect from apprehension through trial existed, all of which favored the police. Trials might be, and in political cases often were, long or indefinitely postponed.

Overall, the Americans, through repeal and legislative ordinance, sought some amelioration of the intensely repressive police and court system of the Japanese Government General, which severely curbed human rights, and some effort in the direction of habeas corpus. These efforts were, however, far too slight and far too scantily administered to cut through the bias of Japanese procedures— inherited by Korean judicial personnel—in favor of the police and the prosecutors. These efforts were, for example, unaccompanied by any systematic retraining effort of the kind, after January 1946, given Korean veterans of the Japanese Army in the Constabulary Military Academy. Nor did the press seek to explain or publicize the new procedures. Under such circumstances, for example, the petition system was neither known nor operated. The vast corpus of Japanese law remained more or less untouched, together with almost all Koreans who had been trained within and committed to implementing the old system. After the military coup of 1961, the Park regime did repeal the Japanese laws, but the overwhelming majority of the "new" statutes had content of Japanese origin. In essence, the means by which Japan repressed Korean political freedom are used by South Korean authorities today to a similar end, long after the Japanese themselves have been unshackled from these restraints.

The Ordinances and Appointment Orders of USAMGIK were

continued in force under Article 100 of the new Constitution of the Republic of Korea, adopted July 1948. Gradually they were amended and dropped by the development of Korean law. Occasionally, one or two were later cited, usually in the context of oppressive acts such as press closings. The more liberal American legislation, procedures, or legal opinions were, however, generally uncited. By and large, ordinances in the human-rights field made so little impression on the system of justice or on human rights as a whole in South Korea that their passing was unnoticed. So far as can be ascertained, the opinions of the U.S. advisers to the Department of Justice have never been translated or published in the language of the country in whose legal tradition they were designed to form a part.

Obstacles to Reform

Legal reform was frustrated, not only by the weight of the security system, a lack of reform intention, and an unbroken continuity with the colonial period, but also by a lack of technical expertise. Military Government had no single American expert on Japanese law nor did any Western expert on Korean law exist anywhere. Military Government was fortunate in having several competent and devoted American officers with legal training and two very distinguished authorities on continenal law, Dean Pergler, a senior Czech legal expert, and Dr. Ernst Fraenkel, a German lawyer, both émigrés. These did their skilled best but were too few and isolated, both within Military Government and within the Korean community, to have much lasting influence.

No careful or comprehensive review of existing Japano-Korean law was therefore possible. What was done was spotty. Certain specific laws were revoked, replaced, or newly legislated to change the existing situation: child labor law, abolition of the Economic Police Department, abolition of the Local Affairs Section of the Secretariat, the Chosun Stock Exchange, the Finance Control Corporation, as well as the rubrics cited above. Only rarely, as with child labor, did these relate to human rights. The General Repealing Clause of Ordinance 11 did, but its controlling definition of laws "enforcement of which would cause discriminations on grounds of race, nationality, creed or political opinions" was too vague for legal precision, insufficiently incorporated into removals from or substitutions to the Japanese code, and too controversial to achieve effectiveness in an environment where laws were largely viewed as punitive and practice was unused to interpretations seeking the protection or enlargement of human rights. Similar factors curbed the effectiveness of Ordinance 11's human-rights-motivated Section III, Limitations on Punishment. These attempted general repeals and limitations, and therefore remained largely dead letters, being from time to time, with all too little protest, violated, as, for example, with the retroactive provisions of the 31 December 1960 "Law Concerning the Restriction of the Civil Rights of Those Who Committed Anti-Democratic Acts" legislated by the Democratic Government under student pressure;[30] the Political Purification Law of November-December 1980, which, over thirty-five years later, also violated all the limitations of Section III.

In essence, Korean society lay, in these early post-Liberation years, beyond the effective reach of law. The hurt thereby sustained was not limited to this period but cast its shadow over succeeding decades. It is possible that, if greater reform had even been attempted—as under the U.S. Occupation in Japan—it would have excited greater violence to frustrate it. The essential irrelevance of legal process undoubtedly underlay the paucity and aridity of attempts at reform. Probably over—some experts say well over—95 percent of the corpus of written law, chiefly Japanese in origin, as it existed in Chōsen at the end of the colonial regime was transmitted unchanged as the corpus of law for an independent Republic of Korea. Much remained for some years even in Japanese text. The chief change for many years was that it gradually underwent the easy process of being translated into Korean.

By this large-scale and rather uncritical transference, the legal means by which the Japanese had controlled—in the Korean view repressed—society continued in place, ready for the Japanese-trained Korean judiciary and police to use the same purposes again. Thus, the infamous Press Law of the 11th year of the Kwangmu era (1907), forced through the supine late-Chosŏn bureaucracy by the Japanese to control Korean newspaper criticism of their then-mounting controls, was still used with USAMGIK's press-licensing Ordinance 88 by Syngman Rhee to shut down several important newspapers between September 1948 and May 1949, nationalizing one of them, the *Seoul shinmun*, in June 1949. On 7 April 1948, the Seoul Appellate Court had declared the law of Kwangmu no longer valid but on

21 May 1948, the Supreme Court pronounced some key sections of the law still valid; on 9 August 1948, the Police Chief, foreseeing its imminent use, triumphantly trumpeted its continued existence. It took special legislation of the National Assembly on 19 March 1952, during one of the few brief periods when that body wielded some independent power, finally to end this historic remnant of Japan's repression in Korea.[31]

A second major obstacle to American efforts to reform the legal system proved to be the social and administrative disorder of the period. In the end, neither American troops nor American legal concepts could successfully bring order from the chaos that followed the collapse of Japan's ubiquitous colonial administration. Transferal of the vast and well-recorded industrial and landed properties left behind was accomplished with substantial legality owing to the central economic controls of the state. But, for the hundreds of thousands of houses, small structures, furniture, utensils, art objects, books now suddenly at the mercy of long-deprived Koreans and of the army of refugees, some 4,000 per day strong, who flung themselves without lodging or possessions against these assets, control was impossible. Property was occupied, squatted on, confiscated, sequestered, and stolen all over the country on a scale that beggared comparisons with postwar conditions in Japan or Germany. Amazingly, there were few attacks on Japanese persons. But a general atmosphere of illegal or extra-legal exchanges of property suddenly flourished in which it was extraordinarily difficult to establish a concept of rights or of the privacy of possessions.

Such extra-legality spread likewise to the institutions of the country. As in Manchuria and northeast China, the long struggle against Japan was superseded—almost overnight—by the struggle between right and left. The pathetic remaining Japanese sank rapidly into irrelevance. Instead, whoever had force used it to establish right, power, property, and position against leftist (or rightist) opponents. Police were first in the fray but not far behind them were the more populous youth groups, often used as terror groups against the left, which in its turn had also used terror. The ironic result was that Koreans were more often helpless against physical violence than were the Japanese. Seoul's tough Northwest Youth Association of P'yŏngan province refugees became notorious for its cruel use of bamboo staves to quell unrest and rebellion on Cheju Island. The notorious Great

Korea Democratic Young Men's Association leader, the gangster Kim Tu-han, and 14 members, were tried for beating to death 2 leftist youth association members whose bodies were found on 20 April 1947.[32] They got off with a small fine, whereupon USAMGIK, dissatisfied with this civil process, sent the trial to a military commission. USAMGIK, however, somewhat in the Government General tradition, had its own youth group, formed in mid-1946 around and largely by General Yi Pŏm-sŏk with USAMGIK support and blessing. It lasted until the Korean War as the Racial Youth Corps and under other names, though all youth groups were ordered and amalgamated into the Taehan Youth Corps by President Rhee in 1949. The 1936–1945 tradition of forming large, semi-legal mass social organizations subject to special governmental privileges and direction has lessened somewhat but never been broken.[33] It lurks behind the Democratic Republic of the Park era and the Democratic Justice Party of the Chun years as well as in official civil-defense, anti-Communist and veterans organizations.

The Problem of Political Confrontation

The increasing confrontation between politics and force flamed into a massive, month-long series of bloody strikes beginning on 25 September 1946 that assumed rebellion proportions. Scores of police were mutilated and killed by an incensed populace, headed by workers organized within leftist unions, especially the South Korean Railroad Workers Association. Scores of rioters were also killed and countless more wounded. General Hodge looked for Communist instigation. Investigations identified not one identifiable North Korean agent.[34] Recommendations for police restraint and dismissals of police chiefs by the moderate Coalition Committee which Military Government was seeking to put together were ignored. Arrests mounted. New vengefulness was added to police brutality. By June 1947, there were almost 22,000 in jail, at least 7,000 of them political prisoners. The original labor-union movements were increasingly repressed; a right-wing one was established and force-fed by the government. In 1949, Rhee ordered all unions combined into the Korean Federation of Trade Unions. Except in 1960–1961, a truly free labor-union movement has never thereafter been permitted.

The October 1st Rebellion, as it came to be known, was the Tet offensive of the Korean left. Not only were long-term leftists suppressed, but many who had joined in the heat of action were also cut down. In Washington, on the other hand, American determination wavered. Combined with the failure of the Joint Commission discussions to lead toward unification in 1946 and 1947 and declining budgetary support for the American armed forces, the October Rebellion aroused a perception of insolubility and of potential danger for American troops. Korea was seen as a trap. Other problems in Greece and Turkey claimed priority for a rapidly shrinking U.S. military establishment. The Pentagon insisted on the decision in late 1947 to withdraw U.S. troops, to create a separate, rightist South Korean government under Syngman Rhee, and to make a feeble U.N. the source of ultimate protection against any possible invasion. With this step, the U.S. attempts to initiate reform were abandoned, though implementation of reforms already decided on—as with land distribution—continued. The Japanese-trained elements on whom USAMGIK had relied against the political and social movements dominant in the first postwar year were confirmed in power.

LAW AND POLITICS IN THE REPUBLIC OF KOREA, 1948–1950

The Elections of 1948

The 1948 elections represented some improvement in the attempt to base government on popular will. Turning the Korean question over to the United Nations in the fall of 1947 broadened the decision-making process that had heretofore been largely confined to the American military. It added civilian U.N. opinion to the overall planning process and representation of several parliamentary traditions—Australia, Canada, China, El Salvador, France, India, the Philippines, and Syria (the Ukraine refused to serve)—in implementing and overseeing the carrying out of free elections throughout Korea under the United Nations Temporary Commission on Korea (UNTCOK). A Soviet proposal that Koreans should be summoned to the U.N. to participate in this decision was skillfully circumvented by Mr. Dulles. North Korea refused to admit the Commission north of the 38th parallel and held closed elections in the north on 25 August 1948, for a Supreme People's Assembly, claiming that this election had also been implemented in the south with 77.8 percent of eligible voters there participating.[36] The Commission then, from the U.N. resolution of 26 February 1948, moved with considerable reluctance to observe elections "in as much of Korea as is accessible to it."

The elections were opposed by the north and boycotted by leftists, many moderates, and even some rightists like Kim Ku in the south. Riots in February 1948 caused 37 deaths and over 8,000 arrests in southern Korea.[37] Confrontation mounted. Extremists of right and left formed terrorist bands. U.S. Military Government authorized police to deputize bands of "loyal citizens" as Community Protective Associations. Between 29 March and 19 May 1948, 589 persons were killed, including 44 on election day, 10 May.[38] Despite some 1,047 cases of SKLP "assaults and violences," UNTCOK succeeded in prevailing on General Hodge to maintain an at least pro forma legality of the SKLP and to encourage a fair election law, registration procedures, and a major information program which greatly raised public consciousness of electoral process.[39] Almost 8 million voters, 79.7 percent of the potential electorate, registered. Of these, 95.5 percent or 75 percent of the electorate,[40] voted on 10 May. Police encouragement and pressure certainly affected the high rates of participation, but, on the whole, forceful means were little evidenced and secrecy of the ballot was maintained. Confrontation, threat, force, and illegality remained: The election was essentially invalidated amid great violence on Cheju Island. But process and the involvement of people in government or in steps leading to government took a forward step in this first mass election in Korean history. The election results were accepted by the U.N. and its non-Communist members, and the government established was supported by the U.N. and recognized by increasing numbers of its member states. The overwhelmingly rightist character of the first Assembly, however, reflected the boycott of the elections by most non-rightists which vitiated any true reflection of popular opinion.[41]

The Constitution

The Republic of Korea Constitution of 1948 and the processes invoked to give it birth improved measurably on the floundering attempts of a foreign military government to cope with law in postcolonial Korea. Syngman Rhee, elected by 188 out of 198 votes to be

Chairman of the new National Assembly, appointed the members of the Constitution-Drafting Committee. These had few qualifications for constitution drafting (only 5 out of the seated 198 assemblymen were lawyers or judges) and availed themselves little of the opportunity to consult with the foreign international law experts attached to military government. They nonetheless extensively consulted Korean experts, especially Mr. Yu Chin-o, and fashioned in a remarkably brief month and a half a Constitution adopted and promulgated on 17 July 1948.

Korean leaders in 1948 saw in democracy the approved path toward progress, enlightenment, and international prestige. The Constitution sought democracy and equality of opportunity, resting "the sovereignty of the Republic of Korea (R.O.K.) . . . in the people" and "respecting and guaranteeing the liberty, equality, and initiative of each individual."[42]

Rights and duties were specified in Chapter II as equality before the law, "personal liberty," freedom of domicile, freedom from trespass and unlawful search, freedom of private correspondence, "the freedom of speech, press, assembly, and association," "the right of property," "equal opportunity of education," "the equality of men and women," and "the rights to elect public officials and hold office," such officials to be "at all times responsible to the people."

These brave new intentions, however, allowed their own blight. Listed freedoms were guaranteed "except as specified by law," "except in accordance with law," and "with the provisions of law." Finally, Article 28 stipulated that "laws imposing restrictions upon the liberties and rights of citizens shall be enacted only when necessary for the maintenance of public order or the welfare of the community." Such "necessaries" lay open to strong executive option.

On paper, the legislature was awarded considerable powers, including that of overriding a presidential veto by two-thirds of a quorum and of instituting impeachment proceedings against the president, the vice-president, Cabinet members, judges, and other officials designated by law when they violated constitutional provisions. The Assembly, by two-thirds vote, also elected the president for a 4-year term and consented to the president's appointment of the prime minister. There was, however, no provision for dissolution of the National Assembly in case of disagreement with the prime minister and his Cabinet and no means of Cabinet control by the legislature in case of disagreement. The only means by which the Assembly could exert control was by deadlocking government through failing to pass the budget. There was also an emergency clause in Article 57, similar to Article 48 of the Weimar Constitution, which made Assembly confirmation of emergency measures mandatory. A vote of two-thirds of all assemblymen was also needed for constitutional amendment.

The judiciary was, consistent with Sino-Korean-Japanese tradition, considerably less powerful and independent than the legislature. The chief justice was appointed by the president with the consent of the National Assembly for an unspecified term; other judges were appointed by the president for 10-year terms, and hence amenable to presidential direction.

Constitutionality of laws was to be decided by a committee under the vice-president, composed of 5 Supreme Court justices and 5 National Assembly members. The committee was, in fact, never appointed. In South Korea as in the north, legal review of constitutionality was never implemented. Police were centrally administered for the entire country.

Threats to the System

The establishment of a Korean government on 15 August 1948 did not quiet or end unrest. In the major Yŏsu-Sunch'ŏn Rebellion from 19–27 October 1948, an R.O.K. regiment, bound for the suppression of lasting leftist violence on Cheju Island, mutinied and held two South Chŏlla cities, over several thousand dying before the Rebellion was contained and defeated. Cruelty was rife on both sides. Evidence of major subversion surfaced in the constabulary. Already on 29 April 1948, between 40 and 100 South Korean soldiers from a constabulary company sent that month to Cheju Island had defected to the guerillas.[43]

Major arrests, terror, and legislative and judicial attempts to curb and eliminate subversion followed these threats to the south. Seven hundred arrests were made in the week following the Rebellion, including the incarceration and torture of the later President of Korea, Major Park Chung Hee. Eighty-nine thousand arrests were made between 4 September 1948 and 30 April 1949.[44] The constabulary lost one-third of its officer-NCO corps. Even after this, in May

1949, two additional battalions defected to North Korea. Torture ubiquitously accompanied arrests, especially as constabulary CIC activity heightened under General "Snake" Kim Ch'ang-yong.[45] Insurgency, sometimes serious, continued until a few weeks before the Korean War and was finally stamped out in April 1950. Popular attitudes were deeply etched by this extended struggle.

Effects on Law: Arrest and Terror

The legal system, as we have seen, buckled under the strain: Jails could not hold the torrents of prisoners. A National Security Law, first of a series now 43 years old, was rushed through the Assembly and promulgated on 1 December. It made communism, up to then nominally a legal part of the South Korean political system, a crime. It branded as criminals those who "in collusion with a betrayer sought to consolidate or group together with the object of disturbing the tranquillity of the state," a provision so vague as to endanger any opposition. The influence of Korean traditional view of law as moral education inspired such provisions as Article II: "In case it is deemed proper, the court may suspend pronouncing sentence on an accused and at the same time detain him for re-education." Article 17 provided for "re-education camps." Urgent initiatives by the American Embassy during consideration of the bill by Assembly specialists succeeded in removing, as violating the Universal Declaration of Human Rights (proclaimed by the U.N. a few days later on 10 December) as well as USAMGIK Ordinance No. 11, the ex-post-facto penalty provisions from the bill's text. By spring of 1950, inspection by the National Assembly revealed that 50 to 80 percent of some 58,000 prisoners were charged with National Security Law violations, twice as many prisoners as had been held in the entire peninsula under Japan during the height of World War II.[46]

Between September 1948 and May 1949, the government closed 7 important newspapers and one news agency. Many reporters were arrested and several important publishers or editors, like Dr. Ha Kyŏng-tŭk, the moderate, anti-Communist publisher of the *Seoul sinmun* and Korea's first Harvard PhD, were removed. On 7 December 1948, the Minister of Education ordered the directors of all educational institutions to file detailed personal histories of all teachers with a view to firing "leftists." Numbers of bureaucrats were arraigned.

Clear intimidation of the judiciary was equally obvious. Judges and prosecutors were privately warned regarding the conduct of national-security cases. In December 1949, in one of the few such occurrences since the start of legal specialization among government officers, 21 judges and prosecutors, among them a former vice-prosecutor-general, Kim Yong-chae, were arrested, held without trial, and then accused ex post facto of failing to leave the SKLP at a time when it was a legal organization and of having formed a cell from 23 July 1949, on.[47] Guilt was sometimes inferred from SKLP membership, even though the suspect had no demonstrable SKLP connection during any part of the period covered by the prosecution statements. From the lightness of the sentences given could one alone surmise that even the authorities doubted the depth of their guilt. The methods employed can be inferred from the Minister of Justice's 27 December 1949 press statement that prosecutors should be increased so they would "strictly inspect the cells where the suspects are detained so that police will not torture them."[48]

THE *PŬRAKCHI* TRIAL

The Accused

Between November 1949 and February-March 1950, there occurred a trial whose scale and importance catalyzed and crystallized the procedures and directions of the previous post-Liberation years and established a pattern which has continued to govern political trials in South Korea for over thirty years since. Relative to its importance, it has been given remarkably little historical and legal attention.[49]

On 18 May 1949, a young representative of the 1st Korean National Assembly named Yi Mun-wŏn was arrested by the South Korean police. A month later, on the close of the Assembly sessions, after which Assembly permission for arrest had no longer to be obtained, 10 more assemblymen were arrested and jailed, including the Assembly's Vice-Speaker, a well known independence leader, Kim Yak-su; 5 more arrests of assemblymen followed during the summer; by 7 October, 16 assemblymen, nearly 8 percent of the Assembly, had been jailed, along with a lawyer and also a campaign-manager nephew of a prominent defendant.[50] Of these, 13 Assemblymen were tried and, on 14 March 1950, sentenced to from 1.5 years to 10 years in jail, forfeiting both their Assembly seats and their careers.[51] A lasting precedent for the use of a subservient judiciary to prop up a dominant executive was set. The Assembly, cowed, lost a power it has rarely, if ever, recaptured and which remains today a distant memory.

The Charges and Hearings

The government contended in the prosecution that Assemblymen No Il-hwan and Yi Mun-wŏn joined the South Korea Labor Party (SKLP) and organized a group or cell (*pŭrakchi* in Korean; *fraktsiya* in Russian) within the National Assembly, which acted as a Communist cell responsive to the requests and initiatives of the SKLP transmitted through its agents. Such acts were culpable under Articles 1, 3, and 4 of the National Security Law and Section 4 of the Military Government Ordinance 19, 30 October 1945.[52]

Fourteen hearings were given the defendants in the Seoul District Court from 17 November 1949 until 4 February 1950. Yi Mun-wŏn waited five months in jail without trial and ten others waited four; a cowed National Assembly expressed concern over such delay, habitual though it was in the Korean legal system. After pleading from 10–13 February, all defendants were declared guilty and sentenced on 14 March 1950. All defendants were in jail in Seoul pending a possible appeal in June when the Korean War broke out and, in three days, North Korean forces took Seoul, opened all jails and freed all prisoners. One imprisoned assemblyman evaded capture, made his way to Pusan and, despite his sentence, has since lived in the south openly and in freedom, though in obscurity. All the others were taken or went north with the North Korean forces, where, after brief publicity, they disappeared in comparative obscurity, though they were later members of the Front for Peaceful Unification of the Fatherland in P'yŏngyang. All had to leave their families behind and remarried in North Korea. Several are now dead, including Kim Yaksu (d. 1965), Yi Mun-wŏn, and No Si-kwan. The political careers of all were effectively ended by the *pŭrakchi* affair. War swept away such little attention as was publicly given the case. Despite its importance at the time, Korean writers have consigned the incident to brief mention as anti-government conspiracy.

Political Background of the Charges

The accusations against the defendants concerned their sponsorship in the Assembly of foreign-troop withdrawal resolutions. On 13 October 1948, 46 backers introduced a resolution proposing the withdrawal of all foreign troops (U.S. and Soviet) from Korea. (A contrary resolution backed by the R.O.K. government asking U.S. troops to stay was approved 5 November instead.) On 4 February 1949, another resolution for the withdrawal of foreign forces was introduced by 72 members and again not passed. On 18 March 1949, 63 Assemblymen brought a message to the U.N. Commission urging the withdrawal of U.S. tactical units. This withdrawal had been decided on by late 1947 in Washington, approved by the U.N., and was within three to twelve months of being completed in March of 1949.[53] The defendants took part in these *démarches* as part of an informal group known as "the young progressives." Their acts created tension with the executive which became critical when, on June 1949, the Assembly passed two demands for the resignation of the State Council. The arrests of 10 assemblymen and the murder of the chief remaining opposition politician, Kim Ku, followed these resolutions within a few days.[54]

Concomitantly, the suspected assemblymen had been involved in a quite different effort: the National Assembly attempt to punish those Koreans who had collaborated with the Japanese in such ways as to harm the Korean national cause. Two hundred and ninety-three of 527 suspects on such charges had been indicted under an Anti-National Acts Punishment law passed by the Assembly and promulgated 8 January 1949. Prominent among those indicted were 25–50 leading policemen. Many officials in the judicial system, including the judge and prosecutor in the *pŭrakchi* case, had originally been products and appointees of the Japanese system. To avoid a possible conflict of interest, the Assembly had created a Special Investigating Committee, Police Force, Prosecutor's Office, and Court to bring these men to justice. One hundred and eighty-three such suspects, many of them prominent, had just been arrested on 9 May 1949, and trials were in progress precisely as the assemblymen were being arrested. On 5 July, the first 16 were sentenced. Plans to arrest active police chiefs in early June resulted in the sudden appearance of a "National Enlightenment Association" in Pagoda Park, Seoul, which accused 3 of the soon-to-be-arrested assemblymen of being Communists, beat one up, attempted to force entry to the Assembly on 2 June, and staged a march on the Special Investigating Committee on 3 June. The Committee in turn arrested 2 Seoul metropolitan police chiefs as "anti-nationalists." In response, over 50 police went on strike and then arrested 35 members of the Special Investigating Committee headquarters, confiscating its records. On 11 June 1949, in response to police pressure, President Rhee dissolved the special police. Arrest of the assemblymen, including No Il-whan, Sŏ Yong-kil, and Kim Yak-su, who had been prominently involved in the movement to punish collaborators, followed within days.[55]

The Legal Case

The indictment designates No Il-whan and Yi Mun-wŏn as ringleaders, alleging that No was approached by a certain Yi Sam-hyŏk and Yi by a certain Ha Sa-pok, both described as South Korea Labor Party agents. It states that the resolutions for troop withdrawal, the petition to UNCURK, attempts to amend the Constitution for a cabinet-responsible system, votes of non-confidence in the Prime Minister and against the budget were all made following, and obedient to, discussions with these agents. The other defendants were charged with having knowingly collaborated with No and Yi in this program.

The indictment was based on the confessions of the defendants obtained in their cells by the prosecutor. Their confessions were corroborated by a document, titled Evidence No. 1, alleged to have been extracted from "the secret parts" of a woman, Chŏng Chae-han, apprehended by the police at Kaesong on 16 June 1949, the week following the police-Assembly confrontation. This document was supposed to represent secret information of the SKLP sent to North Korea, describing in detail the steps taken by the defendants to carry out the instructions of the SKLP and its agents.

In the sessions in open court, the defendants denied having joined the SKLP or collaborated with its agents. Messrs. No and Yi admitted to having conferred several times with Messrs. Ha and Yi[56] but asserted—without contradiction—that Messrs. Ha and Yi had never revealed themselves as Communists to No and Yi, who had no knowledge of their SKLP background. Under the National Security Law, knowledge of the hostile nature of an organization is indispensable for punishment, which can also be given only if the defendant is privy to "knowledge of the plot." All defendants emphasized that, in introducing a motion for withdrawal of armies from Korea, they were motivated exclusively by consideration that Korea as a sovereign nation should not be occupied by foreign armies; that the motion of withdrawal accorded with the U.N. resolution of 12 December 1948; and that their policy did not deviate from repeated statements of the President of the R.O.K. and the Korean Ambassador to the United States.

The defense submitted a long list of witnesses including Mme. Chŏng, whose body, as averred, had enveloped Evidence No. 1, and Messrs. Ha Sa-pok and Yi Sam-hyŏk, the agents with whom No and Yi had dealt. All (both?) were apparently in custody. The prosecutor objected to questioning all the proposed witnesses for the defense because, "first, the witnesses for the accused have nothing to do with the trial, and, second, these witnesses might make false statements in an effort to protect the accused." (14th hearing). Following the request of the public prosecutor, all requests for examination of witnesses for the defense were disallowed by Judge Sa. The judge allowed all 3 witnesses requested by the prosecution, and called one of his own choice as well.

The prosecution introduced many documents, chief among them the alleged report of the SKLP (Evidence No. 1). No effort was made to establish the genuineness of this document, although counsel for the defense repeatedly questioned its admissibility. The public prosecutor read into the record a statement allegedly made by Chŏng Chae-han in which she "acknowledged that Evidence No. 1 shown was the original message sent to North Korea by her." Though the record indicated that Chŏng was then under arrest by the R.O.K. government, neither judge nor prosecutor explained why she could not be called nor why she had "nothing to do with the trial." Informal questioning of legal and police officials during the years since have divulged absolutely no trace of the existence of a Chŏng Chae-han either in prison or out. There was similarly no explanation for the failure to call Ha and Yi to the witness stand or for the view that these persons (this person) who appear on almost every page of the indictment and are prominent throughout the hearings had "nothing to do with this trial."

The judge also read the prosecution statement to contradict direct court evidence as in the 5th hearing when defendant No Il-hwan denied knowing that the SKLP had consumed 1,300,000 wŏn of party funds to complete the petition of UNCOK: "It was quite unnecessary to use any money for submitting the petition," he testified, to which the judge retorted: "Why do you say you don't know? It is stated in the record."

All such procedures violated Korean law and the continental law on which it is based, since they breached the principle of Unmittelbarkeit (immediacy) that all testimony must be presented to courts in its most immediate form. The defense lawyers, rightly but unavailingly, objected to this procedural violation in the case of Evidence No. 1 (2nd hearing, 11 February 1960). Nevertheless, Evidence No. 1 was constantly treated by the courts as if it had been authenticated and its contents, like those of the prosecutor's statements, were treated as being true, even when they conflicted with otherwise uncontroverted direct court evidence.

Confession

The prosecutor's summary of the case relied almost exclusively on the confessions made outside the court by the defendants before the military police, the regular police, and the public prosecutor. These confessions were in no case corroborated by the statements of the defendants in open court.

The cause of this discrepancy was repeatedly revealed in court. Defendant Yi Mun-wŏn, when asked why he confessed that he had become a secret member of the SKLP, answered: "I confessed falsely because of the torture I was given." Yi also repudiated a confession to the prosecutor on grounds that the interrogations took place at the office of the military police: "If I had not confessed, I would have received more torture from the military police." (2nd hearing). When asked why he had confessed to joining the SKLP, defendant No Il-hwan pointed out: "This confession was made to the military police forces. The reason I made it was that my health could not bear the torture I was given." (5th hearing). Defendant Kim Pyŏng-hoe stated in the 6th hearing that he confessed he thought No Il-hwan was almost certainly an SKLP member "because I could not bear the torture." Defendant Hwang Un-ho declared he had admitted to having hosted a party (in connection with "the plot") only "when I was tortured by the military police. This was because I was under arrest by the police and needed consolation. I was afraid of torture." During the 13th hearing, Yi Mun-wŏn recalled Prosecutor O's threat to send him back to the military police if he denied certain specific facts.

When not averring torture, the defendants said in open court that differences between their confessions and their open statements to the judges were accounted for by the fact that the military and civil police "both wrote down anything they wanted to write." (Ch'oe T'ae-kyu and Kim Ok-chu, 7th hearing.) Despite this and without explanation, the prosecutor's summary statement referred consistently to out-of-court confessions rather than to open-court statements.

At no time did the prosecution attempt to deny the application of torture to these elected representatives of the Korean people. Defense lawyer Ch'oe Yong-sik indicated that Prosecutor O had demanded that the defense present evidence of torture. In view of the fact that the prosecutor objected to all motions of the defense to call for witnesses and was supported in all such objections by the judge, it is safe to assume that the same would have occurred had a motion been made to call witnesses regarding torture.

Again, the procedures of continental and Japano-Korean law were clearly violated here. Korean law (or the Japanese Criminal Code of 1922 then in effect in South Korea) knows no rules of evidence comparable to those of common law countries and regulates evidence by the discretion of the court, which can admit or deny confessions as evidence or motions to examine witnesses. It is recognized in civil-law countries, however, that the discretion of the court in matters of evidence requires fairness and justice and is incompatible with arbitrary decisions. If the discretion of the court in admitting or rejecting evidence is abused, it is, for example, recognized in German law (the model for Japano-Korean law) that such abuse of discretion represents a violation of the law sufficient to justify an appeal for the reversal of the decision.[57] The consistent use of confessions in the *pŭrakchi* case was improper not only because they were denied in open court for reasons that were not rebutted but also because confessions can hardly be used in civil-law procedure as conclusive evidence when, as in this case, the police officers concerned did not report verbatim the statements of the defendants but summarized in their own words what they regarded as essential.

Remote Evidence and Bias

The court's tolerance for accepting and using questionable evidence for the prosecution was as great as its intolerance in hearing evidence for the defense. Much such evidence was allowed in violation of the principle of immediacy. The following was accepted as relevant to proving that representative Sŏ Yŏng-kil's election (in Asan in May 1948 against Yun Po-sŏn) was sponsored by the SKLP:

> Judge: What is your candidate number? Is it correct that your number was 2?
> Sŏ: Yes, mine was number 2 and Mr. Yun Po-sŏn [later President of Korea] had number 1.
> Judge: Your candidate number being 2, leftists disguised as night watchmen beat their sticks twice, meaning that leftists wanted their fellow leftists to vote for candidate number 2. They also fired signal lights twice with the same meaning. Is this true?
> Sŏ: No.

So leading was this elaborate question as to arouse the suspicion that Judge Sa perceived his role to be that of the defendant's instructor in his testimony. Such an impression is strengthened by, among others, the following two questions of Judge Sa's: "Why, in view of the fact that you were elected over those prominent figures in the nationalist camp, isn't it very likely that you got many votes from leftists?" And later: "You were greatly indebted to the cooperation of leftists during the election campaign and you should be deeply obliged to them and would have attempted to return something of their good will." (Laughter from the court.)[58]

In contrast to Judge Sa's use of far-fetched circumstantial evidence for the prosecution is his denial of apparently far less remote circumstantial evidence for the defense. Defendant Hwang Yun-ho asked through his lawyer that the chief of the Yŏsu police be heard as a witness for him on the alleged grounds that the police chief had been rescued by Hwang at the risk of his life during the Communist occupation of Yŏsu in late October 1949, sixteen months before the hearing. Judge Sa denied this request.

Rejection of statements of the defense on clearly biased grounds also characterized the trial. The defendants consistently declared that their requests for the withdrawal of foreign armies meant both Soviet and American forces. As Sin Sŏng-kyun stated, such resolutions were necessary to the implementation of the U.N. resolution of 12 December 1948. Both the prosecutor and Judge Sa, however, repeatedly insisted that proposals to withdraw occupying armies from Korea were only Communist propaganda tricks.

Judge Sa insisted in the 3rd hearing, "You have always asked for foreign armies' withdrawal but actually you wanted only the United States Army withdrawal." In examining Pak Yun-wŏn during the 6th hearing, the judge said: "Do you know what happened in Greece? The U.S. Army withdrew from Greece but the Soviet Army did not withdraw. As a politician you should know this sort of thing."

Or to Kim Pyŏng-hoe: "Why did you not propose the withdrawal of the North Korean People's Army to the U.N. Commission if you respected U.N. decisions?" Or, in the 3rd hearing to Kim Yak-su: "Did you realize that insistence upon U.S. Army's withdrawal was on instruction of the SKLP in order to disturb the work of the U.N. Commission?"

The court's view, hammered in with lecturing from the bench that proposals for foreign troop withdrawal represented only a Communist position (when it demonstrably accorded with U.N. and U.S. views) showed clear bias.

Hearsay Evidence

Blatant hearsay evidence was also used against the defendants, the trial repeatedly violating the best-evidence rule. Thus, in examining defendant Yi Ku-su in the 10th hearing, the judge regarded the following relevant evidence:

The same procurator, namely Ch'oe Pong-yŏl of the Seoul District Procurator's office, investigated a police private named Kim Chong-hwa of Sang-ri Police Box, Kosŏng. According to this policeman, although he himself did not cover the meeting, he heard from a fellow policeman named Kang Han-t'ae, who is now in jail, that Yi Ku-su had told an audience around 5 o'clock sometime in the middle of March this year (1949) that the R.O.K. would soon be driven into a serious predicament by a large loan from the United States. At that time, according to him, he could plainly see that the vicious and subversive intention underlying your speech was to overthrow the government of our republic and call a conference of political leaders of south and north to work out a plan for establishing a Central Government."

Yi Ku-su: "I know nothing about it."

The written statement of a prosecutor on the investigation of a policeman who reported a story told by another policeman was not only admitted by the court as evidence, but the conclusions thus indirectly imputed by a jailed policeman from a speech of one of the defendants were also considered proper expert-opinion evidence.

Impeachment of Evidence

In the 14th hearing, the prosecutor called to the stand a witness who had served as a police spy in prison in order to collect evidence against the main defendant. When the defense attorney asked witness Kim Chŏng-sŏk what he had done before the liberation of Korea, Mr. Kim retorted "You can't ask that." The court refused to induce the witness to answer this relevant question. Since Kim Chŏng-sŏk testified to having been asked to cooperate with the authorities in secret and to pretend to be a Communist, his profession in the spy-ridden world of pre-Liberation Korea may readily be imagined. Its relevance to his reliability as a witness is clear.

Evaluation of the Evidence

Up to the calling of witnesses, the government's case against the 13 assemblymen rested on confessions which were challenged as being obtained under duress; documentary evidence which had not been authenticated; and testimony of defendants in open court which denied or varied widely from their reported confessions.

On 20 January 1950, following an adjournment of two weeks requested by the prosecutor, the prosecution introduced as witness Yi Chae-nam who testified in court to being a member of the Central Committee of the SKLP and the boss of the absent Ha Sa-pok and Yi Sam-hyŏk. Mr. Yi appeared before the court in such weakened condition that he had to sit to give his testimony; no questions, however, were raised about that.

Mr. Yi testified that, under orders from the SKLP, he had approached No Il-hwan, whom he had known when he and No had been *Dong-A ilbo* reporters. He was not optimistic about his contact, since he knew No to be a strong nationalist who hated SKLP chief Pak Hŏn-yŏng and had actively participated in exposing a Communist counterfeit ring in 1946 (the "Nonomiya incident"). Mr. Yi testified to finding that "No's political views remained nationalistic as he was in the days when I knew him on the newspaper." Mr. Yi found that No's unification plans differed from the SKLP's, No saying that it was improper to carry out foreign troop withdrawal. Neither No nor Yi Mun-wŏn were persons, Yi found, who "would gladly join in our front." The SKLP "never thought of them except as those who acted on their own beliefs." Failing with No, Yi turned him over to Ha Sa-pok who also reported to Yi that No was difficult, "does not obey what other people say unconditionally," and insists "on maintaining his own opinion."

Asked whether the motion on troop withdrawal had been introduced on SKLP instructions, Yi answered: "As a matter of fact, withdrawal of matter of the alien armies was discussed among National Assembly members without our knowledge." Regarding the message to UNCOK, Yi testified that the SKLP "did not want the delivery of letters but wanted withdrawal to be passed in the National Assembly." "In the end," Mr. Yi said, "our activity in the National Assembly ended in failure."

Witness for the prosecution Chŏng Ha-kyŏng, also under arrest for violation of the National Security Law, testified to having approached Ch'oe T'ae-kyu: "When I asked him whether he could propose troop withdrawal in the National Assembly, he said it was impossible." Witness Chŏng stated explicitly that he had never told defendant Ch'oe of his Communist Party membership. Chŏng felt defendant Hwang Yun-ho "seemed to hate him" and was not interested in Chŏng's proposals. No Il-hwan warned Hwang against seeing Chŏng. Nor was Yi Mun-wŏn more amenable. Witness Chŏng, evidently a SKLP member, testified that he was "positive that No Il-hwan and Yi Mun-wŏn were not members of the SKLP." The attempt of the prosecutor to prove that No and Yi were members or agents of the SKLP ended in failure.

The attempt to identify Evidence No. 1 similarly miscarried. Witness Chŏng testified that the forms he used in reporting to the SKLP differed from Evidence No. 1. Central Committee Member Yi, to whom Ha Sa-pok regularly reported, testified he did not know who wrote Evidence No. 1, nor did he know anything about it until he read of it in the Seoul newspapers after the defendant's arrest. The alleged author of Evidence No. 1, Ha Sa-pok, was not introduced as a witness, quite possibly, one may speculate, because he might have denied having written Evidence No. 1. It is difficult otherwise to explain how the man to whom he reported did not know about the document; or how Ha could keep his identity a secret if he induced No and Yi to join the SKLP; or how they could be described as joining when SKLP members said they didn't. Seen in the context of the events of June relating to the attempted prosecution of R.O.K. police for antinational acts, it is anyone's guess whether Evidence No. 1 originated in the SKLP or in the writings of the South Korean police.[59]

The prosecutor's summary dealt almost exclusively with the alleged crimes of No Il-hwan and Yi Mun-wŏn. The other 13 defendants, including 11 assemblymen or 5 percent of the National Assembly, were hardly mentioned. This appears to have been the government's way of communicating its awareness that it had no case against these defendants. It failed to prove that the association between them and SKLP agents was more than casual or that the defendants had any awareness that their contacts were Communists or had any plan to establish a Communist cell within the Assembly.

Moreover, in view of Article 50 of the Korean Constitution then in force ("No member of the National Assembly shall be held responsible to anyone outside the Assembly for any statement or vote occurring within the Assembly"), it is hard to see how the court could allow Assembly resolutions on troop withdrawal to figure so prominently in the prosecution and trial.

Conclusion of Case

The sentencing on 14 March 1950, awarded 10 years in jail to No Il-hwan and Yi Mun-wŏn, 8 to Kim Yak-su and Pak Yun-wŏn, 6 to 4 others, and 3 to the other 5 assemblymen, including Ch'oe T'ae-kyu, Yi Ku-su, Sŏ Yŏng-kil and Sin Sŏng-kyun. With these last defendants, the use of hearsay, remote, and unconvincing evidence had been particularly marked. All sentences were far lighter than guilt on charges of such seriousness could have been expected to bring.[60] The differences between the sentences of the two main conspirators and the others were also less than the emphases in the prosecutor's summary implied. The system did not, in fact, permit a defendant in a political case to be found innocent, since the government had to be protected from a perceived loss of face.[61] Light sentencing was therefore the apparent means used—here as elsewhere—to signify innocence or inadequate proof of guilt. Certainly the principle of Japano-

Korean and civil law that no person can be punished in a criminal trial unless his guilt has been established in open court was massively breached.

The intended political effect was also achieved. The Assembly, cowed, did not challenge the government again until 1952. The trials of suspects in the Anti-National Acts cases were fatally weakened. Some staggered on through the summer of 1949; most collapsed. Only 2 or 3 suspects (out of nearly 300 charged) served any sentence at all, and even these, though sentenced to long confinements, were soon released; cases against the others were quietly dropped. The police chiefs named by the Assembly investigation were never touched. The South Korean effort to punish collaborators with the Japanese ended in failure to punish and in the political death of the issue. In North Korea, results were different; the wide difference in handling the collaborator issue has been one of the fundamental gaps between South and North Korea.[62]

THE LEGACY OF LEGAL PRACTICE

The use of political trials to quell opposition has continued to the present day. On 26 May 1952 in Pusan, during the middle of the war, some 45 of the then opposition majority in the National Assembly who were currently threatening President Rhee's re-election, were taken into custody on their way to the Assembly on the pretext of not displaying identification to the military police; most were not released for two days, and 4 were further detained. On 19 June 1952, 14 defendants, half of them assemblymen, were sent before 7 military and 3 civilian judges on charges of "Communist conspiracy" under the National Security Act. Defense lawyers were not made available prior to the trial's recess on 21 June. As in the *pŭrakchi* case, the Home Minister again claimed that a plot was discovered when a Communist agent was rounded up with "valuable documents" that were never divulged.

In this instance, the trial was prematurely suspended when the Martial Law Commander released almost all assemblymen on trial and had them marched to the Assembly Hall on 4 July 1952 to pass constitutional amendments proposed by the President that crippled the Assembly's power over him. The charges against the accused subsequently melted away, and nothing more was heard either of "valuable documents," of "Communist conspiracy," or of the threat of trial. The defendants were mostly well-known anti-Communists, and included refugees from North Korea.[63]

The trial, torture, and execution of reporter-politician Chŏng Kuk-ŭn from 1952–1954 on charges of being a Communist agent, though less well known in detail, was observed by U.S. and U.N. officials who recalled improprieties in the use of evidence and failure to call relevant witnesses. Mr. Chŏng's execution had to be delayed so that he could recover sufficiently from torture to stand up and be dispatched. He was apparently prosecuted as a warning to former Prime Minister Yi Pŏm-sŏk, whose political protégé he was. Yi Pŏm-Sŏk never regained his political prominence.

The trial during 1955–1957 of Lt. General Kang Mun-pong and other officers for the murder of Lt. General "Snake" Kim Ch'ang-yong revealed, according to witnesses and one of the panel members, use of remote evidence, misuse of evidence, and both the introduction of questionable witnesses for the prosecution and the denial of apparently relevant defense witnesses, in a manner reminiscent of the *pŭrakchi* trial.[64]

A particular landmark was the trial from 1958–1959 of former Minister of Agriculture, Assembly Vice-Speaker, and opposition presidential candidate Cho Pong-am and some of his associates on charges of being Communist agents allegedly reporting to a Communist superior who could not be introduced to the courtroom because he was in Japan. Written and indirect evidence again took the place of calling key witnesses, including the alleged agent in Japan on whom almost the entire case depended. The defendants were tortured; indeed, in this instance, the main evidence was retracted because it had been obtained under duress and the prosecution lost the first trial appeal. Conviction and rapid, almost secret, execution of Cho was railroaded through in response to evident executive pressure.

After the 1960 Revolution, Liberal Party leaders were tried on ex post facto charges by the Democratic regime and the Democratic cabinet, and in 1961 chief leaders were tried on especially preposterous charges by the coup leaders, convictions being obtained with marked irregularities by a specially designated "Supreme Prosecutor General." Generals guilty of nothing but loyalty to the lawful Democratic regime were tried and, in one case, retried on the same charges; the judge, when asked by one defendant, a senior major general, why he was thus placed in double jeopardy, replied that he would have to answer the question outside the courtroom.

Thereafter, trials of factional dissidents within the ruling party, like General Pak Im-hang and Kim Tong-ha, were marked by hearsay evidence, obstructions to defense, and especially heavy use of torture.[65] In 1962, civilian politicians like Yun Kil-chung and Yi Tong-hwa and groups like the People's Reform Party faced trumped-up charges of conspiracy, remote evidence, remote deductions from key witnesses not in the country, torture, forced confessions, discrepancy between in-trial and outside-trial evidence, leading questions, and double jeopardy, as illustrated in the *pŭrakchi* trial. Nor did the trials of those kidnaped from Germany in the 1967 "Berlin Incident" which, *inter alia*, permanently undermined the health of Prof. Yun I-sang, Korea's most prominent modern composer, show improvement. Through the trial of Socialist Kim Ch'ŏl, concluded on 6 December 1971, and the trial of 22 and executions of 8 members of the so-called Korean Revolutionary Party in 1975, such trials descend to those of the Kwangju Incident in 1980–1981, starring Kim Dae Jung and many others, with little change of style. The only change detectable was that the trials of the late 1960s and 1970s attracted somewhat greater international press attention, and that the reviewing statement of the Korean Supreme Court in the Kim Dae Jung case was considerably longer than written explanations offered in the other cases cited.[66]

Legal Codes in the Rhee Era: Persistance of Japanese Elements

The years of the Syngman Rhee regime were active ones in the process of introducing Korean codes of many kinds to replace—or at least more or less to "Koreanize"—Japanese codes which had approached being the complete basis of Korea's experience with modern law. A review of this entire subject lies well beyond the scope of this chapter; nor is a review of all aspects of new codification relating to human rights or of the educational changes developed in Korean law faculties to inculcate and support the new codes within the competence of this author.

Mention must be made, however, of the chief South Korean effort during the years of the Rhee Administration (1948–1960) bearing on the human-rights field: the coming into force on 3 October 1953, of the Korean Criminal Code, the first autonomous modern Korean code in this field, superseding the Japanese Criminal Code of 1908, which had been imposed on Korea in 1913 and had remained in effect for the next forty years.[67]

This code, still in effect, represents a comingling of the heritage of the Japanese Code (based dominantly on the German Code of 1871), of some notions of Anglo-American criminal law, and of a comparatively small residue of the more ancient Sino-Korean heritage, particularly as it relates to criminal and inheritance law in a familial context.[68] In a rough sense, one can say that Anglo-American law tends to give effect to maximum individual freedom as against the state, whereas German law has been rather oriented to the protection of state interests. Seoul National University Professor of Criminal Law, Dr. Paul K. Ryu (Yu Ki-ch'ŏn) finds that the 1953—and other— "Korean legislation was . . . a compilation of divergent views among which the German views predominated."[69] Significant in this connection is his observation that trial by jury, even though introduced into Korea by Japanese law, never then or now set down roots in Korean soil, a development Dr. Ryu ascribes to the persistence of the Confucian notion of social superiors with directive duties and qualifications with whose directives a lack of understanding on the part of subordinates must not be allowed to impose impediment. The ancient tendency of law to function as an adjunct far less resorted to than in the West for the government's policing of society has likewise continued to persist. Relative reluctance to resort to and have confidence in legal process was reflected in the inordinately small proportion of lawyers to the population—only 600 for a population of 23,000,000 midway through the Rhee era. The prestige of and educational support for the Japanese system on the whole also persisted. Dr. Ryu notes that "Japanese decisions are regarded in Korea not as binding but as persuasive authority."[70]

Finally, there is a general characteristic of Korean criminal law which the new code contains and which, before the code was formulated, the *pŭrakchi* trial already strikingly illustrated: the extreme tendency to prove crime not only—not perhaps even primarily—as determined by result (*Erfolgsdelikte*), that is, by the injury done (*Verletzungsstrafrecht*), but as based simply on intent (*Willensstrafrecht*). The extremely leading questions and biased comment of the judge in the *pŭrakchi* trial appears to illustrate the concept of criminality based on the suspect's intent to endanger the community and its ideological identification, a kind of *Gefahrdungsstrafrecht*. Thus "Did you realize that insistence upon U.S. Army withdrawal was an instruction of the SKLP in order to disturb the work of the U.N. Commission?" and other cited instances. In theoretical terms, this represents an extreme subjectivist position, implicitly threatening to human rights. More controversially, one is struck by the apparent proximity of this position to that expressed in the National Socialist Memorandum on Criminal Law of the Prussian Ministry of Justice in 1933, the *locus classicus* of the Nazi position on law. The essence of the Korean government's position in the *pŭrakchi* trial was not that an attempted resolution on troop withdrawal was, in itself, illegal—or even that it resulted in harm (since it was defeated and in any case did not have the power to determine the withdrawal decision)—but that its *intent* was deemed criminal, that it was solicited for harmful purpose, and was hence considered criminal even if the connection between solicitation and act remained unproved. In essence, this was precisely the Nazi position in the Nazi formulation of Section 49a of the German Penal Code: "Whoever solicits another to commit a felony or to participate in a felony shall be punished as an instigator even if the crime was not carried out or was carried out independently of the solicitation."[71]

Codes and Practice: Steps Toward Human Rights

The picture of legislation and practice regarding human rights had its better as well as its less encouraging side during the period as a whole. The American Military Government did sweep aside numbers of the most obviously repressive measures of the Japanese period and started several more liberal practices which—even when not always observed—persisted in part because, once started, they came to be regarded as the needed baggage of a more enlightened modern state and were not easy to sweep aside.

The ordinances of American Military Government included No. 17, of 24 September 1945, abolishing the Economic Police Department in the bureau of the police, hence removing the police permanently from their former supervisory functions over elements of the economy.[72] An ordinance of 23 July 1946 established a Department of Labor, continued ever since as an important institutional step in advancing the role, if not always the rights, of labor. Ordinance No. 107, of 9 September 1946, established a Bureau of Women's Affairs, a step concentrating somewhat greater attention of the role and rights of women. Ordinance No. 112, of 18 September 1946, regulating child labor sought to correct some of the great abuses of the Japanese and previous eras in exploiting the work of young children under conditions endangering their health, safety, and future well-being; improprieties here continued but the overall situation certainly improved. Similarly, Ordinance 121, of 7 November 1946, attempted to establish maximum working hours after the gross exploitation visited on Korean workers by Japan during the war years. Though Korean employers continue, relative to developed nations, to exploit their workers in the above and other respects, the ground won has never been completely lost; Korea has not returned to the dark days between 1938–1945.

Less liberal in result was Ordinance 88, of 29 May 1946, Licensing of Newspapers and Periodicals, which continued an old continually abusive practice which has persisted into 1987, abridging freedoms of expression otherwise supposed to be protected in other ordinances.[73]

In the judicial field, a limited habeas corpus remedy was provided by Section 8 of the Department of Justice's Instructions to Judges (also, apparently, known as "Appointment Order") of 19 November 1945, a provision unknown in Japanese law. The opinion of Captain Stanley N. Ohlbaum cited above makes it clear that questions of its scope and the complexities aroused by its emplacement within a complex alien law without educational changes have limited its effectiveness.[74]

The judicial power of the police chief under Japanese law was effectively abolished in a Department of Justice Instruction of 9 October 1945, as were 6 other Japanese laws on punishing convicts, preliminary imprisonment, reservation of public order, publication, the protection of political convicts, and treatment of shrines. Instructions to prosecutors were also issued. A more major measure, for some time delayed, was Ordinance 176 of 20 March 1948, Changes in Criminal Procedures. This ordinance, *inter alia*, provided in Section 3 that "no person shall suffer restraint of body except pursuant to a warrant of arrest issued by a court, stating the name of the person to be arrested and the offense with which he is charged." Though exceptions to this, allowed for instances of *in flagrante delicto*, and so forth, were fairly numerous and though, also, court issuance of such warrants at prosecutors' requests was routine, offering little curb to unreasonable state prosecution, the fact that prosecutors could no longer act unilaterally had some significance. When the Code of Criminal Procedure was drawn up and promulgated as Law No. 341 on 23 September 1954, somewhat similar wording was included in Chapter 10, Articles 113–115.[75]

Examination of the Code of Criminal Procedure and the manner in which it has operated in the ensuing years could occupy a far larger space than is available here. No chapter of the present length can present final conclusions on the period. One cannot, however, escape the general conclusions of several experts, including Dr. Hahm Pyong-Choon,[76] that law, the judiciary, the conduct of trials, and attention to human rights are matters that have adhered to Korean tradition most closely and have changed more slowly and reluctantly than almost any other area of Korea's culture and life.

U.S. Foreign Policy and Human Rights in South Korea

JEROME ALAN COHEN *and* EDWARD J. BAKER

Like the Shah's Iran, the Republic of Korea under Park Chung Hee too must be a special case for Americans. True, neither General Park Chung Hee's overthrow of Korea's short-lived democratic government in 1961, nor the two-stage coup of General Chun Doo Hwan in the 1961 case, had the legitimately elected President Yun Po-sŏn asked his American ally to suppress the usurpers, the United States asked his American ally to suppress the usurpers, the United States would probably have done so. Yet, in both instances, once the new leaders seized power, the American attitude toward them gradually changed from suspicion and hostility to unenthusiastic acquiescence to strong support, despite their increasingly repressive rule. And, in South Korea, American support has been indispensable to the survival of any government and of the republic itself.

POST-WAR U.S.-KOREAN RELATIONS TO 1972

Of course, the special responsibility of the United States for basic freedoms and other fundamental human rights in South Korea long antedated the advent of the Park regime. Americans not only played the key role in liberating Korea from Japanese colonial oppression at the end of World War II but also agreed to the Soviet occupation of the northern part of the peninsula while U.S. forces occupied the southern part. While the U.S.S.R. and its Korean sympathizers converted the north into a totalitarian Communist system, the American occupiers taught people in the south as much about authoritarian practices as about democratic principles in the process of bringing order out of chaos and creating a government that would be responsive to both American interests and ideology. When postwar attempts to establish a united government for the entire peninsula failed, it was the United States that took the initiative in establishing the Republic of Korea under U.N. auspices in the south while the Communists established the Democratic People's Republic of Korea (D.P.R.K.) in the north, thus perpetuating the novel and tragic division of the Korean people. When, following the 1948 withdrawal of U.S. forces from the R.O.K., its Communist rival sought to unify the peninsula by force in 1950, the United States led the foreign coalition that under the U.N. banner went to the defense of the R.O.K. At the end of that bloody stalemate, the United States concluded the Mutual Security Treaty of 1954 with the R.O.K., obligating the United States to come to the defense of South Korea "in accordance with its constitutional processes." Washington thereafter continued to provide military and economic aid to the R.O.K. that at last report totaled over $13 billion, in addition to stationing forces at a cost that has now reached well over $12 billion.[1] Moreover, because South Korea was alienated from all its neighbors—the Communist regimes that controlled China, the Soviet Union and North Korea, and the detested former colonial ruler, Japan—and largely isolated from the rest of the world, the overall American impact upon the R.O.K. was immense. Americans not only became the defenders of South Koreans but, in trade, investment, politics, cultural life, and education, also became their mentors and big brothers. American contacts with South Korea were far more intimate than those with Iran, and U.S. influence over its people and their values were correspondingly greater.

From 1948 to 1965, the United States did not hesitate to use its enormous influence over the R.O.K. for many purposes. Although government under the U.S. Army, 1945–1948, had offered only a flawed and ambiguous model of democratic rule, after the R.O.K. was established, Washington, under both Democratic and Republican administrations, intervened on a number of occasions to press the autocratic Syngman Rhee to curb some of the worst excesses of his often-arbitrary presidency. Some of these American interventions took the form of public scoldings. In March 1950, for example, Secretary of State Dean G. Acheson sharply reminded the Rhee regime that "U.S. aid, both military and economic, to the Republic of Korea has been predicated upon the existence and growth of democratic institutions within the Republic."[2] Such ad hoc admonitions and behind-the-scenes pressures could not alter the nature of Rhee's government. That task was left to the students of Korea, who, in the spring of 1960, after rigged national elections and a subsequent cover-up, went into the streets and removed Rhee from office. But the American pressures, and Rhee's awareness that greater abuses might elicit even sterner reactions, did place limits upon his arbitrariness. Furthermore, U.S. pressure at least made clear to the Korean people that the United States did not endorse his authoritarianism. The U.S. position was surely not an irrelevant factor in the calculations of those who overthrew Rhee and gave Koreans the only year of unrestricted political freedom they had ever known.

During the first few years after Park's 1961 military coup aborted the experiment with democracy, the United States continued to exercise its leverage over the R.O.K.'s new authoritarian rulers as it had over Rhee. Thus, a combination of American and domestic pressures forced Park to don more legitimate civilian clothes in 1963 by holding elections (which he won by only the barest plurality despite his control of the government). Even after the election, Park remained unsure of the American support that was essential to his continuing in office. Nothing in his education and service in the Japanese military and his postwar Korean military experience had equipped him to deal with American politicians and diplomats. Yet, in the circumstances in which he found himself, the challenge of coping with them was especially acute.

Not only was Washington maintaining a policy of equidistance between the new rulers and the then still active opposition forces, who were bolstered by renewed anti-government demonstrations by the students, but Park also had to be concerned about potential rivals within the ruling elite itself. Park sorely needed the U.S. seal of approval to consolidate his power. If he was to prove a more effective vote getter at the next election, he would have to demonstrate to his colleagues and to the people generally that he was an effective aid getter. In view of the pervasiveness of the perception of a "threat from the north," military aid was especially crucial. If Park couldn't get it, the R.O.K. would need someone who could. Thus, as late as 1965, American leverage over the R.O.K. seemed powerful, and it was coupled with a continuing will to use it, if only on occasion, to moderate some of the regime's worst abuses against human rights and efforts to suppress pluralistic elements in society.

The American involvement in Vietnam markedly changed Korean-American relations. In order to sustain that tragic adventure, the United States badly needed Korean combat forces in Vietnam beginning in late 1965. The American request for R.O.K. troops made the war a veritable heaven-sent opportunity for Park. He seized this opportunity, as well as American insistence upon Seoul's normalization of relations with Tokyo, to wring out of the United States everything that he could have hoped for as support. The results were dramatic.

Through a series of policies and public and private utterances and gestures the United States made clear to Koreans and the world that its earlier doubts about Park had dissipated and that American ties with the R.O.K. were closer than ever. Vice-President Hubert Humphrey visited Seoul in February 1966 and sought to overcome the uncertainty inherent in the U.S. treaty commitment to come to the defense of the R.O.K. "in accordance with its constitutional processes."[3]

President Johnson visited Seoul in November of the same year and "reaffirmed the readiness and determination of the United States to render prompt and effective assistance to defeat an armed attack against the Republic of Korea,"[4] a new rhetorical flourish that Koreans hopefully depicted as indicating a stronger American tie. And, as early as July 1965, the U.S. Commander in Korea and Ambassador Winthrop Brown had jointly pledged that there would be no reduction in U.S. force levels on the peninsula.[5]

The new and unabashed American support for the regime and for Park as an individual put an end to the U.S. policy of maintaining equidistance between the party in power and its opposition. This crucial shift in the balance of political forces in Seoul was facilitated by the fact that the opposition parties and intellectuals of democratic persuasion, who had never given up the illusion that the American political establishment was at least secretly with them, found themselves in the unenviable position of opposing the single most important U.S. policy of the day regarding Korea—the dispatch of Korean troops to Vietnam.[6]

Washington's new-found enthusiasm for Park was also manifested in the language best understood by South Koreans anxious about their security—military aid. It rose dramatically from the all-time low of $124 million in 1964 to a whopping $480 million in 1969 and $556 million in 1971.[7] Whatever may have been the functional utility of such lavish spending by the United States, its symbolic significance was enormous. Park was a president who could really deliver—or, rather, acquire—the means of safeguarding Korean security.

This change in U.S.-R.O.K. relations elicited a reaction from North Korea that further strengthened Park's hand. The response of the North was to exacerbate the already tense situation on the Korean peninsula through a host of incidents that culminated in 1968 in the doomed commando attack upon the Blue House (Park's White House), the seizure of the U.S. intelligence ship *Pueblo*, and the shoot-down of a U.S. EC-121 reconnaissance plane. These actions reinforced the image shared by South Koreans and Americans of a North Korea bent upon aggression, and this in turn facilitated Park's program for imposing unity upon the unruly, aspiring democrats in the south.

The advent of the Nixon and Ford Administrations only exacerbated the situation. When, beginning in the mid-1960s, Washington ceased exercising the leverage over Seoul that it formerly employed to curb the worst abuses of the R.O.K.'s authoritarianism, it had done so on pragmatic grounds. The new Republican Administration, however, transformed this recent practice into a matter of high principle, invoking the shibboleth of "nonintervention in the internal affairs of another state" against Americans and Koreans who sought a return to the earlier U.S. practice of applying various pressures toward stimulating South Korea's rulers to grant their people certain minimal political and civil rights. This gave Park the clearest signal that he could move ahead in the early 1970s with measures far more repressive than those he adopted during the first decade of his rule. Thus, two of the less well known casualties of the Vietnam War were democracy and human rights in Korea.

In October 1972, President Park Chung Hee declared martial law and dissolved the National Assembly as the first formal steps toward ending the then existing constitutional system and substituting in its place the so-called *Yusin Constitution*. Subsequently, Park's "revitalizing reforms" narrowed the differences between the totalitarian north and the supposedly "free" south in their respect for human rights.

HUMAN RIGHTS IN THE R.O.K. UNDER THE YUSIN SYSTEM, 1972–1979

"Human rights practices in Korea have been carefully considered in formulating this proposed security assistance program."[8] So reads the U.S. Defense Department's "Congressional Presentation" for the fiscal year 1978 security-assistance program, which sought to justify the appropriation of $28,400,000 for military aid to the R.O.K.

This statement highlights several important policy concerns. What weight should the United States attach to human rights considerations while seeking to maintain the peace and security of East Asia? What "human rights" should U.S. policy be concerned with? To what extent are they being observed? What policies can effectively promote the observance of human rights in Korea?

This summary of developments from 1972 to 1979 will focus on political and civil rights rather than economic and social rights, for it is the former that have created the major controversy inside and outside Korea. At the time, observers plainly differed over the costs and benefits of the R.O.K.'s developmental strategy that made the country increasingly dependent upon foreign capital and resources, and they debated such matters as whether the R.O.K. had done enough to raise minimum wages and to reduce income differentials among various strata of its population or to improve the status of women. Yet, it seems clear that in many respects the R.O.K. continued to make very impressive, if uneven, economic and social progress. We would not be concerned with South Korea in this volume had the Park regime made commensurate progress in fostering political and civil rights. Instead, what occurred during this period was a tragic retrogression, repression so thorough and comprehensive that it created profound doubts in the United States about the long-run viability of our country's support for the Park regime and even perhaps for the R.O.K. itself.

We shall discuss three aspects: (1) state officials' arbitrary violation of the integrity of the person outside the judicial system; (2) arbitrary manipulation of the judicial system for purposes of political repression; and (3) restraints upon freedoms of expression.

Arbitrary Violations of the Person

Political murder per se did not become a staple of life under the Yusin system as it has at various times in certain Communist countries and as in the 1970s in Uganda, to cite only the leading non-Communist example. Nevertheless, there have been cases of "mysterious" deaths. For example, on 16 October 1973, Professor Ch'oe Chong-kil, who spent the years 1970–1972 at Harvard Law School on a Harvard-Yenching fellowship, was picked up by the Korean Central Intelligence Agency shortly after having lamented, in a supposedly secret faculty meeting, police brutality against some of his colleagues and students at Seoul National University's Law Faculty. He was never seen alive again. Four days later, the government announced that Ch'oe had been arrested on charges of spying for North Korea and that, after making a full confession, he had committed suicide by jumping out of the window of an interrogation center. Yet, the occupant of a neighboring cell, later released, claimed that he heard screams from Ch'oe's cell followed by silence and the rapid summoning of medical help; the accusation of spying was never substantiated; Ch'oe's supposed confession was never published; and the report of his "suicide" has been treated with the utmost skepticism. The fact that his widow, a medical doctor, was denied permission to examine the corpse hardly inspired confidence in what appears to have been a hastily contrived story.[9]

Even more mysterious was the subsequent death of the ardent patriot and intellectual leader Chang Chun-ha. Chang, a Magsaysay Award winner and former National Assemblyman and publisher, had initiated a "one million citizens petition for a democratic amendment of the *Yusin Constitution*" in late 1973. When the movement began to snowball, gathering roughly 500,000 signatures, the Park regime put an end to it in early 1974 by invoking newly promulgated "emergency decrees."[10] These authorized up to 15 years in prison for any person who "asserted, introduced, proposed, or petitioned for revision or repeal" of the *Yusin Constitution*.[11] Chang was arrested with his colleagues, was "hanged upside down and simultaneously . . . burned with a flame on several parts of his body," and then sentenced to the maximum term by a court martial rather than regular court.[12] Domestic and foreign pressures later forced the regime to release Chang and hundreds of intellectuals, students, and religious and military figures condemned by the military tribunals. Shortly afterward, however, Chang, an experienced mountain climber who had once conquered the formidable mountains of Western China, was reported to have fallen to his death from a cliff while climbing a hill near Seoul. The prosecutor's office accepted the story of a man who had been alone with Chang just before he fell and who claimed that death must have resulted from a hiking accident. After a newspaper reported a variety of suspicious circumstances casting doubt on this claim, the editor was arrested. Many others were puzzled about the death of "perhaps the only man who could have revived an effective opposition to President Park Chung Hee's Government,"[13] but no one could afford to be too curious.

Kim Dae Jung, the charismatic democrat who made such an impressive showing against Park in the 1971 presidential election that Park put an end to such elections, was undoubtedly targeted for a similar fate. After kidnaping Kim from a Tokyo hotel room and spiriting him out of Japan by ship in August 1973, the KCIA was on the verge of dumping him overboard, bound, gagged, and weighted, when a nationwide outcry in Japan and vigorous behind-the-scenes diplomacy by the United States saved Kim's life.[14] Kidnaping itself, of course, is one of the most flagrant violations of the person short of murder.

Obviously, mysterious deaths and kidnapings had a profoundly chilling effect upon those who might wish to speak out against the policies of the Park regime as Ch'oe, Chang, and Kim did, each in his own way. Yet, far more intimidating was the widespread use of torture following arbitrary arrest. This is why Yun Po-sŏn characterized the Park regime as "government by torture," for at least during the early and mid-1970s it was highly dependent upon pervasive and systematic violations of human bodies and minds to maintain its control. The "Genghis Khan cooking" to which Chang Chun-ha was subjected when the KCIA ran a flame over his body is only one of many techniques Park's government used. The reports of Amnesty International and other organizations that investigated KCIA torture during this period have documented how cold water was forced up the nostrils through a tube, how electric shocks were applied to the genitals, toes, and other sensitive parts, and how people were hung from the ceiling and spun around, beaten and kicked mercilessly, stripped naked in sub-zero weather and doused in water, made to stand or sit without sleep for days on end, and subjected to various forms of psychological intimidation.[15]

Most of those tortured were unknown to the press and the outside world. Those whose detention tended to attract publicity were often better treated. Nevertheless, even well-known persons suffered physical abuse if their behavior was considered sufficiently provocative, as in the cases of Ch'oe, Chang, and Kim. In 1975, after students recently paroled from jail spoke out against the tortures they had suffered, 13 former opposition National Assemblymen revealed that they too had been tortured shortly after President Park seized emergency powers in the autumn of 1972. One of them, Ch'oe Hyŏng-u, son of one of South Korea's most noted politicians, was paralyzed at least temporarily from the waist down as a result of this mistreatment. In his statement to the National Assembly, he noted that several cattle dealers had recently been arrested for forcing their animals to drink a large amount of water to increase their weight just before they were sold for slaughter. Ch'oe asked: "Why haven't the KCIA and other agents who used water torture on national assemblymen been arrested? Are the assemblymen less important than the cattle?"[16]

In those circumstances, it was not surprising that the Park regime went to great lengths to hinder congressmen like Donald Fraser and agencies like Amnesty International from interviewing victims of Park's terror.[17] Of course, after their release from interrogation centers and torture chambers, most victims were extremely reluctant to talk about their experiences, out of fear that government agents might make good their threats to retaliate against those breaking silence. In some cases, shame was also a factor. For example, in his speech to the National Assembly, Ch'oe Hyŏng-u declined to reveal details of his wife's torture on the ground that human decency prevented him from describing it. A number of women students who protested against Park's repression were arrested by the KCIA, tortured, and repeatedly raped, as in the case of several Ewha University students in late 1973.[18] Understandably, most of these rape victims have also kept silent about their ordeal.

In many cases, people were tortured not so much to elicit information and evidence from them as to intimidate them. Large numbers of persons were detained, interrogated, tortured, and then released after a few days, with no thought apparently given to bringing any legal proceeding against them. In other cases, torture was applied for the specific purpose of obtaining evidence to be used in criminal prosecutions. One well-known instance of this involved Sŏ Sŭng, a handsome Korean resident of Japan who had gone to South Korea to study at Seoul National University and who was prosecuted for espionage. By the time he appeared in court after interrogation by the KCIA, his body and face were horribly burned as a result of a suicide attempt he claimed he was driven to by torture. His eyelids and ears had disappeared, his fingers had adhered together, and his eyeglasses had to be bound to his head. His condition presented a certain challenge to interrogators who operated under bureaucratic requirements that the accused authenticate his confession by placing his fingerprints upon it. Since Sŏ had no fingerprints left, his captors proved as imaginative as they were punctilious by having him authenticate his confession with a toe print.[19] Although the *Yusin Constitution* maintained the previous constitution's prohibition of torture, there was no constitutional basis for excluding confessions obtained through torture from evidence because the new constitution pointedly failed to retain its predecessor's ban on the admission of coerced confessions.[20]

One could detail other gruesome cases,[21] but the point is clear—if actual deaths were relatively few, savageries at the hands of torturers turned hundreds of articulate and conscientious Koreans who were involved in the democratic movement into the living dead, suffering from both physical damage and psychological trauma. As Koreans say, their sickness had gotten to the marrow of their bones, and the fear lingered on, although resort to torture appears to have temporarily diminished after 1976.

Arbitrary Manipulation of the Judicial Process

If such drastic methods had to be used to obtain evidence for formal legal proceedings, the pressure became enormous to distort those proceedings in order to prevent revelation of the methods of extracting the evidence as well as the dubious nature of the evidence itself. Thus, the judicial process inevitably became corrupted in various ways, despite the continuing claim of regime spokesmen that the independence of the judiciary was guaranteed by the Constitution, and was not subject to interference by anyone.[22] The classic case during the Yusin period was the 1974 conviction of 22 members of the so-called "People's Revolutionary Party" for allegedly having organized to overthrow the government and replace it with a regime sympathetic to North Korea.

The trial was held not before a regular court but before a military tribunal established by the 1974 emergency decrees. Hearings were closed, with only one member of each defendant's family allowed to attend. The "confessions" were admitted into evidence, even though they were extracted under hideous forms of torture. Moreover, 42 prosecution witnesses testified in the absence of defense lawyers, who were apparently under house arrest at the time. In any event, the defense was not permitted to question prosecution witnesses and statements. No defense witnesses were allowed. Government-controlled media proclaimed the guilt of the accused before judgment was rendered. No foreign journalists were permitted at the trial because, according to the Prime Minister, "[t]here was too great a risk they might misunderstand and misrepresent what happened in court."[23] In April 1975, after the Supreme Court had upheld the 8 death sentences and all but 2 of the prison sentences meted out—but before the accused could exercise their rights to petition the Supreme Court for retrial and petition the President for mercy—the 8 condemned to death were unlawfully hanged, despite assurances from the Public Prosecutor's Department that no executions would take place until the accused had an opportunity to exhaust their rights. The government cremated the bodies of a number of those executed, thereby preventing any examination for signs of physical torture. After a careful investigation that pieced together a coherent account of this case, Amnesty International concluded that the charges against the so-called PRP has been fabricated, just as a 1964 prosecution of the same group had been.[24]

Because of the outcry in Korea and abroad against those judicial murders—even the normally timid U.S. Department of State protested—and because resort to courts martial for punishing civilians is generally unattractive, military tribunals did not subsequently play a large role in Park's continuing rule by emergency decree. Yet, the regular courts that had to deal with subsequent political prosecutions behaved in a most irregular fashion. This was demonstrated by the trial of Kim Dae Jung and the 17 other prestigious leaders who, on 1 March 1976, issued a declaration of national conscience calling upon President Park to resign and restore democratic government. The March First Group was immediately prosecuted for violating Emergency Decree No. 9, a Draconian catch-all that prohibited "disseminating falsehood," opposing the new constitution that guaranteed Park's one-man rule, and "publicly defaming" the emergency decree itself.[25] The three levels of judicial proceedings that resulted in long prison sentences for the principal "offenders," and even longer deprivations of political and civil rights for virtually all, mocked minimal standards of fairness.

Although the accused and their families demanded an open and free trial, the admission of friends and relatives was restricted to limited numbers of ticket holders, and the trial was conducted in what the *Washington Post* reporter on the scene called "an atmosphere of intimidation and hostility."[26] Since the defendants were charged with disseminating "groundless rumors" and misrepresenting facts, they sought to call a variety of witnesses to demonstrate the truth of what they had stated, but the court permitted only three. The only defense witness allowed to testify in support of their statements on the economy was taken to the KCIA office prior to his court appearance; by the time he testified, he had become a prosecution witness. This economist, who had often criticized the regime's reliance upon foreign lenders and investors, dropped his head and kept silent when questioned by the defense. Frustrated by the court's refusal to allow the testimony and documentary evidence they sought to introduce, and also frustrated by the regime's refusal to allow them freely to confer with the defendants who were in detention, defense attorneys finally walked out in protest.

The bizarre nature of the trial is best illustrated by the fact that the accused were not permitted to challenge the validity of the decree they were charged with violating because, by its terms, it had prohibited judicial scrutiny. Moreover, despite the fact that the prosecutors were permitted to quote passages from the March First declaration to support their case, the defendants were precluded from showing why those statements were accurate. Nevertheless, in the hope of giving the appearance of a fair trial, the defendants were allowed to deliver long orations, often including opinions that would bring arrest outside the courtroom, since the court was confident that the heavily censored news media would give the public no hint of the views expressed. "These aren't legal proceedings," one diplomat declared. "They remind you of showcase trials in Communist countries."[27]

There was never any danger that the defendants' arguments might persuade the court. Not only were the judges precluded by law from considering challenges to the emergency decree itself, but Park's "revitalizing reforms" had also subjected the judiciary to a reappointment process that had long since screened out the less cooperative elements. Scores of judges had been purged, including 9 of the 10 Supreme Court judges who constituted the majority vote in a landmark decision that aroused Park's ire just before "revitalization."[28] Thus, one can well understand why the March First Group called for the creation of a judiciary truly independent of the political authorities and capable of protecting the people against tyranny.[29]

Denial of Freedoms of Expression

The March First Group also called, among other things, for rescission of the repressive "emergency decrees" without which Park apparently believed he could no longer rule: release of political prisoners; renewal of freedom of speech, press, and assembly; restoration of the legislative system that was abolished in 1972 in favor of Park's current parliamentary charade; and enjoyment by industrial and agricultural workers of the right to organize and strike. This implicitly suggested the lack of basic freedoms of expression. It also served as the foundation of the government prosecution of the group for violating Presidential Emergency Decree No. 9. Promulgated on 13 May 1975, that decree prohibited "fabricating or disseminating false rumors or misrepresenting facts" and "denying, opposing, misrepresenting, or defaming the Constitution; or asserting, petitioning, instigating, or propagandizing revision or repeal of the Constitution by means of assembly, demonstration, or through public media such as newspapers, broadcasts, or press services; or by other such means of expression such as writings, books, or recordings."[30] Also prohibited was any act openly defaming the emergency decree itself. Alleged violaters were subject to arrest, detention, confiscation, and search without a judicially approved warrant. Those convicted were to receive not less than one year in prison, and no maximum sentence was specified. They were also subject to suspension of civil rights, including the rights to run for office and to vote, for up to ten years.

Emergency Decree No. 9 was the capstone of an effort to suppress all dissenting views. It was surely not required in order to prohibit Communist or other revolutionary activity, for such acts had long been banned by formally enacted legislation that was itself of an all-encompassing type. The National Security Law, enacted shortly after Park's 1961 coup, mandated harsh felony punishments for "[a]ny person who has organized an association or group for the purpose of . . . disturbing the state" or who prepared or conspired to do so.[31] Such "anti-state organizations," if they "operate along the lines of the Communists," were further dealt with in the companion Anti-Communist Law. That legislation provided up to seven years at hard labor for "[a]ny person who has praised, encouraged, or sided with anti-state organizations or members thereof on foreign Communist lines or benefited the same in any way through other means."[32]

The only requirement for conviction under the Anti-Communist Law was that the conduct in question be deemed to have benefited an anti-state organization. No subjective intention on the part of the actor to aid such an organization need be proved. In these circumstances, as the Amnesty International report pointed out, "any dissent is capable of being characterized as a benefit to an anti-State organization,"[33] an assessment vindicated by the government's conviction under this law of the courageous lawyer Han Sŭng-hŏn, for publishing an essay that opposed the death penalty as morally indefensible, and of the poet Kim Chi-ha, for stating that the government neglected the rights of the poor and under-privileged and that the KCIA used torture to extract false confessions.

The Kim Chi-ha case is a good example of how, under the Anti-Communist Law, criticism of violence was regarded as more subversive than advocacy of violence. Because so much of the Park regime's power rested upon the apparatus of violence—the KCIA, the Army Counterintelligence Corps, the police, and the Capital Guard Division—to criticize violence was to challenge the existence of the regime. Thus, as Kim Chi-ha discovered, one could talk about torture only on pain of oneself suffering further torture and punishment. Kim, whose death sentence was commuted to life imprisonment thanks to outraged public opinion at home and abroad, was subsequently released. But, when he exposed the torture inflicted upon the defendants in the "People's Revolutionary Party" case, his life sentence was revived, and he was sentenced to an additional seven years in prison, where with but brief interruption he remained in complete isolation, unable to have even toilet paper because he once used this material to record a statement which was then smuggled out and published. By revealing the torture of the alleged PRP members, he was found to have benefited a supposedly "anti-state organization." Moreover, anyone who had "praised, encouraged, or sided with" Kim Chi-ha ran the risk of a similar conviction.

Another example of resort to the Anti-Communist Law to suppress expression is the 1978 conviction of purged university professors Paek Nak-ch'ŏng and Yi Yŏng-hŭi for having published a translation of a volume of academic essays on China by respected Western scholars, including Harvard professors John K. Galbraith and Ross Terrill. The defendants were sentenced to terms of hard labor for "inciting" sympathy for Peking and "praising" the Chinese Communist revolution, but it seemed clear that the real reason for their conviction was that they had both consistently published criticism that offended the government.[34]

Emergency Decree No. 9 went one step further than the Anti-Communist Law. It eliminated even the objective requirement of proving that the conduct in question benefited an anti-state organization. If any person simply spoke out against Park's "revitalizing reforms," advocated revision of the *Yusin Constitution,* or criticized the emergency decree, he or she could be convicted and sentenced to long deprivation of freedom and loss of political and civil rights,[35] as were Kim Dae Jung and other democratic leaders for precisely such statements.

Having "legally" suppressed all forms of expression at home in an effort to prevent domestically inspired political change, the Park regime also sought to suppress Koreans' expression abroad in order to deny foreigners access to unfavorable facts and opinions concerning the regime and thereby to reduce external pressures for change. In March 1975, Park had a captive National Assembly pass a new law creating the crime of "slander against the state." Article 104, Section 2, of the Criminal Code now provided:

All Koreans who commit the following crimes outside of the country will be liable to sentences of up to seven years of imprisonment: slandering any national body which has been established by the Constitution or spreading rumors or distorting facts about any such body; also all other activities which may harm the welfare and interest of or defame the Republic of Korea.[36]

The new law also prohibited Koreans from committing such acts inside their country in association with foreigners or foreign organizations and provided up to ten year's suspension of civil rights for any violator. It is remarkable that a regime that so often claimed that it sought to inform foreign audiences about Korea, that it wished foreign news agencies would report more accurately, and that it welcomed visitors who sought the truth should go so far to frustrate attainment of those goals. Moreover, in late 1977, Park's National Assembly adopted a law authorizing confiscation of the property of overseas Koreans whose words or written work had benefited an "anti-state organization" and who declined to return to Korea in response to a prosecutor's summons.[37] As a Korean journalist told a visiting American who asked whether he had any message for the people of the United States: "Just say that by law, now, we are not allowed to discuss our country with foreigners. That should tell them enough."[38]

The effective suppression of dissent during the Yusin period was far more than a matter of criminal legislation and prosecution, or even of resort to occasional mysterious deaths and widespread detention and torture. By a comprehensive program of administrative measures—some authorized by legislation, others covert—the Park regime imposed increasingly severe restraints upon such pluralistic elements as the highly centralized society possessed. The Park Government curbed the independence of the legal profession as well as that of the courts.[39] Journalists were equally unsuccessful in resisting suppression.[40] The regime also increasingly tightened its grip upon the universities, while trying to develop a new Yusin ideology of "Korean-style democracy" to replace the democratic ideals upon which the R.O.K. was founded. Park used both the carrot and the stick in an effort to achieve conformity among faculty and students.[41] The government also had to devote extraordinary attention to muzzling Protestant and Catholic religious leaders, many of whom were among the most unyielding critics of repression.[42] Although defenders of Park's repression often sought to give the impression that the only people affected by denials of human rights were politicians, intellectuals, journalists, judges, lawyers, and Christians—with the last especially portrayed as a tiny elite unrepresentative of the populace at large—this was refuted by the regime's obstruction of efforts by factory employees to organize unions, bargain collectively, and resort to strikes in the hope of improving minimal wages and working conditions in an economy that needed to rely on cheap labor to lure foreign investments and boost exports.[43]

THE YUSIN SYSTEM

An initial reading of the Yusin Constitution of 1972 seemed to suggest support for many basic human rights.[44] The chapter on the rights and duties of citizens opened with a ringing declaration that "[a]ll citizens shall be assured dignity and value of human beings, and it shall be the duty of the State to guarantee such fundamental rights of the people to the utmost."[45] And there were reassuringly unqualified provisions that "[a]ll citizens shall enjoy personal liberty,"[46] and "[n]o citizen shall be tortured or compelled to testify against himself in criminal cases."[47] Nevertheless, a number of specific guarantees were qualified on their face. Freedoms of speech, press, assembly, and association were promised "except as provided by law," and "[t]he right to association, collective bargaining, and collective action of workers shall be guaranteed within the scope defined by law."[48] Laws restricting all freedoms and rights might be enacted "when necessary for the maintenance of national security, order, or public welfare."[49] Moreover, whenever the president merely "anticipated" a threat to the national security or public safety and order, the new Constitution authorized him to take emergency measures to "temporarily suspend the freedom and rights of the people prescribed in this Constitution" and disallowed any judicial review of presidential actions.[50] And, in similar circumstances, the Constitution also authorized the president to declare martial law and take special measures suspending basic rights.[51]

Even Korean constitutional-law scholars confessed that the Yusin governmental form eluded definition. One called it "Leadership Presidency";[52] another, "Presidential Absolutism," a kind of "republican monarchy" that "has boldly put an end to the past oscillation between the classical presidential and parliamentary systems."[53] Professor Han T'ae-yŏn, a co-drafter, was surprisingly straightforward in his treatment of "the nature of the government form" under the Constitution: It remains a presidential form of government, "albeit in an adulterated form ... the concentration of power in the presidency inevitably entails the personalization of political power."[54]

Even more disturbing, of course, was the fact that the Park regime systematically acted in violation of those constitutional norms that on paper it claimed to respect. Finally, the Yusin constitutional system not only frustrated any legitimate challenge to Park's monopoly of political and lawmaking powers, but also condemned as illegal and unconstitutional any peaceful attempt to alter the system. In these circumstances, comparisons with the theory and practice of constitutionalism in the Communist world were inevitable.

THE TRANSITION FROM PARK TO CHUN

In South Korea, the 1980s began on 26 October 1979 when Kim Chae-kyu, Director of the Korean Central Intelligence Agency (KCIA), shot and killed President Park Chung Hee at a dinner party, putting an end to Park's lifetime presidency.

The shortcomings of the Yusin system and the problems of U.S. human-rights and security policy toward Korea were highlighted by the assassination and the political events of succeeding months which brought an end to the Yusin system and saw the introduction of the even more tightly controlled political system of Chun Doo Hwan. Park's assassination was closely related to the growing crisis in human rights and to the existence of varying strategies within the government for dealing with these developments.

Prior to the summer of 1979, the Park Government had been successfully able to deal separately with the political opposition—"legal" and "illegal"—and the growing labor problems. The growth of both was directly related to South Korea's burgeoning industrialization and urbanization. The Yusin coup itself had been intended to redress the growing demographic edge that urbanization brought to the numerical strength of the New Democratic Party (NDP), just as the tough labor laws and harsh tactics of the government during the 1970s had supplanted the relatively more liberal labor policies of the 1960s.

When the NDP invited female workers of the bankrupt Y.H. Industrial Company to use party headquarters for a sit-down strike, the government was faced with a real possibility that these two significant groups might join forces in opposing the government. When 1,000 riot police armed with clubs and shields invaded the building at 2 A.M. on 11 August, they seriously beat a number of NDP National Assembly members, party staffers, reporters, and union members. One woman worker, Kim Kyong-suk, died during the melee in an as yet unexplained fall from a fourth-floor window.[55] As the crisis escalated, on 4 October NDP leader Kim Young Sam was expelled from the National Assembly and the NDP members resigned en masse in protest. Subsequently, riots erupted in Pusan and Masan, and serious disagreement grew within high counsels of the government as to whether increasingly harsh measures of suppression should be used. These disputes led to Kim Chae-kyu's assassination of Park and the eventual seizure of power by General Chun Doo Hwan.

In the relatively liberal atmosphere that prevailed in the period after the assassination, it became apparent that opposition was by no means limited to a "small group of Westernized, Christian intellectuals," as Park's apologists had often charged. According to a national opinion survey by the Social Science Research Institute of Seoul National University—the first poll of its kind since 1972—72.8 percent of the respondents felt that "democratization" was more important than "economic development." That the Korean people could sustain a democracy was the belief of 89.2 percent. "Expansion of human rights and freedom" was regarded as the most important aspect of political development by 23.3 percent, "strengthening national security" by 20 percent, "social justice through fair distribution" by 15.4 percent, and the independence of the legislature and judiciary by 12 percent.[56]

Even President Ch'oe Kyu-ha, who as Prime Minister at the time of the assassination succeeded Park, agreed that the Constitution had to be amended and promised that he would promote freedom. On 7 December, he rescinded Emergency Decree No. 9, the 1975 presidential decree banning all criticism of the Yusin Constitution, and released 68 political prisoners held under it.[57] December also saw the release of the 5 prominent democratic leaders and 3 union members arrested in connection with the Y.H. Incident.

This is not to say that all restrictions on public debate were removed. In late November, Ham Sŏk-hŏn and 122 others were arrested for a peaceful protest against indirect presidential elections. There were credible allegations that at least 20 of them were systematically beaten at the Army Security Command Headquarters.[58]

On the night of 12 December 1979, General Chun took several thousand troops from the area between Seoul and the Demilitarized Zone and used them to stage an intra-military putsch, which resulted in several deaths and the arrest of between 30 and 40 senior generals, including the martial-law commander, Chŏng Sŭng-hwa, who was accused of complicity in the assassination of Park. Chun's brother-in-law, General Yi Hŭi-sŭng, was named martial-law commander. The troops were under the operational control of the United States-Republic of Korea (R.O.K.) Combined Forces Command formally under the authority of General John Wickham, the highest ranking U.S. officer in Korea. He apparently had no foreknowledge and was reportedly furious about this violation of the chain of command.

Although there was general speculation that the 12 December action was the first step in an attempt by Chun to move into the place of President Park, the participants described the incident as an action necessary to get to the bottom of the assassination and to eliminate corruption in the military. For some months Chun and his colleagues made no further public moves.

During the early months of 1980, many groups made proposals for constitutional revision. Most drafts called for a parliamentary form of government and strengthened protection for basic human rights. Public debate was vigorous and was widely covered by the press, despite the fact that the nation had been placed under a limited form of martial law immediately after the assassination. Some of those described as "Yusin Remnants"—holdovers from Park's Democratic Republican Party—argued for the Yusin Constitution. Many who had openly opposed Park argued that the *Yusin Constitution* should be replaced quickly with a constitution based on popular consensus. In the National Assembly, a joint committee equally representing Park's party, the Democratic Republican Party (DRP), and the NDP set about drafting a new constitution. The Assembly draft was made public in early May.

During this period, three major political figures emerged in opposition. One was Kim Dae Jung, who had run against Park in the 1971 election and became well-known internationally in 1973 when he was kidnaped from Tokyo and nearly killed by the KCIA. Kim had spent most of the time since 1973 in prison or under house arrest. His political and civil rights remained suspended until 29 February 1980. Another was Kim Young Sam, who as head of the NDP played a major role in the events preceding Park's assassination. The third was Kim Jong Pil, who was the planner of the 1961 coup, the founder of both the KCIA and the DRP, and a major figure of the Park years.

Under the martial-law decree, labor activity was even more restricted legally than it had been before the assassination; now permission from the martial-law authorities was required for all assemblies.[59] Nevertheless, in an atmosphere in which most people assumed there would soon be a more democratic government, the pent-up demands of the workers burst forth in numerous strikes calling for wage increases, improved working conditions, and an end to repressive labor laws and KCIA interference. By May, there had been more than 700 labor disputes. Workers demanded wage increases of as much as 50 percent, and management conceded average increases of 25 percent.[60] In the most serious incident, 3,000 miners in Sabuk went on a rampage and seized the Kangwŏn province town of 52,000 after their union president agreed to a 20-percent wage increase instead of the 42 percent the union had demanded. Armed with dynamite and rifles, the miners battled the police and ransacked company officials' homes. The miners were subsequently put down by force and coerced into accepting the 20-percent increase, but it was made retroactive for four months and they were promised a bonus.[61] Most disputes, however, did not become violent and remained on company property. Despite the fact that such labor actions were illegal, the *New York Times* reported, "'The government seems to have an unstated policy that these [strikes] are all right so long as they do not disturb the social order.'"[62] Strikers and business agreed that the lack of government intervention on behalf of business was a key reason that workers, after years of tight control, chose this method to make their demands.[63]

As winter turned to spring, demonstrations began on the university campuses over issues of campus democracy. Students called for voluntary student organizations with elected officers to replace the organizations school administrations had set up and staffed with hand-picked appointees. They demanded an end to the KCIA presence on campus and the dismissal of administrators and professors who had advanced themselves by supporting Park's dictatorship. On 16 April, Chun appointed himself acting director of the KCIA, despite a provision in the governing law prohibiting a military man on active duty as director. This action provoked much criticism, especially on the campuses.

Beginning in May, campus demonstrations increased dramatically. Students were calling for an end to martial law; the dismissal of Chun, President Ch'oe, and Prime Minister Sin Hyŏn-hwak; the prompt drafting of a new constitution; and early elections. The students announced that they would take to the streets on 15 May if martial law had not been lifted by that time, and they did so in great numbers. As many as 100,000 students demonstrated in downtown Seoul on the 15th. They were met with tear gas. Riot police equipped with gas masks, shields, and clubs attacked the students, beating many. Hundreds were injured. Many were arrested.

As 22 May, the date for the opening of the National Assembly, approached, both major parties announced that they were prepared to vote to end martial law. On the evening of 15 May, Prime Minister Sin issued a special appeal to the students, asking for time and promising to take their demands into consideration. The students responded by calling off demonstrations, and on 16 May they were back in their classes. Student leaders met to discuss the situation. On 17 May, an expanded, nationwide martial law was declared. All political activity was prohibited, the National Assembly was dissolved, censorship was imposed on the press and media, all colleges and universities were closed, strikes were banned, and it was forbidden to be absent from work "without a good reason."[64] Student leaders were arrested en masse; Kim Dae Jung and many of his followers and associates were rounded up; and Kim Young Sam was placed under house arrest. Public discussion of political issues, including a new constitution and elections, ceased.

When demonstrations against the new martial-law decree broke out on 18 May in Kwangju, a city of 800,000 in Kim Dae Jung's home province in southwestern Korea, instead of riot police Chun sent paratroopers—not under the Combined Forces Command—to put down the demonstrators. When the paratroopers brutally attacked the peaceful demonstrators, allegedly bayoneting some to death, the populace arose and drove out the troops. Chun sent regular Army units, released on 16 May from the operational control of the Combined Forces Command shortly before the declaration of martial law, to surround and, later, retake the city by force. During the ten days before the Army retook the city, the citizens broadcast appeals for United States mediation, but the U.S. Department of State did not respond.[65] By official count, 191 people were killed in the Kwangju Incident, including 23 soldiers and 4 police officers; 122 persons were wounded and 730 were slightly injured. Responsible private estimates, however, put the number of civilian dead as high as 1,200 with many more injured or missing.[66] Ten years after the events, the circumstances of the transfer of the operational control of the troops used in retaking Kwangju remained under dispute, and many critics continued to assert that the U.S. government shared in the responsibility for the suppression there.

During an ensuing series of "purification" drives, 10 important political figures connected with the Park Government, including Kim Jong Pil, were arrested and accused of enriching themselves by abusing their positions. In June, they were released without being prosecuted in return for a promise to resign all public positions and "return" about $147 million (85.3 billion *wŏn*) in "illegally-amassed wealth."[67] Several hundred high government officials and about 8,000 lower officials and employees of banks and state-owned enterprises were purged. Newspapers, under strict military censorship, were also forced to fire about 400 reporters. One hundred and seventy-two periodicals, including prestigious intellectual journals, were deprived of their licenses to publish.[68] Some 37,000 "hoodlums" were rounded up for re-education in military camps. Although the "purification" drives created much outrage and fear, they also elicited some popular support, because of built-up resentment against corruption.

On 8 August, an unnamed high-ranking U.S. military officer was quoted in the *Los Angeles Times* to the effect that the United States government had decided to support Chun Doo Hwan as the R.O.K.'s next president:

[A]sked whether the United States would support Chon [*sic*] as president even if his present policies of political suppression and a lack of broad political participation in government continue[d], [h]e replied, "Yes, provided that he comes to power legitimately and demonstrates, over time, a broad base of support from the Korean people and does not jeopardize the security situation . . . here—we will support him, because that, of course, is what we think the Korean people want." Saying Chon had come to power "legitimately," the U.S. military official made it clear the United States was asking that constitutional requirements be observed in form but not in substance.[69]

The military official also indicated that Chun might soon replace President Ch'oe Kyu-ha as President "in name as well as in fact."

In the same interview, the U.S. military official was quoted as saying:

Peace and stability are important to the United States here, and national security and internal stability surely come before political liberalization. . . . I'm not sure democracy the way we understand it is ready for Korea or the Koreans ready for it. . . . Korea seems to need a strong leader. For a variety of reasons, many of them rather curious, Chon seems to have emerged as a leader, an unnatural one— but nonetheless a leader. And lemming-like [sic], the people are kind of lining up behind him in all walks of life.

The following day Chun identified the high-ranking military official to a *New York Times* reporter as General John Wickham.[70]

These comments were widely quoted in the South Korean and American press. The coverage they received in South Korea was particularly extensive:

Beginning with Friday's evening editions and running through Sunday morning, newspapers in Seoul established what may be a record in world journalism. For two days, every newspaper published the same news story—written in one or the other of two interviews' versions—as the top item of the day. Not even newspapers in Communist countries have done that. Operating under both South Korean military censorship and military orders specifying what news should be emphasized, the phenomenon had significance that extended beyond journalism.[71]

A week later, President Ch'oe resigned and, on 27 August, Chun had himself elected president under the *Yusin Constitution* until an election could be held under a revised constitution.

On 14 August, after being held incommunicado for more than two months and questioned for as long as fifteen hours a day, Kim Dae Jung and his 23 associates were put on trial on charges including violation of the martial-law decrees, conspiring to foment revolution, and formation of an anti-state organization.[72] On 17 September, the court martial sentenced Kim to death and his codefendants to sentences of from two years to life.[73]

There was a strong international reaction, especially in Japan, where popular resentment over the 1973 kidnaping persisted. The Japanese government was alarmed that the prosecution of Kim violated the "political settlement" reached between the two governments shortly after the kidnaping. According to that agreement, Japan would not pursue charges that the R.O.K. had violated its sovereignty provided that Kim was granted the right to travel to Japan and was not charged for any of his activities in Japan prior to his abduction.[74]

In the indictment, Kim was accused of founding and heading the Hanmint'ong, a group of Korean residents in Japan who opposed the Park Government and supported Kim. In 1978, the R.O.K. Supreme Court ruled that the Hanmint'ong was an anti-state organization, and it was referred to as such in the indictment. The only direct connection Kim had had with the Hanmint'ong was to participate in initial organizational activities in Japan before he was kidnaped. Aware of the Japanese government's alarm that Kim's prosecution might violate the "political settlement," the R.O.K. government at first maintained that the parts of the indictment discussing Kim's activities in Japan were only included as background and then intimated that the National Security Law charge had been dropped. This was not true; the only charge against Kim that carried the death penalty was that based on Article 1 of the National Security Law—forming and being the ringleader of an anti-state organization. Although the Japanese government did not make any official protest against this violation of the "political settlement," it did suspend aid and made it clear that Kim's execution would force the reevaluation of its relations with the R.O.K.[75]

The question of Kim's death sentence permeated U.S.-R.O.K. relations throughout the fall of 1980 and into early 1981. Although a State Department spokesman had earlier characterized the charges against Kim as "far-fetched," the Carter Administration cautiously expressed its "intense interest and deep concern," for fear that too strong a reaction might increase the likelihood of the sentence's being carried out.[76] The Chun Government knew that the Carter Administration would react strongly to Kim's execution and, even before the U.S. presidential election, the likelihood that Kim would actually be executed was greatly lessened when Ronald Reagan indicated that, if he were elected, he also would react strongly. The issue was defused on 24 January 1981 when, in a bargain with the United States, Kim's death sentence was commuted and reduced to a life sentence.

This announcement was made twenty-four hours after it was announced that Chun would be the first foreign head of state to be received by President Reagan. On 25 January, Chun decreed an end to martial law and designated 25 February as the date for presidential elections under the new Constitution, a document that had been drawn up secretly and ratified in a referendum on 22 October 1980, without opportunity for substantial debate.

On 25 February, after a campaign in which his forthcoming trip to Washington was prominently featured, Chun was elected President by the approximately 5,000-member electoral college established by the new Constitution. The vote was unanimous except for 2 ballots that were declared invalid.

Chun's election to the presidency under the new Constitution completed the process of the transition from Park to Chun. However, Chun continued to face serious questions about the legitimacy of his government because he came to power by the use of force and was considered by many to be responsible for the killings in Kwangju. During the Park years, it had been considered axiomatic that "even the death of a single student can bring about the fall of a government."[77] The legitimacy problem was compounded by problems in the economy, financial scandals involving people close to the President and his wife, and the continued inability of the government to provide ways for people to express views that didn't coincide with the government's. The U.S. State Department report on human rights in the R.O.K. for 1983 diplomatically avoided reference to the deaths in Kwangju and the economic problems but nevertheless pointed out that there was a legitimacy problem:

Governmental legitimacy in Korea derives from the ruler's ability to preserve national security, promote prosperity, maintain domestic harmony, and, increasingly to reflect the popular will in questions of public policy. The current government, which assumed power with primarily military support in 1980, has had problems with the last two points; hence to many Koreans the degree of legitimacy it enjoys is still open to question.[78]

HUMAN RIGHTS UNDER THE GOVERNMENT OF CHUN DOO HWAN, 1980–1987

The human-rights situation in the Republic of Korea remained as bad or worse during the early years of the Chun Government as in the last years of the Park Government. The State Department estimated the number of political prisoners to be 325 at the end of 1983, despite the fact that about 80 political prisoners were released in 1982 and about

300 were released in 1983. According to the report, this represents "about a 15-percent decrease from the comparable 1982 figure," but the report for 1982 states that there were between 300 and 400 political prisoners in that year, which makes it hard to determine how the "decrease" was calculated.[79] Such a "decrease" can be achieved in a situation where so many political prisoners have been released only by replacing those released with new ones. The number of political prisoners in South Korea during the second half of 1977 was generally estimated at 200 to 250.[80] At the end of 1978, the Department of State estimate was 180 to 220 and that of church groups in South Korea about 280. The number of political prisoners had obviously decreased from the levels it reached in 1980 and 1981 during the process of the military takeover and consolidation, but it was higher in 1983 than it had been in 1977 and 1978.

The Constitution of the Fifth Republic appeared to afford greater protection than the *Yusin Constitution* for some rights.[81] For example, in Article 11 habeas corpus and the exclusion of coerced confessions from evidence were guaranteed as they had been before the *Yusin Constitution*. The restrictive clause "except as provided by law" was removed from the guarantees of freedom of residence, occupation, correspondence, speech, assembly, and association. The phrase "within the scope provided by law" was stricken from the guarantees of labor's rights to organize and bargain collectively, although not from the most important right—the right to take collective action.

These protections were largely rendered hollow by laws passed by the Legislative Council for National Security (LCNS) which, according to Article 6(1) of the Supplementary Provisions of the Constitution, "shall assume and exercise the functions of the National Assembly from the date this Constitution enters into force to the day prior to the first convening of the National Assembly under this Constitution." The Constitution did not provide a mechanism for choosing the members of the LCNS, and they were apparently selected by President Chun. The enactments of the LCNS are of particular importance because Article 6(3) of the Supplementary Provisions of the Constitution stated "Laws legislated by the [LCNS] . . . shall remain valid, and may not be litigated or disputed for reasons of this Constitution or other reasons." Under these provisions, as a State Department report noted:

In preparation for lifting martial law in January 1981, the legislature [LCNS] enacted 189 laws that profoundly affected the political system. Election laws were promulgated, sharply limiting political organizing and campaigning. Other laws established strict government control over the press, public assembly and demonstrations, and labor organizations. The security services were reorganized and the police and security agencies were given power to suppress social and civil disturbances that the government believed could endanger national security.[82]

Even more important than these legal restrictions on rights apparently given unqualified guarantee by the Constitution was the fact that practice often simply ignored the Constitution. In this, as in other respects, there was considerable continuity with the preceding Park government.

The most glaring example was torture or other harsh treatment by police or security agencies, practiced frequently under both governments. Freedom from torture is widely recognized as one of the most basic human rights. Article 5 of the Universal Declaration of Human Rights provides: "No one shall be subjected to torture or to cruel, inhuman, or degrading treatment or punishment." The Declaration recognizes no instance in which torture is justifiable. Article 10(2) of the *Yusin Constitution* stated: "No citizen shall be tortured or be compelled to testify against himself in criminal cases." Nevertheless, while the *Yusin Constitution* was still in effect under martial law, Kim Dae Jung and his co-defendants were held incommunicado for more than two months and questioned for up to fifteen hours a day throughout this period. All 23 of the defendants in the case repudiated their confessions at the trial.[83] Kim testified, "'Sometimes my clothes were stripped off' and the questioners 'stopped just short of torture' . . . 'I was extremely tired mentally as well as physically, so I signed some statements against my will, thinking I could deny them in court.'"[84] A number of the other defendants testified at the trial that they had made or signed statements only because they had been severely beaten.[85] The allegations, though credible, and in the case of incommunicado detention incontrovertible, were ignored by the court in rendering its decision.

The torture alleged in this prominent case was not unusual. Torture also was widely alleged in political cases under martial law.[86] At least 200 students, journalists, and others who were active and outspoken following Park's assassination were arrested after 17 May; in most cases their interrogations were allegedly carried out under torture. In the most extreme case, Reverend Im Ki-yun died in July 1980 after being interrogated by the military authorities for a week.[87]

Article 11(2) of the new Constitution guaranteed freedom from torture in the same words as the *Yusin Constitution*, but Article 11(6) strengthened the guarantee by adding:

> In case a confession is determined to have been made against a defendant's will by means of torture, violence, intimidation, unduly prolonged arrest, deceit, etc., or in case a confession is the only evidence against a defendant, such a confession shall not be admitted as evidence toward a conviction nor shall punishment be meted out on the basis of such a confession.

In spite of this restoration of an earlier constitutional safeguard excluding coerced confessions, in many political and politically sensitive trials after the new Constitution went into effect, including the prosecution of those accused of the 1982 arson at the U.S. Cultural Center in Pusan, serious allegations of torture made by defendants on the stand were ignored by the courts.[88]

The several hundred students detained annually by the Chun Government for demonstrating are generally believed to have been routinely subjected to beatings at police stations.[89] In 1982, there were several allegations of torture-related deaths. "An unemployed politician, Kim Chong-do, claimed, in a letter dictated from a hospital shortly before his death there, that the police had beaten him for five days to extract a confession, and that those beatings and poor medical treatment were responsible for his serious condition."[90] In the other case, Pak Kwan-hyŏn is alleged to have died in October after leading a hunger strike in Kwangju Prison to protest having been tortured.[91]

"[D]etainees about to be released [are] routinely required to sign a statement that they have not been tortured during their incarceration; thus, reports of torture are difficult to confirm or dismiss."[92] Nevertheless, reports were consistent enough and numerous enough that most observers believed the practice to be widespread.

The belief that torture was a common practice was so widespread that even the controlled press raised the question "When will the torture stop?" In a 1981 murder case without political overtones, a conviction was overturned on the ground that the only evidence was a coerced confession. In 1982, in four widely publicized non-political criminal cases, the courts found the defendants had been tortured and rejected their confessions. In several of the cases, this resulted in an acquittal. In one case, a suspect was freed after the Minister of Home Affairs admitted before the National Assembly that the police had tortured him.[93]

In 1984 the Department of State reported:

Accusations of torture diminished in 1983 compared to past years. . . . [but t]he use of excessive force by the police, despite high-level efforts to reduce or eliminate it, has proven to be a pervasive and ingrained problem. The most notable case in 1983 was the death in March of a business executive [Kim Kun-jo] in Pusan, following a beating by a police lieutenant who was interrogating him in a non-political case. The lieutenant was sentenced to seven years imprisonment and the Home Affairs Minister apologized and vowed to fire any policeman using similar tactics.[94]

Although the Chun Government appeared willing to punish the responsible official in a non-political matter such as the Kim Kun-jo case, there was little public debate about torture in political cases until near the end of Chun's term. In 1985 and 1986, international attention was drawn to the case of Kim Kŭn-t'ae, tortured into false confession while being interrogated under the National Security Act. The Seoul press, operating under strict government guidance, covered the subsequent lawsuit filed by Kim's relatives against the Home Minister and senior police officials.[95] The domestic press also covered the aftermath of the June 1986 incident in which a policeman beat and sexually tortured a labor organizer, Kwŏn In-suk. After extensive legal maneuvering, the policeman involved was sentenced to five years in prison and the state was assessed a civil penalty of $45,000.[96] Finally, there was widespread public outcry and press reportage, often in violation of government guidelines, concerning a government cover-up in early 1987 following the January death of student activist Pak Chong-ch'ŏl during interrogation by police officers.[97] Negative public reaction to this incident as well as to issues of constitutional reform played an important part in precipitating the political crisis of June 1987, discussed in the next chapter.

Although freedoms of assembly and association were flatly guaranteed by the Fifth Republic Constitution (Article 20[1]), the Law on Assemblies and Demonstrations, which was already strict but was made even stricter by the LCNS in December 1980, prohibited specified categories of assembly, including those considered most likely to undermine public order or cause social unrest. . . . Under this law, police have at times intervened, as in June 1983 when they entered a Protestant church at the end of a student meeting, maltreated participants, and damaged the church. The government later apologized. The law also requires that demonstrations of all types and outdoor political assemblies be reported in advance to the police. Violation of the law carries a maximum sentence of seven years or a fine of about $3,750. Prior to the December 1983 amnesty, approximately 250 persons, or more than half of all Korea's "prisoners of conscience" were imprisoned for violation of this law; typically, such persons were [student demonstrators]. . . . In 1983, the courts grew harsher in punishing violations of [this law]; whereas in 1982 most violators received 12 to 18 month sentences, in 1983 sentences of two to three years were more common.[98]

Freedoms of speech and press also were guaranteed by the Constitution (Article 20[1]). In practice, however, the expression of opposition points of view was severely limited. During the Park years, tens of journalists were imprisoned and hundreds lost their jobs for practicing independent journalism. Under General Chun's 1980 interregnum, the martial-law authorities continued this pattern by incarcerating journalists, forcing newspapers to fire almost 400 reporters, and closing down 172 periodicals. The mass media were then "reorganized." Several private broadcasting systems "voluntarily" merged with the government system. The Christian Broadcasting System was forced to stop broadcasting news and advertisements. The several private news services were merged into one headed by the former Minister of Culture and Information, greatly diminishing the variety of news sources available.[99]

Overt censorship ended with the abrogation of martial law in February 1981, but the new arrangements coupled with involuntary self-censorship give the government firm control over the press. According to the State Department, "The domestic media engage in self-censorship, according to guidelines the Government regularly issues to editors. Journalists who ignore these guidelines or go too far in their criticism have been picked up for questioning, and there has occasionally been government pressure on their employers to fire them."[100] In 1982, two editors of a Seoul newspaper were allegedly "arrested and tortured for printing material considered critical of President Chun."[101]

The effectiveness of this system of self-censorship was illustrated in May 1982 when, for several weeks, the media did not mention the fact that a key figure in the "curb-market scandal" was the President's wife's uncle, Yi Kyu-gwang. The fact that Yi was related to the President's wife was widely known already. Therefore, once it became clear that he was involved in the scandal, it was necessary to control the damage by allowing the press to mention his name and relationship to the President and then assert that Yi was not receiving special treatment because of it. Since one of President Chun's major themes on taking power had been "purification" of corruption, this was an extremely sore point.

Former NDP leader Kim Young Sam's 1983 hunger strike provided another illustration of the effectiveness of the system of press control. "This strike went unreported in the Korean media except for vague and veiled references for more than three weeks until the man concerned was released from house arrest and ended his hunger strike. When the press finally did carry the story, it was done just once in all papers, under very specific guidelines."[102]

The Chun Government feared freedom of the press for literature as well as for journalism. For example, in June 1982, the authorities seized and shredded the as-yet unsold 6,000 of the 10,000 copies printed of a new edition of some poems of the well-known Kim Chi-ha shortly after it was published. It also suppressed a novel, *Taesol "Nam"* by the same author, published in December 1982.

The Constitution specifically guaranteed academic freedom (Article 21) as well as the closely related freedoms of expression and conscience (Article 21). Nevertheless, in practice they were severely restricted. Academics were no freer than journalists or novelists to write or speak about sensitive topics. It was also quite unsafe to say anything critical of the government in the classroom, since the campuses were thoroughly infiltrated with informers and plainclothesmen. Every professor was familiar with the fate of others who had been dismissed for their writings or their outspokenness and, as a result, self-censorship was assiduously practiced in academia. The 86 professors dismissed for political reasons in 1980 remained out of work, although the Minister of Education, former Seoul National University president Kwŏn Yi-hyŏk, announced in December 1983 that they would be allowed to return to teaching but only at universities other than those from which they were dismissed.

The limited nature of intellectual debate on matters of the greatest importance to the future of the country was well illustrated by a case involving two of these dismissed professors, noted historian Kang Man-kil and former journalist and journalism professor Yi Yŏng-hŭi. Along with Reverend Cho Sŭng-hyŏk of the Korea Christian Social Problems Research Center, they were detained at the end of 1983 and formally arrested on 10 January 1984 on suspicion of violating the National Security Law.

Cho was accused of "organiz[ing]" primary-and secondary-school teachers . . . into a group to analyze national unification issues as presented in school social-studies textbooks and also to criticize the government's policy on unification."[103] Cho was said to view "the government's unification policy as a scheme to perpetuate the division of Korea . . . [and to prefer] the North Korean-proposed Koryŏ Confederation System as a reasonable approach to unification."[104] Kang and Yi were arrested for giving lectures to the group in which they were accused of describing North Korea's 1950 invasion of South Korea as "a legitimate anti-imperialism struggle to build the nation state," accepting the North Korean proposal for unification, and suggesting that South Korea must become a socialist state. All three of these men had long been critics of the government and had suffered for it. Kang was dismissed from Korea University and Yi from Hanyang University in 1980. Both Yi and Cho had been imprisoned in the past.

Given the serious nature of some of the charges against them, it was surprising that they were released "on probation" on 14 February, ostensibly because they had "confessed to the charges, repented, and pledged to follow the anti-Communist line in the future." The prosecution also indicated that there had been petitions on their behalf.[105] There are several possible explanations in addition to the official one. The prosecution may have decided that its case was so weak that it did not want to make it, even though it almost certainly could have won. The prosecution's purpose may have been only to cow the academic community, and it may have concluded there was no need to go further. Or the petitioners, which included many abroad, may have included the U.S. government or other foreign governments which the R.O.K. government did not wish to displease.

Students comprise the other major group in the academic community. A sizeable percentage feel themselves to be part of a long tradition of nationalist, patriotic student activism. The most striking manifestation of this tradition was the 1960 Student Revolution in which massive student demonstrations against a corrupt, dictatorial government sparked the overthrow of Syngman Rhee. Modern student activism, however, really began with the March First Independence Movement against Japanese rule in 1919 and has continued to the present. In a sense, students have seen, and continue to see, their role as that of the conscience of the nation struggling against dictatorial rule and corruption and for democracy and national dignity.

Park rightly feared student activism and directed many resources toward controlling or suppressing it. General Chun declared nationwide martial law on 17 May 1980, largely because of the massive student demonstrations occurring daily in downtown Seoul. Students also played an important role in the Kwangju Uprising. Many were arrested or dismissed from school after 17 May.

For some time thereafter, the campuses were relatively quiet, and some thought the student movement had died. In fact, however, it had gone underground and reorganized into smaller more radical groups prepared to carry out sudden, limited operations rather than massive protests.[106] There were some demonstrations in the fall of 1981, and the number gradually increased. Twenty-eight incidents were officially reported in the spring of 1982, 41 in the fall of 1982, and 128, involving the arrest of 226 students, in the spring of 1983.[107]

A major campus issue in these demonstrations was the graduation-quota system introduced by Minister of Education Yi Kyu-ho in 1981. This system required each university department to enroll 30 percent more students as freshmen than they would graduate and then "flunk out" the lowest 30 percent in the course of their studies. It was argued that this would raise the quality of education by forcing students to study harder. It is certainly true that the existing system in which everyone who entered graduated did not encourage some students to study hard. But the graduation-quota system did not require meeting a certain standard to graduate; it required that 30 percent not make it. Students strongly opposed this system and organized against it. Professors, administrators, and parents also opposed the system. In August 1983, the quota system was revised and virtually abolished.[108]

Beyond campus issues, the basic concern of the student movement had been a desire for democratization: constitutional revision providing for a popularly elected president, free elections, freedom of the press, academic freedom, a more equitable distribution of income, a cleaning up of corruption based on economic and political power, a less "dependent" form of economic development, and so forth. In a society dominated by a group based on military power, many students felt they had to strive for these ideals, which they believed most Koreans shared. The Chun Government and others argued that restriction of student activities is not the same as restriction of academic freedom because the role of students is to study, and not to make political demands. This argument was not convincing to those students passionately concerned about the welfare of the country who wanted to be able to read about, write about, and openly discuss forbidden or sensitive subjects, because they believed those subjects were important for the country.

In the fall of 1983, there were a great many demonstrations on campuses. In addition to protesting government interference with academic life and repressive government in general, as mentioned above, these demonstrators protested against U.S. support for the Chun Government, and specifically against President Reagan's visit to Seoul as a symbol of such U.S. support.

The demonstrations were put down with violence, for the most part by plainclothesmen called *chapsae*. The *chapsae* were not typical police undercover agents passing as students but hoodlums who took little trouble to be inconspicuous. When a demonstration started, they immediately gathered and attacked the students. During these demonstrations, many students were taken away; some were detained for some time; many were arrested.[109] Outside the gates of the universities on the routes toward the city, heavily equipped, uniformed riot police were assembled in great numbers to intervene if necessary and to see to it that demonstrations did not leave the campuses. The massive demonstration that students planned to stage in downtown Seoul the day before President Reagan's arrival could not materialize.

Several forms of punishment were used against student activists during the Chun years. Many were jailed, most for violation of the Law on Assemblies and Demonstrations. In 1983, before the year-end amnesty, approximately 250 people, mostly students, were in prison for violation of this law. In 1983, several hundred other students were punished by being drafted into the Army before finishing school.[110] The most common form of punishment for students was expulsion from school. Between 17 May 1980 and the end of 1983, a total of 1,363 students were expelled: 538 in 1980, 300 in 1981, 198 in 1982, and 327 in 1983.[111]

On 21 December, the Minister of Education announced that the 1,363 dismissed students could return to their schools if they repented their past "wrongdoings." Minister Kwŏn went on to say that the government would try to prevent campus unrest in the future "through persuasion and guidance . . . instead of resorting to punishment."[112] The Ministry also indicated that steps would be taken to help students who had been convicted or were awaiting trial. One hundred and thirty-one former students were affected by the amnesty of 22 December.[113] Forty-eight more were released on 8 February 1984. The formerly jailed students also were to be allowed to return to school if they repented.

This show of leniency did not defuse campus unrest. Student demonstrations continued through 1984, 1985, and 1986, steadily becoming more focused on political rather than campus issues and more anti-American in tone. Students threw themselves into the 1985 National Assembly election campaign with some effect, working for candidates such as Yi Ch'ŏl, a former student activist who had been sentenced to death during the Park era. They also played a major role in the 1986 series of New Korea Democratic Party rallies to amend the constitution to provide for direct presidential elections. The most notable of these was held in Inch'ŏn in May 1986 by the New Korea Democratic Party. It resulted in a violent clash between several thousand young people—students and workers—and the police. According to the police, the demonstrators started the trouble by throwing stones. According to the NKDP, however, the demonstrators fought back in response to an unprovoked police tear-gas attack. In an attempt to end the constitutional-amendment movement, the government exaggerated the severity of this incident, suggesting it was one of the worst since the establishment of the R.O.K. in 1948. The government also portrayed the incident as part of a plot to establish a leftist government through a violent uprising. Eventually, 129 people, including the well-known democratic activist Reverend Mun Ik-hwan, were arrested in connection with the Inchon Incident.

As has been the case throughout the history of the Republic of Korea, violent suppression of protest and exaggeration of the leftist threat soon led to greater protest. One of the more tragic developments of 1986 was a rash of at least 6 student suicides. In one case, a Seoul National University student shouted denunciations against domestic dictatorship and U.S. imperialism, set himself on fire, and jumped from a fourth floor balcony before a crowd of 3,000 assembled to hear Reverend Mun speak.[114]

This round of demonstrations culminated in a gathering of some 2,000 students from 26 universities at Kŏn'guk University in eastern Seoul on 28 October 1986. This demonstration lasted for four days before it was dramatically and violently ended by a police attack. The incident and its aftermath clarify the political situation in which the debate about constitutional revision was occurring.[115] The students, proclaiming themselves a "patriotic student committee against outside forces and dictatorship," burned effigies of President Reagan and Japanese Prime Minister Nakasone Yasuhiro. According to the police, the students also put up "seditious wall posters," including one describing the Korean War as "a pan-national struggle for liberation from . . . American imperialist rule over South Korea." A banner displayed on a building said, "Let's overthrow [the Chun regime?] and establish an independent government of the [Korean] people."[116]

After the initial demonstration, students trying to leave the campus clashed with police at the gate. In what had become a ritual in such situations, the police fired tear gas and the students fought back by throwing rocks. When the police charged into the demonstrators "brandishing their heavy shields and swinging clubs . . . some residents near the campus gates shouted, 'Don't hit the kids, don't hit them.'" The police took approximately 250 students into custody. Driven back into the campus, the students ran into five campus buildings. According to the police, they took with them at least 750 petrol bombs and nearly 200 bags of rocks. According to international radio and television reports, the students threatened to set the building and themselves on fire if the police attacked. Police continued to ring the buildings, preventing any students from leaving. After a four-day siege, on the morning of 31 October between 6,500 and 8,000 riot police attacked:

Soon after riot police began storming the buildings, two police helicopters swooped, dropping tear gas canisters into the structures, while fire engines pelted students with water cannons. As the police fought their way into the buildings, students hurled a barrage of rocks, petrol bombs and burning furniture pieces at them. . . . The demonstrators retreated to the roofs . . . When police tried to spread thick safety mattresses and nets around the occupied buildings . . . the protestors above doused the buildings with gasoline and ignited them with gasoline bombs. Flames leaped high into the cold morning air and soon the whole campus was covered in a thick pall of black smoke. Two helicopters then appeared above, shooting water cannons on the students and . . . flammable objects. Police on the ground, aided by 30 fire engines, fired more tear gas shells.[117]

According to Seoul Police Chief Yi Yong-ch'ang, 42 students, 34 police officers, and 2 firemen were injured during the 90-minute battle. One Seoul National University sophomore, Hong Wan-gi, remained in serious condition after undergoing six hours of brain surgery. Yi also said that 1,219 students from some 22 universities were taken custody in the incident. The president of the university said that the campus suffered $2.7 million in damage.

As the Associated Press description makes clear, the "occupation" of the buildings resulted from the fact that the police broke the normal pattern by driving the students back into the campus, forcing them to seek refuge, and preventing them from drifting away from the engagement. Many critics of the government have blamed both the four-day siege and its violent end entirely on the government.

In another unusual action during the following week, more than 1,200 of the demonstrators taken into custody were formally arrested. Both the large numbers of students initially taken in and the extent of the formal charges were unprecedented in Korean police and prosecutorial practice, which usually focused on a small number of those characterized as "key activists."

The suppression of the Kŏn'guk Incident and the subsequent attempt to eradicate the student movement led to a brief period of quiescence on the campuses. However, in the course of these operations against the student movement, the police killed Seoul National University student Pak Chong-ch'ŏl while interrogating him, setting off a round of demonstrations that, by 29 June 1987, had forced the government to accede to the popular demand for a constitutional amendment.[118]

As these demonstrations progressed, both police and demonstrators became more violent. Police fired staggering amounts of tear gas—351,000 canisters and grenades during June 1987 alone.[119] Demonstrators did not always wait to be attacked before they attacked. Many arrested demonstrators no longer fit within Amnesty International's definition of a Prisoner of Conscience—a person who has been detained for the expression of his or her views and who has neither used nor advocated violence. Nevertheless, they maintained that their violent actions against the riot police were in reaction to continuous police violence against them. The general South Korean public has often disapproved of student views that they perceive as pro-north, too anti-American, or too violent. As evidenced by the way the general populace joined the students in June 1987, however, the South Korean public apparently agreed that the degree of violence employed by the students during this period was a reasonable response to their accumulated just grievances against the authorities.

Although the new Constitution seemed to provide greater freedom than the *Yusin Constitution* for the labor movement, the labor movement, operating under the Labor Union Law as amended by the LCNS in December 1980, was more tightly circumscribed legally and practically under Chun than under Park.[120] In a sense, the very definition of a union was changed from an industry-wide organization to a unit permitted to be organized only by those employed in a given workplace. Under the new requirements, a minimum of 30 workers or one-fifth of the workers in a company had to petition before a union could be formed (Article 13).

Workers wishing to organize could not receive assistance or guidance from any outside organization including a national union or the Korean Federation of Trade Unions, which in any case was under tight government control (Article 12[2]). This provision, though drawn broadly, was primarily directed against organizations like the Urban Industrial Mission, which was blamed by the government for instigating the Y.H. Incident. Such outside intervention in organizing can be punished by imprisonment for up to three years and a fine of up to 5,000,000 *wŏn* (Article 45[2]).

Individual unions could form an association with others in the same industry, but the local union was the bargaining unit unless special government permission was granted for the association to do the bargaining (Articles 13 & 33). This severely limited the power of the workers in the bargaining process.

A union could be dissolved or ordered to select new officers if it was deemed likely to violate the labor law or harm the "public interest" (Article 32). The Ch'onggye garment workers union, which was a symbol of the workers' refusal to give up pressing for their rights during the 1970s, was dissolved under these provisions. Officers dismissed under this provision and officers of unions dissolved under it were barred from serving as union officers for three years (Article 23[2.2]).

Those who had served prison terms could not serve as officers and those who had received suspended sentences could not serve until two years after receiving the suspension (Article 23[2.1]. These provisions were consonant with the general principle of banning individuals punished for violating the law from public positions, but they were powerful obstacles to effective unions in a situation where individuals were often dismissed from union positions or convicted of crimes for ordinary union activities. Under these legal circumstances, "government and employer influence . . . greatly exceeded that of unions in setting wages and resolving other major labor issues."[121]

These legal changes were accompanied by other harsh measures. A large number of unionists were detained, interrogated, and forced to resign from their jobs. On the job, workers were physically abused by police, goons, and in some cases even fellow workers, apparently instigated by government and management. The Control Data and Wŏnp'ung Textile labor disputes were particularly rife with such problems and attracted considerable international attention.[122] Of events in the Wŏnp'ung Textile dispute Chŏng Sŏn-sun, the president of the union, has written:

[O]n 27 September 1982 around 12:40 p.m. . . . some 40 men . . . which included . . . Yang Pyŏng-uk and other male employees and the superintendents of the working place suddenly broke down the labor-union office doors and . . . dragged out the labor-union representatives and . . . staff members . . . Then they began to recklessly demolish objects in the office . . . Dragging out the room dividers, they nailed them across . . . the entrances, completely sealing [the office] off. They also cut off the telephone cords . . . They illegally confined [me] and the accountant of the . . . union, Kim In-suk [until] 5:30 a.m. . . . and kept [us] awake all night . . . forc[ing] us to kneel on the cement floor for over 12 hours, continuing to threaten our lives and assaulting and beating us . . . [T]hey uttered all kinds of slander, curses, and abusive language . . . In the midst of this effort to create this hellish and ominous atmosphere, they continued to demand [my] resignation . . . When they finally realized they could not compel [me] to resign . . . Yang Pyŏng-uk shouted, . . . "Drag that bitch away and get rid of her." Then they threw me onto the cement floor outside the office door . . . [T]hen [they] carried [me] to the factory main gate and threw [me] down. Then a car came along and [I] was forced into [it] . . . [T]hey continued to demand [my] resignation . . . When [I] adamantly refused they threw [me] out [of the car] . . . almost unconscious and . . . barefooted . . . When the women [employees] tried to enter the labor union office after realizing that [I] was being held hostage and was being assaulted, [30 male employees of the Kukje Group which owns Wŏnp'ung Textile and 30 other male employees and supervisors of the textile company] picked up and threw down some of the women employees and recklessly kicked them. They [seriously injured] Pak Sun-ae [union vice-president], Yi Ok-sun [general secretary], and Pak Hae-suk [a union member] . . . [T]he plain-clothed police and the riot police . . . did nothing to settle this serious and dangerous situation. They only walked around the factory grounds . . . as if they were there to guard the factory. They pretended that nothing was going on . . . These facts clearly show that this is a conspiracy schemed by the company and supported by the police to destroy this democratic labor union.[123]

Even though the repressive laws and actions of the Chun Government greatly reduced the number of labor actions, the Wŏnp'ung and Control Data labor disputes demonstrated that the desire of workers to organize effectively to promote their welfare, so evident in the period between 26 October 1979 and 17 May 1980, was not dead. The problem was covered up but not solved.

In summary, it is clear that, during the first four years of Chun's rule, there was a consistent pattern of gross violation of human rights recognized internationally as well as by the R.O.K. Constitution. The way this pattern was generated by legal manipulation and practice, which simply ignored constitutional and legal provisions, has been described above, but the fundamental reason that this situation was possible was the concentration of power in the hands of the government, particularly the President. This power allowed the government to prevent citizens from challenging violations of their guaranteed rights in either the courts or the political arena.

As the foregoing suggests, a person prosecuted for a political offense could not expect a fair trial from the South Korean judicial system during the Chun period. Under the Constitution, the president no longer appointed all the judges at all levels as under the *Yusin Constitution*, but he did still appoint the chief justice, with the consent of the National Assembly. He also appointed the other justices of the Supreme Court, and for this the consent of the Assembly was not required. The chief justice appointed all the other judges. Chun's first appointments replaced 5 Supreme Court justices who resigned without explanation on 9 August 1980. "[S]ome observers believe at least 4 had voted against sustaining the death sentence accorded presidential assassin Kim Chae-gyu."[124] The trial of Kim Dae Jung on a death-penalty offense began on 14 August.

A mission of the International Commission of Jurists in May 1979, the final year of the Park regime, concluded that only about 20 lawyers were willing to handle political cases and that most of these had been harassed or disciplined as a result; that the independence of the judiciary had been undermined to the point that the courts could not give a defendant in a political case a fair trial; and that no such defendant had been acquitted of all the charges against him since the enactment of the *Yusin Constitution.*[125]

Unfortunately, this situation was not improved under the Fifth Republic. Credible allegations of torture were ignored, exculpatory evidence was ignored, and defendants were sometimes convicted on the basis of uncorroborated confessions. Clearly no person could speak critically of the government and then vindicate himself in court if prosecuted. Under Chun, as under Park, the judiciary in political trials was something analogous to a sentencing machine.[126]

Although the Supreme Court had had the power to review and determine the constitutionality of laws from 1963 until the *Yusin Constitution of 1972,* it was abolished then because of a case in which the Supreme Court held a law unconstitutional against the arguments of the government. After that, as in most judicial systems, this power was vested in a specially designated body. In the South Korean case, the courts were required to refer such questions to the Constitution Committee of 9 members appointed by the President. The Constitution Committee never rendered a decision in its 15-year existence.[127]

Article 12[2] of the Constitution provided, "No restriction shall be placed on the political rights of any citizen . . . by means of retroactive legislation." However, a retroactive political "purification" law passed by the LCNS under the Supplementary Provisions banned approximately 800 individuals, mostly former politicians, from political activity until after the next presidential election in 1988. Upon review, the number was reduced to 567. Still banned were most democratic leaders, notably Kim Dae Jung and Kim Young Sam, as well as some government workhorses of the Park years like Kim Jong

Pil and his 9 fellows in unjust enrichment. In February 1983, President Chun lifted the ban on 250 of them and, in February 1984, he "took his second reconciliatory political step by freeing 202" more, leaving 115 individuals still banned, including of course the "three Kims."[128] The remainder were freed for political activity over the rest of Chun's term, culminating with Kim Dae Jung in July 1987.

Another enactment of the LCNS abolished all existing political parties, even though the history of political parties in the Republic of Korea extended back to 1948. Of course, the newly risen parties had ties to the old parties. The ruling Democratic Justice Party was composed of members of both the former ruling and opposition parties, as well as representatives of other fields, particularly the military. The other two major parties were each tied more clearly to one of the parties of the past. The Korea National Party was composed of former members of Park's DRP and the Yujŏng-hoe, the latter body comprising the one-third of the National Assemblymen hand-picked by the president under the *Yusin Constitution*. The Democratic Korea Party was founded by members of the former opposition New Democratic Party.

The activities of the political parties were severely restricted:

Koreans, other than those under [the] political ban, are free to belong to and participate in the activities of political parties. However, these political parties have had difficulty attracting mass followings for a number of reasons. The government can and does veto their choices of leaders, candidates, and policy positions; the government may dissolve any party it deems contrary to "basic democratic order"; and the electoral laws put time and fiscal constraints on campaigning, which cause all parties, and particularly the opposition, significant difficulties in publicizing their programs. Limitations of freedom of the press also cause opposition parties particular difficulties.[129]

As the presidential election approached in February 1981, there was no doubt that Chun Doo Hwan would be elected under the new Constitution of the Fifth Republic. In addition to having control of the military and the Defense Security Command, he had already become interim president with the extensive powers given that office by the *Yusin Constitution*. These were strong advantages for a candidate, especially for a candidate whose only credible opponents were banned from participating in politics.

During the 1979–1980 interregnum, the desire to have a directly, popularly elected president was widely expressed. However, under the new constitution and

the 1980 Presidential Election Law, the President is chosen by an electoral college of about 5,000 members. By law, presidential campaigns are brief and candidates restricted in campaigning, including both the amount they may spend and the methods they may use to appeal to the voters. In the 1981 presidential election, these restrictions, together with the authorities' careful screening of the electoral college candidates, resulted in the virtual absence of effective opposition to incumbent President Chun Doo Hwan who won by a nearly unanimous electoral vote.[130]

The degree of power in the hands of the president, the banning of strong political figures, and the weakness of the political parties rendered all but meaningless the National Assembly, which had already been seriously weakened by the Yusin system. The U.S. State Department characterized the National Assembly as follows:

The National Assembly, although politically weak, is important as a forum for the expression of divergent views on the Government's programs. Legislation normally originates with the executive branch, although the Assembly has at time [sic] passed or blocked laws contrary to the President's wishes. *Members of the Assembly, who serve a four-year term are Korea's only directly elected public officials. The election laws passed in 1981 provided for a proportional representation system that reserves 92 of the Assembly's 276 seats (exactly one-third) for members appointed by the parties, with two-thirds of those seats awarded to the party which gains a plurality of the popular vote.* In the Assembly elections of March 1981, the authorities brought various forms of pressure to bear to discourage some potential candidates but did not interfere with the voting. Of the 184 Assembly seats to be filled by election, the Government party ran candidates for 92, of which it won 90, along with a 38-percent plurality of the popular vote. The government party was accordingly awarded 61 proportional seats giving it a comfortable majority [of 151 of 276 or 54.7 percent]. [emphasis added][131]

Critics of the R.O.K. government may have felt that this overrated the importance of the National Assembly, but it does clearly show that the U.S. government, at some level, realized how weak the National Assembly is. Since President Chun headed the ruling Democratic Justice Party, which had 54.7 percent of the votes, and obviously had a good deal of influence over the 25 members belonging to the Korea National Party, it strained credulity to believe that the

National Assembly would pass or block much legislation contrary to the wishes of the President. The February 1985 National Assembly election demonstrated that this situation would change only with reform of the electoral system created by the Chun Government. Under a proportional formula, the ruling party received 53 percent of the seats in the National Assembly while winning only 35 percent of the popular vote.[132]

The lengths to which the government would go to silence criticism even in this tamed National Assembly were demonstrated clearly by the fate of Representative Han Yŏng-su, who was outspokenly critical of the government in the Assembly in May of 1982 and during a visit to the United States at the invitation of the International Communications Agency the following month. Immediately upon his return to Seoul, Representative Han was arrested, prosecuted, and sentenced to two years on charges of adultery. Observers agreed that the government's handling of the case represented an act of political reprisal.[133]

Under such political circumstances, a citizen who sought redress for violation of his constitutional or legal rights could hardly expect strong political support from any existing political group or aspire to build a political base of his own.

PROBLEMS OF U.S. KOREA POLICY

The dramatic succession of political events during the transition from late 1979 to early 1981 and the repressive nature of the government of the Fifth Republic created a number of political problems for the United States. The assassination itself demonstrated the questionable nature of a basic assumption of the policy thinking of all the U.S. administrations at least since the Johnson Administration: that security in the Korean peninsula and human rights there could be dealt with as two distinct issues. Events seemed to have vindicated the contention of American and Korean critics of U.S. policy that protection of human rights is a necessary condition for stability and security.

U.S. policymakers proved to be less than adept in coping with the aftermath of the assassination. Although it was widely known that General Wickham was upset over Chun's use of troops from the Combined Forces Command on the night of 12 December without first seeking proper permission, no public statement of reprimand or protest was issued for this breach of the chain of command.[134] This was seen by many as indicating tacit U.S. approval for the coup. Particularly damaging to the standing of the United States in the eyes of many Koreans was General Chun's manipulation of the South Korean media to suggest U.S. support for everything that had taken place in Kwangju. The R.O.K. government disinformation campaign overwhelmed the U.S. Embassy's efforts to clarify the distinction between the paratroops—not under the Combined Forces Command—that perpetrated the initial killings in Kwangju and the regular R.O.K. army forces released from the Command that had subsequently supervised the withdrawal of the paratroops and retaken the city.

General Wickham's previously quoted remarks about South Korea's unreadiness for democracy and assertion that the United States had decided to support Chun as president, which helped pave the way for Chun to take that office, though disavowed at the time by a State Department spokesman, were not officially repudiated by the U.S. government until June 1989, when the State Department issued an official statement concerning the events of 1979 and 1980. Until that statement, no serious attempt was made to inform the South Korean people that the United States had not completely supported Chun's rise to power.

For the second time in a decade, a U.S. presidential campaign in which neither candidate wished to make an issue of Korea policy gave an opportunity for a South Korean ruler to institute sweeping, self-serving political and institutional changes. Once elected, President Reagan deliberately intervened in South Korean politics by inviting Chun to the United States before Chun was elected under the new Constitution. This enhanced Chun's stature and tied the new American administration tightly to him.

As the frequency of events and crises in South Korea calling for immediate American response diminished after early 1981, so did the frequency with which new charges were added to the indictment of U.S. Korea policy by its critics. This did not, however, prevent the growth of anti-American feeling. Such feeling was particularly common among students, and explicit criticism of the United States became a regular feature of student demonstrations. There were reports in the mid-1980s that as many as 35 percent of the students at Yonsei University and more than 50 percent at Seoul National University harbored anti-American sentiment, directed specifically against American support for the Chun Government. It is not opposition to American political ideals, which are in fact widely shared by Korean students.[135] Since anti-Americanism has not been a regular or common feature of student protest in the past in South Korea, this ought to be a matter of serious concern to U.S. policymakers.

In February 1982, growing anti-American sentiment was seriously exacerbated by a news report quoting U.S. Ambassador Richard Walker as characterizing Korean university students as "spoiled brats."[136] Many Koreans were extremely upset over this. The Ambassador went to some lengths to explain that he had been misquoted and quoted out of context. Although his explanation was accepted by some opposition leaders, it was still widely believed that he made the remark.

Anti-American feeling has been expressed in more than words. In the fall of 1981, students at Kangwŏn University burned an American flag. In September 1981, an arson attempt was made on the U.S. Cultural Center in Kwangju. On 18 March 1982, there was a daytime arson attack on the U.S. Cultural Center in Pusan in which a student using the library was killed, two others injured, and the library itself gutted. Leaflets found nearby criticized the U.S. government for supporting the Chun Government and called on the U.S. to pull its troops out of Korea. Ten people, mostly students, were charged under the National Security Law with conspiring in, planning, or taking part in the arson attack in attempt to overthrow the government. Sixteen other were charged with harboring them or assisting them in avoiding arrest.[137]

Subsequent attacks by students and dissidents against U.S. facilities in South Korea, none as serious as the attack on the Pusan Cultural Center, occurred sporadically during the remainder of the Chun period. Most were firebombings or attempted occupations. A record number of some two dozen such incidents took place in 1988 and as many again in 1989, accompanied by a like number of similar attacks on government and ruling-party facilities.[138]

Anti-Americanism is not limited to students. In circles already critical of the Reagan Administration's policy of indiscriminate support of the Chun Government, President Reagan's visit to Seoul, 12–14 November 1983, was further reason for criticism. Many Koreans could not understand why Reagan was visiting Seoul at a time when the visit could be taken only as support for Chun. Before and during the visit, visible security measures were ubiquitous. These measures were obviously intended not only to protect the American President but also to prevent him from witnessing any dissent. They were effective. The massive demonstration called for by students to protest the visit did not materialize because of the security measures.

During his visit, President Reagan made several references to democracy and human rights. At a state dinner he emphasized that "[d]emocracy and freedom of opinion are virtues the free world must cherish and defend." Addressing the National Assembly, he said that the United States "welcomes the goals you have set for political development and increased respect for human rights." In his strongest comment on human rights, he told a group of businessmen, academics, human-rights activists, and journalists that the United States pays close attention to human rights in Korea, "not because we believe our security commitment gives us a right to intervene in your internal affairs but simply because such issues are at the center of our political ideology."[139] In these statements, President Reagan supported human-rights ideals, but he made no explicit criticism of the Chun Government's human-rights record. Nevertheless, critics of the Reagan Administration were pleased that he raised the subject.

During the visit, the approximately 150 or so critics of the government, including 45 who had signed a letter to President Reagan urging him to pay special attention to human rights, were placed under house arrest or taken into custody. When asked about this crackdown, White House spokesman Larry Speakes said "I am not aware of it, and I don't think [President Reagan] has been told anything about it. . . . We do not interfere in the internal affairs of another country, particularly a host country." Later in the day, Speakes told reporters that a South Korean official had told National Security Adviser Robert McFarlane that "no one had been placed under house arrest" and that there had been "no expansion of prohibitions against political activities."[140] This reaction to human-rights violations carried out by the R.O.K. government for the specific purpose of making the visit go more smoothly undermined whatever impact the President's statements about human rights may have had.

The overall impression given to many Koreans by the visit was that the United States government firmly supported the Chun Government and found its repression understandable and excusable. President Reagan's statement to the National Assembly that "the United States realizes how difficult political development is, when, even as we speak, a shell from the north could destroy this Assembly," could only further that impression.[141]

The Reagan Administration tried to deal with human-rights problems in South Korea primarily by quiet diplomacy. Quiet diplomacy is obviously a useful tool in individual cases. Although Japanese pressure appears to have played the major role, quiet American pressure played a role in convincing the R.O.K. government to release Kim Dae Jung from prison and send him into exile in the United States in December 1982.[142] Quiet diplomacy may also help to ameliorate the human-rights situation in general. Critics of exclusive reliance on quiet diplomacy do not doubt that it is useful but feel that it can be much more effective if combined with public diplomacy and other forms of pressure. Since, by definition, it is difficult to take credit for the successes of quiet diplomacy, it is not of much use as a tool for combating the rise of anti-American feeling.

The problem of rising anti-American feeling can not be wished away. Most observers agree that it is still not widespread, except among students, and that it can be reversed, because there is an immense reservoir of good will toward the United States among Koreans and because many Koreans share American democratic ideals. However, as long as Koreans see their government as repressive and the U.S. government does not take steps to dissociate itself clearly from its repressive aspects, the problem will remain and may worsen.

CHAPTER SEVEN

The 1987 Constitutional Reforms in South Korea: Electoral Processes and Judicial Independence

JAMES M. WEST and EDWARD J. BAKER

INTRODUCTION

For the people of the Republic of Korea, 1987 was a year of momentous political changes. In June, millions of South Koreans participated in nationwide protests against the military dictatorship of Chun Doo Hwan.[1] This massive civil disobedience erupted after Chun attempted to suspend debate over constitutional reforms concerning election of his successor as president. In April, Chun deemed constitutional revision to be an untimely and unnecessary distraction from the nation's task of preparing for the Olympic Games set for Seoul in September 1988. Roh Tae Woo (pronounced No Tay Ooh), another former general who played a leading role in Chun's 1980 coup d'état, was designated by the ruling junta as the next tenant of the presidential mansion, the Blue House. The people, Chun decided, would have to be satisfied with a "peaceful transfer of power" from one ex-general to another.

On 25 February 1988, Roh Tae Woo did become president of the Republic of Korea, but his path to the Blue House involved some unforeseen detours.[2] Chun's attempt to stonewall constitutional reform failed. The June 1987 groundswell of popular support for democratic reform was so broadly based that the military government had no choice but to rescind its unilateral decision and to negotiate with opposition leaders on major revisions of the *Constitution*. Landmark amendments were adopted in October 1987.[3] Among the most important changes was an amendment restoring presidential elections by direct popular vote.[4]

On 16 December 1987, about 23 million South Koreans, nearly 90 percent of all eligible voters, cast ballots in the first direct presidential election in seventeen years.[5] The election was staged under a pall of possible intervention by military "veto-groups" in case Roh lost.[6] According to the official tally, Roh Tae Woo won a plurality victory with 36.9 percent of the vote.[7] The two principal democratic reform candidates, Kim Young Sam and Kim Dae Jung, obtained 28 percent and 26.9 percent, respectively.[8] The two Kims immediately contested the outcome, alleging pervasive violations of campaign laws and widespread voting fraud. Despite considerable evidence of election irregularities, Roh's 2-million-vote margin of victory seemed decisive to many observers, and the result was more often attributed to opposition disunity than to fraud.[9]

Undeniably, the presidential election was a debacle for the opposition and for human-rights advocates. The failure of the two Kims to put their personal ambitions in perspective not only allowed the ruling junta to keep the presidency for five more years; it permitted Roh Tae Woo to claim the formal legitimacy of having won a direct election. On the other hand, a clear majority of the Korean electorate repudiated military rule. Roh Tae Woo's windfall victory thus cannot be characterized as a plebiscitarian endorsement of military dictatorship, particularly when Roh himself campaigned as an advocate of democratization and did his best to distance himself from the Chun regime's widely condemned human-rights abuses.[10]

In his inaugural address, Roh declared: "The day when freedoms and human rights could be slighted in the name of economic growth and national security has ended. The day when repressive force and torture in secret chambers were tolerated is over."[11] Roh's admission that "slights" of human rights were "tolerated" by the Chun military dictatorship was a studied understatement. It sought to put the best possible face on more than seven years of unrelenting and systematic human-rights violations by the Chun Government.[12]

Since 1980, tens of thousands of South Korean student demonstrators and political dissidents had been detained, arrested, and imprisoned for exercising their constitutionally recognized rights of free speech and assembly.[13] The buses full of riot police parked in the shadows of Seoul's new skyscrapers came to seem permanent fixtures of city life. Trade unionists were brutally repressed under Chun, and political prisoners were routinely beaten and often tortured to extract confessions.[14] All this unfolded in a society subjected to constant propaganda barrages, media censorship, and surveillance by a ubiquitous secret-police apparatus.[15]

Human-rights abuses under Chun, as under Park Chung Hee before him, were directly attributable to military-executive domination of the legislative and judicial branches of government.[16] For almost twenty years, military regimes have arrogated plenary legislative power and imposed Draconian laws, including laws unconstitutional on their face.[17] In political cases, the military and the intelligence agencies have controlled the procuracy (the hierarchy of public prosecutors) and the courts. A Korean human-rights lawyer said of administration of justice under the Chun regime: "Asking why the military gets involved [in what appear to be criminal cases] is like asking why the government is illegal."[18]

The dictatorship has long invoked national security to rationalize its repressive regimentation of South Korean society. The ideological pretext for human rights abuses has been a fanatical anti-Communist demonology. In order to retain power with minimal accountability, the military regime purposely blurred the distinction between political dissent and real threats to national security. For two decades, criticism of the government has been viewed as tantamount to treason: To question the judgment, competence, or motives of the ruling stratum is to echo North Korean propaganda and to open oneself to the charge of "pro-communism" or "impure leftist leanings."[19] Legal processes capable of impartially discriminating enemies of the state from non-violent critics of the ruling junta have been unavailable or, at best, unreliable.

The popular democratization movement of 1987 proved that most South Koreans consider military assessments of internal security threats to have been disingenuously exaggerated in order to facilitate abuses of power. The millions who demonstrated for direct presidential elections were animated not by an idealistic yearning for "democracy" in the abstract, but by a specific goal: They hoped to expel the military from politics. They hoped to disentrench and dismantle the police state of the Chun junta and to limit military authority to genuine defense concerns. Many Koreans saw Roh Tae Woo's victory as a serious setback, a lost opportunity for prompt and efficacious reforms; but hope has not been abandoned. The emergence of this popular hope for democratization and possible practical impediments to its early fulfillment are the topics this chapter endeavors to illuminate.

In what follows, the South Korean constitutional reforms are situated against the complex background of the ongoing movement for democratization. The first section provides an overview of the political events that brought about the Chun dictatorship's surprising volte face in June 1987 and reached an anticlimax with the December 1987 presidential election. Observations are offered on the election campaign, the voting process, and the aftermath of President Roh's inconclusive plurality mandate.

Now that important opposition demands have been codified in the *Constitution*, attention has shifted to implementation of reforms intended to introduce an authentic separation of powers and effective legal protection of civil and political rights. The second section discusses constitutional changes affecting the institutional structure of the legal system, with a primary focus on the independence of the judiciary. Judicial autonomy will be analyzed in the context of several interdependent issues, including (1) legislative oversight of the executive (particularly the intelligence and police apparatuses); (2) judicial appointment processes and security of judicial tenure against political reprisal; (3) establishment of a Constitution Court with power to interpret the *Constitution;* and (4) recent demands for a more politically neutral procuracy and police.

The chapter concludes by recapitulating the basic question: Will the Sixth Republic under President Roh Tae Woo mark a turning point in South Korean history, a decisive turn away from dictatorship and repression toward pluralistic democracy and effective protection of human rights? By surveying recent political developments and outlining structural reforms essential for real human-rights progress, this paper aims to promote a better understanding of the struggle for democracy in South Korea and to argue for a United States foreign policy that is more supportive of that continuing struggle.

THE 1987 PRESIDENTIAL ELECTION: ORIGINS, PROCESS, AND AFTERMATH

How did there come to be a direct presidential election in the Republic of Korea on 16 December 1987? Up until February 1986, the Chun Government had shown no willingness to discuss changes in the indirect "electoral-college" process under the *1980 Constitution*.[20] Up until April 1986, Chun had firmly ruled out any constitutional revision prior to the September 1988 Seoul Olympics. Up until 29 June 1987, calls for a direct presidential election had been alternately ignored and banned by Chun and his junta. Six months later, however, a direct election had been held and the candidate elected was Roh Tae Woo, the man who would have been installed as president if the constitution had never been amended.

To put this complicated chain of events in historical perspective, it would be necessary to go back at least to 1972, when the Park Chung Hee dictatorship declared martial law and imposed the notorious *Yusin Constitution*.[21] At that time, the direct presidential election process was suspended, repressive practices became entrenched, and human-rights abuses grew pervasive.[22] Popular demands for participatory democracy have been continuous in South Korea, and continuously repressed, for more than fifteen years. Here, the commentary will focus on major domestic and international developments of the past several years that engendered the popular movement for democratization and contributed to the constitutional reforms.

Constitutional revision for a direct presidential election process was already a prominent issue in the National Assembly election campaign at the beginning of 1985.[23] Shortly before this election, the first in four years, and the first actively contested election since Chun seized power in 1980, a new opposition party, the New Korea Democratic party (NKDP), was allowed to form and did quite well considering the serious handicaps imposed on it.[24] The NKDP's reform program included an undertaking to press for replacement of the presidential "electoral-college" system with a direct election process.[25]

The indirect "electoral-college" process was generally regarded as no more than a "rubber stamp" for the military junta's presidential choice. In 1981, when it was used to install Chun in the Blue House, "[the] authorities' screening of electoral-college candidates [along with other restrictions] resulted in the absence of effective opposition to President Chun Doo Hwan, who won nearly unanimously."[26] In 1985, some doubted Chun would relinquish the presidency when his term expired in 1988, and many expected that, if he did, he would use the "electoral college" to install a loyal comrade as his successor.

Chun's Democratic Justice Party (DJP) polled 35.3 percent of the popular vote in February 1985, and the two major opposition parties together polled about 49 percent.[27] Despite its minority share of the vote, the DJP wound up with a clear majority in the unicameral National Assembly due to a peculiar "proportional-representation system."[28] This system is one of the main instruments the South Korean military has used to retain a facade of democratic institutions for its authoritarian rule. Under the system, most National Assembly members are popularly elected as representatives of local constituencies.[29] The party winning the most local-constituency seats— regardless of the aggregate popular vote—then receives a disproportionate "bonus" when a fixed pool of non-elective national constituency seats is distributed.[30]

In practice, the national-constituency "bonus" has amplified distortions attributable to intentional malapportionment. Electoral districts were drawn to favor rural constituencies, where the DJP is strongest, and to dilute voting strength in urban constituencies such as Seoul, where the opposition is strong.[31] Without this apportionment bias and without the national-constituency "bonus," an opposition coalition would almost certainly have controlled the National Assembly in 1985. Opposition parties polled almost twice as many votes as the DJP, despite formidable DJP advantages due to the Chun regime's command of local administration, the broadcast media, and vast financial resources.[32] The outcome reflected Chun's unpopularity—the DJP enjoyed little spontaneous support.

Many Koreans viewed the 1985 elections as an indirect referendum that underscored the illegitimacy of the Chun government. From the inception of his regime, Chun had been plagued by legitimacy problems which were seriously exacerbated by the fact that his military forces had shed blood—and not just the blood of rival contestants for power—in the course of taking over. In the wake of Park Chung Hee's 1979 assassination, Chun's coup d'état had dashed high hopes for political liberalization and had left little doubt about his commitment to constitutional democracy.[33] Shortly thereafter, in May 1980, the grisly suppression of the Kwangju Uprising, in which the government admits 200 died and some witnesses claim several thousand were slaughtered, left the nation reeling in shocked disbelief.[34] Eight years later, millions of Koreans look back on these events as unpunished crimes, and Roh Tae Woo is still haunted by these legitimacy problems of his predecessor.[35]

The strong showing of the NKDP in early 1985 led to a gradual consolidation of an organized opposition and to growing popular support for constitutional revision. On 12 February 1986, the NKDP kicked off a national drive to collect 10 million signatures on a petition calling for a set of constitutional amendments which would not only introduce direct presidential elections but also ban military involvement in politics, restrict executive powers, enlarge legislative powers, abolish the proportional representation system, end censorship, and introduce stronger protections of political freedoms and other human rights.[36] An important part, though not all, of this agenda was eventually to be realized in the October 1987 reforms, but, at the time, the Chun regime responded by banning the initiative, arresting NKDP leaders, raiding the NKDP offices to search for lists of petition signers, and escalating threats against Kim Dae Jung and other proponents of reform.[37]

On 24 February, however, the police crackdown on the petition campaign was abruptly called off. On the previous day, President Reagan had made it clear that the United States could no longer support Ferdinand Marcos.[38] The head of the NKDP, Lee Min Woo, who a week before had been picked up by the police for interrogation, suddenly found himself invited to lunch at the Blue House, where President Chun mused that the Philippines were "suffering from a vicious circle of corruption and the weakening of national strength due to a prolonged hold on power by one man."[39]

In the weeks after the ignominious flight of Marcos, Secretary of State George P. Shultz and other Reagan Administration spokespeople repeatedly stated that there was "nothing in common" between the situations in the Philippines and South Korea, but people in Seoul were enheartened by the success of the "people-power" revolution in Manila.[40] The ousters of Marcos and of Jean Claude Duvalier in Haiti looked to many Koreans like a tilt in United States policy away from unconditional support for "friendly dictators." Cardinal Kim Su-hwan seemed to sum up the thoughts of many of his fellow Koreans in his homily of 9 March 1986: "Before they argue that Korea is different from the Philippines . . . political leaders must first show to the Korean people that Korea is free of [the] corruption, torture, political repression, rule by a handful of families, and violation[s] of human rights which were dominant in the Philippines."[41]

The NKDP staged a series of rallies for constitutional reform around the nation between March and June of 1986, in some cases attracting crowds of 50,000 or more.[42] When police blocked a rally at Inchon in May, a major riot ensued, and this incident was used by the Chun regime as a pretext to crack down on dissidents.[43] Major student demonstrations against the Chun dictatorship occurred through the year. In October, at Kŏn'guk University in Seoul, a police siege ended in a violent assault on students; resulting in many serious injuries and numerous arrests.[44] In the face of police repression, student dissent grew more desperate, and at least six protest suicides were witnessed.[45]

Meanwhile, little progress was made in the National Assembly toward negotiating a constitutional revision. A committee had been set up in June 1986, but the DJP repeatedly rejected NKDP proposals to submit the direct-presidential-election question to a popular referendum. The DJP adopted the stance that the revision should introduce a parliamentary system similar to that of Japan in which executive power would be vested not in a president but in a prime minister and a cabinet.[46] Most of the democratic opposition considered this an unacceptable alternative, given that the DJP was likely to retain control of the National Assembly without major election reforms the DJP showed no inclination to accept.

In October 1986, a political tempest broke out over the arrest of an NKDP National Assemblyman on a sedition charge, notwithstanding parliamentary immunity.[47] The day after the arrest, the ruling party proclaimed a "stern, steady crackdown on any groups related to left-leaning activities."[48] This crackdown continued into February of 1987 and, during this period, tens of thousands of the

Chun regime's critics were harassed, detained, and prosecuted. Mint'ongnyon, the largest democratic reform group, with a membership of almost 30,000, was forced to disband "voluntarily."[49] Constitution-revision rallies planned by the NKDP were blocked by deployment of immense police contingents and liberal preemptive use of tear gas.[50] In December 1986, the government arrested journalists Kim T'ae-hong and Sin Hong-bŏm when the journal they edited, *Mal* (Language), printed a copious sampling of the official "information guidelines" the government had been distributing to control the press.[51]

On 12 January 1987, President Chun in his New Year policy message warned the opposition that he would be compelled to make a "momentous decision" if an agreement were not soon reached on the issue of constitutional revision.[52] This generated speculation that Chun might declare a state of emergency, attempt to ram a cabinet-system amendment through, or insist that the next presidential election be conducted under the old "electoral-college" system. Each of these possibilities would have been certain to provoke widespread public outrage and civil unrest.

In the midst of the crackdown, an unexpected bombshell knocked the Chun regime off balance when the 14 January 1987 torture-murder of Pak Chong-ch'ol, a 21-year-old linguistics student at Seoul National University, became public.[53] Pak died while being subjected to "water torture" in an interrogation cell of the Anti-Communist Bureau of the National Police.[54] Despite arrest of two interrogators and dismissal of the Minister of Home Affairs and the Chief of the National Police, the youth's tragic fate provided a focus for long-standing grievances against human-rights abuses, and public outrage over the brutal murder steadily mounted.[55]

Protests and memorial services were held throughout the country, and the NKDP, religious leaders, and human-rights activists proclaimed 7 February as a nationwide day of mourning for Park.[56] These demonstrations marked an important shift to a new phase of more broadly based dissent. Pak was not a student leader and was not known as a radical; hence his murder struck close to home for many Koreans worried about their own children. The crowds turning out around the country were no longer composed entirely of young student demonstrators—there were women as well as men, middle-aged and elderly citizens, laborers, taxi drivers, and white-collar workers.

Pak's killing was a key factor in the process that was to lead to the Chun regime's about face on the issue of a direct election.

On 13 April, in the face of steadily growing popular criticism of his regime, President Chun abruptly declared that he had made his "momentous decision." What he called the "counterproductive debate" on constitutional revision would, he said, have to end and the next president would be elected under the *1980 Constitution*.[57] This astonishing speech offered no legal basis for such an order, which, in purporting to ban public debate, plainly contravened a number of basic constitutional rights of citizens.[58] Chun asserted that continuing debate would jeopardize "the two major national tasks of a peaceful change of government and the Seoul Olympics."[59]

In his insistence that the first peaceful transfer of power in forty years was the most important precondition for accomplishing genuine democratic development,[60] President Chun disregarded two facts. There had been a peaceful succession in 1960, so his stepping down would not have been the first such instance in South Korean history.[61] More important, he ignored the view of the Korean populace that his planned transfer of power to a hand-picked successor, far from promoting democracy, would perpetuate the control of Chun's own military faction.

At that juncture, in April 1987, Chun and his ruling comrades apparently felt that a direct presidential election posed unacceptable risks, not only for their retention of power, but for their personal futures. They foresaw possible loss of the enormous economic power and privilege they had enjoyed for seven years. Moreover, a democratically elected successor would have had a strong incentive to investigate the corruption widely believed to have flourished under Chun.[62] Still more ominously, Chun and the other military commanders responsible for the 1980 massacre at Kwangju faced the possibility of being called to account if a truly open political order came into being in 1988.

Such risks as these evidently led Chun to grasp at the "certainty" of the "electoral-college" system. In case a direct presidential election turned out to be unavoidable, the DJP had formidable means at its disposal to sway the outcome, but it might have required massive fraud to defeat a unified opposition. Such large-scale irregularities might have sparked a nationwide popular upheaval, and that was simply too risky—this was the real lesson of the Philippines for Korean politics (even if, as things later turned out, the split between the two Kims afforded the DJP a welcome escape from that grave dilemma).

Chun's sudden change of course provoked massive student demonstrations which went on from April into the summer. On 1 May 1987, Kim Young Sam delivered a speech in which he compared the "electoral-college" system to elections in North Korea and declared that, without democratic constitutional reforms, the 1988 Seoul Olympics would be "no more than a reenactment of the Berlin Olympics of 1936 under the Nazis."[63] This rhetorical assault drew threats of prosecution under the National Security Act.[64] On 18 May, there were new revelations about a high-level cover-up in the Pak Chong-ch'ol case, setting off yet another round of large-scale demonstrations.[65] The government tried to control the damage of this revelation by arresting eight more police officers and reshuffling the cabinet.[66]

Despite rising unrest, ex-general and DJP chairman Roh Tae Woo was officially nominated as the DJP's presidential candidate on 10 June, as expected.[67] Hundreds of thousands of people took to the streets to protest the DJP succession plans, and civil disobedience continued throughout June. Growing participation of the middle classes in the street protests was manifest, and telling visual images of the demonstrations were broadcast around the world. The government admitted using more than 350,000 tear-gas grenades and canisters against civilians in June 1987—more than were used in all of 1986, itself a year of unusually heavy tear-gas use.[68] The point had been reached at which the government had two survival options: It could either crack down much more ferociously or it could make basic concessions. Blood in the streets of Seoul might have led to boycotts or cancellation of the 1988 Olympics, and this contingency perhaps was a restraint on the military's resort to the martial-law option.

The United States government was growing alarmed at the drift toward possibly grave civil violence. Earlier in the year, Gaston J. Sigur of the State Department had noted that South Korea's security depended "as much on responsive political institutions . . . as upon the mighty military capability it possesses."[69] Mr. Sigur came to Seoul and met with Chun and Roh in the week of 20 June, seeking to help defuse the crisis.[70] Breaking with past practice, Sigur also met with Kim Young Sam and with Kim Dae Jung, who at that time was under house arrest.[71] At a 26 June press conference in Washington, Mr. Sigur called for a political compromise, release of political prisoners, an end to preemptive arrests, and government tolerance of peaceful demonstrations, pointedly stating: "Military steps offer no solutions."[72]

On 29 June 1987, Roh Tae Woo, responding to immense public pressure, announced the about face that directly led to the constitutional reforms. What the Korean press dubbed his "Epoch-Making Eight-Point Reform" included the following concessions:[73]

1. Prompt constitutional revision with direct presidential elections before February 1988.
2. Campaign-law revisions to "ensure maximum fairness and justice" in the presidential elections.
3. Release of political prisoners, except those guilty of treason or serious criminal offenses, and restoration of Kim Dae Jung's civil and political rights.
4. Effective guarantees of basic human rights and an extension of habeas corpus.
5. A free press.
6. Autonomy for local governments and universities
7. Cessation of harassment of and restrictions on political parties.
8. A nationwide campaign against corruption and crime.

Roh offered to resign his chairmanship of the DJP if President Chun refused to endorse his proposals. On 1 July, Chun announced his agreement.[74]

Through the fall, political debate was constant and animated—for the first time in years, open criticism of the government seemed relatively safe. Progress on Roh's eight points remained uneven. For example, in early July, 562 political prisoners were released and the civil and political rights of many dissidents, including Kim Dae Jung, were restored. But as many as 1,300 political prisoners remained incarcerated, drawing protests from the two Kims.[75] Nevertheless, with the presidential election set for December, a new optimism was in evidence. The constitutional revision was quickly hammered out. The amendments were adopted by the National Assembly on 12 October and ratified by popular referendum on 27 October.[76]

There were welcome signs of liberalization in the print media, which began to carry statements critical of the government. In the freer atmosphere after Roh's concessions, hundreds of thousands of long-repressed workers participated in strikes, seeking both equitable wage increases and employer recognition of autonomous unions.[77]

Between July and September, there were over 3,200 strikes and collective actions in South Korean factories and mines, more than had occurred over the preceding five years.[78] The government showed more restraint than it had in the past, and in some cases pressured employers to satisfy worker demands; but it also continued to detain and prosecute hundreds of unionists and student demonstrators for "left-leaning" initiatives.[79]

While on an unofficial visit to the United States in September 1987, Roh Tae Woo was invited, on unusually short notice, to meet with President Ronald Reagan at the White House.[80] Many Koreans resented this invitation as a tacit United States government endorsement of Roh's presidential candidacy, despite assurances from the State Department that the United States had no preference in the upcoming election and that President Reagan would be pleased to meet with opposition figures of similar stature, such as the two Kims.[81] Such explanations were not persuasive to some Koreans, who recalled that Secretary of State Shultz had declined to meet with either of the two Kims during his May 1986 visit to Seoul.[82]

As the election approached, one important question was which candidate the democratic opposition should put forward against Roh Tae Woo: Kim Young Sam or Kim Dae Jung? Each had a strong base of support rooted in over twenty years of reform politics, and neither was inclined to support the candidacy of the other. Calls for them to join forces became more urgent as time passed. A plea for unity issued on 31 October by 122 professors, journalists, religious leaders, and social activists was forceful:

We . . . cannot restrain our anger that, despite the tremendous efforts on the part of the people to struggle for democracy, the image of the democratization movement is being harmed by the competition for the presidency by the two Kims. It is critically important for the cause of democratization to succeed that a single candidate emerge. . . . If this crucial chance is lost due to a split candidacy, the people are likely to lose the will to resist the dictatorship. The major responsibility for this tragic, historical sin, if this opportunity is lost, will have to be borne by the two Kims.[83]

By the end of October, Kim Dae Jung had made it clear he intended to form his own party, the Peace and Democracy Party (PDP).[84] Dire predictions continued, but a merger of the two Kims' parties never materialized.

The campaign saw more debate and more public participation than Korean politics had seen in years. Campaign posters were plastered everywhere, and the pedestrian bridges in the cities were festooned with banners. Millions attended rallies, particularly for the two Kims. Press coverage of the campaign, although extensive, was far from impartial. Roh was consistently given more space and more detailed stories in the newspapers and more time on state-controlled television than the two Kims.[85]

In early December, Korean government sources acknowledged to reporters that the DJP was "running scared," despite the opposition split.[86] Speculation was rife that the military had a number of contingency plans in the works in case it appeared Roh would lose the election. The United States government expressed its concern by issuing a warning that "any group that tried to interfere with the elections would risk American condemnation."[87] Later, immediately after the election, a high-ranking diplomatic source confirmed to a team of American election observers that the South Korean government indeed had had "hairy schemes" ready to deal with Roh's perceived campaign problems, but that these had been shelved when a last-minute poll by an unnamed agency indicated he would win.[88]

In the days leading up to the election, a number of people were badly hurt when branch offices of the Fair Election Monitoring Committee of the National Coalition for Democracy and of the two main opposition parties were attacked by thugs, reportedly armed with steel pipes, knives, axes, and sickles.[89] Money and gifts—such as packages of soap or cigarette lighters bearing Roh Tae Woo's name—were widely distributed. Local officials and the leaders of compulsory neighborhood organizations were reported to be urging people to vote for Roh.[90]

On election day, 16 December 1987, as election returns were broadcast through the night, it gradually appeared that predictions of a Roh victory in the absence of a unified opposition had been well-founded. The official tally showed Roh with 36.9 percent of votes cast, Kim Young Sam with 28 percent, Kim Dae Jung with 26.9 percent, Kim Jong Pil with 8 percent, and four minor candidates with the remainder.[91] On the morning after the election, the two Kims at once claimed the election had been stolen, and the extent of the fraud continued to be debated months later. There were some demonstrations calling for nullification of the election, but most in the opposition majority seemed stunned, disappointed, and exhausted.

The United States government's first reaction on 17 December was to state: "We are pleased that the process appears to have come forward smoothly on the whole. . . . We understand that the actual voting took place in an orderly fashion overall. . . . We are aware of some charges of fraud. It is too soon to draw any conclusions."[92] Even if the characterizations "smoothly" and "orderly" were not intended as conclusions, no time was wasted in drawing some. The following day, in testimony before the House Committee on Asian and Pacific Affairs, Gaston Sigur suggested that the fraud charges might have been excuses by the two Kims for their failure to unite the opposition and stated that "there may have been certain irregularities, but basically no systematic fraud."[93] President Reagan quickly dispatched a congratulatory telegram to Roh, and, in a 19 December radio address, counseled the losers that "the essence of democracy is the willingness to accept the results and perhaps to try again in the next election."[94]

A *Washington Post* editorial on the election stated: "The air is thick with complaints of fraud, but the proof offered so far is thin."[95] The evidence gathered by the opposition may not have proved the massive scale of fraud alleged by the two Kims, but there was sufficient evidence of irregularities to indicate that the impact on the election results was not negligible.[96]

A group of election observers from the United States reported probative evidence of a number of further abuses on election day: death threats, beatings, and other harassment of election observers; money and gifts being distributed to influence votes; multiple or relay voting; a counterfeit ballot; voters being denied issuance of registration cards; and a ballot box illegally removed from a polling station.[97] This United States group called upon the South Korean government to investigate these and other alleged abuses "fully, quickly, and openly."[98] A Catholic group filed a lawsuit in the Korean Supreme Court on 17 January 1988 alleging "'organized and massive fraud' in excess of 2.17 million votes [Roh's margin of plurality]."[99]

Whether the outcome of the presidential election was altered by fraud is a political question for the Korean people to judge, and the reactions of the United States government, other foreign governments, and the international press were part of this political process. Not many Koreans are optimistic that there will ever be a credible legal investigation of the fraud allegations. Disillusionment with the opposition split and widespread acquiescence in the result quickly dissipated pressure on the government to defend against the fraud allegations.

In the period since the election, many South Koreans have been inclined to give Roh a chance to follow through on his promises of reconciliation and democratization. The desire to have a successful Olympics was a factor in the relative calm, a calm that seemed to cut across class lines. Patterns of protest seem to have reverted to their student-dominated pre-1987 form. If Roh takes this as a sign that the broad popular coalition of June 1987 has become fragmented once more, then he may feel little need to fulfill his past promises on human rights. As Choi Jang Jip, a well-known Korean political scientist, has observed: "There has been a continuity in all major aspects of power. It's the same political coalition among military officers, industrialists, and bureaucrats."[100]

In mid-January 1988, Roh established a Committee for the Promotion of Democracy and National Reconciliation, which was charged with making recommendations on implementation of the constitutional reforms, on reconciliation of continuing bitterness over military atrocities during the 1980 Kwangju Uprising, and on other human-rights issues.[101] Regarding Kwangju, most Committee members agreed that a government apology was in order, but a majority opposed reinvestigation of the incident or assessing individual responsibility, a standpoint many in the opposition considered inconclusive, if not irresponsible.[102]

The Committee made some recommendations of crucial importance for human rights in the future—by unmistakable implication denouncing the abuses practiced under Chun. For example, it recommended a substantial contraction in the power of the intelligence agencies, provision for defense attorneys to be present during all interrogations to preclude opportunities for torture, a revision of the National Security Act (long used to prosecute political dissidents for "pro-communism"), and measures for better protection of the courts from "outside influence."[103]

With the political anticlimax of the presidential election now fully in view, the following part moves to a more theoretical plane in order to bring into focus some important pending questions about implementation of the 1987 constitutional reforms. For reasons to be given, the National Assembly elections scheduled for 26 April 1988 acquired crucial significance for the democratization process in South Korea, and this significance cannot be appreciated without an examination of structural issues.

JUDICIAL INDEPENDENCE AND POLITICAL NEUTRALITY OF THE PROCURACY AND POLICE

The Constitutional Reforms: Toward a Rule of Law?

Fundamentally, whether South Korea will actually undergo a transition from dictatorship to a democratic order depends on whether the South Korean people themselves recognize the indispensability of institutional reforms made possible, but not guaranteed, by the new *Constitution.* Some are uncompromisingly pessimistic about the possibility of escaping a "vicious circle." More than two decades ago, a Korean jurist wrote:

A people who have no actual experience of enjoying freedom cannot be expected to know its value. A nation that has had no stable legal order cannot be expected to fight for such a legal order. They must first have an opportunity of witnessing the Rule of Law in actual operation, protecting their freedom and dignity. They will then, and only then, realize the need for a Rule of Law. If people have only had the experience of dictatorship and authoritarianism, they will not be able to appreciate the need for a Rule of Law.[104]

The events of the past years in South Korea show that such extreme pessimism is unwarranted. It is precisely people who have been brutalized by a dictatorship who are most aware of the need for effective legal restraints on state terror. With Roh's election marking a basic continuity in military-executive power, few Koreans expect a Rule of Law to emerge overnight. For the first time in years, however, new political actors, democratically minded legislators and jurists, may have real opportunities to implement meaningful reforms contemplated under the new constitution. Many citizens will be looking to the National Assembly and to the courts for leadership in approaching phases of the movement for democratic reform.

One crucial structural question is whether a viable separation of powers can be introduced. The "vicious circle" argument is valid, but in a different form. Jürgen Habermas recently argued:

A legal system does not acquire autonomy on its own. It is only autonomous to the extent that legal procedures institutionalized for legislation and for the administration of justice guarantee impartial judgment and provide the channels through which practical reason gains entrance into law and politics. There can be no autonomous law without the realization of democracy.[105]

The force of Habermas's argument is apparent when we examine practical issues presently pending with respect to the South Korean constitutional amendments. The analysis must begin with a seeming paradox: Introduction of a separation of powers is *both* the main goal of the constitutional reforms and a threshold precondition for their implementation. On the one hand, separation of powers as a goal refers to a more balanced distribution of power among relatively autonomous executive, legislative, and judicial branches of government. From a legal standpoint, institutionalization of a system of "checks and balances" requires altered allocations of legal powers and immunities if executive domination of the National Assembly and the courts is to be ended. As a threshold precondition for operational reforms, on the other hand, separation of powers presupposes an effective boundary between military and civilian spheres of authority.

One of the recent constitutional amendments does posit a legal boundary between military and civilian domains of jurisdiction, providing that the military's "political neutrality shall be maintained."[106] This provision, mirroring a basic ideal of participatory democracy, is not self-executing, however. The wall between military and civilian authority stands or falls not in the realm of legal formalities but in the realm of practical politics. In South Korea, this boundary depends almost entirely on military self-restraint. As shown above, military self-restraint in South Korea over the past year has been attributable to the scale of popular support for democratic reforms and also to international constraints. These same factors will continue to be pivotal in the future.

If the South Korean military continues to dominate the government as it has in the past, then the constitutional segregation of military and political functions may be no more than a wishful fiction. Looking ahead, there are two routes by which the modern pattern of military-executive supremacy might be broken in South Korea: (1) The higher military command could defer to majority aspirations for democratization and voluntarily relinquish its long-entrenched political supremacy; or (2) an autonomous National Assembly, supported by public opinion and by a more independent judiciary, could undertake legally to curtail the powers of the military and the executive.

President Roh has indicated that the first route will be taken, but that the road to democracy will be slowly traversed, with structural reforms phased in gradually.[107] The second, more expeditious route is favored by most citizens but could be blocked if legal reforms to implement the new *Constitution* are "vetoed" or covertly undermined by the military. These contingencies are taken very seriously by would-be reformers because virtually all the state organs of coercion remain under control of the military factions around Roh.[108]

The military has acquiesced, under popular pressure, in a more democratic *Constitution* as a matter of legal form—that was the general import of Roh Tae Woo's June 1987 concessions and of the constitutional revision process. Many of these formal changes await statutory specification and institutional embodiment. This part focuses on several issues affecting the prospects for expeditious implementation of these legal reforms. First, it examines the potential effect of several constitutional amendments on introduction of a separation of powers in general and of a more independent judiciary in particular. The importance of the April 1988 National Assembly elections will be discussed with respect to legislative implementation of the constitutional amendments and to the expanded role of the legislature in judicial appointment processes. Second, recent developments within the executive branch and the legal profession, particularly demands for a more politically neutral procuracy and police, will be discussed and their bearing on human-rights issues clarified.

Constitutional Amendments

The following are some of the more significant 1987 constitutional changes pertaining to the judicial function.

LEGISLATIVE INVESTIGATION AND OVERSIGHT. A potentially crucial constitutional amendment is Article 61, which provides that the National Assembly "may inspect affairs of state or investigate specific matters of state affairs," with procedures and powers of legislative inquiry to be specified in forthcoming legislation.[109] A former proviso was repealed which had barred legislative investigations that might "interfere with a judicial trial, or a criminal investigation in process or prosecution."[110] In past years, the formal right of the military-dominated National Assembly to interpellate executive officials was seldom consequential.

Article 61 may turn out to be the single most important change bearing on judicial independence, for, in theory, this power could be invoked to investigate (and deter) interventions by the intelligence agencies and other executive organs into political prosecutions and trials. This amendment actually will promote and safeguard a more autonomous judicial process only if its statutory implementation is broad in scope and the executive branch abides by the procedures enacted.

JUDICIAL APPOINTMENT PROCEDURES. Another amendment that enlarges the power of the legislative branch is Article 104(2).[111] Under this provision, the consent of the National Assembly is required, in addition to a (formal) recommendation from the Chief Justice, when the president appoints Supreme Court justices.[112]

Article 104(3) provides that all inferior court judges, that is, judges of the four high courts and of the district and family courts, shall be appointed "by the Chief Justice with the consent of the Conference of Supreme Court Justices."[113] Under the *1980 Constitution,* inferior court judges were appointed by the chief justice (under instructions from the president, as a practical matter), and this change basically restores the pre-*Yusin* collegial process.[114] In conjunction with Article 104(2), this change could limit screening of judicial appointments based on loyalty to the executive as well as reduce political reprisals in the form of punitive non-reappointments.[115]

TENURE OF SUPREME COURT JUSTICES. The tenure of Supreme Court justices is altered from five to six years by Article 105.[116] The presidential term of office has been reduced from seven to five years, with no reelection, so justices will not face reappointment by the president who first appointed them.[117] Nevertheless, this is not a fundamental change. Punitive non-reappointment has been a recurrent problem even at the Supreme Court level, and this change scarcely obviates opportunities for political reprisals in that form.[118] While the system of life tenure "on good behavior" has dangers of its own (which might be addressed through a carefully designed recall procedure), Article 105 seems to mark a vacuous compromise which fails to address the basic problem of a system of judicial tenure in which periodic reappointments open the door to punitive intervention.

SECURITY OF JUDICIAL TENURE. Article 106(1) is slightly modified to provide that judges may not be removed from office "except by impeachment or a sentence of imprisonment or a heavier punishment."[119] The *1980 Constitution* provided for removal in case of "impeachment or criminal punishment."[120] The government commentary on the amendments states that this change confers greater "job security" on judges because "minor offenses resulting in a fine or brief detention constitute no reason for removal of a judge from office."[121] This may come as a relief to traffic offenders on the bench, but its practical significance is limited. It will not protect a judge framed with a charge of corruption or, for that matter, adultery (the charge used to silence human-rights lawyer Yi Byŏng-nin, once chairman of the Korean Bar Association, in 1975).[122] This relatively insignificant, almost symbolic, change on the serious matter of judicial independence suggests a tough negotiation over the amendments. The real underlying issue, whether judges will be secure against possible procuratorial entrapment and blackmail, evidently remains open.

CIVILIAN REVIEW OF MARTIAL-LAW DEATH SENTENCES. Article 110(4) provides for civilian judicial review of death sentences pronounced by military tribunals covered under "extraordinary martial law."[123] This is a progressive change, undoubtedly, yet it is to be hoped that it will not soon be tested.

INTRODUCTION OF A CONSTITUTION COURT. Composition of an independent Korean Supreme Court, the appellate court of last resort in political cases, is crucial for future protection of human rights, but there is another judicial organ which, in theory at least, may have an even greater future impact on human-rights issues. This is the Constitution Court, which under Article 111 of the amended *Constitution* has jurisdiction (1) to review the constitutionality of legislation, (2) to decide cases of impeachment (of the president, supreme court justices, judges, and other high officials), (3) to dissolve political parties, (4) to decide intragovernmental jurisdictional controversies, and (5) to adjudicate "[p]etitions relating to the *Constitution* as prescribed by law."[124]

The official commentary on the new *Constitution* states:

> The principle of the separation of the legislative, executive and judicial powers is basic to modern constitutional democracy. The amended *Constitution* is thus designed to assure that the president will not have excessive power, as he did so often in the past. . . . Any citizen who feels the state has abused his rights can petition the Constitution Court for rectification. . . . The independence of the judiciary is stringently safeguarded. . . . The creation of the Constitution Court is intended to more effectively preserve and defend the *Constitution,* while avoiding the politicization of courts of law due to their involvement in constitutionality controversies.[125]

On paper, the Constitution Court looks very much like the independent judicial organ South Korea has been so sorely lacking since 1972, when Park Chung Hee stripped the Supreme Court of power to review the constitutionality of legislation.[126] When this amendment was adopted, some South Korean jurists were skeptical about the practical significance of the Constitution Court, and some even doubted it would ever render a judgment. It is important to understand the source of this skepticism, although it turned out to be incorrect.

The suggestion that the Constitution Court is a newly created institution is misleading. It is the direct successor of one of the more mysterious state organs inhabiting the annals of Korean history, the Constitution Committee established under Chapter VII of Park Chung Hee's *Yusin Constitution of 1972.*[127] This Committee, which was carried over in the *1980 Constitution* of the Chun dictatorship, never rendered a decision in the fifteen years of its spectral existence.[128] During this same period, the nominal human-rights protections in the *Constitution* were being contravened on a grand scale and without interruption.

The Constitution Court, in fact, does introduce some changes from the old Committee, apart from a more "judicial" and "apolitical" name. Like the Committee, it is composed of nine presidentially appointed members: three selected at the president's discretion, three from among nominees put forward by the National Assembly, and three from among nominees put forward by the Chief Justice.[129]

Although this appointment procedure is preserved, it is newly provided that all nominees to the Constitution Court must be qualified as judges and that the National Assembly must consent to the presidential appointment of one Court member as presiding judge.[130]

Under Park and Chun, both the National Assembly and the chief justice were creatures of the president, so the president also controlled the composition of the Constitution Committee.[131] The only way for the Committee jurisdiction to be invoked was by a kind of certification of a constitutional question from the Supreme Court.[132] This was known to be disfavored. Hence it was never done. Even if a question had been referred, the creatures of a dictator would scarcely have invalidated his edicts, despite clear unconstitutionality.

The Constitution Court cannot pronounce a judgment of unconstitutionality on a statute or an issue raised by petition unless six or more of the nine members of the Court concur.[133] The Supreme Court may be reluctant to refer constitutional questions if the result could be inconclusive—or anomalous, as it would be if a five-judge majority of the Court found a statute unconstitutional but lacked power to invalidate it. One of the ostensible reasons for the separate jurisdiction of the Constitution Court is to take "hyper-political" cases away from the Supreme Court. But it is hard to imagine a more unsatisfactory situation than one in which such a "hyper-political" case is referred to the Constitution Court and results in an inconclusive or anomalous split that merely dramatizes a preexisting polarization of the polity.

The new petition jurisdiction of the Constitution Court is, on the theoretical plane at least, quite revolutionary. Since 1972 there has been no direct procedural route for a South Korean citizen to mount a challenge to the constitutionality of censorship, arbitrary restrictions on assembly, invasions of privacy, or many other dictatorial abuses. It will be a cruel hoax indeed should this petition jurisdiction turn out to be ineffective. At best, the Constitution Court will reflect and coordinate a separation of powers instituted through political processes. It cannot be relied upon to discharge the threshold task of overcoming South Korea's long-entrenched military-executive supremacy. In the short term, if the National Assembly elections result in an opposition majority and this majority succeeds in achieving legislative autonomy, then the Constitution Court may become a very significant factor in the guardianship of human rights. On the other hand, if no true separation of powers can be instituted, the Court will not play a major role.

Problems of Political Bias in the Administration of Justice

The issue of judicial autonomy in South Korea cannot be divorced from the problems of political bias in the administration of justice and illegal conduct of state officers charged with enforcement of the law. The South Korean legal system as it functioned in the past was predicated on a strong presumption that the procuracy and the police could do no wrong, particularly when implementing a standing order to "crack down" on "left-leaning elements." Administrative arms of the military government have been, as a practical matter, more powerful than the courts.[134] This section comments on constitutional, political, and sociological characteristics of the South Korean legal system that will influence whether improved political neutrality in criminal law and more effective vindication of human rights can be achieved in the future.

Independence of the South Korean courts is emphatically a matter not only of constitutional structure, but also of the existential predicament of the jurist. The *Constitution* provides that "Judges shall rule independently according to their conscience and in conformity with the *Constitution* and law."[135] For many judges, however, this duty has been no more than aspirational in political cases, given the practical reality of judicial disempowerment. There are some signs that this duty may at last become more than an aspiration honored in the breach.

One basic correlate of an independent judicial conscience is a presumption of innocence in criminal procedure. Under the Chun dictatorship, there was little room for a presumption of innocence in political prosecutions and trials. The 1987 constitutional reforms, however, have introduced several new provisions intended to revive the presumption of innocence and to strengthen the relative power of the courts vis-à-vis the procuracy and the police.

A new due-process requirement is imposed on the issuance by courts of warrants for arrests, detentions, searches and seizures.[136] This provision is calculated to aid judges in rejecting warrant requests made by prosecutors without any semblance of probable cause. Such requests, including blanket requests for preventive detention of suspected political dissidents, had come to be viewed by prosecutors as the merest formality. In the fall of 1986, for example, more than 75,000 suspected "criminal elements" were reportedly "rounded up" and preventively detained for up to twenty-nine days, usually without being charged with any crime.[137]

Another constitutional amendment provides that persons detained and not indicted are entitled to claim compensation for wrongful arrest.[138] This may turn out to be a significant deterrent to abusively overbroad warrant requests, assuming the courts are able and willing to uphold its clear purpose and award damages.

One of the most important of the criminal-procedure amendments reads:

No person shall be arrested or detained without being informed of the reason therefor and of his right to assistance of counsel. The family, etc., as designated by law, of a person arrested or detained shall be notified without delay of the reason for and the time and place of the arrest or detention.[139]

Police and prosecutors had acquired the habit of detaining political dissidents incommunicado, sometimes for weeks, notifying no one.[140] Many prisoners were tortured during this interval of disappearance.[141] Prosecutors and intelligence operatives also frequently had refused to permit defense attorneys to visit political suspects until after the interrogation was over and the indictment had been drawn up. Often, by the time a defendant had an opportunity to speak with a lawyer, a confession had already been extracted.[142]

The foregoing constitutional changes, though important, do not alter underlying political and sociocultural factors that in the past have hindered efforts from within the legal profession to promote human rights. An outsider raised in an alien culture can treat such matters only impressionistically, but the importance of the problems outweighs the certainty that their treatment will be inadequate.

Cultural factors, such as a rigid status hierarchy based on seniority and *alma mater*, in conjunction with the realities of military power, render it very difficult to challenge arbitrary authority within the legal profession, which in South Korea is a closed and relatively small fraternity.[143] In 1986, there were only 837 judges, 557 public prosecutors, and 1,483 licensed attorneys in a country with a population exceeding 41 million.[144] Compulsory political indoctrination of young jurists, along with constant surveillance, have contributed to an atmosphere of intimidation and self-censorship within the profession.[145] Deference to authority is deeply ingrained in Korean society at large, and in the legal profession the disincentives to dissent are compounded by the risk of forfeiting a hard-earned niche in a highly privileged elite.

Jurists have been expected to adhere to a basic "friend/enemy" distinction grounded in anti-Communist orthodoxy.[146] The executive has reserved the right, for reasons of state which need not be justified, to decide who its enemies are. Anyone who questions the legality of such decisions risks being seen as a friend of enemies, hence as yet another enemy.[147] This blend of civil religion and "ruling-party" discipline, a sort of McCarthyism squared, creates grave practical dilemmas for conscientious judges. Protest resignations have occurred and some individuals have had their judicial careers cut short by punitive non-reappointment because they followed their consciences.[148] Other judges have simply adapted and maintained a safe silence, even when adaptation meant convicting political defendants based on confessions coerced by torture.[149]

Democratization of the South Korean legal system entails a thoroughgoing "rectification of names": Non-violent critics of the ruling party must no longer be stigmatized as "impure" enemies of the state.[150] The judicial duty to rectify names can be impartially discharged only if acquittals of political defendants no longer expose judges to personal risks. Judicial perceptions of conceivable risks can be as effective as unambiguous threats in distorting legal protections of civil and political rights. Past bias in the administration of justice has reflected an authoritarian scorn for the basic principle that decisions of judges in a professional capacity not only need not, but ought not, register judges' personal choices among constitutionally permitted political alternatives.

Under a sophisticated military dictatorship, the courts are invaluable instruments of command because they exude an air of impersonal authority grounded in tradition and consensual rationality. This atmosphere of legitimacy is exactly what leads a dictator to treat judicial independence as an especially intolerable form of insubordination, for righteous legal sanctions must be very carefully aimed and the results closely monitored—the air of legality can be extremely toxic not only to "impure" enemies of the state but to careless dictators as well.[151]

Two widely publicized cases of police brutality under Chun had a major impact on the 1987 democratization process and merit comment here because they illustrate important issues concerning the political neutrality of the South Korean criminal-justice system. The two cases—the mid-1986 sexual-torture case of Ms. Kwŏn In-suk and the January 1987 torture-murder of Pak Chong-ch'ŏl—have focused public attention on judicial independence and on attempted cover-ups of political bias in the highest levels of the procuracy and the police.

Ms. Kwŏn was arrested in 1986 for falsifying job application documents.[152] She had concealed her university background in order to organize factory workers into a trade union.[153] After her arrest, she was subjected to severe sexual abuse by a police interrogator. Through her lawyer, Ms. Kwŏn filed a complaint against the policeman, and, after an investigation, he was fired, but the prosecution declined to arrest or indict him. Kwŏn herself was accused of exaggerating her complaint for the purposes of "damaging the prestige of law-enforcement agencies and abetting and escalating revolutionary anti-establishment struggles."[154] She was convicted in December 1986 and sentenced to eighteen months. In July 1987, she was freed in the political amnesty that followed Roh's 29 June concessions.[155]

Unlike most others, this legal case did not end with the prosecutorial decision not to indict the policeman. A group of prominent attorneys, supported by the Korean Bar Association and public opinion, filed a petition with the Seoul High Court seeking reconsideration of Ms. Kwŏn's criminal complaint.[156] The petition was rejected, but the attorneys appealed to the Supreme Court. In January 1988, their petition was granted, a clear rebuke to the prosecution and to the lower court.[157]

The Prosecutor General promptly called a press conference to announce that the prosecution stood by its decision and had no intention of reopening the case.[158] It was pointedly denied that there had been "outside pressure" on the original decision against indicting the policeman. This did not create a stand-off, however. Ms. Kwŏn's attorneys invoked a little-used provision of the Code of Criminal Procedure under which the court can "appoint a prosecutor from among the advocates [private attorneys] who applied for public prosecution."[159] The attorney named as "special prosecutor" then is empowered to exercise the usual prosecutorial powers, subject to supervision by the presiding judge of investigatory activity.[160]

The Supreme Court decision to go forward with this "special-prosecutor" procedure was, under the circumstances, a progressive development. Observers are cautious about its implications, but it appears that this procedure, with public support marshaled by a freer press, could be invoked in the future by human-rights lawyers to remedy (and deter) at least the most egregious police and prosecutorial abuses. The Kwŏn case is significant because it demonstrates the important role that courageous attorneys can play in exposing human-rights abuses by the police and the procuracy, assuming the judiciary is able and willing to administer justice independently of ruling-party wishes.

The second case, the torture-murder of Pak Chong-ch'ol, (discussed above as a major factor in precipitating the near-revolution of June 1987)[161] suggests that, under the Roh regime, executive obstruction of impartial judicial inquiry into official illegality may remain a significant barrier to responsible law enforcement.

In this case, the physician who had conducted the autopsy of Pak went public with an accusation that the former Chief of the National Police Headquarters, Kang Min-ch'ang, had ordered changes in the autopsy results to minimize public outrage.[162] This testimony was corroborated by a statement by An Sŏng-su, a former prosecutor who had headed the original investigation into Pak's death.[163] An disclosed that he had received orders from the highest levels of the procuracy to "overlook the police cover-up" in the case.[164]

These revelations, given prominent coverage in the recently liberalized press, left the government no choice but to reopen the investigation. Kang was arrested.[165] After only four days, however, the Prosecutor General's Office announced that the investigation was "wrapped up" and there would be no further arrests.[166] This generated opposition protests because higher officials had been publicly implicated in the cover-up, including the former Ministers of Home Affairs and Justice, the former Prosecutor General, and a former Deputy Director of the secret police, the Agency for National Security Planning.[167] According to An, these and other officials had conducted a "countermeasures conference among concerned agencies" to contain public outrage at the young student's brutal murder.[168]

Several of the implicated high officials are influential in Roh Tae Woo's Democratic Justice Party and were planning to run in the approaching National Assembly elections at the time this story broke.[169] Failure to prosecute them generated discontent in the lower echelons of the police. "Officials of the NPH [National Police Headquarters] . . . grumbled that their former chief [was] being made a 'scapegoat,' since he merely followed orders from above and that senior prosecutors who 'connived at the coverup' should also be brought to justice."[170]

Significant factions in the South Korean police force had been growing increasingly weary of being cast as pawns of the unpopular dictatorship. Taking advantage of the new atmosphere of freer public debate after the presidential election, in late January 1988 thirty-five young police officers met and drew up a public statement entitled "Our Views on Police Neutrality."[171] This declaration was issued to the press on behalf of alumni of the National Police College. It stated, in part: "Police neutrality is a prerequisite for the realization of true democracy. . . . Police neutrality is not a thing subject to political compromise, but a precondition if police are to carry out their inherent duty of keeping public security and social order."[172]

This unprecedented movement from within the police apparatus caught the government off guard and provoked an incoherent and disturbing reaction. Initially, Roh's party issued a statement saying that the declaration was a "very affirmative" development.[173] Simultaneously, however, the young police officers were criticized for having gone "outside" channels" by issuing their declaration to the press.[174] An initial indication that the protest would not be disciplined was reversed about a week later, but it was not revealed what discipline would be applied to the police officers who had publicly embarrassed their superiors.

The decision to discipline the police protestors was plainly inconsistent with Roh's campaign promises to promote democratization. It would have been futile, if not dangerous, for the young officers to have registered their concerns through "internal channels," given that their superiors were among the men responsible for past political bias in law enforcement. This protest generated broad public sympathy and support for democratically minded police officers, who repeatedly have been placed in conflictive situations, forcing them to follow orders against their own consciences. The opposition parties renewed calls for an independent "public security commission" to be interposed between the huge national police force and political appointees in the executive ministries.[175] President Roh announced the formation of a commission to study options for promoting police neutrality, but the issue seems destined to remain contentious for some time.

Utopian political theory, from Confucianism to Western liberalism, optimistically supposes the state apparatus to be peopled by politically neutral professionals who put the best long-term interests of the whole nation ahead of short-term interests of factional expediency and self-aggrandizement.[176] One crucial "check and balance" of a separation of powers consists in the stimulus to executive self-policing that arises from the mere existence of external agencies able and willing to publicize abuses of power.[177] Freedom of the press is obviously a precondition for discharge of this essential function of "policing the police." Thus, the Roh regime's attitude toward press freedom, particularly toward calls for a lifting of state controls on television programming, was expected to be an important indicator of its commitment to democratic reform.

CONCLUSION

The dramatic events of 1987 and the presidential election are now history. From an historical rather than a narrowly legal point of view, the fairness of the December 1987 election was a matter not only of the extent of media manipulation, bribery, ballot-box stuffing, or fraud in tallying the results, but also of the good faith of campaign promises and of tacit, yet efficacious, threats of military intervention in case the majority dared to repudiate the "ruling party." The majority dared, but they lost nonetheless, at least in the official history written by the victors.

Whether the 1987 constitutional reforms turn out to mark a watershed in modern Korean history, a triumph of democracy over authoritarian repression, will depend on an ongoing process that will be closely observed by the international community. This process may continue to be an uphill battle for advocates of democracy, who remain handicapped by entrenched government advantages and by factional strife within their own ranks. With the April 1988 National Assembly elections, the democratic opposition has at last made long overdue progress toward internal unification with the recent resignations of both Kim Young Sam and Kim Dae Jung from the chairmanships of their respective parties.[178]

Apocalyptic prophecies of reversion to state terror after the Olympics one hopes will prove unwarranted; but many Korean citizens are concerned about apparent back-pedaling by President Roh Tae Woo on his June 1987 commitments to human rights and democratization.[179] The 27 February 1988 political amnesty left many political prisoners, including Kim Kŭn-t'ae, incarcerated.[180] An important amendment to the National Assembly Members Election Act, rail-roaded through by the DJP at 2 in the morning on 8 March 1988 over strong opposition objections, perpetuated pro-DJP biases in the process for electing legislators.[181] Roh's first Cabinet "of Chun-era holdovers, former military men, law enforcement officials, and natives of his home Kyŏngsang province gave the appearance of more continuity than most Koreans had expected."[182] In what many view as an ominous and totally unacceptable development, outgoing dictator Chun Doo Hwan apparently intends to remain a prominent "elder statesman" and active advisor to Roh.[183]

No conclusions can yet be drawn in such a complex and inconclusive situation as presently exists in the Republic of Korea. The sheer complexity of the aftermath of the presidential election threatens to undo human-rights gains apparently won in the constitutional reforms but not yet consolidated. Whether gains will be consolidated depends in large part on whether courageous leadership is forthcoming from within the government and the legal profession.[184] Many Korean judges, prosecutors, police, military professionals, and others in positions of power privately support an expeditious transition to democracy but have cautiously hedged their bets, because history will continue to be written by the victors and it is not yet clear that democracy will prevail. The outcome of the National Assembly elections, here also, may be crucial in molding self-fulfilling prophecies of progress or retrenchment.

The people of the Republic of Korea are understandably irked by foreign "advice," particularly from the United States, on matters of political self-determination. The present commentary does not presume to pass judgment on matters that only the Korean people are entitled to judge. It aims rather to generate understanding and support in the United States for a South Korean democratization movement that has a long road yet to travel. The argument that the "internal affairs" of South Korea are of no concern to the United States, it will be recalled, has long been a favorite argument of those who uncritically supported the "friendly dictatorship" of Chun.[185]

The historically nearsighted Reagan Administration policy of "quiet engagement" with the Chun regime was wisely, if belatedly, re-evaluated as chaos loomed in June 1987. Over preceding years, however, this policy of foregoing decisive public condemnation of human-rights abuses undermined the strategic interest in South Korean political stability that it purported to serve. It also predictably generated Korean perceptions of United States complicity in the terror practiced by Chun's police state, thereby poisoning the relationship between our two peoples and inflaming the anti-Americanism so evident in Korea today. We will be living for years to come with the bitter hatred and distrust this policy engendered. It is to be hoped that the Reagan Administration's reception of Roh at the White House in September 1987, its quick favorable verdict on the presidential election, and the offical welcome accorded former President Chun in March 1988 do not herald a complete reversion to this ill-conceived policy.[186]

The Reagan Administration was all too willing to praise the Chun and Roh governments for grudging and involuntary concessions to democratization, but, since June 1987, it was reluctant to call attention to the continuing gap between democratic rhetoric and authoritarian reality. The 1987 presidential election, let it be remembered, would never have come about as a result of pressure from the Reagan Administration if the Korean people themselves had not repeatedly laid their lives on the line. Pressure from Washington was inconsequential until the popular movement became too powerful to ignore or repress. The Reagan Administration may congratulate itself for having helped to avert a catastrophe in June 1987, but, to all appearances, it did very little over the preceding six years to push the Chun regime toward democratic reforms.

The Korean people certainly deserve more support for their democratic ambitions than they have received from the United States government up to now. They also deserve more active support from legal professionals, who have a special responsibility to keep United States foreign policy sensitive to human-rights concerns, particularly when policy decisions made in Washington have real and immediate repercussions in a newly democratizing polity engaged in a difficult quest to institute a Rule of Legality.

CHAPTER EIGHT

U.S. Human-Rights Objectives and Korean Realities

DONALD S. MACDONALD

Korea has, for over a generation, been a test case of American commitment to human rights. For the critics, it is a poignant case of paradise lost—a land liberated in 1945 from its own decadent past and from forty years of colonial subjugation, only to be divided by its American and Soviet liberators into two antithetic regimes and then dragged into dictatorship and oppression. In this view, the United States, instead of using its tremendous power to bring forth a just society, abetted political retrogression through a mixture of mindless anti-communism, cynicism, national self-interest, and impotent good intentions.

For the critics, the spectacle is the more painful because of the century-long American association with Korea: the missionary influence on social ideas, education, and public health; the influence of

the American democratic political example on Korea's outward political forms, and on the many leaders who studied and lived in the
United States; the enormous American input of economic, military,
and technical assistance; the American role in turning back the
North Korean aggression; the continuing American role in South
Korea's security, including the presence of 40,000 American military
men and women close to the line of potential combat. Against this
background, it would seem that the United States should have been
able to put the Republic of Korea into the hands of wise and good
people who would build a democratic society worthy of the twentieth century, and to guide them as they built. Instead, the United
States is perceived as reinforcing the hand of usurping oppressors.

Cohen's and Baker's article is a reasoned and well-documented
example of this point of view. It demonstrates the continued preva-
lence of human-rights abuses by the authorities of the Republic of
Korea, and maintains that these abuses have met generally futile protests, or no protests at all, from Korea's American benefactor. Cohen
and Baker find that, although the intensity of abuses has waxed and
waned, it reached unprecedented heights in the years following the
Yusin Constitution of 1972. They cite the abuses—denial of free speech
and assembly, arbitrary arrests, intimidation, torture, murder—
demonstrating that they cannot be accounted for as random arbitrary
behavior of local authorities. They cite the laws of the Yusin period
(1972–1979), giving the president and his security authorities sweeping powers of coercion and control. They maintain that the Korean
people are mature enough to survive the short-term instability that
might result from a relaxation of controls so as to build a modern democratic polity, and hold that the United States should apply measured
sanctions to bring about progress in this direction.

As a long-time observer of Korean affairs, I fully share the authors'
desire to move Korea toward a free and open society, responsive to
popular preferences and ensuring basic rights and freedoms. I differ
with them, however, in the evaluation of American policy and action
to promote this evolution.

Official U.S. policy on Korea from its outset was based on three
points, first expressed in 1946 and then repeated, in similar language,
in subsequent national-policy documents. As stated in 1946, these
were:

—to establish a self-governing Korea, independent of foreign control, and eligible for membership in the United Nations;

—to insure that the national government so established would be a democratic government fully representative of the freely expressed will of the Korean people;

—to assist the Koreans in establishing the sound economy and adequate educational system necessary for an independent and democratic state.

After the Korean War, the emphasis on security implicit in the first of these points became explicit, and assumed high priority, not only because of the objective situation on the peninsula, but also because of American anti-Communist feeling. Americans would spend money for Korea more readily on security grounds than for social and economic development; hence the latter was justified by the former. Nevertheless, I can testify—because I drafted several of the subsequent national-policy papers myself, and participated in carrying them out—that the three original policy goals remained basic elements in American policy formulation and action.

These goals are wholly consistent with those of the critics, although perhaps less specific. The critics' target, therefore, is not the formulation of American policy objectives (except as the sincerity of their formulation may be doubted), but American performance—the gap between these objectives and Korean reality. My basic thesis is that this gap is primarily due, not to lack of American sincerity, attention, or concern, but to the extraordinary difficulties of the process of political and social change—especially the difficulties for an alien power in bringing about such change through non-coercive means. This is not to say that American performance has been perfect: far from it. But it is to say that the judgment of American performance must be made in full recognition of the magnitude of the problems the United States has faced in Korea.

Among these problems, the first is conceptual as well as practical. American government policy and American popular expectation hold that Korea shall evolve as a democratic state. But democracy, by definition, is rule by the people. In a world of sovereign and equal states, only the Koreans can rule Korea as a democracy. The United States could perhaps enforce certain civil liberties over a certain short time span; but to do so would not be democracy—it would be alien rule. It might be argued that, once American pressures had put free and democratic institutions and human-rights guarantees into place, and installed leaders motivated to make these institutions work, then democracy would take root. This is what the British attempted in their colonies; but it didn't work except in India, where the ideas of democracy had three hundred years to develop. This is what the Americans attempted in the Philippines, but it didn't work. Only when the indigenous national political culture nurtures democracy as the highest social priority can democracy and its associated freedoms (and turmoil) endure. Alien imposition of democratic forms, in the absence of indigenous cultural support for them, may actually retard the eventual realization of true democracy by delaying or suppressing necessary internal evolution, while judicious and subtle international influence may over time promote it.

Accordingly, American influence on Korean political behavior has been exerted principally by informal and relatively subtle means. Despite its mistakes, the United States has enjoyed great prestige in Korea, which has reinforced its own economic and military power. It capitalized on this prestige and power to stimulate growth of democratic political institutions through informal social and professional contacts, technical assistance, and large programs for information and exchange of persons, as well as firm diplomatic representations in specific cases. Additionally, American opinions, both Congressional and public, have had significant influence. The prospect of decreasing aid appropriations was sometimes expressly invoked to moderate Korean political behavior (for example, in reversing Syngman Rhee's decision to postpone scheduled elections in 1950). In critical periods, such as elections, the United States encouraged the presence of American journalists as a means of inhibiting political excesses, and welcomed editorial comment. The presence of the United Nations Commission (until 1973) also supported this objective.

Actual American intervention in Korean politics, however, was slight in the active sense; its greatest impact was passive, through Korean perception of its potential. Pressure was applied in certain crises and situations: the 1950 elections, already mentioned; progress toward an open two-party system and a self-regulating responsible press in the mid-1950s, until the power-holders balked at the prospect of losing power; avoidance of opposition incitement to popular uprising following the untimely but natural death of opposition leader Shinicky (Sin Ik-hŭi) in 1956; pressure on the Rhee Administration before and during the infamous 1960 elections, culminating in the "justifiable-grievances" statement which gave a blessing to popular protest; and the civilianization of military rule through a constitution and elections in 1963, to name some examples.

The second great difficulty faced by the United States is the matter of priorities. The Universal Declaration of Human Rights was one of the first great goals of the United Nations after World War II; but it took years to reconcile two opposing points of view as to which rights were more important: freedoms of speech, assembly, religion, due process, and political participation, on the one hand—rights dear to the people of industrialized Western Europe and America; or rights to food, clothing, housing, education, and employment, which the Soviet Union and the developing countries, in their relative poverty, held to be paramount. What use, it was argued, is freedom of speech to a starving person? Why is not coercion justified if it hastens economic progress and the equitable distribution of wealth?

Critics of human-rights abuses seldom take note of the striking progress made by the Republic of Korea in responding to the economic needs (or rights, if you will) of its citizens. When they do, they point to starvation wages, inhuman working conditions, and denial of collective bargaining rights—abetted in some cases by American capital. Yet, the fact is that the Republic's per capita gross national product has increased far more than 10-fold in twenty years; that income inequality in Korea is little greater than in the United States, although at a much lower level; and that the standard of living is rising for all population groups, putting Korea in the threshold of entry into the select company of industrialized countries. The process has brought injustices; but these can be matched by the same injustices in American and European history—a fact that does not excuse injustice but tends to indicate its stubborn universality.

The debate between political and economic rights is still not resolved on the theoretical level. On the practical level, as public opinion polls of the 1960s in Korea showed, the people of a developing nation put higher priority on their climb out of poverty and insecurity than on democracy, which they may have heard about, but never experienced. A shrewd observer of the Korean political scene once remarked to me that, by the mid-1950s, the Korean people discovered the power of the vote; having discovered it, they proceeded to sell it. From the average Korean voters' point of view at the time, conditioned by their culture, history, and economic condition, this was a rational and even a moral choice.

This is not to say that the Korean people are indifferent to democracy and human rights; it is simply to say that, up until now, other things have seemed more important. Korean priorities are now shifting with growing public education, awareness, and affluence, as they have shifted in Europe and elsewhere. For example, a *Dong-A ilbo* poll in January 1980 (during the interim regime following President Park's assassination) indicated that the public put political liberty ahead of economic growth and security. It may also be that Korean governing authorities, for a variety of reasons, lag behind the public in their perception of priorities. Change such as human-rights critics call for is undoubtedly on the way, through evolution or, in the extreme, through revolution. Heretofore, such change has probably been impossible.

The third problem in realizing Korean democracy and human rights lies in basic national character traits, which affect the leadership as much as the people. Koreans are at the same time group-oriented and individualistic; but their loyalty to an institution as large as the state (as distinguished from loyalty to a sovereign ruler) has been weak. They have been conditioned by centuries of Confucian tradition to accept direction from a government hierarchy which is both respected and disliked, but viewed as beyond popular control. Group-oriented, Koreans value family, clan, and provincial loyalties more than any generalized obligations toward humanity as a whole. Individualistic, they strive relentlessly for power and status, both for self-fulfillment and for family betterment. Their perception of public service is so colored by these considerations that they give lower priority to the general good than do their counterparts in industrial democracies. Established hierarchical tradition makes it easy for officials to manipulate the bureaucracy to their own or their factions' advantage. Moreover, the Korean culture, until now, has had little room for compromise of the sort essential in the give and take of democratic politics. Any challenger of the official orthodoxy, now as in the fifteenth century, tends to be viewed as a heretic for whom tools like those of the Spanish Inquisition are appropriate. The quality of mercy toward persons not within one's own group is not a part of the Korean culture.

As early as 1947, President Rhee (who received his Princeton PhD from Woodrow Wilson, and spent forty years in the United States) said publicly that American-style democracy was not suited to the problems of his country. A leading member of the principal opposition party (which was then officially clamoring for democracy) told me upon his return from a trip to the United States in 1956 that the American political system was admirable, but would never work in Korea. A U.S. Embassy appraisal in December 1958 noted, "Little genuine conviction exists among Korean officials of the basic concepts of democratic government. . . . The population has even less understanding in these areas. . . . Danger exists that current malpractices . . . are being identified by Koreans with democracy and free enterprise." The Embassy prophetically added, "It is entirely conceivable that at some future date, . . . democracy and free enterprise institutions could be rejected in favor of other alternatives less desirable in terms of U.S. policy." After the military coup in 1961, its leader and subsequent President, Park Chung Hee, criticized American democracy in his writings. In doing so, I believe he was reflecting a genuine conviction that he and many other Koreans held, and still hold. Human rights and democracy are not, of course, quite the same thing, and lack of faith in the efficacy of importing the American political system does not mean endorsement of cruel or capricious behavior. Nevertheless, there seems to be a significant correlation between democracy and human rights.

The fourth problem of human rights in Korea is the Korean propensity, born of long experience to a small nation among large ones, to manipulate external power for personal or group advantage. Since 1945, the United States has been the preeminent external influence in South Korea. Would-be Korean political leaders have sought to mobilize this influence for themselves and their causes, often by voicing support of political values that the United States approves. Many examples can be cited, starting with the Independence Declaration of 1919, and including the famous Myŏngdong Cathedral Declaration of 1976. As a political officer in Seoul in the 1950s, I personally experienced this kind of pressure from aspiring political leaders to win official U.S. support, overt or implicit, for their groups and activities. It is hard to say where democratic political conviction leaves off and the old Korean principle of *sadaejuŭi* (respect for size or power) begins. I think the attitudes of most Korean opposition figures have been a blend of both; and it is doubtful whether some of these leaders, were they to come to power, would differ very much from their predecessors in the manner of its exercise—if only because the Korean political environment would make it impossible for them to do otherwise and maintain their control. The Chang Myŏn regime— most free and liberal of any in Korean history—was moving toward stricter control, through sheer necessity, when it was overturned; and the Korean people acquiesced in—even welcomed—a return to order and the familiar authoritarian pattern.

On the other hand, Korean political power-holders are quick to condemn their rivals for treasonous appeal to outside influence, and to invoke the growing fires of nationalism as a means of suppressing what in Western Europe would be regarded as normal and healthy opposition. Such outside influence has mostly been attributed to the Communist states: the fate of people like Cho Pong-am (opposition leader executed in 1959) and Kim Dae Jung (for many years in prison and nearly executed), accused of giving aid and comfort to North Korea, demonstrates the point. The power-holders, knowing the American hypersensitivity toward communism, have also condemned their opposition as either ally or dupe of the Communists so as to enlist American influence on their side and prevent it from going to their adversaries. The technique, in some times and places, has worked all too well; Syngman Rhee applied it with great skill.

The fifth problem for the United States in dealing with human-rights matters in Korea is American ignorance and insensitivity regarding the Korean political and cultural system. If the United States had had anything like the thorough understanding and intelligent policy toward Korea at the outset of its occupation that it had toward Japan, history might have been quite different. If representatives of the United States, either official or private, had a reliable chart of Korean society's pressure points, like that of a skillful acupuncturist, and could insert the proper political needles at the right place and time, they might even now be able to bring about certain transformations in Korean political behavior. There have been a few modest successes of this sort, in my opinion—some of them listed above—with a cumulative effect over the years that may eventually be visible. For each of the successes that can be cited, as well as others, there have been many American attempts that produced no immediate effect. Among such attempts were the strident public U.S. government criticisms of Korean human-rights violations of the late

1970s. These and other blunderbuss approaches—such as, if it were ever tried, playing the "North Korean card"—simply increase South Korean insecurity and trauma, arouse Korean resentment, and weaken further the diminishing reservoir of influence the United States still possesses.

Americans still suffer from a bad case of ethnocentrism in their judgment of foreign cultures and political values. The United States not only cannot, but should not, seek to remold the world in its own image. We can usefully join the international community in mutual enforcement of certain basic and generally accepted rights and freedoms. Non-official American critics can exert useful pressure in stimulating awareness of human-rights abuses and promoting a world consensus supporting their elimination. In doing so, however, both the government and non-government critics must be sure that they stand for the rights of all the people, not just of those who draw the attention of the media and the intelligentsia by their political campaigns; and that we keep in mind how many centuries it took our own ancestors to bring us to our present imperfect system, so that demands for reform are realistic enough to promote constructive action, not destructive reaction.

To summarize: I sympathize with the Cohen and Baker goals for Korea; I respect their detailed analysis of human-rights abuses, and agree that the record is a sad one by American standards. But I believe that they are unrealistic in their implicit disregard of Korean history and culture, and in their estimate of the American capacity to induce change. At the same time I believe, as they suggest, that the Korean people are more capable of political evolution than their own leaders appear to realize. As the Koreans redefine their own priorities, change is bound to come, either by peaceful evolution or violent upheaval. The United States can play a useful catalyzing role in the process of change, if its own perceptions of goals and means are realistic, and its actions prudent.

Epilogue

Comparative Perspectives on Human Rights in Korea

LAWRENCE W. BEER

I would like to go beyond comment on the modern Korean human rights experience and to locate that East Asian case within a broader historical, comparative, and theoretical framework. However interesting and significant a nation's story may be in its own right, it is no longer an intellectually adequate approach to fix attention solely on the human-rights behavior of a given country with myopic disregard for its comparative context and theoretical implications. This is particularly so with *human* rights, which attach not to people of a particular category or nation but universally to each person.

PARADOX AND TRAGEDY

The modern history of law and politics of human rights in Korea is replete with paradox and tragedy. Unified in A.D. 668, Korea was one of the world's most ancient and homogeneous territorial states until divided in 1945. In premodern times, the Kingdom of Korea enjoyed considerable autonomy in its internal affairs, while on occasion deferring to China in its external relations, as its model Confucian tributary state. While dynasties and foreign masters came and went in China (Mongols, Manchus, Europeans, and Americans), Korea's Chosŏn dynasty continued from 1392 until replaced by Japan early in the twentieth century. Particularly from the 1870s, Western nations and Japan brought notions of individual rights along with colonialist intrusion into Korean political and economic life. As in later times, competing Korean political interests seemed to cluster around different foreign powers (for example, China, Japan, Russia, the United States), and rival foreign and indigenous ideas contended for domestic ascendancy as the foundation for the Korean modern state.

A few of the paradoxical ironies for human rights in modern Korea are:

(1) That in the decades from the late 1800s, as human rights ideas began entry into Korean society, Koreans came under ever more systematic governmental and foreign controls.
(2) That the first sustained efforts at modern legal development took place as part of Japan's effort ultimately to absorb Korea into its own political culture.
(3) That relatively straightforward human-rights movements like the Equalization Society of the 1920s could not be easily accommodated by nationalists preoccupied with rival visions for achieving independence.
(4) That concerns for human rights and democracy, which were part of the political thought behind the March First Movement (1919) and other pre-Liberation politics, gave way to division, poverty, war, and repression after Liberation in 1945.
(5) That long and savage civil conflicts between 1945 and 1953 only hardened the north-south division and heightened tensions so much in the south as to weaken inclinations to honor democratic rights and liberties.
(6) That no constitution in independent South Korea has outlasted the ruler who presided at its inception.
(7) That widespread support for democratic law and politics among the Korean people has co-existed with torture and repression by successive governments and with uncompromising rigidity on the part of some elements in the opposition.

Culture as well as history affects human rights today. The idea of "human rights" inhering in each person as a human was not part of pre-modern Korean legal culture; but one had duties according to one's place in the sociopolitical hierarchy, and within that context one's sense of duty might well carry with it, even in relations with superiors, a modest expectation that the other recognized a duty to reciprocate, if not in equal kind, at least with humane condescension. Thus, within the Confucian hierarchy of carefully differentiated stations in society, there existed to some degree a "reciprocal-duty consciousness" which in effect, and perhaps in perspective, functioned as a type of qualified individual-rights consciousness.[1] Irresponsibility was not an accepted principle of government or social rule, however often manifested by some elites. However, the notion of human rights established under government policy and formal law, with protective institutions, as developed in parts of the West, was new and alien when Korea was forced to open its ports for intercourse with Japan and the West. Now, more than a century later, human-rights ideas may well be more powerfully integrated into the popular political consciousness than competing Confucian conceptions. As in all world regions, popular preference for human rights does not imply consistent governmental or societal support for a given right in a concrete context. Americans, for example, support free speech in principle, but not for those whose views differ too much from their own.[2]

THE HUMAN-RIGHTS REVOLUTION

Although universalist ideas of individual rights were institutionalized in such eighteenth-century national documents as the American Declaration of Independence and the French Declaration of the Rights of Man and Citizens, the history of human-rights law under international standards is brief.[3] The worldwide diffusion of the human-rights revolution may well be the most important development in twentieth-century law and politics. Human-rights ideas were molded slowly in a cultural matrix of Western law, religion, government, and economics.[4] Human rights became an element in the indigenous government and law of most non-Western countries only with the demise of colonialism and independence after 1945.[5] International and comparative human-rights studies are primarily a post-World War II phenomenon and did not burgeon as a coherent academic field until the 1970s.[6]

In the early 1860s, as slavery was abolished during the American Civil War, multi-lateral human-rights treaty law began with the first Geneva Convention (1864) regarding victims of armed conflict as a result of the Swiss Red Cross movement. By 1949, this reaction against the horrors of war had evolved into four treaties dealing with prisoners of war, wounded and sick combatants, civilians, and civil wars.[7] Between the end of World War I and 1939, treaty law was developed to cover the rights of minorities, workers (by the efforts of the International Labor Organization), and individuals in League of Nations Mandated Territories. In 1926, the long campaign of non-governmental organizations in the Anti-Slavery League issued a treaty outlawing slavery at last.[8] Although Japan represented the non-Western, non-Caucasian world in some international contexts, such as development of the Kellogg-Briand Treaty of Paris (1928) against war, Korea continued in political slavery to Japan.

As turmoil followed liberation in Korea after 1945, collective revulsion at Nazi atrocities—with somewhat peripheral attention to the less-publicized Japanese atrocities in East and Southeast Asia—brought human rights to the center of the world stage for the first time.[9] The current human-rights movement and international law may be dated from acceptance by nations of Article 55 of the United Nations Charter (1945), which reads in part:

(B)ased on respect for the principle of equal rights and self-determination of peoples, the United Nations shall promote:

   a) higher standards of living, full employment, and conditions of economic and social progress and development;

   b) solutions of international economic, social, health, and related problems; and international cultural and educational cooperation; and

   c) universal respect for, and observance of, human rights and fundamental freedoms for all without distinction as to race, sex, language, or religion.[10]

This complex norm of treaty law has served as the basis for later refinements and clarifications of the meaning of human rights, in the 30 articles of the Universal Declaration of Human Rights approved without dissent by the U.N. General Assembly on 10 December 1948,[11] and in agreements more precisely defining various human rights such as the 1966 United Nations International Covenant on Economic, Social, and Cultural Rights and International Covenant on Civil and Political Rights, which came into force for ratifying nations in 1976.[12]

The Declaration, these two covenants, and the 1966 Optional Protocol to the International Covenant on Civil and Political Rights, which provides for implementation machinery, are referred to as The International Bill of Human Rights.[13] Numerous other human-rights instruments have appeared over the years, such as the international Convention on the Elimination of All Forms of Discrimination against Women (1979)[14] and the Convention against Torture and Other Cruel, Inhuman, or Degrading Treatment (1984).[15] In addition, regional efforts continue to develop under the European Convention on Human Rights (1950), the European Social Charter (1961), the Inter-American Convention on Human Rights (1969; in force since 1978), as well as in Arab League, African, and Asian organizations.[16] Since 1979, the most important regional body in Asia has been the Human Rights Committee of the nongovernmental Law Association for Asia and the Pacific (LAWASIA). Among its accomplishments have been the formulation of human-rights principles for Asia, encouragement of the development of sub-regional human-rights commissions, and publication of Asia-wide reports in its *Human Rights Bulletin* and newsletter.[17]

As of 1 January 1985, about 84 countries had become parties to the two major United Nations Covenants, which some had not yet ratified; 34 had signed the Optional Protocol on Civil and Political Rights, which a minority had ratified.[18] The Democratic People's Republic of Korea has acceded to both covenants, but not to any other of the 22 major human-rights agreements; the more democratic Republic of Korea has ratified conventions against racial discrimination, genocide, and prostitution, and for the rights of stateless persons and the political rights of women, but not the covenants.[19]

THE STUDY OF LAW AND HUMAN RIGHTS IN FOREIGN COUNTRIES

The field of human-rights studies, which pursues knowledge and understanding based on impartial scholarly investigation and analysis, labors under a peculiarly heavy burden of complexity, because of the nature of its subject matter, and because of encroachments by human-rights advocates and opponents, governmental and private, domestic and foreign, on dispassionate academic inquiry. While their resources, levels of commitment, priorities, and degrees of effectiveness are wildly diverse, in the late twentieth century governments and national and international organizations almost universally espouse human rights. The United Nations and certain regional bodies take a broad view of such rights, while Amnesty International, for example, focuses on the plight of non-violent "prisoners of conscience." President Jimmy Carter injected a new concern for human rights into American foreign policy in the 1970s, and the Helsinki Accords have advanced pan-European dialogue on related issues. Few who care would have much time or patience with scholars so ungracious and wrongheaded as to ask: Why bother? How can one intellectually justify attribution of such importance to each person as is assumed by human-rights advocates? A fundamental issue to a human-rights theorist, but a suspect distraction to the mass media, the policymaker, and the activist.

As citizens, human-rights scholars are generally proponents of humane treatment of their fellows; but as scholars, their interests may focus on law, social science, history, or theory. Human-rights studies are also a mixture of national, international, and comparative scholarship. One branch of human-rights studies looks at the status of rights within a country, as of civil rights or free speech within the United States. Another cluster of scholars is preoccupied with international law and foreign policy affecting human rights, usually with an eye on the international bill of human rights. And a third group looks at the law and sociopolitics affecting one or more human rights in other countries for the purpose of comparative understanding of different national systems and problems. (Precise knowledge of the internal context of a country's human-rights problems is often hard to come by, but is often a necessary precondition for reliable comment on issues.) Perhaps to a degree unsurpassed by human-rights studies of any other country, such studies of Korea combine all three distinctive dimensions of scholarship, and also carry with them an unusual sense of immediacy and public urgency in the United States and South Korea.

More broadly speaking, human-rights scholars now need to integrate the implications of Asian, African, and other non-Western experience at the very time when those peoples are themselves in the process of selectively blending perennial national understandings of justice with universal human-rights conceptions, Westernized legal institutions, and competing ideologies, and when all nations are grappling with the human-rights implications of revolutions in science, technology, and communications. In fact, it is time that we cast aside the use of terms like "East and West" or "North and South" in favor of a more omni-directional perspective on issues. In one problem area or another, human-rights ideals conflict with the politics of value and power in all legal cultures. (The United States, for example, deals reluctantly with problems in the treatment of Blacks and in the assurance of civilized subsistence to the less fortunate.)[20] More precise knowledge of a system on its own terms, as provided in this book, does not justify or excuse abuses, or give boasting privileges to some countries in relation to others; rather, by clarifying the locus of specific problems in law, society, and politics, studies can mitigate foreign misinterpretation of events and guide the use of limited resources to combat the most severe human-rights violations.

To gain accurate perspective on a foreign human-rights issue, one needs to take into account at least five problems of contemporary American legal studies:[21]

(1) Legal abstractionism, a tendency to restrict attention to formal legal rules or judicial reasoning on a human-rights issue
(2) Legal chauvinism, an inclination to exaggerate the relevance of American law and democratic institutions as a model for other legal cultures
(3) Cultural insularism, treating the norms of the country studied as so unique and self-enclosed that general human-rights principles and the experience of other legal systems are simply disregarded
(4) Evolutionary thinking about human-rights law, assuming that systems do not simply change over time, but also "develop" along certain lines (for example, American; ideological) and become "better"[22]
(5) The difficulty of even bicultural communication about law and human rights in a world that requires multi-cultural discourse in terms of universal standards.

Although inroads have been made by some Asianists, other area specialists, and some law-social science scholars, a mind-set that is rigidly Western (even American) dominates discourse on national, international, and comparative human-rights concerns in our legal, intellectual, and political communities.

To facilitate multi-cultural communication, human-rights studies of a country might well include:

(1) The author's theoretical presuppositions, with which the foreign reader cannot be assumed to agree. Too often an author's principles go unstated, on the assumption they are too obvious and acceptable to all to warrant mention. Starting points matter much to the reader who wishes to discern whether he disagrees with the author on practical judgmental grounds or in basic principle.
(2) The modern legal history of the issue in the country.
(3) Patterns and rules of indigenous social thought, structure, value, and behavior which affect the context of the issue.
(4) Officialdom as it bears on the human right studied (for example, police and judges; an administrative agency overseeing an area of concern, such as worker rights or health care).
(5) The nature of the legal system (for example, civil law, common law, Islamic law, socialist law) and relevant provisions in the country's constitution, statutes, and administrative rules.
(6) Where the courts are reasonably independent and have jurisdiction over human-rights questions, the facts and reasoning of relevant judicial decisions.
(7) Indigenous views of the issue (for example, legal scholars, the mass media, victims, churches, local rights organizations).
(8) Law and social-science findings with respect to the issue as it exists in other countries.

As Korea's future unfolds, scholars of whatever nationality need a richly interdisciplinary approach to human-rights studies in order to convey reality in a precise, fair, and balanced way to the non-specialist, multi-cultural audience. Although not explicitly designed to illustrate a model, the present volume links human rights with policy, culture, and political history in a manner helpful to those who visit Korea. Few analyses of human rights in Asia provide such breadth of context.

CONSTITUTIONS AND RIGHTS IN ASIA

Brief consideration of constitutional developments in other Asian countries and in the world will add perspective on Korea. Only about 20 of the 167 single-document constitutions in the world today date back as far as the 1940s or earlier.[23] The idea of such national legal documents, now the valued property of humankind, derives from the United States Constitution, which alone dates from the eighteenth century; very few countries (for example, Norway, 1814) have constitutions dating from the nineteenth century. More thought-provoking yet, over 100 constitutions in force today, such as those of North Korea (1972) and South Korea (1987), were established in 1970 or later. Only New Zealand, Israel, the United Kingdom, and 3 Islamic states employing the Koran as a constitutional document (Saudi Arabia, Oman, Libya) lack a formal modern constitutional document; and in some of these there is talk of a constitution or a bill of rights analogous to the 1982 Canadian Charter of Human Rights.

In Asia, only the following constitutions date from the 1940s: Japan (1947); Taiwan (Republic of China, 1947, but the territory was under martial law until 15 July 1987); Indonesia (1945, but two other constitutions were used between independence in 1949 and 1959, and a major upheaval occurred in 1965); and India (which has been amended 59 times since 1949).[24] Other Asian constitutions, with their adoption dates, include: Afghanistan (1980), Bangladesh (1972), Brunei (1984), Myamar (Burma) (1974), China (1982), Cambodia (Kampuchea) (1989), Laos (1975), Malaysia (1963), Nepal (1962), Pakistan (1973), Papua-New Guinea (1975), the Philippines (1987), Singapore (1963), Sri Lanka (1978), Thailand (1978), and Vietnam (1980).

The post-World War II era has seen an unprecedented burst of constitutional creativity and experimentation on all continents. Many documents have been short-lived, and the gap between provisions and human-rights practices is wide in some states; but most nations continue to associate modernity, political stability, and legal predictability with maintenance of the same fundamental law over as long a period as possible. Constitutions are usually meant to be "permanent" rather than interim legal statements about a country's principles and government. When they work reasonably well over a considerable time, constitutions tend to take on an almost sacred communal symbolism which itself further reinforces stability. Within a few decades, most countries that became independent between 1945 and 1965 may achieve documentary stability. In some, this will reflect a firmer sense of corporate identity, as well as cultural preferences as to constitutional form and substance; but all are likely to include detailed human-rights provisions echoing United Nations principles.

With national stability, the concerns of leaders about their own legitimacy, about leadership succession, and about internal security and order may diminish in intensity and become less frequently the cause of or excuse for human-rights violations. Such current preoccupations may be especially strong in those countries capriciously carved out in Asia and Africa by colonialists, with boundaries unnaturally combining antagonistic peoples or dividing large ethnic groups between two territorial states or both. In this respect, Korea is a tragic oddity, because its peninsular territory has not been ambiguous or changing over the past 1,200 years and because there is no natural basis for division in colonial history or differences between north and south in language, ethnic group, or religion. Arguably, no other separation in the world has been so complete yet unnatural as that on the Korean peninsula.

More confident rulers and a stronger sense of constitutional identity in the recently defined states may also reduce, rather than increase, tolerance for unorthodoxy and may thus bring more unabashed violations of the human rights of minorities, the press, women, or workers.[25] It is unclear where some Asian states will lie on the spectrum between systematic authoritarianism and exploitation on the one hand and a deep regard for certain human rights under law on the other, once stability and a measure of prosperity are achieved. Alternative Asian perspectives may help intellectuals refine Western justifications for human rights; but some Asian nations seem to have farther to go in integrating human-rights law into the elite consensus than South Korea.

Consider, for example, the overwhelming complexity of Indonesia next to the relative simplicity of Korea. The Constitution and the official Pancasila (Five Principles) of Indonesia legitimize human rights in providing the documentary basis for governing 180 million people on over 13,660 islands spread over 4,000 miles of ocean with hundreds of distinct ethno-linguistic groups and fewer than 1,000 lawyers. Indonesia, like India, Malaysia, Bangladesh, and Pakistan, must balance, and eventually integrate, human-rights law with modern reformulations of Islamic politico-legal thought as Islam emerges again as a coherent world force in the twenty-first century, and as deep cleavages within the Muslim community continue.[26] Thailand may be taken to symbolize the difficulty in some Asian countries besides South Korea—for example, the Philippines, Indonesia, Burma, Pakistan, and China—of integrating the military into a constitutional system sensitive to human rights; but the cosmo-magic kingship system and Buddhism of Thai constitutionalism again make Thailand's problem more delicate than Korea's need to integrate unofficial Confucianism into a democratic state. The Philippines, mixing American and post-colonial legalisms with Catholicism in a sophisticated understanding of constitutional democracy and human rights, is plagued with fractious politics rooted in regional and long-standing socioeconomic divisions which make Korea's divisions in the south seem simple and historically shallow by comparison. But Korea shares with the Philippines and with many East Asian and Southeast Asian countries a version of patron-client, quasi-paternal-filial, and familistic social structure which frames power relations and affects human-rights performance importantly, often negatively.[27] Concrete loyalties have more bite than human-rights abstractions or laws in many situations.

The current age of constitutional fluidity may end within a few decades. It is not clear in 1990 where Korea will stand as the wheels of time turn, whether constitutional stability will be attained, and, if so, whether freedom, personal security, and socioeconomic justice will coexist with governmental firmness, whether Confucianism will yield to the democratic elements in modern tradition, whether the military will withdraw from government and politics, and whether familistic loyalties will accommodate to human-rights law.

TRANSCULTURAL HUMAN-RIGHTS THEORY

The constitutional documents of nations have never been so similar to each other as now, and international human-rights instruments are gaining increasing acceptance as customary international law (if only because few dare repudiate such unexceptionable statements), but their philosophical, ideological, or religious leanings and historical experiences often differ radically in some respects.[28] Long-dominant Western formulations of rights are undergoing transformation as non-Western experience impinges on dialogue in the West. This will surely continue as non-Western formulations of human rights and legal thought grow in influence in the next century. A stronger sense of integration will likely come with the maturation of Islamic human-rights theory, and a stronger sense of community will infuse democratic legalism generally with digestion of the encounter between the

West and other directions. John Locke, John Stuart Mill, and American liberals of both conservative and progressive inclination seem destined to recede in importance, as have the excessively dated and parochial views of Karl Marx and his heirs. It will likely puzzle future American students of human-rights law how legal positivism could have so long dominated legal education in disregard of any rational justification for human rights. Out of Asia and other regions may come the strongest insistence upon what may be the crucial alteration of theoretical understanding of individual human rights: the replacement of an individualist notion of human rights with what I call a "mutualist" conception in a "transcultural" theory.

By "transcultural" I mean applicable to, relevant in any cultural context, inter-subjectively and cross-culturally persuasive. An American conception of individualism, for example, is not transculturally valid; nor is it philosophically convincing, because it tends to reduce the individual to "a naked chooser" without context or natural relatedness to others, and because its attendant conceptions of law and society are peculiar to one nation, or at most to some in some Western countries, and to few elsewhere. Human rights pertain to individuals as "persons-in-community," not as "individuals-in-nature."[29] The term *individualism* has been a major barrier to cross-cultural communication about human rights between Asia and the United States.[30] American individualism is a myth; like Koreans and other Asians, Americans are, in general, social conformists. Moreover, cooperation, compromise, a "team spirit," and Judeo-Christian respect for each person are as essential as competitive politics to the protection of human rights in the U.S. constitutional system. Inaccurately, American rhetoric often presents "individualism" as essential to the possession of individuality, individual dignity, and/or individual rights.

What is essential to any human-rights theory is that it be compatible with philosophical attribution of great, intrinsic, and equal value and dignity to each person as a human without qualifications based on differences of religion, race, sex, wealth, caste, ethnic group, or any other basis for distinction. Philosophically rigorous relativism is incompatible with any persuasive human-rights theory. The human-rights ideal seems best expressed by "mutualism" and democratic constitutionalism. *Mutualism,* unlike words such as *individualism* and *collectivism,* is unencumbered by cultural chauvinism and complex historical argumentation; it implies government and rights based on mutual respect for equal individual dignity. The term well expresses the inherently interdependent and relational nature of individual freedoms, rights, and responsibilities among citizens and between citizens and government.[31]

Among the practical consequences of mutualist respect for each person is a democratically constitutionalist system which institutionalizes the following or analogous features:

(1) Constitutional division of governmental power among two or more organs.
(2) Regularized limits on the amount of governmental power possessed by anyone and on the length of time power is legitimately possessed. In large systems, elections and other legal procedures are used to bring peaceful, routine passage from one national leader or group of leaders to the next.
(3) Sufficient governmental authority and means of coercion under law and constitution to maintain public peace and national security within parameters defined by human rights.
(4) Governmental involvement in socioeconomic problem-solving to meet citizens' subsistence needs and a life compatible with human dignity when the private sector fails to provide this minimum.
(5) Legally protected freedoms of peaceful expression and silence regarding personal and group belief and opinion.
(6) Procedural rights in criminal and civil justice for each citizen equal to the rights of all others within the national community.
(7) Acceptance of the constitution and human rights as the supreme law of the land, by the government and by the general public.

HUMAN RIGHTS IN SOUTH KOREA

The other contributors to this volume illuminate the sociohistorical context. They convey a dramatic sense of conflict between traditional Neo-Confucian thought and government and early modern efforts of intellectual politicians to revolutionize Korea toward modern statehood and protection of human rights under law. They also explain with empathy and dismay that this goal had not yet been achieved in the 1980s. How should we assess the Korean human-rights situation from a comparative perspective?

South Korea seems to have remained a country under rule by military men or "military occupation" through most of its twentieth-century history. Today, the military leadership of the Republic of Korea continues to occupy a position of supra-constitutional power; in choosing its own candidates for national leadership it has shown recurrent disregard for the normal legal accoutrements of constitutional government. In Korea, the supremacy of the military, not the Constitution, has been the dominant pattern, at least since 1961. Yet the legitimacy of this supremacy is widely questioned. Like Park Chung Hee before him, President Chun Doo Hwan resigned from the military to assume the presidency as a civilian, in recognition of the inappropriateness of military rule in Korean constitutional understandings. Roh Tae Woo left the military in 1981, holding a variety of civilian posts in and out of the government before receiving his party's nomination and being elected to the presidency.

Basic living standards among the generality of Koreans have improved markedly in the past twenty years, but the rights of unions and workers have been circumscribed. Studies in this volume and elsewhere[32] indicate relatively strong public support for constitutional rights, and students and other dissenters have proved to be perennially irrepressible. In fact, the degree to which international human-rights ideas have been indigenized in South Korean society, even without the aid of consistent official encouragement, may be unusual among non-Western countries. Contrary to the distinctively American fixation on absolutist wording (as in the First Amendment) as significant to legal protection of rights, defective performance is not traceable at all to constitutional phraseology allowing limitation of rights under law; that phraseology seems unimportant, viewed in comparative perspective. All democracies limit under law all but a few freedoms of the spirit in all traditions of legal draftsmanship.[33]

In Korea, the problem since liberation is that a way has not yet been found in Korean law and politics to divide and restrain governmental power sufficiently to guarantee individual rights. Law itself may not yet have the autonomy necessary for legal protection of rights. Perhaps the judiciary and the National Assembly are not yet institutionalized in relation to the presidency, and administrators and police are not yet democratically professionalized in such a way as to control under law violations of human rights.

But more than the above, the pivotal issue for human rights and for Korean constitutionalism in general may be the succession problem. Transitions are needed on three levels: (1) orderly passage under law and constitution from one president and leadership group to another; (2) peaceful transition from military supremacy to civilian sovereignty and the supremacy of the constitution; and (3) a generational change from current leaders who came to maturity in the 1940s and 1950s out of conditions of colonial oppression, war, indigenous authoritarianism (sometimes under civilians), and economic want, to the next generation of social and political leaders whose seminal experiences were in the 1960s and 1970s, and who would like liberty along with affluence, and somehow a less taut relationship with North Korea.

The issue of generational succession seems of vital concern throughout East Asia. Most dramatically, the People's Republic of China has been in transition since about 1975 from the era of Mao Zedong, Zhou Enlai, and others in a remarkable group of political leaders tracing their lineage back beyond the Long March of the mid-1930s. Twice purged before he assumed the mantle of leadership, Deng Xiaoping is of that earlier generation. His picked people now head the government (Li Peng) and the Chinese Communist party (Jiang Zemin).[34] Until Deng has passed and a new group of leaders has been confirmed in authority by a time of stability, China's succession process will not have ended. Almost concurrently with the generational succession, China is engaged in one of history's more comprehensive law-making efforts, both filling out the broad framework of a modern legal system and adding in the details with civil, criminal, commercial, and administrative laws and rules to replace the pattern of neglect and alegalism of the latter Mao years (1966–1976). How stable the leadership-succession system will prove to be under the living constitution combining the government Constitution of 1982 with party rules and practices remains to be seen. The Tiananmen Massacre of June 1989 only heightened uncertainty further.

On Taiwan, the generation of leaders who came with Chiang Kai-shek from the mainland in the late 1940s is rapidly passing from the scene; the symbolic end of that regime was signaled when Chiang Ching-kuo, his son, passed away in 1988, and indigenous Taiwanese assumed greater authority in relation to mainlanders within the increasingly democratic political culture.

Whether durable North Korean leadership will pass simply from father to son, from Kim Il Sung to Kim Jong Il, is unclear, moreso because there is no precedent since its founding in 1948 for leadership transition in the Democratic People's Republic of Korea, either individual or generational.

Since the end of the Pacific War forty years ago, once set on a new democratic course with Allied Occupation support, Japan has experienced at many junctures an independent and peaceful succession of leadership under law and constitution. The generational succession issue in Japan turns, in part, on the question of whether the emerging generation of political leaders will favor change like current "revisionists" who, in spite of overwhelming popular support for the Constitution, are uncomfortable with constitutional pacifism, democracy, and a powerless emperor; or will continue, with deep and quiet passion, adherence to the Constitution as the country's primary sacred writ, and with a revulsion to militarism and authoritarianism passed on to them by family and teachers who directly experienced the unprecedented horror, shameful aggression, and devastating defeat of World War II. As in South Korea, the form and content of constitutionalism in these other East Asian countries may continue as is or come into new or sharper focus by the turn of the century.

In the absence of a pattern over time of peaceful, predictable, rule-based transition from one national leader to the next, the human-rights element in South Korea's constitutional order has tended to become lost in a recurrent military politics of force and alegal maneuver to secure the national leadership (as in 1961 and 1980), followed by aggressive manifestations of defensive anxiety about gaining full legitimacy and/or retaining presidential power, with the guidance of technocratic and military supporters. At times, there has been a jolting harshness about governmental violations of rights in Korea: Dissenters have not just been arrested and detained, they have also at times been beaten and tortured; journalists and editors of newspapers and magazines have not simply been given coercive guidelines and advice on the political content of publications, they and/or their products have been banned if the level of their cooperation has been deemed inadequate; politicians perceived as possibly viable competitors in electoral politics, such as Kim Dae Jung and Kim Young Sam until 1987, have been subjected to a range of abusive measures to render them politically inoperative; hundreds have been banned from political life; unions have been severely restricted; procedural rights have been violated capriciously; and the freedom of peaceful assembly often denied. Granted that the modes of dissent have at times been quite provocative; political revenge, distaste for tolerance and compromise, and distrust of law as a basis for exercising governmental power may have been among the motivating forces.

Authoritarian cowardice and cruelty have sometimes been matched by uncommon courage. But the tone of voice and political style of both government and opposition have often seemed marked more by stark confrontation over power than by practically oriented negotiations to achieve shared constitutional goals.[35]

Yet there have also been periods of political amnesty and relative freedom, as in the period following the assassination of Park Chung Hee in 1979 and 1980, and as in 1985 and 1987. More important perhaps than the strong electoral showing of the opposition in 1985 were the government tolerance of even harsh opposition criticisms of the regime, the absence of noteworthy violence in highly charged political campaigns, and the willingness of the government virtually to ignore widespread technical violations of the election-campaign law. The scale, persistence, and vehemence of the demonstrations and political rhetoric were seen as a sign that the expanded free speech of the February election period had broken a taboo and started the process of widespread popular expression of long-pent-up demands for democracy. Although the road from the 1985 elections to the autumn 1987 constitutional revision—returning to the direct popular election of the president in force in the 1960s—was by no means direct or predictable, the aura of freedom brightened with that campaign.

In comparative terms, it is unusual for a people to focus so explicitly and often on freedom and democracy themselves as the objects of practical concern in their major acts of political expression—most free speech in the world takes for granted the freedom itself and is for or against some type of concrete interest, such as better garbage collection, getting rid of the rascals in city hall, pollution control, or an end to nuclear weapons. Where freedom of expression is not protected under law, governments do not care to hear such demands to the degree found in South Korea, and so such speech is squelched with dispatch. Ambivalence is not a trait of the serious authoritarian. In Korea, the past pattern of inconsistency and unpredictability in government intent about human rights and democracy makes many wonder, with some doubts and suspicions but also with hope: Whither Korea now?

In the years ahead, should the government succeed in its gamble on restoring constitutional democracy and move towards elimination of torture (and ratify the 1984 U.N. convention against torture), political revenge, military dominance, and political intolerance, then the South Korean government might gain some of the human-rights legitimacy which eluded it as of the time President Chun Doo Hwan stepped down from office in 1988. But human rights seem likely to remain in a precarious position until the ruling group and the opposition leaders become accustomed to peaceful transfers of power under the supreme law of the land, until they leave behind harsh confrontation, and move on to mutualist democratic compromise on the road of constitutional politics.

Notes
Index

NOTES

Introduction, by William Shaw

1. Louis Henkin, "The Human Rights Idea in China," in R. Randle Edwards, Louis Henkin, and Andrew J. Nathan, *Human Rights in Contemporary China* (New York, Columbia University Press, 1986), p. 7–39.
2. John King Fairbank, *Chinawatch* (Cambridge, Harvard University Press, 1987), pp. 1–2, 95, passim.
3. Adda B. Bozeman, *The Future of Law in a Multicultural World* (Princeton, Princeton University Press, 1971), Chapter 1.
4. For a more nuanced interpretation that takes social and economic change into account in explaining Korean attitudes, see Vincent Brandt, "Korea," in George C. Lodge and Ezra F. Vogel, eds., *Ideology and National Competitiveness: An Analysis of Nine Countries* (Cambridge, Harvard Business School Press, 1987), pp. 207–239.
5. Kim Yŏng-su, *Taehan min'guk imsi chŏngbu hŏnpŏp non* (Constitutions of the Korean Provisional Government; Seoul, Samyŏngsa, 1980), p. 86.
6. Bruce Cumings, "The Origins and Development of the Northeast Asian Political Economy: Industrial Sectors, Product Cycles, and the Political Consequences," *International Organization* 38.1:1–40 (Winter 1984).
7. Norman Jacobs, *The Korean Road to Modernization and Development* (1986).

8. Michael E. Robinson, "Colonial Publication Policy and the Korean Nationalist Movement," in Mark R. Peattie, *The Japanese Colonial Empire, 1895–1945* (Princeton, Princeton University Press, 1984), pp. 275–311. In September 1986, the dissident magazine *Mal* published South Korean government press guidelines (*podo chich'im*) issued to the press during the period from October 1985 to August 1986. These guidelines dictated language, orientation, size, and placement of press articles on current political subjects. A selection is translated in *Index on Censorship*, May 1987.

9. Judith Shklar, *Legalism: Law, Morals, and Political Trends* (Cambridge, Harvard University Press, 1986).

10. Kim Ch'ŏl-su, *Sin Han'guk hŏnpŏp yoron* (A new survey of Korean constitutional law; Seoul, Tonga Hagyŏnsa, 1981), pp. 114–115.

11. For the situation in the 1970s, see Adrian W. Dewind and John Woodhouse, *Persecution of Defence Lawyers in South Korea*, Report of a Mission to South Korea in May 1979 (Geneva, International Commission of Jurists, 1979). See the Korean Federal Bar Association's critique of the Act for the Protection of Society in *Korea Herald* (U.S. Edition) 19 December 1986, p. 8. Also, see "NKDP Discloses List of 238 'Illegal' Detainees," *Korea Herald* (U.S. Edition), 1 February 1987, p. 3.

12. For an example, see "We Endorse Kim Dae Jung As Our National Candidate for the Presidency: the Resolution of the United Minjung Movement for Democracy and Unification," published by the Korean Institute for Human Rights in Alexandria, Virginia, 13 October 1987.

13. International League for Human Rights and the International Human Rights Law Group. *Democracy in South Korea: A Promise Unfulfilled* (New York, The International League for Human Rights, 1985).

14. Larry A. Niksch, "Korea: U.S. Troop Withdrawal and the Question of Northeast Asian Stability," Issue Brief, Congressional Research Service, Library of Congress. Washington, D.C., 1980.

15. For an authoritative, if brief, U.S. government statement on the question of "operational control" and the events of December 1979 and May 1980, see "ROK Units under Operation Control of CFC," Public Affairs Fact Sheet, United Nations Command/Combined Forces Command/United States Forces Korea/Eighth United States Army (Seoul, no date), 2 pp. A statement on the U.S. role during the Kwangju Incident by former Ambassador William H. Gleysteen, filtered through the South Korean press, is found in *Tonga ilbo* (Seoul), 14 January 1987, translated in U.S. Embassy Press Translations 87–8, 14 January 1987. Donald N. Clark, ed., *Kwangju* (Denver, Westview Press, 1988) explores various aspects of the Kwangju Incident and U.S.-South Korean relations.

16. William H. Gleysteen, Jr., "Korea: A Special Target of American Concern," in David Newsom, *The Diplomacy of Human Rights* (Lanham, Maryland, University Press of America, 1987), pp. 85–99.

17. The invitation was subsequently criticized by Kim Dae Jung himself as the worst since the mid-1960s of a "series of [U.S.] actions that have shaken the Korean people's trust and gratitude." See "Peace and Unification in Korea

and America's Role in the Restoration of Democracy," in Kim Dae Jung, "Cultural Tradition and Democracy in Korea," in Kim Dae Jung, *Philosophy and Dialogues: Building Peace & Democracy* (New York, Korean Independent Monitor, 1987), pp. 223–234.

18. "Investigation of Korean-American Relations," Report of the Subcommittee on International Organizations of the Committee on International Relations, U.S. House of Representatives, October 31, 1978," p. 42. William H. Gleysteen, Jr., "Korea, A Special Target of American Concern," p. 97–98. Gleysteen states that for six months in 1980 "Kim's fate consumed more of our time than any other matter."

19. "Korea at the Crossroads: Implications for American Policy. A Study Report," (New York: Council on Foreign Relations and the Asia Society, 1987), p. 60; Ralph N. Clough, *Embattled Korea: The Rivalry for International Support* (Boulder and London: Westview, 1987), p. 137.

20. U.S. Department of State, *Country Reports on Human Rights Practices* (annual) (Washington, D.C.: U.S. Government Printing Office).

21. Asia Watch, "A Stern, Steady Crackdown," Supplement to the Report on Human Rights in South Korea (Washington, D.C., February 1987), pp. 106–107. Gaston J. Sigur, "Korean Politics in Transition," (Washington, D.C.: U.S. Department of State, Bureau of Public Affairs, Current Policy No. 917, 1987).

22. Don Oberdorfer, "U.S. Policy Toward Korea in the 1987 Crisis Compared with Other Allies," in Robert A. Scalapino and Hongkoo Lee, eds., *Korea-U.S.-Relations: the Politics of Trade and Security* (Berkeley, Institute of East Asian Studies), p. 179.

23. The new strategy is accurately reflected in the comments of former Ambassador to South Korea William H. Gleysteen, Jr., and Alan D. Romberg, "Korea: Asian Paradox," *Foreign Affairs* (Summer 1987), pp. 1037–1054.

24. 20 February 1987 press conference with James M. Montgomery, Senior Deputy Assistant Secretary of State for Human Rights and Humanitarian Affairs, United States Information Agency Foreign Press Center, Washington, D.C., p. 16.

25. Don Oberdorfer, "U.S. Policy Toward Korea in the 1987 Crisis Compared with Other Allies," p. 180.

26. Telepress conference with James M. Montgomery, Senior Deputy Assistant Secretary of State for Human Rights and Humanitarian Affairs, 16 March 1987. Transcript dated 17 March 1987 in the author's possession, p. 7.

27. Don Oberdorfer, "Carefully Timed U.S. Advice Played Role in South Korean Events," *Washington Post*, 5 July 1987.

28. "United States Government Statement on the Events in Kwangju, Republic of Korea, in May 1980," issued by Department of State, 19 June 1989. For the reaction of a U.S.-based human-rights organization to the report, see "State Department Answer on Kwangju Raises New Questions," *Korea Update* (Washington, D.C.), July 1989, pp. 13–14.

29. Terrence C. Markin, "South Korea in Transition: Establishing a Better

Benchmark to Measure Progress," *Journal of Northeast Asian Studies* (Washington, D.C.) 1.3:51 (Fall 1988).

30. Oberdorfer, "U.S. Policy," p. 180. David I. Steinberg, "U.S. Public Perceptions of Korea," in Robert A. Scalapino and Hongkoo Lee, eds., *Korea-U.S.-Relations: the Politics of Trade and Security* (Berkeley, Institute of East Asian Studies), p. 222.

31. For an example, see Kim Dae Jung, "Cultural Tradition and Democracy in Korea," in Kim Dae Jung, *Philosophy and Dialogues*, pp. 174–185. Similar arguments are found in Kim Dae Jung, *Prison Writings*, tr. Choi Sung-il and David R. McCann (Berkeley, University of California Press, 1987).

32. Tonghwan (Stephen) Moon, "Korean Minjung Theology, An Introduction," in Wonmo Dong, *Korean-American Relations at the Crossroads* (Princeton Junction, The Association of Korean Christian Scholars in North America, Inc., 1982), pp. 12–34. See p. 32.

33. Albert Memmi, *The Colonizer and the Colonized* (Boston, Beacon Press, 1967).

1. Korean Human-Rights Consciousness in an Era of Transition, by Vipan Chandra

1. I refer here to such regimes as those of Iran and Saudi Arabia. The Iranian regime of Ayatollah Khomeini eliminated many of the legal procedures of the Shah's regime in favor of an "Islamic" system of justice. Summary trials, absence of appeals, and swift punishments of those opposed to the new order have been widely reported in the world press since January 1979. The Saudi Arabian regime has always had a similar Islamic system of justice. Recent events in Pakistan indicate movement in the same direction. Egypt under the late Anwar Sadat also eroded much of the secular structure of his predecessor Gamal Abdul Nasser and made the legal system adopt principles recommended by the Koran. This was in contradiction to the popular image of a personally pious but politically modern, secular leader that Sadat enjoyed in the West.

2. For concise treatments of the concept of human rights, see *Common Ground* 4.1 (Winter 1978; Hanover, New Hampshire: The American Universities Field Staff); and Linda L. Lum, ed., *Cross Cultural Aspects of Human Rights: Asia* (Washington, Foreign Service Institute, U.S. Department of State, 1988).

3. Here I am taking the personal position that all human rights in the end ideally can be traced to the three concepts of justice (defined here as a moral category), liberty, and equality, and, unless all three are present in a society, human rights can have only a truncated existence. Perhaps, among Western political thinkers, Rousseau comes closest to this notion. See "Equality in Rousseau and Kant," in C. J. Friedrich, *An Introduction to Political Theory* (New York, Harper and Row, 1967). Cf. Essays by E. F. Carritt, Sir Isaiah Berlin, and Joseph Schumpeter, in Anthony Quinton, ed., *Political Philosophy* (New York, Oxford University Press, 1967).

4. For the utilitarian school's views on this question (also echoed by many other English writers of the era), see the essay "On Representative Government," in Marshall Cohen, ed., *The Philosophy of John Stuart Mill* (New York, Modern Library, 1961); Eric Stokes, *The English Utilitarians and India* (London, Clarendon Press, 1959), esp. "Utilitarianism and Late 19th Century Imperialism," pp. 287–322; Francis G. Hutchins, *The Illusion of Permanence* (Cambridge, Harvard University Press, 1967); and Raghavan Iyer, "Utilitarianism and Empire in India," in Thomas R. Metcalf, ed., *Modern India: An Interpretive Anthology* (New York, MacMillan, 1971).

5. For missionary attitudes on this question, see Arthur H. Smith, *Chinese Characteristics* (New York, Fleming H. Revell, 1894), esp. pp. 314–330. Also see articles by Fairbank, Hutchinson, Cohen, Miller, and Schlesinger in John K. Fairbank, ed., *The Missionary Enterprise in China and America* (Cambridge, Harvard University Press, 1974). Cf. Harold R. Isaacs, *Images of Asia: American Views of China and India* (New York, Harper and Row, 1972). Stuart Creighton Miller's work, *The Unwelcome Immigrant: The American Image of the Chinese, 1785–1882* (Berkeley, University of California Press, 1974), offers much concrete detail on the subject.

It must be mentioned here that not all missionaries thought alike, but most did proceed on the assumption that Christianity produces a special kind of character and temperament which is conducive to the advancement of civilization, and civilization to them meant Western Civilization. The Utilitarians and the missionaries were preeminently cultural parochialists. But both were also incorrigible optimists. The Utilitarians believed that non-Western cultures could be reformed and brought up to the level of the West by the secular means of Western law and Western education. (A cruder version of this belief was Kipling's famous phrase "The White Man's Burden.") Most missionaries thought that, since Western culture and civilization were essentially the fruits of Christianity, their proselitization would transform the world in the Western mold. However, neither the utilitarians nor the missionaries thought that this change could be accomplished quickly. A long period of Western tutelage of the non-Western world was necessary in their view. Hence the amusing sentiment of Western "self-sacrifice" that one often finds in the otherwise clearly imperialistic notion of many nineteenth-century Westerners in Asia and elsewhere in the non-Western world. A few missionaries even welcomed the Opium War as a providential blessing, as part of God's design to offer them an opportunity to serve Him in the land of the heathens by bringing to their dark world the light of Christian civilization.

6. I like to call this the Rotary and Lions Club reasoning. Those with an experience of attendance at meetings of these clubs in Seoul would recall conversations with Korean and Western businessmen in which they supported this line of thinking. In my own experience, other private businessmen and even some conservative Korean Christians have taken such a position.

7. For an appraisal of the gap between the theory and practice of human rights in North Korea, see *Country Reports on Human Rights Practices*, a Report

submitted by the State Department to the House and Senate Foreign Relations Committees, 2 February 1981 (Washington, D.C., Joint Committee
Print, 1981).

8. In the discussion that follows, I have drawn upon some portions of my monograph, *Imperialism, Resistance, and Reform in Late-Nineteenth-Century
Korea: Enlightenment and the Independence Club* (Berkeley, Institute of East
Asian Studies, University of California, 1988). I am grateful to the Institute
of East Asian Studies for allowing me to do so.

9. The five cardinal relationships were: father-son, ruler-subject, husband-wife,
elder brother-younger brother, and friend-friend. The first three of these
constituted special bonds. The five virtues were: humanity, righteousness,
propriety, wisdom, and faithfulness. Sometimes a gloss on these virtues puts
them in this way: righteousness on the part of the father, love on the part
of the mother, brotherliness on the part of the elder brother, respect on the
part of the younger brother, and filial piety on the part of the son. (In this
arrangement, loyalty to the ruler on the part of the subjects was akin to the
virtues informing the father-son relationship.) See Chu Hsi's discussion of
these themes in Wing-Tsit Chan, *A Source Book in Chinese Philosophy*
(Princeton, Princeton University Press, 1963), p. 614.

10. Wing-Tsit Chan, *Reflections on Things at Hand* (New York, Columbia Uni-
versity Press, 1967), pp. 229, 231–232; quoted in Martina Deuchler, "Neo-
Confucianism in Early Yi Korea: Some Reflections on the Role of *Ye*," in
Korea Journal 15.5:13 (May 1975).

11. Ibid., p. 14.

12. Ibid.

13. Deuchler, p. 17.

14. Ibid.

15. The only relationship that categorically admitted the concepts of individual
autonomy and of equality was that between friends.

16. Several chapters in *Virtues in Conflict: Tradition and the Korean Woman
Today*, ed. Sandra Mattielli (Seoul, Samhwa Publishing Co., for the Royal
Asiatic Society, 1977) discuss the status of women in traditional Korea at
considerable length.

17. I am inclined to believe that the Korean language as a vehicle of Korean culture will continue to alter the meaning and role of Western ideas and institutions in the peninsula. As long as rank-consciousness remains a part of
Korean society and the country's language continues to reflect it, the quest
for human rights and democracy in Korea is likely to be frequently marked
by uncertainty and ambivalence.

18. See the observations of Pak Pyŏng-ho in his article "Characteristics of Traditional Korean Law," *Korea Journal* (Korean National Commission for
UNESCO, Seoul) 16.7 (July 1976), especially p. 14.

19. Ibid., p. 11. Sons of concubines suffered discrimination in this regard, as in
many others. See Hahm Pyong-Choon's article on the subject in his book
The Korean Political Tradition and Law (Seoul, Hollym Corporation, for

the Royal Asiatic Society, 1967). In the pages that follow, my debt to the late Dr. Hahm is heavy.

20. This is not meant to imply that the king always personally originated the law but that, as the final source of all legitimacy for legislation, his seal formalized nearly all law as the command of the sovereign. He had the ultimate authority to confer or withdraw such legitimacy.

21. The state was thus technically above the law, not under it. This does not, however, mean that it was always capricious and rode roughshod over popular sentiments and needs. The populist injunctions of the Confucian-Mencian tradition were part of the moral teachings of both the rulers and the people. The remonstrance system allowed another limited constraint on the king's arbitrariness. The *Book of History (Shu Ching)* had said that the insight and watchfulness of Heaven are expressed through the insight of the people. The *Tso Chüan* warned:

> Heaven created the people, placed a ruler above them and charged him to be a pastor; he must not lose this quality. . . . Heaven's love for the people is great; is it possible Heaven would allow a single man to act arbitrarily towards them, give free rein to his whims, and not take into account the nature of Heaven and Earth? Of course not!

Confucius had also sternly said: "Without the trust of the people, the state cannot survive." Similarly, Mencius had admonished that, in the constitution of a state, "the people rank the highest, the spirits of the land and grain come next, and the ruler counts the least." Mencius had also supported the right of a people to unseat a tyrannical government.

On the institution of remonstrance, see Ch'oe Sŭng-hi "Interrelations of the Monarch and the Remonstrants in the Early Yi Dynasty," in *Korea Journal* 15.5. On the *Shu Ching*, the *Tso Chüan*, and the Confucian precepts, see Vitaly Rubin, *Individual and State in Ancient China* (New York, Columbia University Press, 1976), p. 3. On the views of Mencius, see Wm. Theodore deBary et al., eds., *Sources of Chinese Tradition* (New York, Columbia University Press, 1960), I, 86–96.

22. Hahm, p 19
23. Ibid., p. 20.
24. Ibid., pp. 35–39, passim.
25. Ibid., p. 37.
26. Ibid., p. 39.
27. Hahm, p. 43.
28. Ibid., p. 64.
29. Ibid., pp. 63–69, passim.
30. Ibid., p. 68.
31. Ibid., p. 68.
32. Ibid., p. 64–65. A study by William Shaw, *Legal Norms in a Confucian State* (Berkeley, Institute of East Asian Studies, University of California, 1981), offers a useful corrective to Hahm's somewhat exaggerated stress on the punitive role of law and the notion that it was not considered a reliable instrument of social justice in Chosŏn Korea. Shaw offers persuasive evidence that

it was as important as "rule by virtue" and that, under wise and caring rulers, the legal system of Chosŏn Korea was not as capricious as Hahm claims. Yet, it is undeniable that the culture of a stratified society inevitably negates the moral meaning of justice, by which I mean fair play unencumbered by class, race, or sex considerations. To argue otherwise would be to claim, impossibly, that feudal and modern concepts of justice are identical in their aims. Unequal justice is thus another name for injustice. Hahm's reasoning was flawed but his conclusions about Chosŏn society strike me as eminently sound.

33. On the *Sirhak* scholars, see Han Woo-Keun, *The History of Korea* (Seoul, Eul-Yoo Publishing Co., 1970), pp. 316–335; and Michael C. Kalton, "An Introduction to Sirhak," in *Korea Journal* 15.5 (May 1975).

34. Kim Young-Choon, "Chŏndogyo Thought and Its Significance in Korean Tradition," *Korea Journal* 15.5.49.

35. On these matters, see Han Woo-Keun, *The History of Korea*, pp. 354–357, and his Korean language monograph *Tonghaknan kiin e kwanhan yŏn'gu* (A study of the causes of the Tonhak Rebellion; Korean Cultural Research Center, Seoul, 1971). See also Kim Young-Choon's article "Ch'ŏndogyo Thought and Its Significance in Korean Tradition," *Korea Journal* 15.5:49–51.

36. See Han Woo-Keun, *The History of Korea*, p. 362.

37. James B. Palais, *Politics and Policy in Traditional Korea* (Cambridge, Harvard University Press, 1975), p. 177.

38. On these developments, see Palais and Han Woo-Keun, *The History of Korea*, pp. 371–377. Chapters in Martina Deuchler's monograph, *Confucian Gentlemen and Barbarian Envoys: The Opening of Korea, 1875–1885* (Seattle and London, University of Washington Press, 1977), also go into them at length.

39. See Han Woo-Keun, *The History of Korea*, pp. 374–376.

40. Deuchler, *Confucian Gentlemen*, pp. 149–152.

41. Ibid., pp. 152–197, on all these changes.

42. On these developments, see Yi Kwang-nin, *Han'guk kaehwasa yŏn'gu* (A study of the history of enlightenment in Korea; Seoul, Ilchogak publishing Co., 1969).

43. On this theme, see David Kwang-Sun Suh, "American Missionaries and a Hundred Years of Korean Protestantism," in *Korea and the United States: A Century of Cooperation*, ed. Yongnok Koo and Dae-Sook Suh (Honolulu, University of Hawaii Press, 1985).

44. See Yi Kwang-nin, *Kaehwadang yŏn'gu* (A study of the Enlightenment Party), especially Chapters 1–3 (Seoul, Ilchogak Publishing Co., 1973). Chapters in a monograph by Harold F. Cook, *Korea's 1884 Incident* (Seoul, Taewon Publishing Co., for the Royal Asiatic Society, 1972) also are informative on the subject.

45. See the statement of Sŏ Chae-p'il quoted in my dissertation entitled "Nationalism and Popular Participation in Government in Late-19th-Century Korea: The Contribution of the Independence Club" (PhD dissertation, Harvard University, 1977), p. 17.

46. Two good works on Fukuzawa Yukichi's thought in English are Carmen

Blacker, *The Japanese Enlightenment: A Study of the Writings of Fukuzawa Yukichi* (Cambridge, Cambridge University Press, 1964) and Fukuzawa Yukichi, *An Outline of a Theory of Civilization,* tr. David A. Dilworth and G. Cameron Hurst (Tokyo, Sophia University Press, 1973). *The Autobiography of Fukuzawa Yukichi,* tr. Eiichi Kiyooka (New York, Columbia University Press, 1966) is also worth looking at.

47. See Harold F. Cook, *Korea's 1884 Incident,* p. 86.
48. See Yi Kwang-nin, "Progressive Views on Protestantism," *Korea Journal* 16.3:31 (March 1976).
49. See Cook, p. 247.
50. Ibid., pp. 238–244. See also Chŏn Pong-dŏk, "Kaehwagi ŭi pŏp sasang" (Legal thought in the enlightenment period), in *Han'guk sasang taegye* (A survey of Korean thought; (Cultural Research Institute, Sŏnggyungwan University, Seoul, 1977) III, 663–665. The two Sŏ's and Pak later went to the United States. Sŏ Chae-p'il stayed there for a decade, studying in higher education and eventually becoming a medical doctor. See my dissertation, pp. 21–23.
51. See George A. Lensen, *Balance of Intrigue: International Rivalry in Korea and Manchuria, 1884–1899* (Tallahasee, University Presses of Florida, 1982), pp. 27, 108–117.
52. A very detailed study of Pak's memorial is Chŏn Pong-dŏk, "Pak Yŏng-hyo wa kŭ ŭi sangso sŏsŏl" (An introduction to Pak Yŏng-hyo and his memorial), *Tonyang-hak* (Oriental studies) Vol. 8, Special Supplement (Seoul, Oriental Studies Institute, Tanguk University, 1978). See also Young-Ick Lew, "The Reform Efforts and Ideas of Pak Yŏng-hyo, 1894–1885," in *Korean Studies,* Vol. I (Honolulu, Center for Korean Studies, University of Hawaii, 1977).
53. Chŏn Pong-dŏk, "Kaehwagi ŭi pŏp sasang," p. 672.
54. Chŏn Pong-dŏk, "Pak Yŏng-hyo wa kŭ ŭi sangso," pp. 33, 35.
55. Ibid., p. 33.
56. Ibid., p. 55.
57. Ibid., p. 33.
58. Ibid., p. 60.
59. See Yi Kwang-nin, "Hansŏng sunbo wa Hansŏng chubo e taehan il Koch'al" (An examination of the *Hansŏng sunbo* and *Hansŏng chubo*), in *Han'guk Kaehwasa yŏn'gu,* cited above.
60. Chŏn Pong-dŏk, "Kaehwagi ŭi pŏpsasang," p. 671.
61. Ibid., p. 674.
62. Chŏn pong-dŏk, "Sŏyu kyŏnmun kwa Yu Kil-chun ŭi pŏmnyul sasang" (Observations on a stay in the West, and the legal thought of Yu Kil-chun), *Haksulwŏn nonmunch'ong* (Anthology of research papers), No. 15 (Seoul, The Korean Academy, 1976), p. 304.
63. Ibid., p. 305.
64. Ibid., Chŏn Pong-dŏk, "Kaehwagi ŭi pŏp sasang," pp. 684–686.
65. Ibid., p. 685.
66. Chŏn Pong-dŏk, "Sŏyu kyŏnmun kwa Yu Kil-chun," p. 314.

67. Ibid., p. 330.
68. Chŏn Pong-dŏk, "Kaehwagi ŭi pŏpsasang," p. 688.
69. Chŏn Pong-dŏk, "Sŏyu Kyŏnmun kwa Yu Kil-chun," p. 329.
70. Ibid., p. 324.
71. Ibid., p. 315.
72. See on this aspect of the book, Yi Kwang-nin, *Han'guk kaehwa sasang yŏn'gu* (A study of the enlightenment thought of Korea; Seoul, Ilchogak Publishing Co., 1979), pp. 66–67.
73. See Han Woo-Keun, *The History of Korea*, pp. 403–404. See also Jean Chesneaux, *China: From the Opium Wars to the 1911 Revolution* (New York, Pantheon Books, 1976), pp. 85–99.
74. Han Woo-Keun, *The History of Korea*, pp. 409–410.
75. Ibid., pp. 410–415.
76. Ibid., p. 416–427. Also see Homer B. Hulbert, *Hulbert's History of Korea*, ed. C. N. Weems (New York, Hillary House Publishers, Ltd., 1962), II, 243, 267–269.
77. Han Woo-Keun, *The History of Korea*, pp. 424–427; and *Hulbert's History of Korea*, II, 278–279.
78. Han Woo-Keun, *The History of Korea*, p. 432.
79. A good article on Yun is Kenneth W. Wells, "Yun Ch'hi-ho and the Quest for National Integrity," *Korea Journal* 22.1 (January 1982).
80. See my dissertation, p. 35.
81. *The Korean Repository* (1895), II, 401.
82. Ibid., pp. 403–404.
83. *The Independent*, 13 July 1897.
84. Ibid., 14 November 1896.
85. Ibid., 12 July 1898.
86. *Tongnip sinmun* (Korean language edition of *The Independent*), 9 March 1897.
87. *The Independent*, 5 December 1896.
88. For some samples of this oft-repeated theme, see the English and Korean editions of the paper of 21 November 1896, and *Tongnip sinmun*, 16–17 November 1898.
89. *Tongnip sinmun*, 17 November 1898 and 11 January 1898.
90. Ibid., 20 February 1897; 9 March 1897.
91. *Tongnip sinmum*, 17 April 1897.
92. Ibid.
93. This theme, another oft-repeated one, appears prominently in *Tongnip sinmun* on 11 July 1896, 20 May 1897, 21 and 26 November 1898, and 15 December 1898.
94. On the conflicting interpretations of the various exponents of the social-contract theory, see C. J. Friedrich, *An Introduction to Political Theory* (New York, Holt, Rinehart and Winston, 1961), Chapters 23, 26–28.
95. *Tongnip sinmun*, 9 July 1897.
96. Here again many issues of the *Tongnip sinmun* can be cited. The following are especially noteworthy: 11 April, 11 July, and 21 November 1896; 17

April, 21 November, and 15 December 1897; and 4, 11 January, 20 February, 3 March, 4 and 20 May, and 16, 17, 21, and 26 November 1898.

97. *The Independent,* 30 January 1897. See also *Tongnip sinmun,* 17 April 1897.
98. *The Independent,* 23 June 1896.
99. Sŏ often praised General Greathouse for his efforts. See, for example, Sŏ's remarks in *The Independent,* 10 October 1896 and 17 November 1897. See also *Tongnip sinmun,* 29 December 1896.
100. *The Independent,* 23 June 1896.
101. *Tongnip sinmun,* 4 August 1898.
102. *The Independent,* 7 October 1897.
103. *Tongnip sinmun,* 11 April 1896. See also the issues of 15 August 1896, 18 March 1897, and 11 December 1898.
104. Ibid., 5 August and 8 September 1896; and 3 March and 4 May 1897.
105. *The Independent,* 26 March 1898.
106. Numerous issues of *Tongnip sinmun* discuss this theme. For samples, see those of 7, 12 April, 26 July, and 5 September 1896; 1 May, 3 June, 14 August, 5 October, 7 November, and 16 and 28 December 1897; and 10 January, 19, 24 February, 12 April, 3 June, 7 November, and 16 December 1898.
107. Ibid., 7 November 1897.
108. Ibid. See also *The Independent* of 5 November 1898 in which Yun wrote the following memorable words:

>It is a sorely degraded and spiritless people that cannot grumble . . . Wherever there is grumbling there is hope . . . Even our chronic pessimism inclines us to discover some hope in Korea in the grumbling of the people. Grumble on then.

109. Marshal Cohen, *The Philosophy of John Stuart Mill* (New York, The Modern Library, 1961), p. 205.
110. On this theme, too, one finds many editorials. See *Tongnip sinmun,* 7 April 1896; 14 August, 4 December, and 18 December 1897; and 19 February, 12 April, 7 November, and 28 December 1898.
111. Ibid., 27 August 1898. See also the issues of 29 August, 1 September 1896; 28 January 1897; 7 November 1898. CF. *The Independent,* 25 August 1896.
112. Quoted in Peter Duus, *Party Rivalry and Political Change in Taishō Japan* (Cambridge, Harvard University Press, 1968), p. 237.
113. *Tongnip sinmun,* 14–16 April, 1896.
114. Ibid., 16 January 1897, and *The Independent,* 12, 15, 16 January 1897. About 18,000 Koreans were reportedly living in Russian Manchuria at the time. See also Isabella B. Bishop, *Korea and Her Neighbours* (Reprint ed., Seoul, Yonsei University Press, 1970), pp. 223–238.
115. *The Independent,* 16 January 1897. See also *Tongnip sinmun,* 17 January 1897.
116. Ibid., 7 December 1898.
117. Ibid., 27 July 1889.
118. For examples of such admonitions see *Tongnip sinmun,* 7 April, 30 July, and 22 August 1897; and 8 September 1898.
119. *Tongnip sinmun,* 22 December 1896.

120. *The Korean Repository* (1897), IV, 472–473.
121. *The Independent,* 19 May 1898.
122. *The Korean Repository* (1897), IV, 472.
123. Isabella B. Bishop, *Korea and Her Neighbors,* pp. 439–440.
124. H. B. Hulbert, *The Passing of Korea* (Seoul, Yonsei University Reprint, 1969), p. 149.
125. See John E. Sloboda, "Legal Change in Korea, 1876–1910: The Victory of Tradition," Seminar Paper, Harvard Law School, April 1970; and H. B. Hulbert, *The Passing of Korea,* p. 154.
126. Ibid., p. 169.
127. See my article "The Independence Club and Korea's First Proposal for a National Legislative Assembly" in *Occasional Papers on Korea* (Seattle, University of Washington), no. 4, 1975.
128. Unless otherwise indicated, the whole section on law reform is based upon John E. Sloboda's paper cited above. I wish to express my deep appreciation to the author for his contribution to my understanding of late Chosŏn-dynasty law.
129. It is unclear whether traditional Korean legislation defined "public" and "private" in terms of whether an official was acting on or off duty. The Chinese statutes and court proceedings suggest that the determining question was whether offenses were committed with a corrupt or selfish ("private") purpose or not. See Thomas A. Metzger, *The Internal Organization of Ch'ing Bureaucracy: Legal, Normative and Communications Aspects* (Cambridge, Harvard University Press, 1973), pp. 268–269, 281–287.
130. Ibid., p. 33.
131. Ibid., p. 37.
132. Ibid., pp. 37–38.
133. Ibid., pp. 38–39.
134. Edward J. Baker, *The Role of Legal Reforms in the Japanese Annexation and Rule of Korea, 1905–1910* (Studies in East Asian Law, Korea: No. 1; Cambridge, Harvard Law School, 1979).

2. Korea Before Rights, by William Shaw

1. For further discussion of the reception of Neo-Confucianism in Korea, see William Shaw, "The Neo-Confucian Revolution of Values in Early Yi Korea: Its Implications for Korean Legal Thought," in Brian E. McKnight, ed., *Law and the State in Traditional East Asia: Six Studies on the Sources of East Asian Law* (Honolulu, University of Hawaii Press, 1987), pp. 149–171, and Martina Deuchler, "The Tradition: Women during the Yi Dynasty," in Sandra Mattielli, ed., *Virtues in Conflict: Tradition and Korean Women Today* (Seoul, Royal Asiatic Society, 1977), pp. 1–47.
2. Chŏng To-chŏn, *Sambongjip* (Collected writings of Sambong; Seoul, Kuksa p'yŏnch'an wiwŏnhoe, 1961), p. 239.
3. U Chŏng-kyu, *Kyŏngje yaŏn* (*An Outsider's Opinions on Government*), tr. Yi Ik-sŏng (Seoul, Ŭryu munhwasa, 1973), p. 31.
4. Richard Rutt and Kim Chong-un, tr., *Virtuous Women: Three Classic Korean*

Novels. (Seoul, Kwang Myong Printing Company, 1974), pp. 195, 199. The novel is based on an historic incident. Pak T'ae-po for a time received treatment as a moral exemplar in South Korean textbooks. The story of his principled opposition to unjust authority was removed under the Yusin political order of President Park Chung Hee in the 1970s.

5. William Shaw, *Legal Norms in a Confucian State* (Berkeley, Institute for East Asian Studies, University of California, 1982), pp. 46–59, 127–138.

6. *Simnirok* (Records of *simni* review hearings; Seoul, Pŏpchech'ŏ, 1968), I, 276–278. Translated in *Legal Norms*, pp. 237–238.

7. Ibid., 88. Translated in *Legal Norms*, pp. 192–193.

8. Ibid., I, 193–194. Translated in *Legal Norms*, pp. 222–223.

9. Ibid., I, 135–136. Translated in *Legal Norms*, pp. 205–206.

10. For discussion of the petition-drum system in the Chosŏn dynasty, see *Legal Norms*, pp. 85–92.

11. *Chŏngjo sillok, kwŏn* 2, pp. 60b–61a.

3. Between Class and Nation: The Equalization Society of the 1920s, by William Shaw

1. The principal studies in Korean are KimŬi-hwan, "Ilche ch'iha ŭi Hyŏngp'yŏng undonggo" (A study of the *Hyŏngp'yŏng* [Equalization] Movement under Japanese rule), *Hyangt'o Sŏul* (December 1967), pp. 51–90; and, by the same author, "P'yŏngdŭng sahoerŭl wi hayŏ–hyŏngp'yŏng undong," (To achieve an egalitarian society–the Equalization Movement), in *Han'guk hyŏndaesa* (History of modern Korea; Seoul, 1973), VIII, 353–371. The Movement is also mentioned briefly in Herbert Passin, "The *Paekchŏng* of Korea, *Monumenta Nipponica* 12.3–4:27–72 (1956–57).

2. For example, Yi Ki-paek, *Han'guksa ŭi kibon chisik* (Basic knowledge of Korean history; Seoul, 1972), pp. 276–297. About three-fourths of the essays in the chapter on the colonial period are devoted to cultural and other forms of resistance to Japanese rule.

3. Kim Chun-yŏp and Kim Ch'ang-sun, *Han'guk kongsanjuŭi undongsa* (A history of the Korean Communist Movement; Seoul, 1969), II. 29–174. The *Hyŏngp'yŏng* movement is dealt with at pp. 160–174.

4. On the subject of collaboration, see Bruce Cumings, "The Politics of Liberation: Korea, 1945–1947" (PhD dissertation, Columbia University, 1975), pp. 158–160. Yi Ki-paek points out that the movement to foster Korean-managed enterprises was criticized as "meaningless" by socialists (p. 291).

5. Kim Tŏk-han, "Hyŏngp'yŏngsa ŭi naehong gwa hyŏngp'yŏng undong e daehan p'ip'an" (International strife within the Equalization Movement: A critique), *Kaebyŏk* 50: 39–42 (August 1924).

6. Ferdinand Lassalle (d. 1864) was the pioneer German socialist who developed ideas of evolutionary socialism based on the attainment of universal suffrage. Many doctrinal and tactical disputes within the Social Democratic Party of Germany in the late-nineteenth century are to be understood in terms of tension between this perspective and that of Marxists within the party. See David Caute, *The Left in Europe since 1789* (London, 1966).

7. On Yamakawa, see George Beckmann and Genji Okubo, *The Japanese Communist Party, 1922–1945* (Stanford, Stanford University Press, 1965), p. 20. The subsequent shift among Japanese Marxists to the concept of an elite party organization under the influence of Fukumoto Kazuo is discussed in Henry Smith, *Japan's First Student Radicals* (Cambridge, Harvard University Press, 1972), pp. 162–185.

8. Kim Yun-hwan, "Ilcheha Han'guk nodong ŭi chŏn'gae kwajŏng" (The process of development of Korean labor under Japanese imperial rule), in Kim Yun-hwan et al., *Ilcheha ŭi minjok undongsa* (National movements under Japanese imperial rule; Seoul, 1971), p. 295.

9. Kim and Kim, *Han'guk kongsanjuŭi undongsa*, II, 43–44.

10. Robert A. Scalapino and Chong-sik Lee, *Communism in Korea, Vol. I: The Movement* (Berkeley, University of California Press, 1972), p. 70.

11. *Kuksa taesajŏn* (*Encyclopedia of Korean history;* Seoul, 1970), articles on *mujari* (p. 542) and *paekchŏng* (p. 615).

12. *Kyŏngguk taejŏn* (*Great code for governing the country;* Chōsen sōtokufu edition, Keijō, Seoul), p. 476. *Chosŏn wangjo sillok* (Veritable Records of the Chosŏn dynasty; Kuksa p'yŏnch'an wiwŏnhoe ed.) II, 629, 649, 652, 7804 (all Sejong period).

13. Kang Man-gil, "Sŏnch'o paekchŏnggo" (A study of the *paekchŏng* of the early Chosŏn dynasty), *Sahak yŏn'gu* (Studies in history) 18:491–526 (September 1964).

14. Kim Ŭi-hwan, "P'yŏngdŭng sahoe," pp. 354–355.

15. All references to the *Simnirok* are to the Pŏpchech'ŏ edition. *Simnirok* (Records of Simni hearings) Pŏpchech'ŏ ed., 2 vols. (Seoul, 1968).

16. Kim Ŭi-hwan, "P'yŏngdŭng sahoe," pp. 352–353.

17. Ibid.

18. Passin, p. 60.

19. Chang Chi-p'il was of *paekchŏng* origin, but prosperous enough to spend three years at Meiji University in Tokyo. He applied for a position with the Government General on his return to Korea, but withdrew his application in protest when required to submit census documents, upon which the term *butcher* (*tohan*) had been routinely stamped. *Tong-A ilbo* (*TI*), 20 May 1923.

20. All information on the *burakumin* and *burakumin* movements has been taken from George O. Totten and Hiroshi Wagatsuma, "Emancipation: Growth and Transformation of a Political Movement," in George DeVos and Hiroshi Wagatsuma, *Japan's Invisible Race: Caste in Culture and Personality* (Berkeley, University of California Press, 1966), pp. 33–67.

21. Passin, p. 64.

22. This issue was one singled out for mention in a *paekchŏng* manifesto of 1927. See Kim Ŭi-hwan, "Ilche ch'iha," p. 85.

23. Passin, p. 64.

24. Kim Ŭi-hwan, "Ilche ch'iha," pp. 73–74.

25. Hirano Shoken, "Chōsen kōhei undō no gaikan" (An overview of the Equalization Movement of Korea), *Jinruiai* 2:202–227 (Tokyo, 1927). Hirano provided a table showing the occupation of nearly 7,500 *paekchŏng* households;

some 2,300 of these were involved in the sale of meat, while more than 1,400 are listed as farmers. Those employed as butchers ranked third with over 1,200. Hirano did not say whether his information was based on official Government General figures or figures provided by the Equalization Movement; whichever it may be, these were clearly households still identified as of *paek-chŏng* origin.

26. Kim Ŭi-hwan, "Ilche ch'iha," p. 58. Kim states that the survey was conducted as an intelligence measure by the Government General police authorities following the organization of the Equalization Society.

27. Ibid.

28. The following account of the founding of the Equalization Society is based on Kim Ŭi-hwan, "P'yŏngdŭng sahoe," pp. 357–359.

29. Ibid., p. 360.

30. *Tonga ilbo* articles on the Equalization Movement for 1923 and 1924 have been collected and reprinted in *Chōsen gakuhō* (Journal of Korean studies), LX, 155–214. For convenience, I have used these rather than the reduced-format reprint of the original available at Yenching Library. Spot checks have not turned up any inaccuracies in the transition from Korean to Japanese. All citations to the *Tonga ilbo* hereafter are *TI.*

31. *TI,* 20 May 1923.

32. Ibid.

33. Kim Ŭi-hwan, "P'yŏngdŭng sahoe," p. 360.

34. Kim Yun-hwan, p. 317.

35. *TI,* 20 May 1923.

36. Kim Ŭi-hwan, "P'yŏngdŭng sahoe," p. 376.

37. Ibid., p. 362.

38. Ibid., pp. 363–365.

39. *TI,* 26 June, 9 July, 18 August 1923.

40. *Genbun shimbun sashi-osae kiji shuroku* (Records of articles removed from vernacular newspapers), III, 118–119.

41. Kim Ŭi-hwan, P'yŏngdŭng sahoe," pp. 362–363; "Ilche ch'iha," pp. 69–72.

42. Ibid.

43. Kim Ŭk-hwan, "Ilche ch'iha," p. 81. Both labor and tenancy disputes showed a marked rise (in numbers and in number of persons involved) in 1923 and 1924 over previous years, declining somewhat thereafter.

44. Ibid., pp. 85–86.

45. Kim and Kim, pp. 167–168.

46. Ibid.

47. *TI,* 19 August 1924.

48. *TI,* 16 September 1924.

49. Kim and Kim, p. 168.

50. Totten and Wagatsuma, pp. 42ff.

51. Henry Smith, pp. 25ff. According to Smith, student demonstrations at Meiji University were non-political during the period concerned, since they remained limited in scope to one campus and were not ideological in origin. But Smith also demonstrates the ease with which experience in such demon-

strations, even at the middle-school level, could lead to subsequent political activism. Moreover, it is difficult to believe that Chang could have spent three years as a student in Tokyo without witnessing a wide variety of types of student activism.

52. *TI,* 20 May 1923.
53. For a list of such visits, see Akisada Yoshikazu, "Kaisetsu" (Interpretation), appended to the *Tonga ilbo* articles on the Equalization Movement in the *Chōsen gakuhō,* LX, 215–231. Hirano is said to have visited Korea in early summer 1926.
54. Hirano, p. 215.
55. Ibid., p. 217.
56. William O'Neill, *Coming Apart: An Informal History of America in the 1960s.* See the relevant portions on the shift in goals, tactics, and leadership that took place during the decade.
57. *TI,* 27 June 1923.
58. Kim Tŏk-han, "Hyŏngp'yŏngsa ŭi naehong."
59. *TI,* 18 May 1923.
60. Robert A. Scalapino and Chong-Sik Lee, *Communism in Korea, Vol. II, The Society,* p. 764.

4. Nationalism and Human-Rights Thought in Korea under Colonial Rule, by Michael Robinson

1. The following are two examples of such attacks: "Kyehwa wa kapcha" (1923 and 1924), *Kaebyŏk* (Creation) 5.1:2–12 (January 1924); Yi Sŏng-t'ae, "Chungsan kyegŭp igijŏk undong" (The self-serving movement of the middle class), *Tonga ilbo,* 20 March 1923.
2. Kang Tong-chin, *Nihon no chōsen shihai seisakushi kenkyū,* (Tokyo, Tōdai shuppankai, 1979), Chapter 2, Section 2. For a discussion of these reforms in English, see Frank Baldwin, "The March First Movement: Korean Challenge and Japanese Response" (PhD dissertation, Columbia University, 1969).
3. This observation is based on the approaches of standard histories of the colonial period. A good example is the Korea University series *Ilcheha ŭi Han'guk yŏn'gu chongsŏ* (Collected studies on Korea under Japanese rule), 5 vols.; and Kim Chun-yŏp and Kim Ch'ang-sun's *Han'guk kongsanjuŭi undongsa* (The history of the Korean Communist movement), 5 vols. The standard work on the history of the Korean nationalist movement in English also separated "nationalists" from "internationalists"; see Chong-sik Lee, *Politics of Korean Nationalism* (Berkeley, University of California Press), 1964.
4. For a recent study of the "anti-nationalist" trials in post-war South Korea, see Kil Chin-hyŏn, *Yŏksa e tasi mutnunda: panmin t'ŭkwi wa ch'in'ilp'a* (Asking again of history: The anti-national crimes committee and the pro-Japanese group; Seoul, Saminsa, 1984).
5. Kim Chun-yŏp and Kim Ch'ang-sun. pp. 15–22. For a detailed treatment of

the ideology of the Buy Korean Movement, see Kenneth M. Wells, "The Rationale of Korean Economic Nationalism Under Japanese Colonial Rule, 1922–1932: The Case of Cho Man-sik's Products Promotion Society," *Modern Asian Studies* 19.4:823–860 (October 1985).

6. For a groundbreaking study of the origins of Korean capitalism, see Carter Eckert, "The Origins of Korean Capitalism: The Koch'ang Kims and the Kyŏngsŏng Spinning and Weaving Company, 1871–1945" (PhD dissertation, University of Washington, 1986).

7. For a discussion of the moderate nationalist movements, see Michael Robinson, *Cultural Nationalism in Colonial Korea, 1920–1925* (Seattle, University of Washington Press, 1988).

8. Yi Kwang-su. "Minjok kaejoron" (Treatise on reconstruction of the nation), *Kaebyŏk* 3.5:18–72 (May 1922).

9. Ibid.

10. Chŏng Chin-sŏk, *Han'guk ŏllon t'ujaengsa* (The struggle of the Korean press; Seoul; Chŏng'ŭm mungo, 1975).

11. Yi Sŏng-t'ae, "Chungsan Kyegŭp igijŏk undong."

12. "Chosŏn ŭi t'ŭki han ch'ŏji wa i e taehan t'ŭki han kujech'aek" (A special plan for the special conditions of Korea), *Kaebyŏk* 3.1 (January 1922).

13. For a history of the Korean Communist movement and the Comintern's critique of the movement's elitism, see Suh Dae-sook, *The Korean Communist Movement* (Princeton, Princeton University Press, 1967); Lee Chong-sik and Robert Scalapino, *Communism in Korea*, 2 vols. (Berkeley, University of California Press, 1972).

14. See William Shaw's chapter on the Equalization Society in this volume.

5. Human Rights in South Korea, 1945–1953, by Gregory Henderson

1. Various claims of human-rights violations in the north have emanated through the years from defectors reaching the Republic of Korea, the most extensive being accounts in the spring of 1982 concerning the existence of concentration camps in the D.P.R.K. incarcerating some 100,000 political prisoners. Such claims are not subject, as yet, to normal check and authentication, particularly in cases like the foregoing in which a very considerable time elapsed between the defection and the public report. They can, therefore, be neither confidently asserted nor denied.

2. Nena Vreeland and Rinn-Sup Shinn et al., *Area Handbook for North Korea* (DA Pam 550–581, Foreign Area Studies, The American University, U.S. Government Printing Office, 1976), p. 30.

3. Robert A. Scalapino and Chong-Sik Lee, *Communism in Korea*, Vol. II, *The Society* (Berkeley, University of California Press, 1972), pp. 813–818.

4. E. Grant Meade, *American Military Government in Korea* (New York, King's Crown Press, Columbia University, 1951), pp. 221ff., passim.

5. USAMGIK Ordinances were published on separate sheets or small fascicles on poor paper as they were issued and are available in this—now deteriorated—form in major libraries. At Harvard, they are available both in

Widener and at the Law School Library, under the heading KOR 203 F46, *Korea: Laws, statutes, compilations.* The ordinances of the U.S. Military Government (Seoul Official Gazette, Chosŏn haengjŏng ch'ulp'ansa, 1946).

6. Gregory Henderson, *Korea: The Politics of the Vortex* (Cambridge, Harvard University Press, 1968), p. 126.

7. Ibid., p. 138.

8. Ibid., pp. 137–140.

9. As pointed out in E. Grant Meade, p. 55, the *ch'iandae*, the Peace Preservation Forces of the People's Committees (later KPP) took over police functions briefly in late August 1945 where the Japanese police collapsed. They soon yielded this function, but some *ch'iandae* holdovers continued, in some areas, even under Military Government.

10. Henderson, pp. 103–104.

11. Karl Moskowitz, "Current Assets: The Employees of Japanese Banks in Colonial Korea" (PhD dissertation, Harvard University, 1979), p. 381 and passim.

12. Pak Kyŏng-sik, "Taiheiyō sensōjii ni okeru Chōsenjin Kyōsei renkō" (Koreans forced to enter the Pacific War), *Rekishigaku Kenkyū* (Historical research) 297:30–46 (February 1965).

13. Changsoo Lee and George DeVos, *Koreans in Japan: Ethnic Conflict and Accommodation* (Berkeley, University of California Press, 1981), p. 54.

14. Wonmo Dong, "The Japanese Colonial Bureaucracy in Korea, 1910–1945: Patterns of Recruitment and Mobility," paper for presentation at the Social Science Research Council, Conference on Colonial Korea, 2–4 January 1981, New York.

15. Henderson, p. 106.

16. Wonmo Dong, "Japanese Colonial Policy and Practice in Korea, 1905–1945: A Study of Assimilation" (PhD dissertation, Georgetown University, 1965) Chapter 5, pp. 355–363.

17. Dr. John Merrill has pointed out an exception to me: Just after the Yŏsu-Sunch'ŏn Rebellion of October 1948, the Sunch'ŏn prosecutor was accused of taking part in the rebellion and was executed.

18. John K. Oh, *Korea: Democracy on Trial* (Ithaca, Cornell University Press, 1968), p. 9.

19. Henderson, pp. 142–143.

20. Richard D. Robinson, "Korea—Betrayal of a Nation" (unpublished manuscript 1947, available at Harvard-Yenching Institute Library), p. 142.

21. U.S. International Cooperation Administration, "Report on the National Police," Seoul, 1947.

22. GAOR, 4th Session, Report of the United Nations Commission on Korea, Supplement No. 9 (A/936), p. 28. Also Lawrence K. Rosinger, *The State of Asia* (New York, Knopf, 1951), p. 149.

23. *Dong-A ilbo,* 28 December 1948, p. 2.

24. Henderson, p. 160.

25. Ibid., p. 163.

26. Supreme Commanders for the Allied Powers (SCAP), *Summation of Non-*

Military Activities in Japan and Korea, No. 1, September-October 1945 (Tokyo), p. 177.

27. United States Military Government in Korea, Office of the Military Governor, Official Gazette Ordinance 21, Seoul, 2 November 1945.
28. *General Review of Law and Regulations under Military Government,* Korean Legal Research Society, Seoul, date unspecified, perhaps 1971.
29. For this and other principal opinions, see "Selected Legal Opinions of the Department of Justice, U.S. Army Military Government in Korea: Opinions Rendered in the Role of Legal Adviser to the Military Government of Korea and Covering a Period from March 1946 to August 19, 1948," Compilation prepared by the Department of Justice, Headquarters, U.S. Army Military Government in Korea, Seoul, Korea, 2 vols., n.d. available, inter alia, presently in the Treasure Room, Harvard Law School Library, Cambridge, under the call no. KOR 322948. These opinions, though of considerable importance, seem not to have been formally published in either English or Korean.
30. Article 100 in the 1948 Constitution as in *Yukpŏp Chŏnsŏ* (The complete text of the Six Codes; Seoul, Pŏpchŏn Publishing Co., 1976), p. 22.
31. Oh, p. 86.
32. *Han'guk sinmun paeknyŏn* (100 Years of Korean newspapers; Seoul, Han'guk Sinmun Yŏn'guso, 1975), pp. 1130–1132.
33. Robinson, p. 156; *South Korean Interim Government (SKIG) Activities* No. 27, December 1947, p. 166 (published in Seoul by USAMGIK as the continuation after August 1947 of the *USAMGIK Activities in Korea*).
34. Henderson, p. 141.
35. Robinson, pp. 162–165.
36. Robert A. Scalapino and Changsik Lee, *Communism in Korea,* II, 372–373. Though these claims were vastly exaggerated, even American sources confirm the possibility of upwards of 25% of the rural population having voted, mostly for some reform but perhaps 5% for the establishment of a rival government in the north, percentages on Cheju Island being higher. See John Merrill, "The Cheju-do Rebellion," *The Journal of Korean Studies* 2:177 (1980).
37. Oh, p. 8.
38. Ibid., p. 9.
39. UNTCOK recommendations on the election law are contained in U.N. Document A/AC, 19/53 Report of the United Nations Temporary Commission on Korea, 1948. This document, originally restricted, is normally available only at the Hammarskold Library, U.N. Plaza, New York.
40. Soon Sung Cho, *Korea in World Politics, 1940–1950* (Berkeley, University of California Press, 1967), pp. 207–208.
41. For another, less positive, view of the elections, see Harold H. Sunoo, *America's Dilemma in Asia: The Case of South Korea* (Chicago, Nelson Hall, 1949), pp. 63–65.
42. Constitution, General Provisions and Article 5. For text and amendments through 1962, see *Korean Constitution, Election and Political Party Laws*

(Central Election Management Committee, R.O.K. Seoul, Bo Jin Zae Printing Co., 1964).

43. John Merrill, p. 168.

44. GAOR, 4th Session, Supplement No. 9 (A/936).

45. For above, see G. Henderson, "Legal Development and Parliamentary Democracy: The Fraktsiya Incident of 1949" (unpublished paper, Columbia University seminar, 10 April 1972). Also Henderson, pp. 162–163.

46. Henderson, p. 163.

47. Henderson, p. 165.

48. *Dong-A ilbo*, 28 December 1949, p. 1.

49. All hearings of the *pŭrakchi* trial were open to the public. The U.S. Embassy and the U.N. Commission sent senior Korean employees to cover all proceedings in the belief that, since the freedom of the 1948 Assembly election had constituted the basis for the recognition and legitimacy of the South Korean government, the freedom of the representatives so elected bore both on the government's continued legitimacy and also on the development of its democratic institutions.

    The Embassy sent to all hearings two trusted Korean employees who took separate verbatim notes of everything that transpired. A lengthy record of the hearing was prepared from a collation and translation of these notes. This is now available in the National Archives, Washington, D.C., in declassified despatches of the author beginning with Seoul despatch 391, 27 June 1949. The author's despatches on the anti-national acts legislation and the events of May-June 1949 are also available in the archives. A *Dong-A ilbo* text of all or most of the first two sessions exists or existed. Comparison of the Embassy recordings with each other and with this revealed little significant discrepancy, although the *Dong-A ilbo* version identified somewhat differently those actors in the case who were not produced in open court. As with other Korean trials, no official court verbatim record was made, only a summary whose present existence following the record-scattering of the war is moot.

50. Three of the arrested Assemblymen avoided the main prosecution. One was tried in Chŏnju, perhaps to avoid attention; he was sentenced mildly, bailed, and released. The second was released without being charged. The third, a ranking former Department of Commerce official, was briefly tried but not sentenced.

51. It is interesting that 1.5 years is also the lowest sentence handed down in the October-December 1920 sentencing by colonial courts of the 33 independence leaders and their chief accomplices. Japan's Chōsen courts were, however, more lenient: the upper limit of sentence was 3 years. Yi Pyŏng-hŏn, *Sam-il undong* (Seoul, Sisa Sibo-sa, 1959), pp. 808–810.

52. These provided punishment for those who "played leading roles in an association or group established for the purpose of disturbing the tranquillity of the nation"; "joined, with knowledge of its hostile nature, any organization or group established for the purpose of disturbing the tranquillity of the nation in compliance with orders of such an association or group";

caused commission of the crimes prescribed in the Security Law; "rendered assistance with knowledge of a plot by promises or by some methods"; or, under Ordinance 19, "obstructed, attempted to obstruct, or contravened order or announced programs of the Government or because they were engaged in a conspiracy." (Government citation of Ordinance 19 is an interesting demonstration that it did not consider that its new security legislation replaced older Military Government provisions.)

53. Because of the role played by the U.N. Commission message in the prosecution, members of the UNCOK intervened and buried all interest in the case.

54. On 25 June 1949, the Democratic Front for the Unification of the Fatherland was founded at the Moranbong Theatre in P'yǒngyang. Taking their cue therefrom, remaining Communist sympathizers in South Korea launched assaults and sabotage in July and August. Whether this foundation had, in fact, any connection with the *pǔrakchi* incident remains entirely uncertain. The events in the case transpired before the advent of the Democratic Front—though perhaps not before the planning which must have preceded it and which could have borne on the SKLP effort to despatch Yi Chae-nam to contact No Il-hwan (see below). The formation of such a movement, however, undoubtedly raised the level of South Korean apprehension. Once induced by their sentences to go to the north with the Communist invaders who freed them from jail in Seoul, the sentenced National Assemblymen did become active in this organization. (See Scalapino and Lee, pp. 338–390.)

55. The defendants were, except for Kim Yak-su, young. They came from widely scattered districts in South Korea, and had no previous organizational relationship with one another. In fact, their relations with each other had no very deep roots except in the idea of a greater and more neutral independence. No Il-hwan and, for a time, Kim Yak-su (once a leftist-nationalist student in Tokyo) had even been members of the conservative Korean Democratic party, No's family having ties with KDP founder and wealthy patron, Kim Sǒng-su. Sǒ Yong-kil was a devout Christian.

56. Messrs. Ha's and Yi's superior in the SKLP, introduced as a witness for the prosecution, testified that Ha and Yi were one and the same person.

57. For much of the foregoing and following judgments I am indebted to "Comments on the Trials of the National Assemblymen," unpublished memorandum of Dr. Ernst Fraenkel to the U.S. Embassy, Seoul, April 1950, on the *pǔrakchi* case, in the possession of the author. Dr. Fraenkel, legal adviser to the American aid mission and before that to USAMGIK, had practiced law before both the Weimar and the Nazi courts. A copy of this memorandum was handed to President Rhee by Ambassador Muccio in the spring of 1950—without result.

58. In essence, the use of inferential evidence (if "evidence" it can be called) is very little changed in these passages from its use in the following passage in 1589 to convict the great Zen abbot and warrior monk, Sǒsan Taesa, of being in league with a convicted friend. Sǒsan had written:

The capital is like an ants' nest.
The hero is like a dayfly.
Lying quietly under the bright moon.
I hear music in a wind among the pines.

The prosecutor interpreted the poem to mean that the "hero" is Sŏsan's devoted friend, and that the ants referred to the enemies who imprisoned him. Thus, Sŏsan's poem was taken as evidence that he was in league with his friend. Sŏsan eventually was pardoned by the King. Cho Myong-ki. "Prominent Buddhist Leaders and Their Doctrines," *Korea Journal* 4.5:21 (May 1964).

59. Consistent with this hypothesis was the mysterious assassination on 12 August 1949, of Kim Ho-ik, Chief of the central detachment of the political surveillance section of the Seoul Police Bureau and in charge of investigating the *pŭrakchi* case. Mr. Kim, midway in the arrests of the assemblymen, was shot by a man in military uniform carrying the name card of the intelligence chief of the Seoul Police Bureau. The assassin was apprehended minutes after the shooting at a nearby bus stop but was neither arrested nor tried, for reasons never explained but quite possibly connected with the need to prevent the appearance of any evidence that the police—quite possibly Mr. Kim himself—had written Evidence No. 1.

60. For example, Article 98 of the Criminal Code of 1953 provided penalties of "not less than 7 years" up to and including death for acting as a spy or aiding "a spy of an enemy country." Gerhard O. W. Mueller, *The American Series of Foreign Penal Codes,* Vol. II, *The Korean Criminal Code,* translated and introduced by Prof. Paul K. Ryu (South Hackensack, Fred B. Rothman, and London, Sweet and Maxwell, 1960), Article 98, p. 62.

61. More research is needed to determine the extent to which the same was true in political trials of the colonial period in Korea. One defendant in the Samil Independence Movement trial of 1920 was freed as innocent.

62. The political effect is well illustrated by the trial of Kim Yak-su (above.) Mr. Kim has been a well-known fighter for Korean independence from his student days in Japan, was jailed for 10 years in Japanese jails, was tried in an independent Korea by Japanese law administered by a former Government General judge and a Government General prosecutor who used against him a Korean spy formerly in Japanese employ.

63. Henderson, pp. 167–168.

64. Interview with a former R.O.K. general who was a member of the court-martial trial board, Cambridge, Mass., 1965.

65. In 1962, the chief of the U.S. Embassy's Political Section, meeting General Kim Tong-ha unexpectedly at church following his ordeal, found him, only a few months after their last meeting, so altered as to be scarcely recognizable. (Conversation with Counselor Philip Habib, fall 1962.)

66. The question arises whether the description in Korean textbooks of the *pŭrakchi* and other of the above trials as if they were proved cases of subversion does not falsify history.

67. For the observations here I am grateful to Prof. Dr. Paul K. Ryu, Professor

of Criminal Law at Seoul National University of which he has been Law School Dean and President, in Mueller, pp. 1–29.

68. Thus, where a man kills, injures, or harms his or his spouse's lineal ascendant, the punishment is aggravated. Ibid., p. 4.

69. Ibid., p. 21.

70. Ibid., p. 2.

71. Ibid., pp. 11, 19. References to *pŭrakchi* are mine alone.

72. For USAMGIK Ordinances, see notes 5 and 27 above.

73. Cf. Ordinance 11, Section V, Ordinance 19 and Ordinance 158, 30 December 1947.

74. The right of suspects to request the court to review the legality of their arrest or detention was present in the first Park Chung Hee Constitution of 1962, but was deleted from the 1972 (Yusin) Constitution. The 1980 Constitution restored this right. However, under the Code of Criminal Procedure, Art. 214-4, the right does not apply to those accused of serious crimes or violations of the National Security Act. The same right is retained in the 1987 Constitution. During the period of the Chun Doo Hwan Government (1980–1987), opposition sources and the Korean Federal Bar Association claimed that the government often illegally detained political dissidents by taking them in without warrants or other benefits of due process, such as notification of next-of-kin, rights to an attorney, or habeas corpus. "NKDP (New Korea Democratic party) discloses list of 238 'illegal' detainees," *Korea Herald* (U.S. edition), 18 January 1987, p. 8. For discussion of habeas corpus by a constitutional lawyer, see Kim Ch'ŏl-su, *Sin han'guk hŏnpŏp yoron* (New topics in Korean constitutional law; Seoul, Tonga Hagyŏnsa, 1982), p. 183.

75. The Code of Criminal Procedure can be found in *Laws of the Republic of Korea*, translated, edited, and published by the Korean Legal Center (Seoul, 1964), pp. 669–787 (or 1969), pp. 1195–1313. (Volumes are published periodically.)

76. Hahm Pyong-Choon, *The Korean Political Tradition and Law*, (Seoul, 1967).

6. U.S. Foreign Policy and Human Rights in South Korea, by Jerome Alan Cohen and Edward J. Baker

Note on State Department Human Rights Reports

Since 1977 the Department of State has annually submitted a report entitled *Country Reports on Human Rights Practices* to the Senate Committee on Foreign Relations and the House of Representatives Committee on Foreign Affairs. These reports are issued early in the year and cover the preceding calendar year. For example, the report issued on 2 February 1982 covered 1981. In the notes below these reports are cited in the following form: *DOSCR 1981*, p. 639. The date refers to the year covered by the report, not the year of publication.

Material contributed by Jerome Alan Cohen to this chapter has appeared in Peter G. Brown and Douglas MacLean, eds., *Human Rights and U. S. For-*

eign Policy: Principles and Applications (Lexington, Lexington, D. C. Heath, 1979), and is used here with the consent of the publishers.

1. See Center for International Policy, *Human Rights and the U.S. Foreign Assistance Program, Fiscal year 1978, Part 2–East Asia* (Washington, D.C.), p. 46.

2. "Secretary Acheson's Aide-Mémoire to the Korean Ambassador," 7 April 1950, in Donald G. Tewksbury, ed., *Source materials on Korean Politics and Ideologies* (New York, Institute of Pacific Relations, 1950), p. 145.

3. United States Senate, "United States Security Agreement Abroad," *Hearings before the Committee on Foreign Relations,* 91st Cong., 1971, p. 1725.

4. *Dept. of State Bull.,* 21 November 1966, p. 1198.

5. S. R. Larsen and J. L. Collins, Jr., *Allied Participation in Vietnam* (Department of Army, 1975), p. 125.

6. See Elizabeth Pond, "South Korea's New Trouble," *Christian Science Monitor,* 22 May 1974, p. F8, Letter, "Professor Gregory Henderson to *Christian Science Monitor,*" *Christian Science Monitor,* 20 June 1974, p. F8.

7. See U.S. Agency for International Development, *Overseas Loans and Grants and Assistance from International Organizations* (Washington, D.C., 1960), p. 71; ibid. (1974), p. 73.

8. *Congressional Presentation for the Security Assistance Program,* FY 1978, I, 59.

9. See Jerome Alan Cohen, "A Grim Anniversary in South Korea," *Washington Post,* 9 October 1974, p. A18.

10. See Robert Campbell, "Everything's Illegal," *Far Eastern Economic Review,* 21 January 1974, pp. 19–20.

11. See Articles 2 and 5 of "Emergency Measure No. 1," promulgated 8 January 1974; translated in William J. Butler, *Report of Commission to South Korea for Amnesty International* (no date), p. 20 (hereafter Butler, *Report*).

12. Butler, *Report,* p. 26.

13. Roy Whang, "An Opposition Leader's Mysterious Death," *Far Eastern Economic Review,* 12 September 1975, p. 18.

14. Jerome Alan Cohen, "Huh? What? Who, Me? Free Kim Dae Jung," *Los Angeles Times* 8 August 1978, Part II, p. 5.

15. See, for example, "Report of an Amnesty International Mission to the Republic of Korea" (hereafter cited as "Amnesty International Report") in "Human Rights in South Korea and the Philippines: Implications for U.S. Policy," *Hearings before the Subcommittee on International Organizations of the Committee on International Relations, House of Representatives,* 94th Cong., 1st sess., 20 May–24 June 1975, pp. 55–56 (hereafter cited as *1975 Hearings*).

16. "Truth About the Politics of Torture," *Dong-A ilbo,* 28 February 1975 (in Korean).

17. See, for example, Father James Sinnott, "Congressman Fraser Visits Political Prisoners in South Korea," 6 April 1975, printed in *1975 Hearings,* p. 357.

18. There is a discreet and guarded Korean-language account of the widely known Ewha incident by then Dean An In-hŭi of the College of Education, Ewha Women's University, in *Yŏsŏng Tong-A* (Women's East Asian monthly), February 1974, pp. 110–115.

19. See Butler, *Report,* note 11, p. 27. The suicide attempt is reported in *Japan Times,* March 1990, p. 2.

20. See the statement of the late Professor Gregory Henderson, "Human Rights in South Korea: Implications for U.S. Policy," *Hearings before the Subcommittee on Asian and Pacific Affairs and on International Organizations and Movements,* Committee on Foreign Affairs, House of Representatives, 93rd Cong., 2nd sess., 30 July, 5 August, 20 December 1974, p. 86 (hereafter *1974 Hearings*). For an English translation of the pre-1972 Constitution, see Laws of the Republic of Korea (Korean Legal Center, Seoul, 1969), pp. 1–30.

21. See John Saar, "Confession in Seoul: A Tale of Terror," *International Herald Tribune,* 7 July 1977, p. 4.

22. See, for example, John Saar, "Abusing the Law in Korea," *Washington Post,* 1 August 1976, p. C5.

23. The statement was made by Prime Minister Kim Jong Pil in the National Assembly in October 1974. He also explained that the secrecy of the trial was due to lack of court space. *1975 Hearings,* p. 64.

24. "Statement of Brian Wrobel, Amnesty International, London," *1975 Hearings,* pp. 72–73.

25. Article 1 of the Emergency Decree. An English translation of the entire decree may be found in *1975 Hearings,* pp. 6 7.

26. John Saar, "S. Korean Trial: Christians Put Park Dictatorship in Dock," *Washington Post,* 9 August 1976, p. A8.

27. Ibid.

28. In the landmark decision, the Korean Supreme Court held unconstitutional a new statute restricting judical review of legislation. The new statute had required that, in order to decide upon constitutionality, a quorum of two-thirds of the entire court had to hear the case and that two-thirds of the judges present had to concur. The Supreme Court Plenary Collegiate Session, Decision of 22 June 1971. The revamping of the judiciary was carried out during 1972 as part of the Yusin "revitalizing reforms."

29. For a brief account of the March First Declaration and its consequences, see Jerome Alan Cohen, ". . . and a letter from Carter to Kim," *Christian Science Monitor,* 1 March 1977, p. 27.

30. Article 1(B), note 24, above.

31. Article 1. For an English translation of the National Security Law, see *Laws of the Republic of Korea* (3rd ed., Korean Legal Center, Seoul, 1975), pp. 772–775.

32. Article 4(1). For an English translation of the Anti-Communist Law, See *Laws of the Republic of Korea,* note 31, above, pp. 776–780.

33. See Amnesty International Report, *1975 Hearings,* p. 51.

34. See "South Korea: Bad Review," *Newsweek,* 31 July 1978, p. 34. Paek's sentence was suspended.

35. *1975 Hearings,* p. 51.

36. For a discussion of this provision, see *1975 Hearings,* pp. 51–52. In order to adopt the bill containing this provision, the majority of the National Assembly's committee on the Judiciary and Legislation met secretly to con-

sider the bill in the Library of the Assembly, while the opposition committee members were kept locked in the committee room. The plenary session
that considered the bill was held in the cloakroom, while opposition members were kept locked in the main Assembly chamber (p. 52).

37. This law, which extended as well to any Koreans who had sought asylum in
a foreign country, was to be activated when the Minister of Foreign Affairs
notified the Minister of Justice that a violation had taken place. The Minister of Justice would then direct the public prosecutor to conduct the investigation and summon the suspect. In addition to permitting trial in absentia,
the law required that a default judgment be returned against the defendant.
There was no right to counsel or to present evidence. An English translation
of the "Special Act Concerning Punishment of Crimes Against the State,"
as amended in 1980, is in *Current Laws of the Republic of Korea,* 4 vols.
(Seoul, Statutes Compilation and Dissemination Foundation of Korea, 30
September 1985), section X, pp. 45–48.

38. "Statement of the Reverend James P. Sinnott," *1975 Hearings,* p. 46.

39. For an account of the bar association's efforts to protest, written before they
succumbed to the regime's pressures, see Jerome Alan Cohen, "Lawyers, Politics and Despotism in Korea," *American Bar Association Journal,* June 1975,
p. 730.

40. For an observer's account of the vain struggle of Korea's leading newspaper,
see Sinnott, *1975 Hearings,* pp. 45–47.

41. See Andrew H. Malcolm, "400 Professors Ousted in Korea," *New York
Times,* 14 March 1976, p. 1.

42. Amnesty International Report, *1975 Hearings,* p. 57.

43. Testimony of Rev. George E. Ogle, *1974 Hearings,* p. 145.

44. Article 10(5) of the pre-1972 Constitution, repealed by the new Constitution, had contained the guarantee of habeas corpus, and Article 10(6) had
prohibited reliance on coerced confessions.

45. Article 8.

46. Article 10(1).

47. Article 10(2).

48. Article 8 and Article 29.

49. Article 32(2). Obviously this provision is designed to expand the constitutionally permissible limits of restricting basic rights through "laws." The
term *laws* herein denotes statutes passed by the legislature and meeting the
requirements of generality and specificity. It is noteworthy that the 1972
Constitution does not retain its predecessor's provision that even a law
restricting liberties and rights in the public interest cannot be constitutionally valid if it infringes "the essential substances of liberties and rights." Article 32(2) of the pre-1972 Constitution.

50. Article 32(2) and (4).

51. Article 54(1) and (3).

52. Park Il-kyŏng, *The Yusin Constitution* (Seoul, 1973, in Korean), pp. 1, 297.

53. Mun Hong-ju, *The Korean Constitution* (Seoul, 1973; in Korean), p. 332.

54. Han T'ae-yŏn, *A Study of the Constitution* (Seoul, 1973; in Korean), p. 390.

55. *DOSCR 1979*, p. 474. For a detailed description and analysis of this incident, see Scott Kalb, "The Y.H. Incident," *Stone Lion* 11:57–65 (1983).
56. *Dong-A ilbo,* 1 January 1980, p. 1.
57. *Amnesty International Report 1980I*, p. 207.
58. There were even rumors that Ham had been tortured, but he later denied them.
59. For a description of the legal situation of labor under the Yusin system, see Edward J. Baker, "Within the Scope Defined by Law: The Rights of Labor under the Yusin System I & II," *East Asian Executive Reports,* Vol. 1, No. 2, 15 October 1979, and No. 3, 15 November 1979.
60. *Washington Post,* 1 May 1980, p. 16.
61. *Asian Wall Street Journal,* 28 April 1980, p. 16.
62. *New York Times,* May 1980, p. 16.
63. Ibid.
64. For the full text of the Martial Law Decree in Korean, see Yŏnhap T'ongsin, *Yŏnhap Nyŏn'gam 1981,* p. 559. For summaries and partial translations in English, see *DOSCR 1980*, p. 639 ff. and Amnesty International, *Republic of Korea: Violations of Human Rights,* 1981, p. 7.
65. During the siege of Kwangju, one of the authors, having heard about this appeal, called the Korean Section of the Department of State to urge that the United States offer its good offices. He was first told that no response was possible because the request had not been made through proper channels. After a heated discussion, in which it was pointed out that the people of Kwangju were not in a position to pay a proper call on the U.S. Embassy, the exasperated diplomat said, "We have no interests in Kwangju." In response to questions from the South Korean National Assembly, the U.S. government submitted a report concerning these and related events on 20 June 1989. According to the report, " . . . on May 16, military authorities notified CFC officials of their intent to remove the 20th Division's artillery and its 60th regiment from CFC OPCON. The CFC received the Marital Law Command's OPCON retrieval notification while General Wickham was in the United States on official duties. CFC Deputy Commander, Korean 4-star General Baek Sok Chu, responded for the CFC, acknowledging the OPCON release notification, but requesting that other forces be provided to replace the 20th Division troops beings transferred to control of the Martial Law Command." "U.S. Governm,ent Statement on the Events in Kwangju, Republic of Korea, in May 1980," issued by the Department of State 20 June 1989, paragraph 31, pp. 11–12. During the Kwangju crisis, one of the authors was told by Korean section officials at the Pentagon that the United States had to transfer the troops unless it could assert that to do so would threaten the security of the Republic of Korea.
66. These figures were presented by the Minister of Defense, Yu Song-min, "Report on the Kwangju Incident to the National Assembly National Defense Committee, June 7, 1985," reprinted in Donald N. Clark, ed., *The Kwangju Uprising: Shadows over the Regime in South Korea* (Westview Special Studies on Asia, Westview Press, Boulder and London, 1988), p. 91. Other

estimates include those in *DOSCR 1980*, p. 693; and Amnesty International, *Republic of Korea: Violations of Human Rights*, 1981, p. 8.

67. *Korea Herald*, 19 June 1980, p. 1. Kim Jong Pil's share was $37.3 million (21,646,480,000 *wŏn*) and his brother's was $15.9 million (9,229,870,000 *wŏn*). The names of the others and the amounts they "returned" are given in the article. It is not clear what happened to the "returned" money.

68. *DOSCR 1980*, pp. 644–645.

69. *Los Angeles Times*, 8 August 1980, part 1, p. 18.

70. *New York Times*, 9 August 1980, p. A1 "General Wickham discusses his statements to the *L.A. Times*," originally "on background," in Mark Peterson, "Americans and the Kwangju Incident: Problems in the Writing of History," in Donald N. Clark, *The Kwangju Uprising*, p. 63."

71. *Los Angeles Times*, 11 August 1980, p. 10.

72. The full text of the indictment in English is in the *Korea Herald*, 15 August 1980, pp. 2ff.

73. For a complete list of the defendants, the charges against each, and the sentences imposed, see Yonhap T'ongsin, *Yonhap Nyon'gam 1981*, p. 99. Pages 98 through 100 of this book give a chronological account of the case, and the text of the investigative report is given in full on pp. 567–574.

74. *Japan Times*, 2 November 1973, p. 5.

75. For a full discussion of the Kim Dae Jung case in the context of R.O.K.-Japan relations, see Scott Kalb, "Kim Dae Jung—Held for Ransom," *Korea Scope* 3.1:44–50 (March 1983).

76. For the official U.S. reaction to the sentence, see the *New York Times*, 18 September 1980, p. A6. "In a statement [Secretary of State Muskie] said, 'As is well known, we have followed the court martial trial of Kim Dae Jung with intense interest and deep concern. In light of our past comments, we obviously have strong feelings about the extreme verdict which has been handed down. Nevertheless, since the case is subject to judicial review and since the Government of the Republic of Korea is fully aware of our views, we will have no additional comment on the matter at this time.'"

77. This was a reference to the killing of Kim Chu-yŏl by the Masan police in 1960, considered the triggering event in fall of Syngman Rhee.

78. *DOSCR 1983*, p. 812.

79. *DOSCR 1982*, p. 743, and *DOSCR 1983*, p. 813.

80. Congressional Research Service, *Human Rights Conditions in Selected Countries and the U.S. Response* (Prepared for the use of the House of Representatives Committee on International Relations), 25 July 1978, p. 223.

81. For the full text of the Constitution in English, see the *Korea Herald*, 30 September 1980. This is a draft published before the referendum, but there was no subsequent change. For the Korean text, see *Pŏpchŏn 1981* (Seoul, Hyonam sa, 1981), pp. 1–8. For a table comparing the Fifth Republic Constitution article by article with earlier South Korean constitutions, see Kim Ch'ŏl-su, *Sin hanguk hŏnpŏp yoron* (New topics on Korean constitutional law; Seoul, Tonga Hagyŏnsa, 1982), pp. 528–557. In references to the Constitution below, only article numbers will be given. For a more detailed anal-

ysis of the Constitution, see Edward Baker, "The New South Korean Constitution," *Korea Scope* 2.1:17–31.

82. *DOSCR 1981*, p. 626.

83. *New York Times*, 13 September 1980.

84. *New York Times*, 20 August 1980.

85. *Boston Globe*, 13 September 1980, p. 4; *New York Times*, 13 September 1980.

86. Amnesty International, *Republic of Korea: Violations of Human Rights*, 1981, pp. 26–27.

87. Amnesty International, *Torture in the Eighties*, 1984, p. 192.

88. *DOSCR 1982*, p. 743.

89. See, for example, the case of the Pusan National University students cited in *DOSCR 1982*, p. 744.

90. *DOSCR 1982*, p. 744.

91. Amnesty International, *Republic of Korea: Violations of Human Rights*, 1981, p. 193.

92. *DOSCR 1981*, p. 626.

93. *DOSCR 1982*, p. 774.

94. *DOSCR 1983*, pp. 815–816.

95. *Far Eastern Economic Review* (Hong Kong) 20 March 1986, p. 18. For samples of Korean press coverage, see *Chosŏn ilbo* and *Dong-A ilbo* for 30 January 1986.

96. *Korea Herald*, 31 July 1986 (US Edition), p. 8. Press coverage during the initial phase of the investigation closely followed official press guidance. The policeman was sentenced in July 1987. The Seoul District Civil Court awarded Kwŏn In-suk compensation in June 1989. Reuters, 13 June 1989.

97. *Far Eastern Economic Review* (Hong Kong) 5 February 1987, pp. 15–16, and 17 February 1987, p. 44.

98. *DOSCR 1983*, p. 819. For the text of the law, see *Pŏpchŏn 1980* (Seoul, Hyonamsa, 1980), pp. 723–724.

99. *DOSCR 1980*, p. 645.

100. *DOSCR 1983*, p. 819. In 1986, a magazine published by dissident journalists released government press guidelines for the period from October 1985 through August 1986. Some of the guidelines are translated, and the system of press censorship under the Chun Government discussed, in Lek Hor Tan, "South Korea: Guiding the Press," *Index on Censorship* (May 1987), pp. 28–36.

101. *DOSCR 1982*, p. 626.

102. *DOSCR 1983*, p. 819.

103. *Korea Herald*, 13 January 1984, p. 4.

104. Ibid.

105. *Korea Herald*, 17 February 1984, p. 1.

106. For a fuller discussion of the student movement during the Chun period, see Scott Kalb, "An Appraisal of the Student Movement in South Korea Today," in *Korea Scope* 3.3:13–18 (December 1984); and Wonmo Dong, "University Students in South Korean Politics: Patterns of Radicalization in the 1980s," *Journal of International Affairs* 40:2.233–255 (Winter/Spring 1987).

107. Government report presented to the National Assembly on 13 June 1983. See *Korea Times*, 15 June 1983, p. 1.

108. Kalb, p. 15–16.

109. In November 1983, at least 125 students were arrested. Kalb, p. 18.

110. *DOSCR 1983*, p. 819.

111. *Korea Herald*, 24 December 1983, p. 1. It is unclear if these figures include those who were not only expelled but also jailed. We believe they do not.

112. Ibid.

113. *Korea Herald*, 25 December 1983, p. 1. It is not clear how many of these were released from prison and how many were already out but had their rights restored.

114. Edwin O. Reischauer and Edward J. Baker, "A Time Bomb is Ticking in South Korea," *New York Times Magazine* 16 November 1986, p. 51.

115. See the following: *Korea Herald*, 30 October 1986, p. 8; Associated Press story in *Korea Herald*, 31 October 1986, p. 1; and *Korea Herald*, 1 November 1986, p. 8.

116. A photograph showing the banner appears on p. 1 of the *Korea Herald* of 30 October 1986. The object of the verb *overthrow* is not seen and has been interpolated in our translation.

117. *Korea Herald*, 1 November 1986, p. 8. It is not certain whether the student weapons in this incident actually included gasoline bombs, as sometimes stated in the foreign and English-language domestic press. The Korean language term *firebottle* (*hwabyŏng*) is not specific concerning the contents. Students more often have used kerosene in their firebombs. The tactic is still a violent one, but arguably more restrained than the use of the more volatile and dangerous gasoline, also readily available in South Korea.

118. See chapter by West and Baker, pp. 221–252.

119. *Physicians for Human Rights Record*, Issue 1, Fall 1987, p. 1.

120. *Pŏpchŏn 1981*, pp. 2443–2445; Unofficial English translations of labor laws are found in Korean Legal Center, *Laws of the Republic of Korea* (4th ed., Seoul, 1983), and Supplement 1, July 1984, Vol. I, Pt. III (Social Laws), pp. 264–311.

121. *DOSCR 1983*, p. 820.

122. Asia Watch, *Human Rights in Korea*, January 1986, pp. 197–201.

123. Chŏng, Sŏn-sun, "A Bill of Complaint," written 28 or 29 September 1982. In the translated version available to us, Ms. Chong refers to herself in both the first person and the third person. We have made the account consistent by changing all these references to the first person.

124. *DOSCR 1980*, p. 642.

125. DeWind and Woodhouse, *Persecution of Defense Lawyers in South Korea* (International Commission of Jurists, 1979), pp. 57–59.

126. This is a paraphrase of a statement in DeWind and Woodhouse, p. 58, which fit the situation under Chun as well as it did the Yusin system.

127. See Articles 108, 112, 113, and 114 and the Constitution Committee law, *Pŏpchŏn*, 1981, p. 34. Three are nominated by the National Assembly and 3 by the Chief Justice. For further discussion of The Constitution Committee, see chapter by West and Baker, p. 242.

128. *Korea Herald,* 28 February 1984, p. 1.
129. *DOSCR 1983,* p. 822.
130. *DOSCR 1983,* p. 821. In fact, there were no strong candidates who were not under the ban.
131. *DOSCR 1983,* p. 821–822.
132. B. C. Koh, "The 1985 Parliamentary Election in South Korea," *Asian Survey* 25:9.883–897 (September 1987), p. 889.
133. *DOSCR 1983,* p. 746.
134. In 1984 or 1985, the Public Affairs Office of the United States Forces Korea/Eight United States Army issued a brief fact sheet (in English) that noted publicly for the first time that the R.O.K. government had not requested release of the 9th Division prior to the movement of some of its elements to Seoul on the evening of 12 December. Public Affairs Office, United Nations Command/Combined Forces Command United States Forces Korea/Eighth United States Army, "R.O.K. Units Under Operational Control of the Combined Forces Command," n.d., reprinted in Donald N. Clark, *The Kwangju Uprising,* pp. 93–94. According to an official U.S. account, issued only in 1989, General Wickham "formally protested to Korean military leaders" that same night, and "word was sent to Chun Doo Hwan warning him of the dangerous implications of the conflict within the South Korean forces." A strong U.S. statement drafted in Seoul that night had to be issued in Washington, not Korea, the following day "because the Embassy lacked access to the government controlled public media to disseminate it to the Korean people." "United States Government Statement on the Events in Kwangju, Republic of Korea, in May 1980," issued by Department of State, 19 June 1989, pp. 6–7.
135. Kalb, p. 16.
136. *The State,* 14 February 1982, p. 1-C. This story came to the attention of Koreans when it appeared in *Stars and Stripes,* the U.S. Army newspaper published in Korea.
137. Two of the men, Mun Pu-sik and Kim Hyŏn-jang, were sentenced to death and two others to life imprisonment. The death sentences were commuted in January 1983. On 22 September 1983, another bomb exploded at a U.S. Cultural Center in Taegu. One man was killed. No South Korean group claimed credit for this attack, and the R.O.K. government blamed the incident on North Korean infiltrators.
138. United States Department of State, *Patterns of Global Terrorism: 1988* (Washington, D.C., March 1989), p. 39; U.S. Department of State, *Political Violence Against Americans, 1989* (Washington, D.C., 1990).
139. These three quotations are taken from Americas Watch, Helsinki Watch, and Lawyers Committee for International Human Rights, *Failure: The Reagan Administration's Human Rights Policy in 1983* (1984), pp. 67–69.
140. Ibid., p. 68.
141. Ibid.
142. For a discussion of this case, see Kalb, "Kim Dae Jung—Held for Ransom."

7. The 1987 Constitutional Reforms in South Korea: Electoral Processes and Judicial Independence, by James M. West and Edward J. Baker

Note: Mr. Baker visited Korea from 13 to 19 December 1987 as a member of an Election Process Observation Delegation sponsored by the non-profit Council for Democracy in Korea. This delegation included a bipartisan contingent of Congressional staff members as well as academic experts on Korea and on the election process. The present paper does not purport to speak for the Election Process Observer Delegation. Mr. West was in Seoul on a private visit from mid-December 1987 until early February 1988.

The authors are grateful to Jack Tobin, the Harvard Human Rights Program, and the editors of the *Harvard Human Rights Yearbook* for permission to reprint this paper.

1. U.S. Department of State, *Country Reports on Human Rights Practices in 1987* (Washington, D.C., U.S. Government Printing Office, February 1988), p. 728. See generally Sung-Joo Han, "South Korea in 1987–The Politics of Democratization," *Asian Survey* 28:52–61 (January 1988).

2. Roh Tae Woo was inaugurated and the revised Constitution entered into force on 25 February 1988 pursuant to its Supplementary Provisions, Article 1. Citations to and quotations of the 1987 Constitution (*Hŏnpŏp*) of the Republic of Korea refer to Korea Overseas Information Service, *Constitution–The Republic of Korea* (Seoul, October 1987; English translation of the Korean text with Explanatory Notes [hereinafter *Constitution*]). Citations to *Constitution of 1980* refer to the 27 October 1980 *Constitution of the Republic of Korea* in force prior to the recent revision, which is accessible in an unofficial English translation in Korean Legal Center, *Laws of the Republic of Korea* (Seoul, 4th ed., 1983), I, 1–19. For an overview of the *1980 Constitution*, see Edward J. Baker, "South Korea's New Constitution: The Emperor's New Clothes," (a pamphlet published by the North American Coalition for Human Rights in Korea, Washington, D.C., November 1980). *Constitution of 1972* refers to the 27 December 1989 Yusin constitution translated in *Korean Politics in Transition*, (Seattle and London, University of Washington Press, 1975), pp. 357–383.

3. For a textual analysis of the amendments with an immediate bearing on human rights, see Amnesty International, "Republic of Korea (South Korea): Human Rights Guarantees in New Constitution," (a pamphlet, London, AI Index ASA 25/56/87, November 1987). For an overview of South Korean constitutional history since the Republic of Korea was founded in 1948, see Dae-Kyu Yoon, 'Law and Political Authority in Korea,' pp. 144–166 (Boulder, Westview Press, and Kyungnan University Press, forthcoming). We are grateful to Dr. Yoon for making available the updated version of his thorough analysis of Korean constitutional law, a work full of useful empirical information.

4. "The President shall be elected by universal, equal, direct and secret ballot by the people." *Constitution*, Art. 67.

5. "Divided They Fall," *Far Eastern Economic Review,* 31 December 1987, p. 8.

6. See, e.g., "Worry Grows that Korean Army Might Intervene in the Elections," *New York Times,* 10 December 1987, p. A1.

7. *Korea Herald,* 18 December 1987, p. 1.

8. Ibid.

9. For example, one lawyer who observed the election as part of an international mission rather hastily concluded: "What we saw ourselves did not give evidence of massive, wholesale fraud on election day. . . . We simply see no evidence to support the charges. The charges strike us as proceeding from conviction, not from empirical data." "Int'l Rights Group Finds No Evidence of Massive Vote Fraud," *Korea Herald,* 23 December 1987, p. 2.

10. Roh campaigned as a "common man" and as a proponent of "democratization without chaos." See "The Election Show," *Far Eastern Economic Review,* 10 December 1987, pp. 56–57.

11. *Korea Times,* 26 February 1988, p. 2.

12. The best documented and most comprehensive human-rights fact-finding report available on South Korea, written by Dr. James Palais, is in Asia Watch, *Human Rights in Korea* (New York and Washington, 1986 [hereinafter *Asia Watch Report*]). See also International Commission of Jurists, *South Korea: Human Rights in the Emerging Politics* (Geneva, 1987 [hereinafter *ICJ Report*]); Asia Watch, *A Stern, Steady Crackdown: Legal Process and Human Rights in South Korea* (New York and Washington, 1987 [hereinafter *A Stern, Steady Crackdown*]); Amnesty International, *South Korea: Violations of Human Rights,* (London, AI Index AFA/25/21/86, 1986); International League of Human Rights and International Human Rights Law Group, *Democracy in South Korea: A Promise Unfulfilled* (New York, 1985 [hereinafter *ILHR Report*]).

13. Most arrests of student demonstrators and other protestors led to incarceration lasting from several hours up to 29 days. Often, individuals were held and released without being charged or were sentenced by summary procedure to detention. In thousands of cases, however, more serious charges were leveled against political dissidents, leading to longer prison terms and even death sentences. See the sources cited in note 12.

14. *Asia Watch Report,* pp. 182–288, 320–322; *ICJ Report,* pp. 31–34.

15. *ILHR Report,* pp. 113–140.

16. See generally Jang-Jip Choi, "Political Cleavages and Transition in a Military Authoritarian Regime: Institutionalization, Opposition and Process in South Korea, 1972–1986" (unpublished paper, Korea University, 1986).

17. For example, the Basic Press Act, Law No. 3347 of 1980, Laws of the Republic of Korea, III, 122–135, imposed prior restraints on publishing, and the Act on Assembly and Demonstration, as amended by law No. 3278 of 1980, ibid., II, 38–42, imposed prior restraints on assembly despite the freedoms of the press and assembly conferred by article 20 of the *Constitution of 1980.* Numerous student demonstrators and dissidents have been prosecuted under the second statute. One of the 1987 amendments provides: "Licensing or censorship of speech and the press, and licensing of assembly and association shall not be recognized." *Constitution,* Art. 21(2).

18. *A Stern, Steady Crackdown,* p. 8.
19. "[A]nti-communist ideology, a consequence of the Korea [*sic*] war, is used by the government as an instrument to secure its power. There is widespread indoctrination both with anti-communist ideology and, as the [April 1987 International Commission of Jurists] Mission itself experienced when talking to [a government official], with the idea that torture is necessary to fight communism effectively. The danger of such indoctrination is exacerbated by the fact that those struggling for more democracy and greater respect for human rights are labelled as communists and, therefore, it is felt that torture is justified against them." *ICJ Report,* p. 32.
20. See *Constitution of 1980,* Arts. 39–41. The Chun Government's shift in stance at that time is recorded in Korean Overseas Information Service, "Collision to Compromise: Roundtable Discussions between President Chun Doo Hwan and the Leaders of Political Parties on Constitutional Issues," (a pamphlet, 24 February 1986 [hereinafter "Collision to Compromise"]).
21. *Constitution of 1972.* See Ki-Bom Kim, "Revisions of Korean Constitution," in Sang Hyun Song, ed., *Introduction to the Law and Legal System of Korea* (Seoul, Kyung Mun Sa, 1983), pp. 213, 225–230.
22. *Asia Watch Report,* pp. 17–25.
23. See B. C. Koh, "The 1985 Parliamentary Election in South Korea," *Asian Survey* 25:883, 886 (1985).
24. Ibid., pp. 884–897.
25. The *1980 Constitution* had been drafted under martial law without popular input and ratified in a rushed referendum without meaningful opportunity for debate. Yoon, pp. 164–165; Baker, p. 6.
26. U.S. Department of State, *Country Reports on Human Rights Practices in 1985* (Washington, U.S. Government Printing Office, February 1986), p. 807.
27. Koh, p. 889. These 1985 results were strikingly similar to the December 1987 presidential election results, not only in terms of overall shares of the DJP and the opposition, but also in terms of provincial and urban/rural splits. Ibid., pp. 888–893; "Divided They Fall," *Far Eastern Economic Review,* 31 December 1987, pp. 8–9.
28. See National Assembly members Election Act, Law No. 3359 of 1981, Art. 130. The recent 8 March 1988 amendments to this act are discussed in notes 29, 30, and 181 below.
29. In 1985, there were 92 districts, with 2 representatives elected from each district. *IHLR Report,* pp. 86–88. An amendment now provides for 224 single-member districts. *North American Coalition for Human Rights in Korea, Bi-Weekly Report* VII.5:2 (15 March 1988 [hereinafter *NACHRK Bi-Weekly* volume.no.:page (date)]).
30. The national-constituency (NC) seats have been used to dispense patronage and also auctioned off to raise campaign funds. In 1985, there were 92 NC seats and the DJP was allotted two-thirds or 61 based on its plurality of local-constituency (LC) seats. The remaining 31 were shared among the opposition parties according to their LC seats. *ILHR Report,* p. 87. The 1988 amendment provides for 75 NC seats, with the "bonus" amounting to at least

one half of the NC seats. *NACHRK Bi-Weekly* VII.5:2 (15 March 1988).

31. See Koh, pp. 888–890. Redistricting in 1988 continues to contravene the egalitarian apportionment principle of "one citizen-one vote"; the 5 largest cities, with 44% of the population, are allotted only about 34% of the LC seats. *NACHRK Bi-Weekly* VI.5:2 (15 March 1988).

32. The DJP after the election controlled about 53.6% of the National Assembly seats with only about 35.3% of the popular vote. *Asia Watch Report,* pp. 68–69.

33. "Governmental legitimacy in Korea derives from the ruler's ability to preserve national security, promote prosperity, maintain domestic harmony, and, increasingly, to reflect the popular will in questions of public policy. The current [Chun] Government, which assumed power with primarily military support in 1980, has had problems with the last two points; hence to many Koreans the degree of legitimacy it enjoys is still open to questions." U.S. Department of State, *Country Reports on Human Rights Practices in 1983* (Washington, U.S. Government Printing Office, February 1984), p. 812. In a recent interview, Chun stated: "The question of legitimacy does not exist as far as I am concerned. . . . [It] is political rhetoric." *Far Eastern Economic Review,* 11 February 1988, p. 25.

34. The Kwangju Uprising, the military atrocities which provoked it, and its bloody suppression are recounted in *Asia Watch Report,* pp. 36–44. "Several sources tell of soldiers stabbing or cutting off the breasts of naked girls; one murdered student was found disembowelled, another with an "X" carved on his back. . . . They had virtually declared open season on anyone younger than thirty, arresting and beating any they found on the streets. . . . When a mother protested the teasing of her daughter, both were shot dead on the spot." Ibid., p. 37. The broader context, including longstanding allegations of United States complicity in the violence, is examined in Donald N. Clark, *The Kwangju Uprising: Shadows over the Regime in South Korea* (Boulder and London, Westview Press, 1987). For the official U.S. position, see U.S. Department of State, "United States Government Statement on Events in Kwangju, Republic of Korea, in May 1980" (20 June 1989).

35. See, e.g., "Kwangju Case is Regrettable, Unfortunate, Incident: Chun," *Korea Times,* 30 January 1988, p. 1. After eight years, Chun told reporters: "I hope that the unfortunate incident will be smoothly solved at an early date." Ibid.

36. "NKDP: Leading Democratic Reforms in Korea" (undated pamphlet setting forth the constitutional reform program, on file at the *Harvard Human Rights Yearbook*).

37. The government asserted that the petition initiative was illegal because existing provisions for amendment provided that a "proposal to amend the Constitution shall be proposed either by the President or by a majority of the members on the register of the National Assembly." *Constitution of 1980,* Art. 129(1). This interpretation (abusing the familiar canon *expressio unius est exclusio alterius*) ignored the principle that the National Assembly is elected to represent, not to stifle, the freely expressed interests of its constituents. It also reflected contempt for the constitutional rights of citizens to

freedom of speech and to petition the state for redress of grievances. Ibid., Arts. 20, 25.

Among the important 1987 amendments reflecting the 1986 opposition demands are two mutually reinforcing changes: (1) The emergency powers of the President have been scaled back somewhat and declarations of a state of emergency or martial law now will lapse without "prompt" National Assembly approval, *Constitution*, Arts. 76–77; and (2) the National Assembly can no longer be dissolved by presidential decision, *Constitution of 1980*, Art. 57, repealed. These changes, potentially of crucial importance in a future crisis, cannot be examined in detail here.

38. *New York Times*, 23 February 1986, p. 1.
39. "Collision to Compromise," p. 12.
40. See, e.g., *New York Times*, 8 May 1986, p. A1. For further analysis of the impact of United States foreign policy on South Korean domestic politics, see Crystal Nix, "South Korea: United States Policy in the 1987 Presidential Elections," *Harvard Human Rights Yearbook* 1:48–59 (Spring 1988).
41. *New York Times*, 10 March 1986, p. A3.
42. See, e.g. "50,000 Protest Korean Regime," *Boston Globe*, 31 March 1986, p. 1; *New York Times*, 6 April 1986, p. 8.
43. The Chun regime blamed the NKDP for the 3 May riot at Inchon, evidently aiming to alienate the middle classes from the opposition by associating it with radical violence. The Rev. Mun Ik-hwan and other leaders of the United Minjung Movement for Democracy and Unification (*Min-t'ongnyŏn*) were prosecuted for inciting the Inchon violence, an implausible charge for many of the accused. *A Stern, Steady Crackdown*, pp. 53–56. Newspaper articles attributed to unnamed "analysts" even claimed that "radical students" were planning to establish a leftist government in May through a violent uprising. *Korea Herald*, 7 May 1986, p. 1.
44. About 2,000 students from 26 colleges had gathered at Kŏn'guk University to declare the formation of a "patriotic student committee against outside forces and dictatorship." They denounced American imperialism and burned President Ronald Reagan and Prime Minister Nakasone Yasuhiro in effigy. Barricaded within the campus, students were besieged in school buildings for four days before the police attack. 1,400 students were detained and 395 were later indicted, including 34 on National Security Act charges. *Korea Herald*, 30 October 1986, p. 8; *Korea Herald*, 31 October 1986, p. 1; *Korea Herald*, 1 November 1986, p. 9. For a more detailed discussion of this incident, see Chapter 6, pp. 207–208.
45. See Edwin O. Reischauer and Edward J. Baker, "A Time Bomb is Ticking in South Korea," *New York Times*, 16 November 1986 (Magazine), p. 51.
46. Although there would be no emperor, in such a system the president was envisaged as a symbolic head of state not unlike the Austrian president. At the time, it had already become commonplace to speculate that the DJP's ultimate goal was a system similar to that in Japan, in which a multi-member district parliamentary system with apportionment favoring the countryside has allowed a conservative party to retain power continuously since 1948.

47. National Assemblyman Yu Sŏng-hwan had argued in a speech on the floor of the Parliament that the reunification of Korea ought to be given a higher priority than anti-communism. The government claimed his parliamentary immunity was inapplicable because he had distributed copies of his speech to the press. *Korea Weekly Report* 5.28:1 (20 October 1986). An April 1987 human rights mission "asked Ministry of Justice officials what it was in the statement of Assemblyman Yu that endangered national security and they admitted that there was nothing, lamely adding that the matter should be left to the court since it involved an interpretation of law." *ICJ Report,* p. 67.
48. *A Stern, Steady Crackdown,* p. 1.
49. Ibid., pp. 4–5; *Korea Herald,* 11 November 1986, p. 8.
50. One of the authors personally witnessed deployment of about 70,000 riot police at and around an athletic field in Seoul on 29 November 1986 to preempt an NKDP rally. For blocks around, the streets were lined with young men in well-padded uniforms equipped with gas masks, helmets, and shields. Traffic was redirected, nearby subway stops were removed from service, and the area was heavily doused with tear gas.
51. "'Guiding' the Press," *Index on Censorship* 16.5:28–36 (1987). The publication of these guidelines confirmed what had long been obvious—the Chun regime had been "guiding" press coverage of political events. Some were surprised, however, at the remarkable detail of the guidelines, which dealt not only with content (categorized as "possible," "impossible," or "absolutely impossible") but also with the format, space, and relative prominence of stories. Ibid., pp. 30–36. The government was facing frequent quandaries in orchestrating self-censorship because sensitive stories were being quickly and widely disseminated by word of mouth and through underground media. For the newspapers to remain silent on such stories was to risk losing what little credibility they had left, so "guidance" was often devoted to rumor-containment, in addition to run-of-the-mill propaganda and screening of foreign criticism of Chun's human rights record. See "'Guidelines' for the Press," *Far Eastern Economic Review,* 19 March 1987, p. 34.
52. *Korea Herald,* 13 January 1987, p. 1.
53. The story did not appear in the Korean press until 18 January, *Korea Herald,* 18 January 1987, p. 8, by which time knowledge of the incident had been widely disseminated.
54. Pak was being interrogated about the whereabouts of an acquaintance suspected of being a member of a network of student militants. In this case, "water torture" was a simulation of drowning by repeatedly forcing the victim's head under water. *A Stern, Steady Crackdown,* p. 104.
55. *New York Times,* 21 January 1987, p. A6. The Chun Government had long claimed it discountenanced torture, which it attributed to "excessive zeal" of individuals, but, as the Korean Bar Association concluded after interviewing other torture victims, bathtubs were obviously not included in the normal furniture of interrogation cells "to allow suspects to take baths." *ICJ Report,* p. 36.
56. *Korea Herald,* 3 February 1987, p. 1. The government repeatedly warned against holding the planned services and accused the NKDP of seeking to

"reap political gains" from Pak's death and of fomenting unrest "to topple the government and overthrow the current free democratic system through violent means." On 7 February in Seoul, riot police limited entry to Myong-dong Cathedral where a memorial service was being held and fired heavy barrages of tear gas in an attempt to disperse the large crowds that had gathered. Ibid.; *Korea Herald,* 6 February 1987, p. 1; *Korea Herald,* 8 February 1987, p. 1. See also *Korea Weekly Report* 6.3 (10 February 1987).

57. *Korea Herald,* 14 April 1987, p. 1. The speech is excerpted in *ICJ Report,* pp. 17–19. In March, most of the NKDP had deserted the leadership of Yi Min Woo, who had shown an inclination to compromise on the DJP proposal to introduce a parliamentary/cabinet system. The new opposition party, the Reunification Democratic party (RDP), was formed under the leadership of the two Kims, who reaffirmed their commitment to a direct presidential election and renewed their proposal to submit the issue to choice by popular referendum. *Korea Weekly Report* 6.6,8 (19 February & 15 April 1987).

58. The Secretary General of the International Commission of Jurists on 21 April requested the government to explain the legal basis of the ban on debate, but no response was received. *ICJ Report,* pp. 19–20.

59. Ibid., p. 19.

60. *Korea Herald,* 14 April 1987, p. 1.

61. President Syngman Rhee was forced to resign on 27 April 1960, after blatant election fraud precipitated the massive civil disobedience known in Korea as the 19th April Revolution. Hŏ Chŏng was named interim president and there was a peaceful transfer of executive power a few months later from Hŏ's caretaker cabinet to Prime Minister Chang Myŏn (under the short-lived parliamentary system of the Second Republic) with Yun Po-sŏn assuming the (largely symbolic) presidency. Chong-Sik Lee, "Historical Setting," in *South Korea: A Country Study,* Frederica M. Bunge, ed. (Washington D.C., U.S. Government Printing Office, 1982), pp. 31–32.

62. In 1984, Chŏng Nae-hyŏk, the Chairman of Chun's DJP, was implicated in massive corruption and forced to resign and to relinquish ill-gotten wealth, though he was spared prosecution. Far Eastern Economic Review, *Asia 1985 Yearbook,* p. 176 (1984). Corruption was also compounded by nepotism: Yi Kyu-gwang, a former general who happened to be an uncle of Chun's wife, was prosecuted as a conspirator in the monumental Chang Yŏng-ja financial scandal. *Korea Herald,* 19 May 1982, p. 3. More recently, President Chun's younger brother Chun Kyŏng-hwan, former head of the state-sponsored National Saemaul Headquarters, has been arrested after confessing to influence peddling and embezzlement of at least $9.3 million in public funds. "Korean Ex-leader's Brother Arrested in Corruption Case," *Boston Globe,* 31 March 1987, p. 3.

63. The full text of the speech is translated in *North American Coalition for Human Rights in Korea/Update,* Nos. 82–83, pp. 32–38 (Spring 1987).

64. See, e.g., *Korea Herald,* 5 May 1987, p. 1; *Korea Herald,* 10 May 1987, p. 1.

65. *Korea Weekly Report* 6.12 (June 1987).

66. Ibid.

67. "Old Friends: Chun Chooses His Successor," *Time,* 15 June 1987, p. 40. On the day Roh was nominated, demonstrations were organized by the RDP and the National Coalition for a Democratic Constitution, a group formed in late May by over 2,000 leaders of the reform movement. *Korea Weekly Report* 6.13 (29 June 1987).

68. Physicians for Human Rights, "The Use of Tear Gas in the Republic of Korea: A Report by Health Professionals," (a 16-page document, Somerville, Mass., 29 June 1987).

69. Gaston J. Sigur, "Korean Politics in Transition," p. 6 (a speech before the United States-Korea Society of New York, 6 February 1987), reprinted in *Congressional Record* 133:58336 (daily ed. 18 June 1987).

70. *Korea Herald,* 24 June 1987, p. 1.

71. *Korea Weekly Report* 6.13 (29 June 1987).

72. Ibid.

73. A paraphrase based on ibid. and *Korea Herald,* 30 June 1987, p. 1.

74. One news report stated that United States officials believed that Chun and Roh were forced to compromise largely because military leaders, who were under increasing pressure from Washington to exercise restraint, made it plain they would not intervene on the government's behalf. *Newsweek,* 13 July 1987, p. 16.

75. *Korea Weekly Report* 6.14 (9 July 1987).

76. *New York Times,* 13 October 1987, p. A7. The turnout for the referendum was 78%, and 93% of the voters approved the revisions. *Korea Herald,* 29 October 1987, p. 2.

77. See, generally, Asia Monitor Resource Center, *Min-ju No-jo: South Korea's New Trade Unions* (Hong Kong, AMRC, 1987); *Nodongja ŭi pŏt* (The laborer's friend, November 1987, Inaugural Issue). For background on labor repression in South Korea, see *Asia Watch Report,* pp. 182–288; Jang-Jip Choi, "Interest Conflict and Political Control in South Korea: A Study of the Labor Unions in Manufacturing Industries, 1961–1980 (PhD dissertation, University of Chicago, 1983); James West, "South Korea's Entry into the International Labor Organization," *Stanford Journal of International Law* 27: 477–564 (1987).

78. Asia Monitor Resource Center, p. 47 (government statistics).

79. See, e.g., *Korea Herald,* 19 September 1987, p. 3; *Korea Weekly Report* 6.17 (14 October 1987).

80. Roh was invited to Washington D. C. by the National Press Club. Carter J. Eckert and Edward J. Baker, "Reagan Alienates Koreans Needlessly," *New York Times,* 20 September 1987, p. A27.

81. Ibid. Roh's visit was in some respects reminiscent of Chun Doo Hwan's visit to the White House in 1981. "[I]n receiving President Chun of South Korea as one of the first foreign heads of state to visit the White House under the new Administration, President Reagan indicated that Washington would no longer pressure Seoul on human-rights issues ('What happens internally is an internal affair of the Republic of Korea,' a State Department spokesman told reporters at a White House briefing on the Chun visit), but would rather concentrate on building up South Korea's military capacities."

Michael Klare and Cynthia Arnson, *Supplying Repression: U.S. Support for Authoritarian Regimes Abroad* (Washington, D.C., Institute for Policy Studies, 1981), p. 86.

82. Eckert and Baker.

83. *Korea Weekly Report* 6.18 (5 November 1987).

84. Ibid.

85. Personal observations. "Televised news reports consistently showed Mr. Roh surrounded by large crowds, even on days when he had not campaigned; pictures of opposition candidates, on the other hand, frequently highlighted the backs of their heads and showed the sparsely populated fringes of the crowds at their rallies." International Human Rights Law Group, *The 1987 Korean Presidential Election* (Washington, D.C., IHRLG, February 1988), p. 17 [hereinafter *IHRLG Election Report*]).

86. *Washington Times,* 1 December 1987, p. A9.

87. *New York Times,* 10 December 1987, p. A8.

88. One of the authors was a member of this team.

89. Related to one of the authors by eyewitnesses.

90. Related to one of the authors by recipients and eyewitnesses.

91. *Korea Herald,* 18 December 1987, pp. 1–2.

92. U.S. Department of State, "Text of Press Guideline Used at Press Briefing" (received from Political Section of United States Embassy in Seoul on 17 December 1987, copy on file at *Harvard Human Rights Yearbook*).

93. *Korea Herald,* 20 December 1987, p. 1.

94. *Boston Globe,* 20 December 1987, p. 15.

95. Reprinted in *International Herald Tribune,* 19–20 December 1987, p. 4. Some Koreans were angered at what they regarded as an ill-informed and condescending attitude toward the fraud charges in the United States press. The prominent theologian, poet, and democratic activist Rev. Mun Ik-hwan spoke for millions when he replied to the foreign press with a poem entitled "Now is the Right Time to Refuse" (excerpts of unpublished translation, 25 December 1987):

> Yes, they stole some, but not two million votes,
> Say the Christian countries' conscienceless press,
> So he clearly has the mandate to be president—
> Watergate—
> Not a case of stealing votes
> But only using wire-tapping and listening devices,
> Yet for that an incumbent president was impeached and ousted.
> What in hell do you high and mighty American journalists take us for?
> You hypocrites!
> You refused to acknowledge Nixon as president
> But tell us we should gratefully accept a vote-stealer as our president,
> You swindling charlatans!

96. For example, the government admitted after the election that confidentiality was not guaranteed for the 600,000 mostly conscripted members of the military who cast absentee ballots. *Korea Times,* 28 January 1988, p. 2. In one often-cited case, a young soldier Chŏng Yun-gwang allegedly was

beaten to death by his superior on 4 December 1987, just after having cast an absentee ballot for an opposition candidate. *IHRLG Election Report,* pp. 22, 52; Joint Christian Committee of the National Coalition for Democracy, "Election Watch—A Documentation of Cases of Election Fraud," (pamphlet, Seoul, December 1987), p. 6. No credible explanation of this incident has been issued by the government. Kim Dae Jung's party alleged: "One of the fraudulent tactics characteristic of the recent presidential election is the fraud involved in absentee balloting of which the most infamous is the coerced open voting of the military personnel on military bases as well as switching of their ballots after supposedly secret voting. . . . In this manner, at least 500,000 out of 850,000 absentee votes were stolen." The Party for Peace and Democracy, "We Indict 5 Major Scandals of Fraudulent Election," (PPD announcement, 29 December 1987), p. 6, reprinted in *IHRLG Election Report,* pp. 61, 66–67.

At Kuro-gu, a working-class area on the outskirts of Seoul, there was a violent incident after a local resident showed opposition poll watchers a ballot box being illegally transported by government officials—it was concealed under bread and cookies in a private truck. Hundreds of citizens occupied the local polling station to protest this fraud and many were seriously injured on 18 December when 4,000 riot police stormed the building and arrested the protestors. Reported to Carter J. Eckert, a member of the Council for Democracy in Korea observer delegation, by eyewitnesses. An account of the Kuro incident is also given in the recent article that displays an utterly irresponsible blend of black humor, cynicism, and blatant racism: P. J. O'Rourke, "Seoul Brothers," *Rolling Stone,* 11 February 1988, p. 93. "In testimony before the National Assembly, election official [and Supreme Court Justice] Yun Il Yun admitted it was an 'error' for a District Election Management Committee to have transported the box containing absentee ballots to the counting station in Kuro before balloting was completed. He said the mistake was due to the fact that the officials were in too much of a hurry to gather boxes for a speedy count." *IHRLG Election Report,* p. 23 (quoting *Korea Times,* 28 January 1988).

Massive fraud in the computerized central counting process was alleged, but the evidence was largely circumstantial. The opposition claimed it lacked access to direct evidence that would substantiate these allegations. It struck some observers as highly suspicious that the National Coalition for Democracy's parallel central vote count was halted by the government after only 62% of the votes had been tallied and a considerable discrepancy from the official tally had already emerged. *IHRLG Election Report,* p. 64. It also struck many as suspicious that state-controlled television coverage of election returns showed early returns being received most quickly for the regions in which Roh Tae Woo was expected to do best—Roh thus opened a large early lead, and a Roh win appeared likely from the outset. Personal observation.

In addition, an extra edition of the *Seoul sinmun,* a semi-official news organ of the government, reportedly was printed early on 17 December and contained accurate election results that should not have been known until hours later. This was reported by several independent sources, including an American missionary with long experience in Korea. The authors have a copy of this extra edition but were unable to confirm reports that it actually began to be distributed before 6 a.m. on 17 December.

97. "Election Process Observer Delegation to South Korea—Statement," 18 December 1987, reprinted in *IHRLG Election Report,* App. VIII, p. 58. See also Anna Park, "International Election Observation: The 1987 South Korean Presidential Election," *Harvard International Law Journal* 29:423–449 (1988).

98. *IHRLG Election Report,* App. VIII, p. 59.

99. The complainants were the Korean Catholic Priests Council for Justice and the Catholic Election Watchdog Committee. Ibid., p. 29. The opposition parties and the National Coalition for Democracy declined to file law suits they regarded as futile due to lack of an unbiased forum.

100. "In South Korea, More of the Same," *Boston Globe,* 13 March 1988, p. 20.

101. *Korea Times,* 12 January 1988, p. 2.

102. "The panel . . . said that the government should stop describing the street protests that led to the killings as a rebellion, and should characterize them instead as part of a pro-democratic movement." "Seoul Urged to Make Amends for 1980 Massacre," *New York Times,* 24 February 1988, p. A6. See also "Living Bitter Memories," *Far Eastern Economic Review,* 17 March 1988, p. 26. Very recently, the Roh Government did announce a public apology, "Korea Contrite for '80 Killings," *Boston Globe,* 2 April 1988, p. 3.

103. "Roh Should Declare Guarantee of Human Rights," *Korea Times,* 28 January 1988, p. 2; "Gove't Should Carry Out Overall Amnesty," *Korea Times,* 31 January 1988, p. 2.

104. Pyong-Choon Hahm, *The Korean Political Tradition and Law* (Seoul, Hollym Publishers for the Royal Asiatic Society, Korea Branch, 2nd ed. 1971), p. 213.

105. Jürgen Habermas, "Law and Morality," tr. Kenneth Baynes, in *The Tanner Lectures on Human Values* (Salt Lake City and Cambridge, University of Utah Press, Cambridge University Press, 1988), VII, 279.

106. *Constitution,* Art. 5(2). See generally Jang-Jip Choi, "Political Cleavages and Transition in a Military Authoritarian Regime," (unpublished paper, Korea University, 1986). The realpolitik of the martial constitution is well known: "Sovereign is he who decides on the exception." Carl Schmitt, *Political Theology: Four Chapters on the Concept of Sovereignty,* tr. George Schwab (Cambridge and London, The M.I.T. Press, 1988), p. 5.

107. "New Seoul Chief's Aides Dampen Expectations," *New York Times,* 26 February 1988, p. A3.

108. The structure of the military and the internal security apparatus is described in Bunge, ed., pp. 209–253. For an account of the linkage between the South Korean and United States military, see generally Taek-Hyung Rhee, *US-ROK Combined Operations: A Korean Perspective* (Washington, D.C., National Defense University Press, 1986). No comprehensive description of the activities of the large South Korean internal security apparatus has been published. For accounts of Korean Central Intelligence Agency activities in

the past, including surveillance and intimidation of Koreans in the United States who are critical of the military dictatorship, see Subcommittee on International Organizations of the House Committee on Foreign Affairs, 95th Congress, 2nd Session, *Investigation of Korean-American Relations* (Washington, D.C., U.S. Government Printing Office, 31 October 1978), pp. 22–23, 42–44, 89–113; Robert Boettcher, *Gifts of Deceit* (New York, Holt, Rinehart & Winston, 1980), p. 224–240; Thomas P. Gordon & Andrea Darvi, *Secret Police* (Garden City, Doubleday, 1981), pp. 118–119, 262–263, 276; Jai Hyon Lee, "The Activities of the Korean Central Intelligence Agency in the United States," in Irving Horowitz, ed., *Science, Sin, and Scholarship: The Politics of Reverend Moon and the Unification Church,* (Cambridge and London, The M.I.T. Press, 1978), pp. 120–147 (extensive bibliography); and Michael J. Glennon, "Liaison and Law: Foreign Intelligence Agencies Activities in the United States," *Harvard International Law Journal* 25:1 (1984).

109. *Constitution,* Art. 61.
110. *Constitution of 1980,* Art. 97.
111. *Constitution,* Art. 104(2).
112. Ibid.
113. Ibid., Art. 104(3).
114. Yoon, pp. 211–212.
115. Ibid., pp. 203–228. In 1985, punitive transfers of three judges attracted the attention of the Center for the Independence of Judges and Lawyers in Geneva. One of the three was abruptly transferred after publishing an article criticizing the first two transfers. These cases led to opposition attempts to impeach the Chief Justice; however, the DJP blocked the motion. *Center for Independence of Judges and Lawyers Bulletin* 16:21–23 (1985); *A Stern, Steady Crackdown,* p. 111.
116. *Constitution,* Art. 105(1).
117. Ibid., Art. 70. The previous term was seven years. *Constitution of 1980,* Art. 45.
118. Yoon, pp. 211–228.
119. *Constitution,* Art. 106(1).
120. *Constitution of 1980,* Art. 107(1).
121. *Constitution* (Explanatory Notes), p. 59.
122. On the 1971 "Judicial Upheaval," in which prosecutors sought to intimidate the lower judiciary through corruption charges, see Yoon, pp. 218–223. On the case of Yi Pyŏng-nin, see Adrian DeWind and John Woodhouse, *Persecution of Defence Lawyers in South Korea* (Geneva, International Commission of Jurists, 1979), pp. 47–48; Jerome A. Cohen, "Lawyers, Politics and Despotism in Korea," *American Bar Association Journal* 61:730–731 (1975). Under Chun, lawyers continued to be intimidated, disbarred, and prosecuted for political reasons. The case of attorney Pak Se-gyŏng, an associate of opposition leader Kim Dae Jung, is a prominent example. Pak was convicted of treason under martial law in 1980. When his conviction was affirmed in 1985 on appeal to the Supreme Court, two justices questioned the jurisdiction of the military tribunal that had tried Pak. The same two jus-

tices were denied reappointment on 2 April 1986. See *A Stern, Steady Crackdown*, p. 112.

123. *Constitution*, Art. 110(4).

124. Ibid., Art. 111.

125. *Constitution* (Explanatory Notes), pp. 48–50.

126. For an overview of South Korean judicial review since 1948, see Yoon, pp. 231–303; Dai-Kwon Choi, "Law and Social Change: The Korean Experience" (PhD dissertation, University of California, Berkeley, 1976), pp. 208–271.

127. *Constitution of 1972*, Arts. 109–111; Constitution Committee Act, Law No. 2530 of 1972, as amended by Law No. 3557 of 1982, *Laws of the Republic of Korea*, I, 45–54. An ad hoc Constitution Committee under the *1948 Constitution* of the First Republic did review the constitutionality of legislation in seven cases, including two cases in which it struck down laws restricting access to the courts. There had also been a Constitutional Court under the Second Republic (1960–1961), but it had no opportunity to function due to Park Chung Hee's 1961 coup d'état. Yoon, pp. 232–241.

128. *Constitution of 1980*, Arts. 112–114; Yoon, pp. 251–259.

129. *Constitution of 1980*, Art. 112(3) and *Constitution*, Art. 111(3) are the same.

130. *Constitution*, Art. 111(2), 111(4). Under Article 3 of the prior Constitution Committee Act, not only judges but "persons in the position of president, speaker of the National Assembly . . . prime minister, [member] of the State Council [Cabinet], or [an] administrator of the Office of Legislation" were eligible to be appointed to the Constitution Committee.

131. See *IHLR Report*, pp. 126–131.

132. *Constitution of 1980* Art. 112(1); Court Organization Act, Law No. 51 of 1949, last amended by Law No. 3362 of 1981, *Laws of the Republic of Korea*, I, 151–169, Arts. 12–15.

133. *Constitution*, Art. 114(1).

134. "Checking through the political cases already decided, there were few that could be quoted as indicating that independence of justice still exists with regard to political cases in the Republic of . . . Korea. From all cases reported within the last five years [as of mid-1987] there was only one in which the judge set free a person indicted for opposing the government under the National Security Act, and five or six cases were mentioned where the judges gave lesser penalties than those demanded by the prosecution." *ICJ Report*, p. 59.

135. *Constitution*, Art. 103. See Shigemitsu Dando, "The Conscience of the Judge: Its Role in the Administration of Justice," in Edward Wise and Gerhard Mueller, eds., *Studies in Comparative Criminal Law* (Springfield, Illinois, Charles C. Thomas Publishing Co., 1975), pp. 13–14. (Korean provision derived from so-called MacArthur Draft of Japanese constitution of 1946.) See also Sir Ninian Stephen, "Judicial Independence: A Fragile Bastion," in Shimon Shetreet and Jules Deschenes, eds., *Judicial Independence: the Contemporary Debate* (Dordrecht, Boston and Lancaster, Martinus Nijhoff, 1985), pp. 529–540. (This volume contains a broad range of valuable comparative and international assessments of problems of judicial independence.)

136. "Warrants issued by a judge *through due procedures* upon the request of a prosecutor shall be presented in case of arrest, detention, seizure or search." *Constitution*, Art. 12(3) (amendment in italics). This change is intended to do away with a certain kind of "police-state law" which is no law at all: "[T]he 'law' of the police really marks a point at which the state, whether from impotence or because of the immanent contradictions within any legal system, can no longer guarantee through the legal system the empirical ends it desires at any price to attain. Therefore the police intervene 'for security reasons' in countless cases where no legal situation exists. . . ." Walter Benjamin, "Critique of Violence," in *Reflections: Essays, Aphorisms, Autobiographical Writing*, tr. Edmund Jephcott and ed. Peter Memets (New York and London, Harcourt Brace Javanovich, 1978), p. 287. See generally Otto Kirchheimer, *Political Justice: The Use of Legal Procedure for Political Ends* (Princeton, Princeton University Press, 1961).

137. John Hoberman, "Human Rights and the 1988 Seoul Olympic Games," *Human Rights Internet Reporter* 12:11 (1987).

138. *Constitution*, Art. 28. (Previously, compensation was provided only in cases of prosecution and acquittal, which almost never occurred in the thousands of political cases processed between 1980 and 1987.)

139. Ibid., Art. 12(5).

140. U.S. Department of State, *Country Reports on Human Rights Practices in 1987*, p. 731.

141. Ibid., p. 730; Amnesty International, "The Constitutional Assembly Case" (a pamphlet, London, AI Index ASA 25/57/87, December 1987). The Agency for National Security Planning detained 12 ex-student radicals in late 1986 and early 1987 for up to 8 weeks without warrants—the accused claimed confessions to National Security Act violations were coerced by beatings, electric shock, water torture, and other abuses. *A Stern, Steady Crackdown*, pp. 87–107.

142. Under Article 11(4) of the *1980 Constitution*, suspects theoretically had the right to "prompt assistance of counsel." In practice, however, the police and prosecution commonly denied defense attorneys access to their clients on the grounds that interrogation was in process or, less often, that isolation was required "to prevent the destruction of evidence or to maintain investigatory secrets." *A Stern, Steady Crackdown,* p. 72.

143. For background on legal education and career paths in the legal profession in South Korea, see Yoon, pp. 176–185; Sang-Chol Kim, "Legal Education in Korea: Problems and Suggestions," (working paper, Seoul Conference on the Law of the World, 6–11 September 1987), available from World Peace Through Law Center, Washington, D.C.

144. Yoon, p. 196-I.

145. For example, in the early 1980s a number of top law students were blacklisted because of participation in student demonstrations against the 1980 Chun coup and were not permitted to enter the Judicial Training Institute until they had gone through extensive interrogations by intelligence agencies to verify their "repentance." They were also in some cases required to submit to loyalty oaths. Young judges, as part of their ideological training

in the *Saemaul* (New Village) Program, have been required to attend "retreats," where, after long days of exhortation, they may have been required to share lodgings with an "ideological mentor," i.e., a politically "reliable" senior executive-branch official. For background on anti-Communist indoctrination, see Gregory Henderson, "The Politics of Korea," in *Two Koreas–One Future?* John Sullivan and Roberta Foss, eds., (Boston and London, American Friends Service Committee/University Press of America, 1987), pp. 112–114.

146. For the classic Hobbesian-authoritarian interpretation of this distinction, see Carl Schmitt, *The Concept of the Political*, tr. George Schwab (New Brunswick, Rutgers University Press, 1976), pp. 19–58; see also Paul Hirst, "Carl Schmitt's Decisionism," *Telos* 72:15 (1987). For criticism of Schmitt's legal realpolitik, see Franz Neumann, *The Rule of Law: Political Theory and the Legal System in Modern Society* (Leamington Spa, Heidelberg, and Dover, N.H., Berg, 1986), pp. 293–298.

147. Judges who displease the government have in the past been accused of Communist sympathies. Yoon, p. 221.

148. Ibid., pp. 221–228.

149. In January 1987, the Korean Catholic Justice and Peace Commission charged that "the judiciary encourages torture by refusing requests to deny the admissibility of an alleged confession since it has been obtained by torture." *ICJ Report*, p. 60. Article 12(2) of the *1987 Constitution* provides: "No citizen shall be tortured or compelled to testify against himself in criminal cases."

150. Suk Jo Kim and Edward J. Baker, "The Politics of Transition: Korea After Park" (unpublished paper, Harvard Law School, East Asian Legal Studies Program, 1980). For background on rectification of names, see Geoffrey Mac-Cormack, "Rectification of Names in Early Chinese Legal and Political Thought," *Archiv fur Rechts- und Sozialphilosophie* 72:378 (1986).

151. For these reasons, a dictatorship must destroy the generality of law–it cannot be allowed to turn back on the command structure–as well as the boundary between law and morality: The dictator claims a *moral* authority that is identified with the fate of the whole nation and is therefore put above possible challenge; the mere legal powers of any official role would be specifiable and thus too confining. See Franz Neumann, *Behemoth: The Structure and Practice of National Socialism 1933–1944* (New York and Evanston, Harper and Row, 1963, reprint of 1944 rev. ed. published by Oxford University Press), pp. 451–455.

152. Details of the case are reported in *A Stern, Steady Crackdown*, pp. 94–98, 104, and in *ICJ Report*, pp. 37–41.

153. See *Asia Watch Report*, pp. 107–108; James M. West, "The Suboptimal 'Miracle' of South Korean State Capitalism," *Bulletin of Concerned Asian Scholars* 19.3:60, 68–71 (1987).

154. *A Stern, Steady Crackdown*, p. 96.

155. *Korea Weekly Report* 6.14 (9 July 1987).

156. The petition alleged "a systematically executed crime of deliberate sex tor-

ture, planned by senior police officers [and which went beyond the] conventional torture or brutality we have often seen." *ICJ Report*, p. 38.

157. *Korea Times*, 31 January 1988, p. 3.

158. Ibid.

159. Code of Criminal Procedure, Law No. 341 of 1954, as amended Art. 265, in *Laws of the Republic of Korea*, X, 137.

160. Ibid.

161. See text for notes 53–56.

162. "NPH Chief Knew Park Died of Torture," *Korea Times*, 13 January 1988, p. 3. The lack of an independent observer at the postmortem, the failure to provide the family with the possibility of conducting their own independent examination, the hasty cremation which did not allow the family time to view the body, and the lack of a full and independent investigation of the case all point to the conclusion that the police were concealing more than they revealed." *ICJ Report*, pp. 36–37.

163. "New Disclosure of Coverup Attempt in Torture Death Case Becomes Hot Political Issue," *Korea Times*, 14 January 1988, p. 2.

164. "Prosecution to Reinvestigate Park's Torture Cover-Up Case," *Korea Times*, 14 January 1988, p. 3.

165. *Korea Times*, 16 January 1988, p. 1.

166. "Probe in Cover-Up Wrapped Up," *Korea Times*, 17 January 1988, p. 3.

167. *Korea Times*, 14 January 1988, p. 1.

168. Nae-Bok Han, "A Skeleton in the Closet," *Korea Times*, 2 February 1988, p. 8.

169. *Korea Times*, 14 January 1988, p. 1.

170. Nae-Bok Han, p. 8.

171. *Korea Times*, 31 January 1988, p. 1.

172. Ibid.

173. Ibid.

174. Ibid.

175. "RDP Seeks Commission to Ensure Political Neutrality of the Police," *Korea Times*, 2 February 1988, p. 2.

176. See generally John W. Dardess, *Confucianism and Autocracy* (Berkeley, Los Angeles, & London, University of California Press, 1983), pp. 43–84. The *1987 Constitution* provides: "(1) All public officials shall be servants of the entire people and shall be responsible to the people: (2) The status and political impartiality of public officials shall be guaranteed as prescribed by law." *Constitution*, Art. 7.

177. "All actions relative to the rights of other men whose underlying principles are not susceptible to public scrutiny are unjust, meaning that an action I am forced to undertake in secret is not only obviously unjust, but such that, were it made public, the reaction would render its realization impossible." Norberto Bobbio, "The Future of Democracy," *Telos* 61.3:10 (1984). (Quoting Kant's *Perpetual Peace*).

178. *Korea Herald*, 9 February 1988, p. 1; "Three Parties Near Agreement for Collective Leadership System," *Korea Herald*, 19 March 1988, p. 1.

179. See *Boston Globe*, 9 February 1988, p. 20; "Rough Road Ahead," *Far Eastern Economic Review*, 3 March 1988, p. 30; Clyde Haberman, "Skeptically, Koreans Await Demonstrations of Democracy," *New York Times*, 7 February 1988, Sec. 4, p. 2.

180. Only 2 of the 26 political prisoners adopted by Amnesty International as "prisoners of conscience" were among the 109 persons released. *NACHRK Bi-Weekly* 7.5:4 (15 March 1988). The Korean Council of Churches stated in a telephone interview on 2 April 1988 that, as of 1 April 1988, more than 600 political prisoners had not been released.

181. "DJP Railroads Election Law Revision Through Assembly," *Korea Herald*, 8 March 1988. The amendments, in addition to perpetuating malapportionment, "disallowed open counting of absentee ballots and prohibited parties from holding rallies, organizing support groups, or bringing national leaders in to local districts on behalf of candidates. These restrictions give the government a significant advantage in rural districts, where the population is sparse and wholly dependent on the government for agricultural inputs and markets, while making it extremely difficult for the democratic movement to play a legal role in the election campaign." *NACHRK Bi-Weekly* 7.5:2 (15 March 1988). The rationale for these DJP-imposed legal restrictions on opposition-party campaign activities (if they express any policy beyond partisan advantage) is unclear; yet it would seem that a compelling state interest would be necessary to justify restrictions, that, prima facie, appear to be of doubtful constitutionality. The establishment of political parties shall be free, and the plural party system shall be maintained. . . . Political parties . . . shall have the necessary organizational arrangements for the people to participate in the formulation of the political will." *Constitution*, Art. 8(1)-(2). Such restrictions also contravene point 7 of Roh's 29 June 8-point commitment. See text accompanying note 73.

182. "In South Korea, A New Cabinet Full of Old Faces," *New York Times*, 20 February 1988, p. 20. There was no change in the key portfolios of Justice (controlling the procuracy), Home Affairs (controlling the national police), Foreign Affairs, and Finance. Two new members of the Cabinet had been high officials in the secret police, the Agency for National Security Planning, the powers of which Roh has pledged to scale back. *Boston Globe*, 20 February 1988, p. 3. An opposition spokesperson reacted with this statement: "[T]he new government has revealed its intention to commit injustices in the coming general election [for the National Assembly] by keeping ministers who engineered fraud in the presidential election last year." *Korea Herald*, 20 February 1988, p. 1. Roh's party also announced its slate of National Assembly candidates, which excluded several of Chun's close cronies and showed sensitivity to popular disgust with past nepotism, but nevertheless exhibited a basic continuity with what the *Korea Herald* called "the Fifth Republic's power elite." The 219 DJP candidates included 28 military men, notably Chun junta stalwarts, Chŏng Ho-yŏng, Hŏ Sam-su, and Yi Hak-bong as well as ex-Minister of Home Affairs Sŏ Chŏng-hwa and ex-secret police director Yu Hak-su. *Korea Herald*, 19 March 1988, p. 1.

183. There have recently been disputes over the status of the Advisory Council

of Elder Statesmen (ACES), a body established in 1980 and carried over in Article 90 of the 1987 constitution. Chun, as the outgoing president, is automatically Chairman of ACES, the functions of which are to be determined by statute. In the past, ACES was of no practical significance, but Chun and his supporters sought to expand the ACES staff and to enact legislation that would require the government to seek and follow ACES "advice" on national security matters. This plan predictably threatened to rekindle public outrage and to damage DJP prospects in the forthcoming National Assembly election; hence, it was scaled back. See *Bi-Weekly* 7.5:3 (15 March 1988).

184. A Seoul law professor recently wrote: "Our jurists have never made an issue of the discrepancies between existing and formal laws, between street and classroom laws, and between realistic laws and laws upon which examinations are based, although they know of them more clearly than anyone else. Our jurists have been apathetic to the reality of the law, which is so thorough in serving power but not in serving the people, the bearers of sovereignty. They are insensitive to the bitter criticism that the law is strong toward the weak but weak toward the strong." Chong-Dae Pae, "Reflections on and Prospects for Our Jurisprudence—Centered on Criminal Jurisprudence," *Korea Journal* 27.7:4,5 (1987). See also Suk Jo Kim, "A Theory of Pseudo-Community: The Formal Law in Korea," in Song, ed., pp. 70–111.

185. See note 81.

186. Chun was invited to pay a visit to the White House on 23 March 1988 (and thereafter to be given tours at the Pentagon and the Central Intelligence Agency), a move some Koreans construed as a signal that the Reagan Administration found nothing wrong with a continued role for Chun in Korean politics. "Korea's Former Leader to Visit D.C. Next Week," *Boston Globe,* 17 March 1988, p. 18. The United States government decision to roll out the red carpet one more time for ex-dictator Chun and also the growing pressure from Washington on trade issues probably will fuel an already dramatic rise in anti-Americanism among Koreans across the political spectrum. "Anger at America Becomes Common Cause for Many Koreans," *Korea Herald,* 2 March 1988, p. 4.

Epilogue: Comparative Perspectives on Human Rights in Korea, by Lawrence W. Beer

1. William Shaw, "Korea Before Rights" in this volume. For analogy in less-Confucian feudal Japan, see Lawrence W. Beer, *Freedom of Expression in Japan: A Study in Comparative Law, Politics and Society* (New York, Kodansha International/Harper & Row, 1985), Chapter 3; hereafter cited as *Freedom.*

2. On problems of liberty where well institutionalized, see Harry Street, *Freedom, the Individual and the Law,* 5th ed. (New York, Viking Penguin, 1982); Beer, *Freedom;* and William Spinrad, *Civil Liberties* (Chicago, Quadrangle Books, 1970).

3. David P. Forsythe, *Human Rights and World Politics* (Lincoln, University of Nebraska Press, 1981), pp. 1–21.

4. On the development of human rights in the West, see Richard P. Claude, ed., *Comparative Human Rights* (Baltimore, Johns Hopkins University Press, 1976), Chapter 1. On the Western need for revivification of its legal tradition by interaction with the non-West, see Harold Berman, *Law and Revolution* (Cambridge, Harvard University Press, 1984).

5. C. G. Weeramantry, *Equality and Freedom: Some Third World Perspectives* (Colombo, Hansa Publishers, 1976).

6. The founding by Richard Pierre Claude of *Universal Human Rights* (now *Human Rights Quarterly*) in 1979 may be taken to mark the growth of the interdisciplinary field of human-rights studies into healthy adolescence.

7. Forsythe, pp. 6–8.

8. Ibid., pp. 6–7; Hurst Hannum, ed., *Guide to International Human Rights Practice* (Philadelphia, University of Pennsylvania Press, 1984), pp. 4–6; generally, Paul Sieghart, *The Lawful Rights of Mankind: An Introduction to the International Legal Code of Human Rights* (Oxford, Oxford University Press, 1985), and Albert P. Blaustein, ed., *Human Rights Source Book* (New York, Paragon, 1987).

9. Arnold Brackman, *The Other Nuremberg: The Untold Story of the Tokyo War Crimes Trials* (New York, William Morrow, 1987).

10. Forsythe, p. 8; United Nations, *United Nations Action in the Field of Human Rights* (New York, United Nations, 1980), pp. 5–6; hereafter cited as *UN.*

11. Resolution 217 A(III) of the General Assembly, 10 December 1948; UNIFO (ed.), *International Human Rights Instruments of the United Nations, 1948–1982* (Pleasantville, UNIFO Publishers, 1983), pp. 5–7, hereafter *UNIFO.*

12. Ibid., pp. 86–100; *UN,* pp. 12–14.

13. *UN,* pp. 8–10.

14. United Nations General Assembly Resolution 34/180, 18 December 1979; entered into force on 3 September 1981. *UNIFO,* pp. 150–154. This source also includes the record of each nation in ratifying the major human-rights instruments.

15. United Nations General Assembly Resolution 39/46 of 10 December 1984; *Amnesty International Report 1985,* pp. 10–11, 353–357; Sieghart.

16. Forsythe, pp. 15–18; *UN,* pp. 8–22 especially.

17. For information on the Human Rights Committee, contact LAWASIA, 170 Phillip St., Sydney, NSW 2000, Australia.

18. *UNIFO,* p. 170; *Amnesty International Report 1985,* p. 11.

19. Ibid., pp. 163, 167.

20. J. S. Auerbach, *Unequal Justice: Lawyers and Social Change in Modern America* (New York, Oxford University Press, 1976).

21. Beer, *Freedom,* pp. 21–28.

22. Max Rheinstein, "Legal Systems: Comparative Law and Legal Systems," *International Encyclopedia of Social Sciences* (New York, Macmillan, 1968), IX, 208. He sees the tasks of law as social control, conflict resolution, adaptation and social change, and norm enforcement. Though hope is essential for

the human-rights revolution, whether there are grounds for optimism in a given case is an empirical question not to be facilely answered.

23. The ratification dates of constitutions were provided by Albert P. Blaustein, Rutgers University Law School, Camden, January 1990.

24. On Asian constitutions, see Lawrence W. Beer, *Constitutionalism in Asia: Asian Views of the American Influence* (Berkeley, University of California Press, 1979, and Baltimore, OPRSCAS, University of Maryland School of Law, 1989), especially pp. 4–8; hereafter *Constitutionalism*. See also, Lawrence W. Beer, ed., *Constitutional Systems in Late Twentieth-Century Asia*, forthcoming.

25. Lawrence W. Beer, "Freedom of Expression in Japan and Asia: Some Comparative Prespectives," in M. Shimizu, ed., *Nihonkoku Kempo no Riron* (Tokyo, Yuhikaku Publishing Co., 1985), p. 730; Harry M. Scoble & Laurie S. Wiseberg, eds., *Access to Justice: Human Rights Struggles in Southeast Asia* (London, Zed Books, 1985); B. Obinna Okere, "The Protection of Human Rights in Africa and the African Charter on Human and Peoples' Rights: A Comparative Analysis with the European and American Systems," *Human Rights Quarterly* 6.2:141 (May 1984); L. J. Macfarlane, *The Theory and Practice of Human Rights* (London, Maurice Temple Smith, 1985). Macfarlane's book is outstanding for clear conciseness and realistic balance.

26. Majid Khadduri, *The Islamic Conception of Justice* (Baltimore, Johns Hopkins University Press, 1984).

27. Lucian Pye, *Asian Power and Politics* (Cambridge, Harvard University Press, 1985).

28. Richard P. Claude, "The Case of Joelito Filartiga and the Clinic of Hope," *Human Rights Quarterly* 5.3:275 (August 1983).

29. Beer, *Freedom*, pp. 30–37; Macfarlane.

30. Robert Bellah et al., *Habits of the Heart* (Berkeley, University of California Press, 1985).

31. Beer, *Freedom*, pp. 28–37.

32. L. L. Wade, "South Korean Political Culture: An Interpretation of Survey Data," *Journal of Korean Studies* 2:1 (1980).

33. John Henry Merryman, *The Civil Law Tradition* (2nd ed. Stanford, Stanford University Press, 1985).

34. Zhao Ziyang, confirmed as General Secretary of the Chinese Communist Party at the 13th National Party Congress, 1 November 1987, has since been replaced by Jiang Zemin.

35. Among sources are the annual *Amnesty International Report*, U.S. Department of State's *Country Reports on Human Rights Practices*, Raymond Gastil's *Freedom in the World* (Freedom House), and publications of the Human Rights Committee of LAWASIA, and Asiawatch. See Asiawatch, *Human Rights in Korea* (New York, Asiawatch Committee, 1985).

SUGGESTED READINGS

Amnesty International. *Annual Report on Human Rights.*

Amnesty International. *South Korea: Violations of Human Rights.* London, 1986.

Asia Watch. *Assessing Reform in South Korea: A Supplement to the Asia Watch Report on Legal Process and Human Rights.* Washington, D.C., 1988.

Asia Watch. *A Stern, Steady Crackdown: Legal Process and Human Rights in South Korea.* Washington, D.C., 1987.

Asia Watch. *Human Rights in Korea.* Ed. James B. Palais and Bruce Cumings. Washington, D.C., 1986.

Asia Watch, International Human Rights Law Group and American Center of International PEN. *Freedom of Expression in the Republic of Korea.* Washington, D.C., 1988.

Asia Watch and Minnesota Lawyers and International Human Rights Committee. *Human Rights in the Democratic People's Republic of Korea.* Washington, D.C., and Minneapolis, 1988.

Gleysteen, William H., Jr. "Korea: A Special Target of American Concern." In David Newsom, *The Diplomacy of Human Rights.* Lanham, Maryland, University Press of America, 1987.

International Commission of Jurists. *South Korea: Human Rights in the Emerging Politics.* Report of a mission, April 1987, 1987.

International League for Human Rights and the International Human Rights Law Group. *Democracy in South Korea: A Promise Unfulfilled.* New York, 1985.

Kim Dae Jung. *Prison Writings.* Berkeley, University of California Press, 1986.

United States Department of State. *Country Reports on Human Rights Practices.*

NAME INDEX

Romanization of Korean personal names generally follows the McCune-Reischauer system, with minor modifications in some chapters. For a small number of prominent persons, the journalistic standard is used, e.g. Park Chung Hee, rather than Pak Chŏng-hŭi. For Koreans whose English-language work is cited, names are romanized as published.

South Korean Labor Party (SKLP), 147, 151, 152, 154, 155, 156, 160, 161, 162, 167

South Korean Railroad Workers Association, 145

Special Act Concerning Punishment of Crimes Against the State, 309n37

State Tribunal (Chosŏn dynasty), 74

Suiheisha (Levelers' Society), 98, 102, 107

Supreme Commander for the Allied Powers (SCAP), 123, 128, 139–140

Supreme Court, 9, 181, 183, 195, 235, 243, 247; in reform government of 1894, 74, 75; validates portions of Press Law of 1907, 144; review opinion in 1980 Kim Dae Jung case, 165; in People's Revolutionary Party case, 181; purges of, 183; under Chun Doo Hwan government, 211–212

Swiss Red Cross, 268

Taehan Youth Corps, 145

Taiping Movement, 40

Taiping Rebellion, 57

Taoism, 35, 40

Tale of Queen Inhyŏn (*Inhyŏn wanghujŏn*), 82

Tangun myth, 19

Thoughts on the Cause of the Present Discontents, 70

Thirty-eighth parallel, 125

Tonga ilbo. See Dong A ilbo

Tonghak Movement, 40–41, 48; rebellion (1893–1894), 56–58, 60, 97

Tongnip sinmun, See *The Independent*

torture, 236, 280; post-Liberation continuation of Japanese practices, 133, 141; following Yŏsu-Sunch'ŏn Rebellion (1948), 138, 150; in *purakchi* case (1949), 156–157; case of Chŏng Kuk-ŭn (1952), 164; case of Lt. General Kang Mun-bong and others (1955–1957), 164; case of Cho Pong-am and others (1958–1959), 164; cases of General Pak Im-hang and Kim Tong-ha, 165; cases of Yun Kil-chung and Yi Tong-hwa (1962), 165; case of People's Revolutionary Party (1962), 165, 181–185; case of Yun I-sang (1967), 165; case of Chang Chun-ha, 178, 179, 180; case of Ch'oe Hyŏng-u, 179; case of Ehwa University students (1973), 180; case of Kim Chi-ha, 184–185; prohibited in *Yusin Constitution,* 187; case of Ham Sŏk-hŏn and others (1979), 190; case of Kim Dae Jung and others (1980), 198; case of Reverend Im Ki-yun

(1980), 198–199; under government of Chun Doo Hwan, 198–200, 201, 223, 236, 246–249, 329n141; case of Kim Chŏng-do (1982), 199; case of Kim Kunjo (1983), 200; case of Kwŏn In-suk (1986), 200, 246–249; case of Pak Chongch'ŏl (1987), 200, 208, 229–230, 231, 245–249; 266, 280, 321n54–55, 330n149, 330n156, 331n162; Convention Against Torture and Other Cruel, Inhuman, or Degrading Treatment (1984), 269, 281; prohibited in 1987 *Constitution,* 330 n149, 330n156

Treaty of Paris (1928), 268

Treaty of Shimonoseki (1895), 58

Union of Soviet Socialist Republics, 125, 126, 172

United Nations, 155, 158, 172, 257; Temporary Commission on Korea (UNTCOK), 146, 147; Commission on Korea (UNCOK), 153, 156, 167, 256; Commission for the Unification and Rehabilitation of Korea (UNCURK), 154; General Assembly, 268; Charter, 268

United States Army Military Government in Korea (USAMGIK), 123, 128–130, 173; centralization under, 129; appropriation of Japanese-held industries and land; Ordinances, 129, 140–143, 150, 152, 167, 168; erosion of private property concept under, 130; politics under, 131; economic dislocation under, 132–133; police under, 136–138; Department of Justice, 141; Coalition Committee, 145; Instructions to Judges, 168; Bureau of Women's Affairs, 146, 168

U.S. Congress, 15

U.S. Cultural Center in Kwangju, attempted arson (1981), 217

U.S. Cultural Center in Pusan, arson (1982), 199, 217

U.S. Department of Defense, 176

U.S. Department of State, 15, 17–18, 181–182, 193, 197, 200, 201, 214, 231, 233; Country Reports on Human Rights Practices, 2, 15, 22, 196, 197, 198, 200, 201, 214, U.S. Government Statement on the Events in Kwangju, Republic of Korea, in May 1980, 17, 18, 216, 311n65, 314n134, 319n34; reaction to 1980 Kim Dae Jung trial, 195, 287n18; U.S. Embassy Seoul, 259

U.S. House of Representatives, 235

U.S. Information Agency, 17

U.S. policy toward human rights in Korea:

Studies in East Asian Law
Harvard University

1. *Law in Imperial China Exemplified by 190 Ch'ing Dynasty Cases* (*translated from the* Hsing-an hui-lan) *with Historical, Social, and Juridical Commentaries.* By Derk Bodde and Clarence Morris. Cambridge: Harvard University Press, 1967.
2. *The Criminal Process in the People's Republic of China, 1949–1963: An Introduction.* By Jerome Alan Cohen. Cambridge: Harvard University Press, 1968.
3. *Agreements of the People's Republic of China, 1949–1967: A Calendar.* By Douglas M. Johnston and Hungdah Chiu. Cambridge: Harvard University Press, 1968.
4. *Contemporary Chiense Law: Research Problems and Perspectives.* Edited by Jerome Alan Cohen. Cambridge: Harvard University Press, 1970.
5. *The People's Republic of China and the Law of Treaties.* By Hungdah Chiu. Cambridge: Harvard University Press, 1972.
6. *China's Practice of International Law: Some Case Studies.* Edited by Jerome Alan Cohen. Cambridge: Harvard University Press, 1972.
7. *The Internal Organization of Ch'ing Bureaucracy—Legal, Normative, and Communication Aspects.* By Thomas A. Metzger. Cambridge: Harvard University Press, 1973.
8. *People's China and International Law: a Documentary Study.* By Jerome Alan Cohen and Hungdah Chiu. Princeton: Princeton University Press, 1974.
9. *The Chinese Communist Treatment of Counterrevolutionaries, 1924–1949.* By Patricia E. Griffin. Princeton: Princeton University Press, 1976.
10. *The T'ang Code: General Principles, Volume I.* Translated and edited by Wallace Johnson. Princeton: Princeton University Press, 197?.
11. *Chinese Legal Tradition under the Mongols: The Code of 1291 as Reconstructed.* By Paul Heng-chao Ch'ien. Princeton: Princeton University Press, 1979.
12. *Essays on China's Legal Tradition.* Edited by Jerome A. Cohen, R. Randle Edwards, and Fu-mei Chang Chen. Princeton: Princeton University Press, 1980.
13. *Legal Norms in a Confucian State.* By William Shaw. Berkeley: Institute of East Asian Studies, University of California, 1981.
14. *The Lê Code: Law in Traditional Vietnam, A Comparative Sino-Vietnamese Legal Study with Historical-Juridical Analysis and Annotations.* Translated and edited by Nguyễn Ngọc Huy and Ta Van Tai with the cooperation of Trần Văn Liêm for the translation. Athens: Ohio University Press, 1987.
15. *The Vietnamese Tradition of Human Rights.* By Ta Van Tai. Berkeley: Institute of East Asian Studies, University of California, 1988.
16. *Human Rights in Korea: Historical and Policy Perspectives.* Edited by William Shaw. Cambridge: Council on East Asian Studies, Harvard Unviersity, 1990.